THE LANGUAGE OF LITERATURE

THE *InterActive*
READER™ PLUS

for English Learners

McDougal Littell
A HOUGHTON MIFFLIN COMPANY

Evanston, Illinois • Boston • Dallas

Reading Consultants, *The InterActive Reader™Plus*

Sharon Sicinski-Skeans, Ph.D. Assistant Professor of Reading, University of Houston-Clear Lake; former K–12 Language Arts Program Director, Spring Independent School District, Houston, Texas.
Olga Bautista Reading Coordinator, Will C. Wood Middle School, Sacramento, California.

Senior Consultants, *The Language of Literature*

Arthur N. Applebee Professor of Education, State University of New York at Albany; Director, National Research Center on English Learning and Achievements; Senior Fellow, Center for Writing and Literacy.
Andrea B. Bermúdez Professor of Studies in Language and Culture; Director, Research Center for Language and Culture; Chair, Foundations and Professional Studies, University of Houston-Clear Lake.
Sheridan Blau Senior Lecturer in English and Education and former Director of Composition, University of California at Santa Barbara; Director, South Coast Writing Project; Director, Literature Institute for Teachers; Past President, National Council of Teachers of English.
Rebekah Caplan Coordinator, English Language Arts K–12, Oakland Unified School District, Oakland, California; Teacher-Consultant, Bay Area Writing Project, University of California at Berkeley; served on the California State English Assessment Development Team for Language Arts.
Peter Elbow Professor of English, University of Massachusetts at Amherst; Fellow, Bard Center for Writing and Thinking.
Susan Hynds Professor and Director of English Education, Syracuse University, Syracuse, New York.
Judith A. Langer Professor of Education, State University of New York at Albany; Director, National Research Center on English Learning and Achievements; Director, Albany Institute for Research on Education.
James Marshall Professor of English and English Education, University of Iowa, Iowa City.

Acknowledgments

Miriam Altschuler Literary Agency: "The Treasure of Lemon Brown" by Walter Dean Myers, *Boys' Life,* March 1983. Copyright © 1983 by Walter Dean Myers. Reprinted by permission of Miriam Altschuler Literary Agency on behalf of Walter Dean Myers.

Susan Bergholz Literary Services: Excerpt from *The Anaya Reader* published as "The Magic of Words" by Rudolfo Anaya. Copyright © 1995 by Rudolfo Anaya. First published as "In Commemoration: One Million Volumes" in *A Million Stars: Millionth Acquisition for the University of New Mexico General Library,* edited by Connie Capers Thorsen (University of New Mexico Press, 1982). Reprinted by permission of Susan Bergholz Literary Services, New York. All rights reserved.

Continued on page 449.

ISBN-13: 978-0-618-31019-7   ISBN-10: 0-618-31019-3

14 15 16–DWI–08 07

Table of Contents

Introducing *The InterActive Reader™ Plus*

The InterActive Reader™ Plus is a new kind of literature book. As you will see, this book helps you become an active reader. It is a book to mark on, to write in, and to make your own. You can use it in class *and* take it home.

An Easy-to-Carry Literature Text

This book won't weigh you down—it can fit as comfortably in your hand as it can in your backpack. Yet it contains works by such important authors as . . .

Edgar Allan Poe, whose classic horror story "The Tell-Tale Heart" sends chills down the spine.

Toni Cade Bambara, whose short story "Raymond's Run" explores physical, spiritual, and mental challenges.

Anne Frank, whose struggle to survive the Holocaust is detailed in her diary and recreated in a popular drama.

You will read these selections and other great literature—plays, poems, stories, and nonfiction. In addition, you will learn how to understand the texts you use in classes, on tests, and in the real world, and you will study and practice specific strategies for taking standardized tests.

Help for Reading

The InterActive Reader™ Plus helps you understand many challenging works of literature. Here's how.

Before-You-Read Activities A prereading page helps you make connections to your everyday life and gives you a key to understanding the selection.

Preview A preview of every selection tells you what to expect.

Reading Tips Reading tips give useful help throughout.

Focus Each longer piece is broken into smaller "bites" or sections. A focus at the beginning of each section tells you what to look for.

Pause and Reflect At the end of each section, a quick question or two helps you check your understanding.

Read Aloud Specific passages are marked for you to read aloud. You will use your voice and ears to interpret literature.

Reread This feature directs you to passages where a lot of action, change, or meaning is packed in a few lines.

Mark It Up This feature invites you to mark your own notes and questions right on the page.

Vocabulary Support

Words to Know Important new words are underlined. Their definitions appear in a Words to Know section at the bottom of any page where they occur in the selection. You will work with these words in the Words to Know SkillBuilder pages.

Personal Word List As you read, you will want to add some words from the selections to your own vocabulary. Write these words in your Personal Word List on page 434.

SkillBuilder Pages

After each literary selection, you will find these SkillBuilder pages:

> **Active Reading SkillBuilder**
>
> **Literary Analysis SkillBuilder**
>
> **Words to Know SkillBuilder** (for most selections)

These pages will help you practice and apply important skills.

The InterActive Reader™ Plus for English Learners

The InterActive Reader™ Plus for English Learners provides all of the literature selections and all of the features from the *InterActive Reader™ Plus*. Special additional features include:

Section summaries A brief summary helps get you started with each section or chunk of the text.

More About . . . These notes provide key background information about specific elements of the text such as historical events, scientific concepts, or political situations needed for understanding the selection.

What Does It Mean? These brief notes clearly explain any confusing words, phrases, references, or other constructions.

English Learner Support Here you will find special help with vocabulary, language, and culture issues that may interfere with understanding the selection.

Reading Check These questions at key points in the text help you clarify what is happening in the selection.

Links to *The Language of Literature*

If you are using McDougal Littell's *The Language of Literature*, you will find *The InterActive Reader™ Plus* to be a perfect companion. The literary selections in the reader can all be found in that book. *The InterActive Reader™ Plus* lets you read certain core selections from *The Language of Literature* more slowly and in greater depth.

Read on to learn more!

Academic and Informational Reading

Here is a special collection of real-world examples to help you read every kind of informational material, from textbooks to technical directions. The strategies you learn will help you on tests, in other classes, and in the world outside of school. You will find strategies for the following:

Analyzing Text Features This section will help you read many different types of magazine articles and textbooks. You will learn how titles, subtitles, lists, graphics, many different kinds of visuals, and other special features work in magazines and textbooks. After studying this section you will be ready to read even the most complex material.

Understanding Visuals Tables, charts, graphs, maps, and diagrams all require special reading skills. As you learn the common elements of various visual texts, you will learn to read these materials with accuracy and skill.

Recognizing Text Structures Informational texts can be organized in many different ways. In this section you will study the following structures and learn about special key words that will help you identify the organizational patterns:

- Main Idea and Supporting Details
- Problem and Solution
- Sequence
- Cause and Effect
- Comparison and Contrast
- Argument

Reading in the Content Areas You will learn special strategies for reading social studies, science, and mathematics texts.

Reading Beyond the Classroom In this section you will encounter applications, schedules, technical directions, product information, Web pages, and other readings. Learning to analyze these texts will help you in your everyday life and on some standardized tests.

Test Preparation Strategies

In this section, you will find strategies and practice to help you succeed on many different kinds of standardized tests. After closely studying a variety of test formats through annotated examples, you will have an opportunity to practice each format on your own. Additional support will help you think through your answers. You will find strategies for the following:

Successful Test Taking This section provides many suggestions for preparing for and taking tests. The information ranges from analyzing test questions to tips for answering multiple-choice and open-ended test questions.

Reading Tests: Long Selections You will learn how to analyze the structure of a lengthy reading and prepare to answer the comprehension questions that follow it.

Reading Tests: Short Selections These selections may be a paragraph of text, a poem, a chart or graph, or some other item. You will practice the special range of comprehension skills required for these pieces.

Functional Reading Tests These real-world texts present special challenges. You will learn about the various test formats that use applications, product labels, technical directions, Web pages, and more.

Revising-and-Editing Tests These materials test your understanding of English grammar and usage. You may encounter capitalization and punctuation questions. Sometimes the focus is on usage questions such as verb tenses or pronoun agreement issues. You will become familiar with these formats through the guided practice in this section.

Writing Tests Writing prompts and sample student essays will help you understand how to analyze a prompt and what elements make a successful written response. Scoring rubrics and a prompt for practice will prepare you for the writing tests you will take.

User's Guide

Connect to Your Life

These activities help you see connections between your own life and what happens in the selection.

Key to the Selection

This section provides a "key" to help you unlock the selection so that you can understand and enjoy it. One of these four kinds of keys will appear:

• **What You Need to Know**—important background information.

• **What's the Big Idea?**—an introduction to key words or concepts in the selection.

• **What Do You Think?**—a preview of an important quotation from the selection.

• **What to Listen For**—a chance to examine the sound and rhythm of a piece.

Before You Read

Connect to Your Life

Have you ever chosen to spend time alone? Have you ever felt lonely? What do you think is the difference between being lonely and being alone? Use the spaces below to list feelings and experiences that show the difference.

Lonely . . .

Alone . . .

Key to the Story

WHAT'S THE BIG IDEA? An orphanage is an institution for the care of children whose parents have died or whose parents can no longer take care of them. At the time of the story, orphanages were more common than they are today. What images come to mind when you think of an orphanage? See if your images match the images in the story.

lonely children

Orphanage

20

A MOTHER in MANNVILLE

by Marjorie Kinnan Rawlings

PREVIEW In this story, a friendship develops between a writer who has rented a cabin in the mountains and a boy who comes from a nearby orphanage to chop wood for the writer. What will it take for these two people to reach out to each other?

21

PREVIEW

This feature tells you what the selection is about. It may also raise a question that helps you set a purpose for reading.

And there's more!

User's Guide *continued*

1 FOCUS

Every selection is broken down into parts. A Focus introduces each part and tells you what to look for as you read.

2 ▐ MARK IT UP ⟩

This feature may appear in the Focus or in the side column next to a boxed passage. It asks you to underline or circle key details in the text.

3 📖 As the story begins . . .

Each part of the selection begins with a brief summary. The bulleted sentences tell you what to expect in the part you will read next.

4 English Learner Support

This feature helps you understand difficult words and phrases in the English language. Some notes explain ideas from American culture. When you see words in blue type, look for this feature in the side column.

5 ▐ MORE ABOUT . . .

When you see a circled word or phrase in the text, look for a More About note that provides more information about the circled topic.

---

3 📖 As the story begins . . .

- The narrator, a writer, is staying at a cabin near an orphanage.
- Jerry is a 12-year-old boy who lives at the orphanage. He will help the narrator chop wood.

4 English Learner Support
Culture

Social Services An *orphanage* is a public institution that provides care for children whose parents are either dead or unable to care for them.

5 ▐ MORE ABOUT . . .
RHODODENDRON There are many kinds of rhododendron. One kind is the mountain laurel. It is a shrub with clusters of flowers. When in full bloom, the shrubs might look like a carpet or covering on the hills.

The InterActive Reader PLUS
22 For English Learners

---

1 FOCUS

The narrator describes where she goes to be by herself. Find out about the place and about Jerry, an orphan who comes to help her.

▐ MARK IT UP ⟩ Circle details that help you picture the setting. An example is highlighted.

The orphanage is high in the Carolina mountains. Sometimes in winter the snowdrifts are so deep that the institution is cut off from the village below, from all the world. Fog hides the mountain peaks, the snow swirls down the valleys, and a
10 wind blows so bitterly that the orphanage boys who take the milk twice daily to the baby cottage reach the door with fingers stiff in an agony of numbness.

"Or when we carry trays from the cook house for the ones that are sick," Jerry said, "we get our faces frostbit, because we can't put our hands over them. I have gloves," he added. "Some of the boys don't have any."

He liked the late spring, he said. The rhododendron was in bloom, a carpet of color, across the
20 mountainsides, soft as the May winds that stirred the hemlocks.[1] He called it laurel.[2]

"It's pretty when the laurel blooms," he said. "Some of it's pink and some of it's white."

I was there in the autumn. I wanted quiet, isolation, to do some troublesome writing. I wanted mountain air to blow out the malaria[3] from too long a time in the subtropics. I was homesick, too, for the flaming of maples in October, and for corn shocks and pumpkins and black-walnut trees and the lift of hills. I found
30 them all, living in a cabin that belonged to the orphanage, half a mile beyond the orphanage farm. When I took the cabin, I asked for a boy or man to come and chop wood for the fireplace. The first few

---

1. **hemlocks:** coniferous evergreen trees belonging to the pine family.
2. **laurel:** an evergreen shrub or tree with aromatic leaves.
3. **malaria** (mə-lâr′ē-ə): a disease in the blood caused by the bite of a mosquito.

days were warm, I found what wood I needed about the cabin, no one came, and I forgot the order.

I looked up from my typewriter one late afternoon, a little startled. A boy stood at the door, and my pointer dog, my companion, was at his side and had not barked to warn me. The boy was probably twelve
40 years old, but undersized. He wore overalls and a torn shirt, and was barefooted.

He said, "I can chop some wood today."

I said, "But I have a boy coming from the orphanage."

"I'm the boy."

"You? But you're small."

"Size don't matter, chopping wood," he said. "Some of the big boys don't chop good. I've been chopping wood at the orphanage a long time."

I visualized mangled and <u>inadequate</u> branches for
50 my fires. I was well into my work and not inclined to conversation. I was a little <u>blunt</u>.

"Very well. There's the ax. Go ahead and see what you can do."

6 Pause & Reflect

FOCUS

Read to find out more about Jerry, the orphan boy.

MARK IT UP As you read, circle passages that describe Jerry.

I went back to work, closing the door. At first, the sound of the boy dragging brush annoyed me. Then he began to chop. The blows were rhythmic and steady, and
60 shortly I had forgotten him, the sound no more of an interruption than a consistent rain. I suppose an hour and a half passed, for when I

WORDS TO KNOW
inadequate (ĭn-ăd′ĭ-kwĭt) *adj.* not good enough for what is needed
blunt (blŭnt) *adj.* abrupt; rudely straightforward or honest

---

Pause & Reflect

1. Where does the story take place? (**Clarify**)

2. Review the details that you circled. Describe the setting of the story during *one* of the following seasons. (**Visualize**)

Season: winter/spring/autumn

Description:

As the story continues . . .

- Jerry chops wood for the narrator.
- Jerry visits with the narrator before supper.

A Mother in Mannville   23

---

6 Pause & Reflect

Whenever you see these words in the selection, stop reading. Go to the side column and answer the questions.

Pause-and-Reflect questions at the end of every section follow up the Focus activity at the beginning of each section. They give you a quick check of your understanding.

---

7 WORDS TO KNOW

Important **Words to Know** are underlined in each section. Definitions are given at the bottom of the page.

And there's more!

Student Model

These pages show you how one student used *The InterActive Reader™ Plus for English Learners* for "A Mother in Mannville."

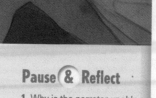

Note how this student used the following symbols:

* marks a place where something is important—a main idea, topic sentence, or important detail.

? marks a place where something is unclear or confusing.

! marks a surprising or critical fact, or a turning point in the action—not just a main idea but a major event or theme.

Pause & Reflect

1. Why is the narrator unable to return to the cabin on Sunday night? **(Cause and Effect)**

There is fog, and it is too dangerous to drive in it.

2. Once again, Jerry proves that he has integrity. What does he do when the narrator's return is delayed? **(Summarize)**

When the narrator does not return, Jerry still feeds the dog, this time with his own food.

As the story continues . . .

• Jerry tells the narrator about his mother.

• The narrator reacts to this news.

for him. And it seemed to me that being with my dog, and caring for him, had brought the boy and me, too, together, so that he felt that he belonged to me as well as to the animal.

"He stayed right with me," he told me, "except when he ran in the laurel. He likes the laurel. I took him up over the hill and we both ran fast. There was a place where the grass was high, and I lay down in it 200 and hid. I could hear Pat hunting for me. He found my trail and he barked. When he found me, he acted crazy, and he ran around and around me, in circles."

We watched the flames.

"That's an apple log," he said. "It burns the prettiest of any wood."

We were very close.

He was suddenly <u>impelled</u> to speak of things he had not spoken of before, nor had I cared to ask him.

"You look a little bit like my mother," he said. 210 "Especially in the dark, by the fire."

"But you were only four, Jerry, when you came here. You have remembered how she looked, all these years?"

Pause & Reflect

FOCUS

As Jerry and the narrator sit by the fire, Jerry begins to speak about his mother.

MARK IT UP As you read, circle words and phrases that describe the narrator's reaction to hearing about Jerry's mother.

WORDS TO KNOW
impel (ĭm-pĕl′) *v.* to drive, force, or urge to action

"My mother lives in Mannville," he said.

For a moment, finding that he had a mother shocked me as greatly as anything in my life has ever done, and I did not know why it disturbed me. 220 Then I understood my distress. I was filled with a passionate

resentment that any woman should go away and leave her son. A fresh anger added itself. A son like this one—The orphanage was a wholesome place, the executives were kind, good people, the food was more than adequate, the boys were healthy, a ragged shirt was no hardship, nor the doing of clean labor. Granted, perhaps, that the boy felt no lack, what blood fed the bowels of a woman who did not yearn over this child's
230 lean body that had come in parturition[7] out of her own? At four he would have looked the same as now. Nothing, I thought, nothing in life could change those eyes. His quality must be apparent to an idiot, a fool. I burned with questions I could not ask. In any, I was afraid, there would be pain.

"Have you seen her, Jerry—lately?"

"I see her every summer. She sends for me."

I wanted to cry out, "Why are you not with her? How can she let you go away again?"

240 He said, "She comes up here from Mannville whenever she can. She doesn't have a job now." **?**

His face shone in the firelight.

"She wanted to give me a puppy, but they can't let any one boy keep a puppy. You remember the suit I had on last Sunday?" He was plainly proud. "She sent me that for Christmas. The Christmas before that"— he drew a long breath, savoring the memory—"she sent me a pair of skates." **?**

"Roller skates?"

250 My mind was busy, making pictures of her, trying to understand her. She had not, then, entirely deserted or forgotten him. But why, then—I thought, "I must not condemn her without knowing."

"Roller skates. I let the other boys use them. They're always borrowing them. But they're careful of them."

What circumstance other than poverty—

---

7. **parturition** (pär′tyōō-rĭsh′ən): childbirth.

She is angry. Does she have her own children?

WHAT DOES IT MEAN? The words in blue mean "What kind of a mother could give birth to Jerry and then allow him to live at the orphanage?"

English Learner Support
Vocabulary

Figure of Speech *Burned with questions* means that the narrator felt a strong desire to ask questions.

Is this why he doesn't live with his mother, because she has no job?

Before You Read

Connect to Your Life

In "Raymond's Run" a girl named Squeaky has responsibility for her mentally disabled brother, Raymond. Have you ever taken care of someone? What was fun about the experience? What was challenging? Fill in the chart.

TAKING CARE OF SOMEONE

I liked the experience because _____

_____

_____

The experience was challenging because _____

_____

_____

Key to the Story

WHAT'S THE BIG IDEA? As Squeaky takes care of Raymond, her relationships with him and with other girls in the neighborhood change. Squeaky's ideas about herself change too. Use the concept web to describe changes you have undergone as you've grown up.

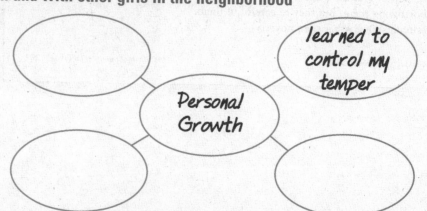

learned to control my temper

Personal Growth

Raymond's Run

by Toni Cade Bambara

PREVIEW Squeaky lives in a tough inner-city neighborhood and cares about two things: her brother Raymond and running.

- Squeaky, the narrator, is going for a walk with her older brother Raymond.
- Squeaky is a runner and she wins many races.
- Another girl named Gretchen will try to beat Squeaky in an upcoming race.

READING TIP If you are having trouble understanding a passage in this story, try reading it aloud to a classmate. Together you can figure out Squeaky's use of slang.

REREAD the boxed text. What does Squeaky do best? **(Clarify)**

FOCUS

In this section you meet Squeaky, who takes care of her brother Raymond.

MARK IT UP As you read, underline details that help you get to know her. An example is highlighted.

I don't have much work to do around the house like some girls. My mother does that. And I don't have to earn my pocket money by hustling; George runs errands for the big boys and sells Christmas cards. And anything else that's got to get done, my father does. All I have to do
10 in life is mind my brother Raymond, which is enough.

Sometimes I slip and say my little brother Raymond. But as any fool can see he's much bigger and he's older too. But a lot of people call him my little brother 'cause he needs looking after 'cause he's not quite right. And a lot of smart mouths got lots to say about that too, especially when George was minding him. But now, if anybody has anything to say to Raymond, anything to say about his big head,[1] they have to come by me. And I don't play the dozens[2] or believe in
20 standing around with somebody in my face doing a lot of talking. I much rather just knock you down and take my chances even if I am a little girl with skinny arms and a squeaky voice, which is how I got the name Squeaky. And if things get too rough, I run. And as anybody can tell you, I'm the fastest thing on two feet. There is no track meet that I don't win the first place medal. I use to win the twenty-yard dash when I was a little kid in kindergarten. Nowadays, it's the fifty-yard dash. And tomorrow I'm subject to run the
30 quarter-meter relay all by myself and come in first,

---

1. **big head:** enlarged skull as a result of Raymond's hydrocephalus (hī′ drō-sĕf′ə-ləs), a medical condition with symptoms that include swelling of the brain caused by too much fluid.

2. **play the dozens:** exchange rhyming insults.

WORDS TO KNOW
relay (rē′lā) *n.* a race in which each team member has a turn to finish a set part of the race and is then replaced by another team member to finish the next part

second, and third. The big kids call me Mercury[3] 'cause I'm the swiftest thing in the neighborhood. Everybody knows that—except two people who know better, my father and me. He can beat me to Amsterdam Avenue with me having a two-fire-hydrant head start and him running with his hands in his pockets and whistling. But that's private information. 'Cause can you imagine some thirty-five-year-old man stuffing himself into PAL shorts to race little kids? So
40 as far as everyone's concerned, I'm the fastest and that goes for Gretchen, too, who has put out the tale that she is going to win the first-place medal this year. Ridiculous. In the second place, she's got short legs. In the third place, she's got freckles. In the first place, no one can beat me and that's all there is to it.

I'm standing on the corner admiring the weather and about to take a stroll down Broadway so I can practice my breathing exercises, and I've got Raymond walking on the inside close to the buildings, 'cause he's
50 subject to fits of fantasy and starts thinking he's a circus performer and that the curb is a tightrope strung high in the air. And sometimes after a rain he likes to step down off his tightrope right into the gutter and slosh around getting his shoes and cuffs wet. Then I get hit when I get home. Or sometimes if you don't watch him he'll dash across traffic to the island in the middle of Broadway and give the pigeons a fit. Then I have to go behind him apologizing to all the old people sitting around trying to get some sun
60 and getting all upset with the pigeons fluttering around them, scattering their newspapers and upsetting the wax-paper lunches in their laps. So I keep Raymond on the inside of me, and he plays like

---

3. **Mercury:** in Roman mythology, the swift messenger of the gods.

WHAT DOES IT MEAN? *PAL* means "Police Athletic League," a group that organizes sports events for children.

MARK IT UP How does Squeaky describe Gretchen, her rival? Underline the words and phrases Squeaky uses. (Visualize)

MORE ABOUT . . .

BREATHING EXERCISES Serious runners often practice breathing techniques. They might breathe in, hold their breath for a few seconds, and breathe out as they walk. This helps them breathe evenly during a race.

English Learner Support

Vocabulary

Slang The words in blue mean that Raymond chases the pigeons and they begin to fly.

Pause & Reflect

How does Squeaky feel about herself? Check two words that apply. **(Infer)**

❏ proud
❏ competitive
❏ embarrassed
❏ discouraged

⌐ **As the story continues . . .**

• Squeaky describes the differences between herself and her classmate Cynthia Proctor.

[WHAT DOES IT MEAN?] *High-prance* means "lift the knees up high when walking."

English Learner Support
[Vocabulary]

Figure of Speech The words in blue mean that she fell on purpose but made it look like an accident.

he's driving a stagecoach which is O.K. by me so long as he doesn't run me over or interrupt my breathing exercises, which I have to do on account of I'm serious about my running, and I don't care who knows it.

Pause & Reflect

FOCUS

Squeaky compares herself to Cynthia Procter. Read to find out how they are different.

Now some people like to act like things come easy to them, won't let on that they practice. Not me. I'll high-prance down 34th Street like a rodeo pony to keep my knees strong even if it does get my mother uptight so that she walks ahead like she's not with me, don't know me, is all by herself on a shopping trip, and I am somebody else's crazy child. Now you take Cynthia Procter for instance. She's just the opposite. If there's a test tomorrow, she'll say something like, "Oh, I guess I'll play handball this afternoon and watch television tonight," just to let you know she ain't thinking about the test. Or like last week when she won the spelling bee for the millionth time, "A good thing you got 'receive,' Squeaky, 'cause I would have got it wrong. I completely forgot about the spelling bee." And she'll <u>clutch</u> the lace on her blouse like it was a narrow escape. Oh, brother. But of course when I pass her house on my early morning trots around the block, she is practicing the scales on the piano over and over and over and over. Then in music class she always lets herself get bumped around so she falls accidentally on purpose onto the piano stool and is so surprised to find herself sitting there that she decides just for fun to try out the ole keys.

WORDS TO KNOW
clutch (klŭch) *v.* to grasp and hold tightly

And what do you know—Chopin's waltzes[4] just spring out of her fingertips and she's the most surprised thing in the world. A regular <u>prodigy</u>. I could kill people like that. I stay up all night studying the words for the spelling bee. And you can see me any time of day practicing running. I never walk if I can trot, and

100 shame on Raymond if he can't keep up. But of course he does, 'cause if he hangs back someone's liable to walk up to him and get smart, or take his allowance from him, or ask him where he got that great big pumpkin head. People are so stupid sometimes.

Pause & Reflect

FOCUS
Squeaky runs into her rival, Gretchen, and Gretchen's friends.

MARK IT UP As you read, circle details that help you understand how Squeaky reacts to these girls.

So I'm strolling down Broadway breathing out and breathing in on counts of seven, which is my lucky number, and here comes
110 Gretchen and her <u>sidekicks</u>: Mary Louise, who used to be a friend of mine when she first moved to Harlem from Baltimore and got beat up by everybody till I took up for her on account of her mother and my mother used to sing in the same choir when they were young girls, but people ain't grateful, so now she hangs out with the new girl Gretchen and talks about me like a dog; and Rosie, who is as fat as I am skinny and has a big mouth where Raymond is
120 concerned and is too stupid to know that there is not

---

4. **Chopin's** (shō-pănz') **waltzes:** works by the 19th-century pianist and composer Frédéric Chopin.

WORDS TO KNOW
prodigy (prŏd′ə-jē) *n.* a person with an exceptional talent
sidekick (sīd′kĭk′) *n.* a close friend

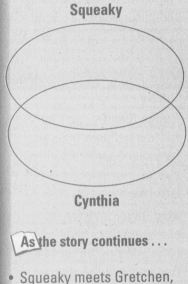

Pause & Reflect

How are Cynthia and Squeaky alike? How are they different? Write one similarity in the middle and one difference in each outer ring. (**Compare and Contrast**)

Squeaky

Cynthia

As the story continues . . .

- Squeaky meets Gretchen, Mary Louise, and Rosie.
- Rosie says that Squeaky may not win the May Day race.
- The girls try to tease Raymond but Squeaky defends him.

English Learner Support
Culture
Setting Harlem, the setting of the story, is a section of Manhattan. Manhattan is one of the five burroughs, or areas, of New York City.

English Learner Support
Language

Proverb *Throw stones* comes from the proverb "People who live in glass houses shouldn't throw stones." Because Rosie has flaws of her own, she shouldn't judge Raymond.

English Learner Support
Culture

Dodge City Dodge City, Kansas became famous for violent gunfights in its streets and saloons in the late 1800s.

May Day Many towns celebrate the arrival of spring on the first of May. Games, parades, dances, and races are all part of the fun.

WHAT DOES IT MEAN? By *all salty*, Squeaky means that Rosie is being bold and rude.

WHAT DOES IT MEAN? A *mule team* is a group of two or four mules hitched together to pull a wagon or stagecoach. Remember that Raymond is pretending to drive a stagecoach.

a big deal of difference between herself and Raymond and that she can't afford to throw stones. So they are steady coming up Broadway and I see right away that it's going to be one of those Dodge City scenes 'cause the street ain't that big and they're close to the buildings just as we are. First I think I'll step into the candy store and look over the new comics and let them pass. But that's chicken and I've got a reputation to consider. So then I think I'll just walk straight on
130 through them or over them if necessary. But as they get to me, they slow down. I'm ready to fight, 'cause like I said I don't feature a whole lot of chitchat, I much prefer to just knock you down right from the jump and save everybody a lotta precious time.

"You signing up for the May Day races?" smiles Mary Louise, only it's not a smile at all. A dumb question like that doesn't deserve an answer. Besides, there's just me and Gretchen standing there really, so no use wasting my breath talking to shadows.
140 "I don't think you're going to win this time," says Rosie, trying to signify with her hands on her hips all salty, completely forgetting that I have whupped her behind many times for less salt than that.

"I always win 'cause I'm the best," I say straight at Gretchen who is, as far as I'm concerned, the only one talking in this ventriloquist-dummy routine.[5] Gretchen smiles, but it's not a smile, and I'm thinking that girls never really smile at each other because they don't know how and don't want to know how and there's
150 probably no one to teach us how, 'cause grown-up girls don't know either. Then they all look at Raymond who has just brought his mule team to a standstill. And they're about to see what trouble they can get into through him.

"What grade you in now, Raymond?"

---

5. **ventriloquist-dummy routine:** Squeaky thinks that all the girls are speaking Gretchen's thoughts, like dummies being controlled by a ventriloquist.

"You got anything to say to my brother, you say it to me, Mary Louise Williams of Raggedy Town, Baltimore."

"What are you, his mother?" sasses Rosie.

160 "That's right, Fatso. And the next word out of anybody and I'll be their mother too." So they just stand there and Gretchen shifts from one leg to the other and so do they. Then Gretchen puts her hands on her hips and is about to say something with her freckle-face self but doesn't. Then she walks around me looking me up and down but keeps walking up Broadway, and her sidekicks follow her. So me and Raymond smile at each other and he says, "Gidyap," to his team and I continue with my breathing

170 exercises, strolling down Broadway toward the ice man on 145th with not a care in the world 'cause I am Miss Quicksilver[6] herself.

Pause & Reflect

FOCUS

Squeaky arrives at the park for the race. What happens before the race begins?

MARK IT UP As you read, underline details that help you picture what happens.

I take my time getting to the park on May Day because the track meet is the last thing on the program. The biggest thing on the program is the May Pole dancing, which I can do without, thank you,

180 even if my mother thinks it's a shame I don't take part and act like a girl for a change. You'd think my mother'd be grateful not to have to make me a white organdy dress with a big satin sash and buy me new white baby-doll shoes that can't be taken out of the box till the big day. You'd

6. **Miss Quicksilver:** a reference to the speed with which quicksilver (the liquid metal mercury) flows.

Pause & Reflect

1. Circle the word that *best* describes Squeaky's reaction to Gretchen, Mary Louise, and Rosie. **(Infer)**

  angry   frightened

  jealous   timid

2. What are the most important points that Squeaky makes when she talks to the girls? Check two. **(Main Idea)**

  ❏ Squeaky is the best runner.

  ❏ Raymond is smarter than Rosie.

  ❏ Nobody should mess with Raymond.

As the story continues . . .

• Squeaky arrives at the park and gets her race number from Mr. Pearson.

English Learner Support
Culture

May Pole A May Pole is a pole with ribbons attached. People hold the ribbons and dance around the pole. This tradition is part of the May Day celebration.

think she'd be glad her daughter ain't out there prancing around a May Pole getting the new clothes all dirty and sweaty and trying to act like a fairy or a flower or whatever you're supposed to be when you should be trying to be yourself, whatever that is, which is, as far as I am concerned, a poor Black girl who really can't afford to buy shoes and a new dress you only wear once a lifetime 'cause it won't fit next year.

I was once a strawberry in a Hansel and Gretel pageant when I was in nursery school and didn't have no better sense than to dance on tiptoe with my arms in a circle over my head doing umbrella steps and being a perfect fool just so my mother and father could come dressed up and clap. You'd think they'd know better than to encourage that kind of nonsense. I am not a strawberry. I do not dance on my toes. I run. That is what I am all about. So I always come late to the May Day program, just in time to get my number pinned on and lay in the grass till they announce the fifty-yard dash.

I put Raymond in the little swings, which is a tight squeeze this year and will be impossible next year. Then I look around for Mr. Pearson, who pins the numbers on. I'm really looking for Gretchen, if you want to know the truth, but she's not around. The park is jam-packed. Parents in hats and corsages and breast-pocket handkerchiefs peeking up. Kids in white dresses and light-blue suits. The parkees[7] unfolding chairs and chasing the rowdy kids from Lenox[8] as if they had no right to be there. The big guys with their caps on backwards, leaning against the fence swirling the basketballs on the tips of their fingers, waiting for all these crazy people to clear out the park so they can play. Most of the kids in my class are carrying bass

REREAD the boxed text. What does the text tell you about Squeaky? (Draw Conclusions)

English Learner Support

Culture

Races In official races, competitors often wear numbers on their shirts so that they may be easily identified.

What does Squeaky do when she arrives at the park?

---

7. **parkees:** park employees.
8. **Lenox:** a street in the Harlem section of New York City.

220 drums and glockenspiels[9] and flutes. You'd think they'd put in a few bongos or something for real like that.

Then here comes Mr. Pearson with his clipboard and his cards and pencils and whistles and safety pins and 50 million other things he's always dropping all over the place with his clumsy self. He sticks out in a crowd because he's on stilts. We used to call him Jack and the Beanstalk to get him mad. But I'm the only one that can outrun him and get away, and I'm too 230 grown for that silliness now.

"Well, Squeaky," he says, checking my name off the list and handing me number seven and two pins. And I'm thinking he's got no right to call me Squeaky if I can't call him Beanstalk.

"Hazel Elizabeth Deborah Parker," I correct him and tell him to write it down on his board.

"Well, Hazel Elizabeth Deborah Parker, going to give someone else a break this year?" I squint at him real hard to see if he is seriously thinking I should lose 240 the race on purpose just to give someone else a break. "Only six girls running this time," he continues, shaking his head sadly like it's my fault all of New York didn't turn out in sneakers. "That new girl should give you a run for your money." He looks around the park for Gretchen like a <u>periscope</u> in a submarine movie. "Wouldn't it be a nice gesture if you were . . . to ahhh . . . "

I give him such a look he couldn't finish putting that idea into words. Grownups got a lot of nerve 250 sometimes. I pin number seven to myself and stomp away, I'm so burnt. And I go straight for the track and

9. **glockenspiels** (glŏk′ən-spēlz′): musical instruments having tuned metal bars that are played with light hammers.

WORDS TO KNOW
periscope (pĕr′ĭ-skōp′) n. a tube-shaped optical device that lets one see into an area beyond the area he or she is in; a periscope is used by submarines to see above the surface while remaining underwater

---

WHAT DOES IT MEAN?
Bongos are an attached pair of drums usually held between the knees of a seated player and played by beating with the hands. Each drum is about a foot tall.

English Learner Support
Culture

Stilts When Squeaky says *he's on stilts,* she means "he is very tall and thin." *Stilts* are poles that one stands on to walk above the ground. Stilts make people look very tall and are often used as a toy for amusement.

Fairy Tale "Jack and the Beanstalk" is a children's story about a boy named Jack who climbs a magic beanstalk. By calling Mr. Pearson "Jack and the Beanstalk," Squeaky and her classmates are teasing him and comparing his height to that of the tall beanstalk.

WHAT DOES IT MEAN? *Burnt* means "angry."

WHAT DOES IT MEAN?
Concrete jungle means that the city is like a jungle.

Pause & Reflect

What does Mr. Pearson want Squeaky to do? (Question)

 **As the story continues...**

- Squeaky and Gretchen get ready for the race.
- Raymond gets ready to join the race from the other side of the fence.
- Squeaky races to the finish line.

English Learner Support

Vocabulary

Slang *Psyching* means "causing someone to feel nervous."

stretch out on the grass while the band winds up with "Oh, the Monkey Wrapped His Tail Around the Flag Pole," which my teacher calls by some other name. The man on the loudspeaker is calling everyone over to the track and I'm on my back looking at the sky, trying to pretend I'm in the country, but I can't, because even grass in the city feels hard as sidewalk, and there's just no pretending you are anywhere but in
260 a "concrete jungle" as my grandfather says.

Pause & Reflect

FOCUS

Squeaky watches the other races and then goes to the starting line for the fifty-yard dash. Read to find out what goes through her mind before and during the race.

The twenty-yard dash takes all of the two minutes 'cause most of the little kids don't know no better than to run off the track or run the wrong way or run smack into the fence and fall down and cry. One little kid, though, has got the good sense to run straight for the white ribbon up
270 ahead so he wins. Then the second-graders line up for the thirty-yard dash and I don't even bother to turn my head to watch 'cause Raphael Perez always wins. He wins before he even begins by psyching the runners, telling them they're going to trip on their shoelaces and fall on their faces or lose their shorts or something, which he doesn't really have to do since he is very fast, almost as fast as I am. After that is the forty-yard dash which I used to run when I was in first grade. Raymond is hollering from the swings 'cause he
280 knows I'm about to do my thing 'cause the man on the loudspeaker has just announced the fifty-yard dash, although he might just as well be giving a recipe

for angel food cake 'cause you can hardly make out what he's saying for the static. I get up and slip off my sweatpants and then I see Gretchen standing at the starting line, kicking her legs out like a pro. Then as I get into place I see that ole Raymond is on line on the other side of the fence, bending down with his fingers on the ground just like he knew what he was doing. I 290 was going to yell at him but then I didn't. It burns up your energy to holler.

Every time, just before I take off in a race, I always feel like I'm in a dream, the kind of dream you have when you're sick with fever and feel all hot and weightless. I dream I'm flying over a sandy beach in the early morning sun, kissing the leaves of the trees as I fly by. And there's always the smell of apples, just like in the country when I was little and used to think I was a choo-choo train, running through the fields of corn 300 and chugging up the hill to the orchard. And all the time I'm dreaming this, I get lighter and lighter until I'm flying over the beach again, getting blown through the sky like a feather that weighs nothing at all. But once I spread my fingers in the dirt and crouch over the Get on Your Mark, the dream goes and I am solid again and am telling myself, Squeaky you must win, you must win, you are the fastest thing in the world, you can even beat your father up Amsterdam if you really try. And then I feel my weight coming back just 310 behind my knees then down to my feet then into the earth and the pistol shot explodes in my blood and I am off and weightless again, flying past the other runners, my arms pumping up and down and the whole world is quiet except for the crunch as I zoom over the gravel in the track. I glance to my left and there is no one. To the right, a blurred Gretchen, who's got her chin jutting out as if it would win the race all by itself. And on the other side of the fence is

REREAD the boxed text. In the space below, draw a picture of what Squeaky sees in her dream. (**Visualize**)

English Learner Support

Language

Metaphors The pistol shot is the sound that signals the start of the race. *Explodes in my blood* is a metaphor, or comparison, telling how Squeaky's whole body reacts to the shot. *Flying past* means that she is moving very quickly, like a bird.

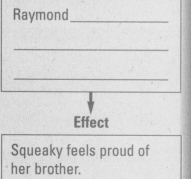

1. **MARK IT UP** Circle details on pages 13 and 14 that tell you the different thoughts that Squeaky has while running her race. **(Clarify)**

2. What does Raymond do during the race that makes Squeaky feel proud of him? Fill in the chart below. **(Cause and Effect)**

Cause

Raymond_____

_____

↓

Effect

Squeaky feels proud of her brother.

As the story ends . . .

• There is a delay in announcing who won the race.

• Squeaky gets an idea from watching Raymond run.

Raymond with his arms down to his side and the
320 palms tucked up behind him, running in his very own style, and it's the first time I ever saw that and I almost stop to watch my brother Raymond on his first run. But the white ribbon is bouncing toward me and I tear past it, racing into the distance till my feet with a mind of their own start digging up footfuls of dirt and brake me short. Then all the kids standing on the side pile on me, banging me on the back and slapping my head with their May Day programs, for I have won again and everybody on 151st Street can walk tall for
330 another year.

Pause & Reflect

FOCUS

All at once, winning is no longer important to Squeaky. Read to find out what Squeaky realizes about Raymond.

MARK IT UP As you read, underline words and phrases that reveal Squeaky's new plans for the future.

"In first place . . ." the man on the loudspeaker is clear as a bell now. But then he pauses and the loudspeaker starts to whine. Then static. And I lean down to catch my breath and here comes Gretchen walking back, for she's overshot the finish line too, huffing and
340 puffing with her hands on her hips taking it slow, breathing in steady time like a real pro and I sort of like her a little for the first time. "In first place . . ." and then three or four voices get all mixed up on the loudspeaker and I dig my sneaker into the grass and stare at Gretchen who's staring back, we both wondering just who did win. I can hear old Beanstalk arguing with the man on the loudspeaker and then a few others running their mouths about

what the stopwatches say. Then I hear Raymond
350 yanking at the fence to call me and I wave to shush
him, but he keeps rattling the fence like a gorilla in a
cage like in them gorilla movies, but then like a dancer
or something he starts climbing up nice and easy but
very fast. And it occurs to me, watching how smoothly
he climbs hand over hand and remembering how he
looked running with his arms down to his side and
with the wind pulling his mouth back and his teeth
showing and all, it occurred to me that Raymond
would make a very fine runner. Doesn't he always
360 keep up with me on my trots? And he surely knows
how to breathe in counts of seven 'cause he's always
doing it at the dinner table, which drives my brother
George up the wall. And I'm smiling to beat the band
'cause if I've lost this race, or if me and Gretchen tied,
or even if I've won, I can always retire as a runner and
begin a whole new career as a coach with Raymond as
my champion. After all, with a little more study I can
beat Cynthia and her phony self at the spelling bee.
And if I bugged my mother, I could get piano lessons
370 and become a star. And I have a big rep as the baddest
thing around. And I've got a roomful of ribbons and
medals and awards. But what has Raymond got to call
his own?

   So I stand there with my new plans, laughing out
loud by this time as Raymond jumps down from the
fence and runs over with his teeth showing and his
arms down to the side, which no one before him has
quite mastered as a running style. And by the time he
comes over I'm jumping up and down so glad to see
380 him—my brother Raymond, a great runner in the
family tradition. But of course everyone thinks I'm
jumping up and down because the men on the

English Learner Support
Language

Similes A simile is a comparison of two things using *like* or *as*. Note the similes in blue. Imagine a gorilla rattling a cage. Then imagine a dancer moving smoothly and easily. Do these images help you visualize Raymond's actions?

READING CHECK   What does Squeaky realize about Raymond?

[WHAT DOES IT MEAN?] The words in blue mean "a reputation as the most talented or successful person in the neighborhood."

Why do you think the story is called "Raymond's Run" rather than "Squeaky's Run"? Discuss your response in a group. **(Analyze)**

loudspeaker have finally gotten themselves together and compared notes and are announcing, "In first place—Miss Hazel Elizabeth Deborah Parker." (Dig that.) "In second place—Miss Gretchen P. Lewis." And I look over at Gretchen, wondering what the "P." stands for. And I smile. 'Cause she's good, no doubt about it. Maybe she'd like to help me coach Raymond; she obviously is serious about running, as any fool can see. And she nods to congratulate me and then she smiles. And I smile. We stand there with this big smile of respect between us. It's about as real a smile as girls can do for each other, considering we don't practice real smiling every day, you know, 'cause maybe we too busy being flowers or fairies or strawberries instead of something honest and worthy of respect . . . you know . . . like being people. ❖

390

Pause & Reflect

Active Reading SkillBuilder

Cause and Effect

Events in a plot are linked to each other through **cause-and-effect** relationships. The event that happens first is the **cause;** the one that follows, or results, is the **effect.** As you read "Raymond's Run," use the following chart to write down major events in the plot (the effects). Then explain why these events happen (the causes). One example has been done.

What Happens: Effect	Why It Happens: Cause
The big kids call her Mercury.	Squeaky is the "fastest thing in the neighborhood."

Literary Analysis SkillBuilder

Plot

A story's **plot** is made up of events that can be divided into rising action, climax, and falling action. The **rising action** develops as the main character encounters conflicts. Rising action leads to the **climax,** or turning point, of the story, which is the point of highest interest. In the **falling action,** or **resolution,** the conflicts are resolved, and the story is brought to a close. Use the diagram below to jot down the events in "Raymond's Run" that make up the rising action, the climax, and the falling action.

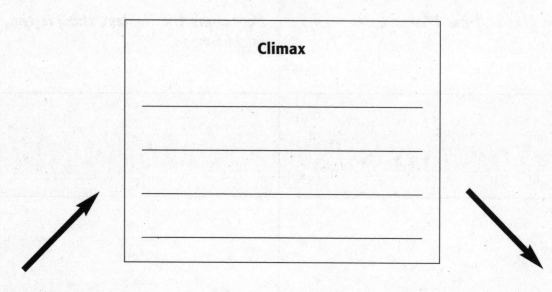

Climax

_____

_____

_____

_____

Rising Action

Squeaky takes Raymond for a walk on Broadway.

_____

Falling Action

_____

_____

_____

Words to Know SkillBuilder

Words to Know

clutch	periscope	prodigy	relay	sidekick

A. Decide which word from the list is closest in meaning to the underlined word or words. Then write the word in the blank line on the right.

1. Squeaky boasted that she could win the quarter-meter <u>race</u>. _____

2. She expected Cynthia to <u>grasp</u> the lace on her blouse in surprise. _____

3. Cynthia liked people to think she was a <u>person with exceptional talent</u>. _____

4. Squeaky missed her <u>close friend</u>, Mary Louise. _____

5. Some sort of <u>device to see over a crowd</u> would be useful to many people. _____

B. Answer each question by writing one of the Words to Know in the blank.

1. What is a synonym for *grasp*? _____
   (1)

2. What is another word for *pal* or *buddy*? _____
   (2)

3. What device is used on submarines to see above the surface of the water? _____
   (3)

4. How would you describe a person who has exceptional talent? _____
   (4)

5. What type of race uses several team members, each of whom finishes a part of the race? _____
   (5)

Before You Read

Connect to Your Life

Have you ever chosen to spend time alone? Have you ever felt lonely? What do you think is the difference between being lonely and being alone? Use the spaces below to list feelings and experiences that show the difference.

Lonely . . .
_____
_____
_____

Alone . . .
_____
_____
_____

Key to the Story

WHAT'S THE BIG IDEA? An orphanage is an institution for the care of children whose parents have died or whose parents can no longer take care of them. At the time of the story, orphanages were more common than they are today. What images come to mind when you think of an orphanage? See if your images match the images in the story.

Orphanage

lonely children

A MOTHER in MANNVILLE

by Marjorie Kinnan Rawlings

PREVIEW In this story, a friendship develops between a writer who has rented a cabin in the mountains and a boy who comes from a nearby orphanage to chop wood for the writer. What will it take for these two people to reach out to each other?

- The narrator, a writer, is staying at a cabin near an orphanage.

- Jerry is a 12-year-old boy who lives at the orphanage. He will help the narrator chop wood.

English Learner Support

Culture

Social Services An *orphanage* is a public institution that provides care for children whose parents are either dead or unable to care for them.

MORE ABOUT . . .

RHODODENDRON There are many kinds of rhododendron. One kind is the mountain laurel. It is a shrub with clusters of flowers. When in full bloom, the shrubs might look like a carpet or covering on the hills.

FOCUS

The narrator describes where she goes to be by herself. Find out about the place and about Jerry, an orphan who comes to help her.

MARK IT UP > Circle details that help you picture the setting. An example is highlighted.

The orphanage is high in the Carolina mountains. Sometimes in winter the snowdrifts are so deep that the institution is cut off from the village below, from all the world. Fog hides the mountain peaks, the snow swirls down the valleys, and a
10 wind blows so bitterly that the orphanage boys who take the milk twice daily to the baby cottage reach the door with fingers stiff in an agony of numbness.

"Or when we carry trays from the cook house for the ones that are sick," Jerry said, "we get our faces frostbit, because we can't put our hands over them. I have gloves," he added. "Some of the boys don't have any."

He liked the late spring, he said. The rhododendron was in bloom, a carpet of color, across the
20 mountainsides, soft as the May winds that stirred the hemlocks.[1] He called it laurel.[2]

"It's pretty when the laurel blooms," he said. "Some of it's pink and some of it's white."

I was there in the autumn. I wanted quiet, isolation, to do some troublesome writing. I wanted mountain air to blow out the malaria[3] from too long a time in the subtropics. I was homesick, too, for the flaming of maples in October, and for corn shocks and pumpkins and black-walnut trees and the lift of hills. I found
30 them all, living in a cabin that belonged to the orphanage, half a mile beyond the orphanage farm. When I took the cabin, I asked for a boy or man to come and chop wood for the fireplace. The first few

---

1. **hemlocks:** coniferous evergreen trees belonging to the pine family.

2. **laurel:** an evergreen shrub or tree with aromatic leaves.

3. **malaria** (mə-lâr′ē-ə): a disease in the blood caused by the bite of a mosquito.

days were warm, I found what wood I needed about the cabin, no one came, and I forgot the order.

I looked up from my typewriter one late afternoon, a little startled. A boy stood at the door, and my pointer dog, my companion, was at his side and had not barked to warn me. The boy was probably twelve
40 years old, but undersized. He wore overalls and a torn shirt, and was barefooted.

He said, "I can chop some wood today."

I said, "But I have a boy coming from the orphanage."

"I'm the boy."

"You? But you're small."

"Size don't matter, chopping wood," he said. "Some of the big boys don't chop good. I've been chopping wood at the orphanage a long time."

I visualized mangled and <u>inadequate</u> branches for
50 my fires. I was well into my work and not inclined to conversation. I was a little <u>blunt</u>.

"Very well. There's the ax. Go ahead and see what you can do."

Pause & Reflect

FOCUS

Read to find out more about Jerry, the orphan boy.

MARK IT UP > As you read, circle passages that describe Jerry.

I went back to work, closing the door. At first, the sound of the boy dragging brush annoyed me. Then he began to chop. The blows were rhythmic and steady, and
60 shortly I had forgotten him, the sound no more of an interruption than a consistent rain. I suppose an hour and a half passed, for when I

Pause & Reflect

1. Where does the story take place? (Clarify)

2. Review the details that you circled. Describe the setting of the story during *one* of the following seasons. (Visualize)
   Season: winter/spring/autumn
   Description:

As the story continues ...

• Jerry chops wood for the narrator.
• Jerry visits with the narrator before supper.

WORDS TO KNOW
inadequate (ĭn-ăd′ĭ-kwĭt) *adj.* not good enough for what is needed
blunt (blŭnt) *adj.* abrupt; rudely straightforward or honest

stopped and stretched, and heard the boy's steps on the cabin stoop, the sun was dropping behind the farthest mountain, and the valleys were purple with something deeper than the asters.

The boy said, "I have to go to supper now. I can come again tomorrow evening."

70 I said, "I'll pay you now for what you've done," thinking I should probably have to insist on an older boy. "Ten cents an hour?"

"Anything is all right."

We went together back of the cabin. An astonishing amount of solid wood had been cut. There were cherry logs and heavy roots of rhododendron, and blocks from the waste pine and oak left from the building of the cabin.

"But you've done as much as a man," I said. "This is a splendid pile."

80 I looked at him, actually, for the first time. His hair was the color of the corn shocks, and his eyes, very direct, were like the mountain sky when rain is pending— gray, with a shadowing of that miraculous blue. As I spoke, a light came over him, as though the setting sun had touched him with the same suffused glory with which it touched the mountains. I gave him a quarter.

"You may come tomorrow," I said, "and thank you very much."

He looked at me, and at the coin, and seemed to want to speak, but could not, and turned away.

90 "I'll split kindling tomorrow," he said over his thin ragged shoulder. "You'll need kindling and medium wood and logs and backlogs."

At daylight I was half wakened by the sound of chopping. Again it was so even in texture that I went back to sleep. When I left my bed in the cool morning, the boy had come and gone, and a stack of kindling

REREAD the boxed text. Why is the narrator surprised by what Jerry has done? (Cause and Effect)

English Learner Support
Vocabulary

Farming Term *Corn shocks* are piles of corn stalks set upright in a field for drying.

MORE ABOUT . . .
BACKLOGS are large logs put in the back of a fireplace. These logs burn longer than medium logs, which are put in the middle of the fireplace. Medium logs burn longer than kindling, which is put near the front to get the fire started.

WORDS TO KNOW
kindling (kĭnd'lĭng) *n.* pieces of dry wood or other material that can be easily lighted to start a fire; tinder

was neat against the cabin wall. He came again after school in the afternoon and worked until time to return to the orphanage. His name was Jerry; he was twelve years old, and he had been at the orphanage since he was four. I could picture him at four, with the same grave gray-blue eyes and the same—independence? No, the word that comes to me is "integrity."[4]

The word means something very special to me, and the quality for which I use it is a rare one. My father had it—there is another of whom I am almost sure—but almost no man of my acquaintance possesses it with the <u>clarity</u>, the purity, the simplicity of a mountain stream. But the boy Jerry had it. It is bedded on courage, but it is more than brave. It is honest, but it is more than honesty. The ax handle broke one day. Jerry said the wood shop at the orphanage would repair it. I brought money to pay for the job, and he refused it.

"I'll pay for it," he said. "I broke it. I brought the ax down careless."

"But no one hits accurately every time," I told him. "The fault was in the wood of the handle. I'll see the man from whom I bought it."

It was only then that he would take the money. He was standing back of his own carelessness. He was a free-will agent, and he chose to do careful work, and if he failed, he took the responsibility without subterfuge.[5]

And he did for me the unnecessary thing, the gracious thing, that we find done only by the great of heart. Things no training can teach, for they are done on the instant, with no <u>predicated</u> experience. He found a cubbyhole beside the fireplace that I had not noticed. There, of his own accord, he put kindling and "medium"

---

4. **integrity** (ĭn-tĕg′rə-tē): moral uprightness; honesty.
5. **subterfuge** (sŭb′tər-fyo͞oj′): anything used to hide one's true purpose or avoid a difficult situation.

WORDS TO KNOW
clarity (klăr′ĭ-tē) n. the quality of being easily seen; clearness
predicated (prĕd′ĭ-kā′-tĭd) adj. established; assumed **predicate** v.

MARK IT UP Reread the boxed text. Circle the sentences that explain what the narrator means by the word *integrity*. (Clarify)

WHAT DOES IT MEAN?
Bedded means "based" or "built upon."

WHAT DOES IT MEAN?
Standing back of his own carelessness means that Jerry was willing to accept the responsibility for breaking the ax.

English Learner Support
Vocabulary
Idioms *Of his own accord* means "on his own, without being told."

Metaphor In line 138, the narrator compares her sudden understanding of Jerry to a lifted curtain that offers a clear view of what has been hidden.

Pause & Reflect

1. Which of the following words best describes Jerry? Circle one. (Clarify)

   hard-working

   carefree

   angry

2. In the space below, describe something Jerry does that shows integrity. (Evaluate)

As the story continues . . .

- The narrator asks Jerry to take care of her dog Pat.
- The narrator does not return at the expected time.

wood, so that I might always have dry fire material ready in case of sudden wet weather. A stone was loose in the rough walk to the cabin. He dug a deeper hole and steadied it, although he came, himself, by a shortcut over the bank. I found that when I tried to return his thoughtfulness with such things as candy and apples, he was wordless. "Thank you" was, perhaps, an expression for which he had had no use, for his courtesy was <u>instinctive</u>. He only looked at the gift and at me, and a curtain lifted, so that I saw deep into the clear well of his eyes, and gratitude was there, and affection, soft over the firm granite of his character.

He made simple excuses to come and sit with me. I could no more have turned him away than if he had been physically hungry. I suggested once that the best time for us to visit was just before supper, when I left off my writing. After that, he waited always until my typewriter had been some time quiet. One day I worked until nearly dark. I went outside the cabin, having forgotten him. I saw him going up over the hill in the twilight toward the orphanage. When I sat down on my stoop, a place was warm from his body where he had been sitting.

Pause & Reflect

FOCUS

The narrator goes away for a weekend, leaving Jerry in charge of her dog. Read to find out how Jerry manages while the narrator is away.

He became intimate,[6] of course, with my pointer, Pat. There is a strange <u>communion</u> between a boy and a dog. Perhaps they possess the same singleness of spirit, the same

---

6. **intimate** (ĭn′tə-mĭt′): marked by close association or familiarity.

WORDS TO KNOW
instinctive (ĭn-stĭngk′tĭv) *adj.* having a natural tendency; spontaneous
communion (kə-myōōn′yən) *n.* close relationship in which deep feelings are shared; intimacy

kind of wisdom. It is difficult to explain, but it exists. When I went across the state for a weekend, I left the dog in Jerry's charge. I gave him the dog whistle and the key to the cabin and left sufficient food. He was to come two or three times a day and let out the dog and feed and exercise him. I should return Sunday night, and Jerry would take out the dog for the last time Sunday afternoon and then leave the key under an agreed hiding place.

My return was belated, and fog filled the mountain passes so treacherously that I dared not drive at night. The fog held the next morning, and it was Monday noon before I reached the cabin. The dog had been fed and cared for that morning. Jerry came early in the afternoon, anxious.

"The superintendent said nobody would drive in the fog," he said. "I came just before bedtime last night and you hadn't come. So I brought Pat some of my breakfast this morning. I wouldn't have let anything happen to him."

"I was sure of that. I didn't worry."

"When I heard about the fog, I thought you'd know."

He was needed for work at the orphanage, and he had to return at once. I gave him a dollar in payment, and he looked at it and went away. But that night he came in the darkness and knocked at the door.

"Come in, Jerry," I said, "if you're allowed to be away this late."

"I told maybe a story," he said. "I told them I thought you would want to see me."

"That's true," I assured him, and I saw his relief. "I want to hear about how you managed with the dog."

He sat by the fire with me, with no other light, and told me of their two days together. The dog lay close to him and found a comfort there that I did not have

When does the narrator return?

WHAT DOES IT MEAN? The *superintendent* is the person in charge of the orphanage.

English Learner Support
Vocabulary
Figure of Speech *I told maybe a story* means that he said something he wasn't sure was true.

for him. And it seemed to me that being with my dog, and caring for him, had brought the boy and me, too, together, so that he felt that he belonged to me as well as to the animal.

"He stayed right with me," he told me, "except when he ran in the laurel. He likes the laurel. I took him up over the hill and we both ran fast. There was a place where the grass was high, and I lay down in it and hid. I could hear Pat hunting for me. He found my trail and he barked. When he found me, he acted crazy, and he ran around and around me, in circles."

We watched the flames.

"That's an apple log," he said. "It burns the prettiest of any wood."

We were very close.

He was suddenly <u>impelled</u> to speak of things he had not spoken of before, nor had I cared to ask him.

"You look a little bit like my mother," he said. "Especially in the dark, by the fire."

"But you were only four, Jerry, when you came here. You have remembered how she looked, all these years?"

Pause & Reflect

FOCUS

As Jerry and the narrator sit by the fire, Jerry begins to speak about his mother.

||| **MARK IT UP** > As you read, circle words and phrases that describe the narrator's reaction to hearing about Jerry's mother.

"My mother lives in Mannville," he said.

For a moment, finding that he had a mother shocked me as greatly as anything in my life has ever done, and I did not know why it disturbed me. Then I understood my distress. I was filled with a passionate

WORDS TO KNOW
impel (ĭm-pĕl′) v. to drive, force, or urge to action

resentment that any woman should go away and leave her son. A fresh anger added itself. A son like this one—The orphanage was a wholesome place, the executives were kind, good people, the food was more than adequate, the boys were healthy, a ragged shirt was no hardship, nor the doing of clean labor. Granted, perhaps, that the boy felt no lack, what blood fed the bowels of a woman who did not yearn over this child's lean body that had come in parturition[7] out of her own? At four he would have looked the same as now. Nothing, I thought, nothing in life could change those eyes. His quality must be apparent to an idiot, a fool. I burned with questions I could not ask. In any, I was afraid, there would be pain.

"Have you seen her, Jerry—lately?"

"I see her every summer. She sends for me."

I wanted to cry out, "Why are you not with her? How can she let you go away again?"

He said, "She comes up here from Mannville whenever she can. She doesn't have a job now."

His face shone in the firelight.

"She wanted to give me a puppy, but they can't let any one boy keep a puppy. You remember the suit I had on last Sunday?" He was plainly proud. "She sent me that for Christmas. The Christmas before that"—he drew a long breath, savoring the memory—"she sent me a pair of skates."

"Roller skates?"

My mind was busy, making pictures of her, trying to understand her. She had not, then, entirely deserted or forgotten him. But why, then—I thought, "I must not condemn her without knowing."

"Roller skates. I let the other boys use them. They're always borrowing them. But they're careful of them."

What circumstance other than poverty—

WHAT DOES IT MEAN? The words in blue mean "What kind of a mother could give birth to Jerry and then allow him to live at the orphanage?"

English Learner Support
Vocabulary
Figure of Speech *Burned with questions* means that the narrator felt a strong desire to ask questions.

---

7. **parturition** (pär′tyŏŏ-rĭsh′ən): childbirth.

1. Complete the following
sentence. (Draw Conclusions)

*When Jerry tells the
narrator that he has a
mother, the narrator
feels* _____

_____

_____

2. What most confuses the
narrator about Jerry's
mother? Check one. (Infer)

❏ why she gave him
skates

❏ how she could bear to
give him up

❏ how she lost her job

As the story ends . . .

- The narrator plans to leave.
- Jerry does not say
goodbye.
- The narrator stops at the
orphanage before she goes.

WHAT DOES IT MEAN?
Thistledown refers to the
silky, featherlike hairs that
are part of the thistle plant.

"I'm going to take the dollar you gave me for taking care of Pat," he said, "and buy her a pair of gloves."

I could only say, "That will be nice. Do you know
260 her size?"

"I think it's 8½," he said.

He looked at my hands.

"Do you wear 8½?" he asked.

"No. I wear a smaller size, a 6."

"Oh! Then I guess her hands are bigger than yours."

I hated her. Poverty or no, there was other food than bread, and the soul could starve as quickly as the body. He was taking his dollar to buy gloves for her big stupid hands, and she lived away from him, in Mannville, and
270 contented herself with sending him skates.

"She likes white gloves," he said. "Do you think I can get them for a dollar?"

"I think so," I said.

I decided that I should not leave the mountains without seeing her and knowing for myself why she had done this thing.

Pause & Reflect

FOCUS
The narrator prepares to
leave the mountains.
Read to find out what she
discovers before she
leaves.

The human mind scatters its interests as though made of thistledown, and every wind
280 stirs and moves it. I finished my work. It did not please me, and I gave my thoughts to another field. I should need some Mexican material.

I made arrangements to close my Florida place. Mexico immediately, and doing the writing there, if conditions were favorable. Then, Alaska with my brother. After that, heaven knew what or where.

And after my first fury at her—we did not speak of her again—his having a mother, any sort at all, not far away, in Mannville, relieved me of the ache I had had about him. He did not question the anomalous[8] relation. He was not lonely. It was none of my concern.

He came every day and cut my wood and did small helpful favors and stayed to talk. The days had become cold, and often I let him come inside the cabin. He would lie on the floor in front of the fire, with one arm across the pointer, and they would both doze and wait quietly for me. Other days they ran with a common <u>ecstasy</u> through the laurel, and since the asters were now gone, he brought me back vermilion maple leaves, and chestnut boughs dripping with imperial yellow. I was ready to go.

I said to him, "You have been my good friend, Jerry. I shall often think of you and miss you. Pat will miss you too. I am leaving tomorrow."

He did not answer. When he went away, I remember that a new moon hung over the mountains, and I watched him go in silence up the hill. I expected him the next day, but he did not come. The details of packing my personal belongings, loading my car, arranging the bed over the seat, where the dog would ride, occupied me until late in the day. I closed the cabin and started the car, noticing that the sun was in the west and I should do well to be out of the mountains by nightfall. I stopped by the orphanage and left the cabin key and money for my light bill with Miss Clark.

---

8. **anomalous** (ə-nŏm′ə-ləs): differing from the general rule; abnormal.

WORDS TO KNOW
  abstracted (ăb-străk′tĭd) *adj.* lost in thought so as to be unaware of one's surroundings; absent-minded, preoccupied
  ecstasy (ĕk′stə-sē) *n.* intense joy or delight; bliss

REREAD the boxed text. Why does the narrator decide not to go to see Jerry's mother? (Cause and Effect)

WHAT DOES IT MEAN?
Vermilion means "bright red or orange." *Boughs dripping with imperial yellow* means "branches full of beautiful yellow leaves."

Pause & Reflect

1. Complete the following sentence. (Clarify)

At the end of the story, the narrator finds out that Jerry

_____

_____

_____

2. What was your reaction to learning the truth about Jerry's mother? (Connect)

Why do you think Jerry tells the narrator that he has a mother? Discuss your answer in a small group. (Infer)

320 "And will you call Jerry for me to say goodbye to him?"

"I don't know where he is," she said. "I'm afraid he's not well. He didn't eat his dinner this noon. One of the other boys saw him going over the hill into the laurel. He was supposed to fire the boiler this afternoon. It's not like him; he's unusually reliable."

I was almost relieved, for I knew I should never see him again, and it would be easier not to say goodbye to him.

330 I said, "I wanted to talk with you about his mother—why he's here—but I'm in more of a hurry than I expected to be. It's out of the question for me to see her now too. But here's some money I'd like to leave with you to buy things for him at Christmas and on his birthday. It will be better than for me to try to send him things. I could so easily duplicate—skates, for instance."

She blinked her honest spinster's eyes.

"There's not much use for skates here," she said.

Her stupidity annoyed me.

340 "What I mean," I said, "is that I don't want to duplicate things his mother sends him. I might have chosen skates if I didn't know she had already given them to him."

She stared at me.

"I don't understand," she said. "He has no mother. He has no skates." ❖

Pause & Reflect

Active Reading SkillBuilder

Visualizing

You **visualize** when you form a mental picture from a written description. Good readers use details supplied by the writer to picture characters, settings, and events. Making pictures in your mind can be one of the great pleasures of reading. The drawing below can help you visualize the events of "A Mother in Mannville."

- On pages 23–24, the narrator describes Jerry chopping and piling wood. Add the woodpile and woods to the drawing to show their locations.

- On page 26, the narrator mentions a stone walk and a stoop outside the cabin. Add the walk and stoop to the drawing. Label the "loose stone" to show its location.

- As you read, notice the hill that both the narrator and Miss Clark mention. Its location depends in part on where you visualize the mountains, the town of Mannville, and the fields of laurel. You may wish to add these details and others to the drawing or add arrows to show where they are in relation to the drawing.

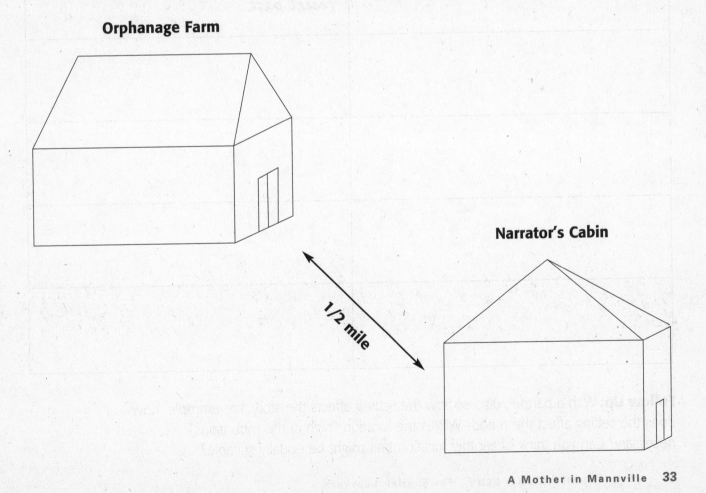

Orphanage Farm

Narrator's Cabin

1/2 mile

Literary Analysis SkillBuilder

Setting

The **setting** of a story, poem, or play is the time and location where the action occurs. The setting may be a backdrop, with no effect on what happens, or it may be important to the action of the story. Clues about time and place are often scattered throughout a story. In "A Mother in Mannville," the location is stated, but the time period is not. Use the chart below to jot down setting details that you find in "A Mother in Mannville." Then make an inference based on each clue that you find. Try to determine whether the story takes place in the present, the recent past (50–100 years ago), or the distant past (several hundred years ago).

Detail from the Story	Inference
The narrator uses a typewriter.	The use of a typewriter implies the recent past.

Follow Up: With a partner, discuss how the setting affects the story. For example, how does the setting affect the mood? Why is the location "high in the mountains" necessary? Can you think of another location that might be equally suitable?

Words to Know SkillBuilder

Words to Know

abstracted	clarity	ecstasy	inadequate	kindling
blunt	communion	impel	instinctive	predicated

A. Write the Word to Know that belongs in each numbered blank.

It looks like something chewed up by a cat.
Oh, what could (1) you to wear such a hat?

_____
(1)

For pounding a nail, a hammer ought to do it.
A shoe is (2); it's just not up to it.

_____
(2)

A parent's love is (3), so a mom or a dad
Can still feel affection for a most unpleasant lad.

_____
(3)

It's good to be candid and up-front,
But it can be foolish to be too (4).

_____
(4)

Proofread all your papers if the goals you have are higher
Than using them as (5) when you start a fire.

_____
(5)

I can't remember when I ever felt so fine.
I tell you, I'm in (6). I think I'm on cloud nine.

_____
(6)

B. Fill in each blank with the correct Words to Know.

1. The _____ between the narrator and the boy
   was shaken when he spoke of his mother.

2. The responsibility the narrator gave Jerry was _____
   on Jerry's reliable work habits.

3. _____ by thoughts of packing up and moving,
   the narrator forgot about the boy's mother.

4. Jerry understood with perfect _____ that once
   again he was alone.

Before You Read

Connect to Your Life

Have you ever planned something that turned out differently than you expected? Use the space below to write or illustrate how you imagined the event. Then show what actually happened.

| What I thought it would be like | What really happened |

Key to the Story

WHAT'S THE BIG IDEA? A ransom is the exchange of money for something or someone who has been held captive. Have you ever read or heard about a ransom? Complete the word web by writing words that come to mind when you think of the word *ransom*.

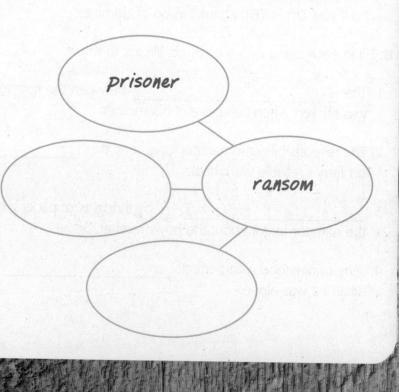

prisoner

ransom

The Ransom of Red Chief

BY O. HENRY

PREVIEW Two professional criminals think that they've found a quick and easy scheme to make money. Will their plan work the way they expect?

As the story begins . . .

- The narrator and Bill are in Alabama.
- They are looking for a way to make money.
- They think of a plan.

English Learner Support

Language

Simile *As flat as a flannel-cake* is a simile—it compares the town to a flannel-cake. *Flannel-cake* is another term for a pancake. The simile means that the town is very flat.

Why do the men think that Summit is a sensible place to carry out their plan?

WHAT DOES IT MEAN?

Constables are town officers responsible for keeping the peace. *Lackadaisical* means "lazy." *Bloodhounds* are dogs with a good sense of smell, often used to track and catch criminals.

FOCUS

The narrator and his friend, Bill, think up a money-making plan. Read to find out about the narrator and this plan.

MARK IT UP As you read, underline details that tell you something about their scheme. An example is highlighted.

It looked like a good thing; but wait till I tell you. We were down South, in Alabama—Bill Driscoll and myself—when this kidnapping idea struck us. It was, as Bill afterward expressed it, "during a moment of temporary mental apparition";[1] but we didn't
10 find that out till later.

There was a town down there, as flat as a flannel-cake, and called Summit, of course. It contained inhabitants of as undeleterious[2] and self-satisfied a class of peasantry[3] as ever clustered around a Maypole.

Bill and me had a joint capital of about six hundred dollars, and we needed just two thousand dollars more to pull off a fraudulent[4] town-lot scheme in Western Illinois. We talked it over on the front steps of the hotel. Philoprogenitiveness,[5] says we, is strong in
20 semi-rural communities; therefore, and for other reasons, a kidnapping project ought to do better there than in the radius[6] of newspapers that send reporters out in plain clothes to stir up talk about such things. We knew that Summit couldn't get after us with anything stronger than constables[7] and, maybe, some lackadaisical bloodhounds and a diatribe or two in the Weekly Farmers' Budget. So, it looked good.

---

1. **apparition** (ăp′ə-rĭsh′ən): a sudden or unusual sight; Bill means an "aberration," a moving away from the normal to the unusual.
2. **undeleterious** (ŭn-dĕl′ĭ-tîr′ē-əs): harmless.
3. **peasantry** (pĕz′ən-trē): the social class made up of farmers, tenants, and workers.
4. **fraudulent** (frô′jə-lənt): false.
5. **philoprogenitiveness** (fĭl′ō-prō-jĕn′ĭ-tĭv-nəs): love for children or one's own children.
6. **radius**: range or area.
7. **constables** (kŏn′stə-bəlz): the police.

WORDS TO KNOW
diatribe (dī′ə-trīb′) *n.* condemnation; bitter, abusive criticism

We selected for our victim the only child of a prominent citizen named Ebenezer Dorset. The father was respectable and tight, a mortgage fancier and a stern, upright collection plate passer and forecloser. The kid was a boy of ten, with bas-relief[8] freckles and hair the color of the cover of the magazine you buy at the newsstand when you want to catch a train. Bill and me figured that Ebenezer would melt down for a <u>ransom</u> of two thousand dollars to a cent. But wait till I tell you.

Pause & Reflect

FOCUS

The kidnapping does not go smoothly. Read to find out what happens when the narrator and Bill kidnap the boy.

MARK IT UP ⟩ As you read, underline details that help you **visualize**, or imagine, the boy.

About two miles from Summit was a little mountain, covered with a dense cedar brake.[9] On the rear elevation of this mountain was a cave. There we stored provisions.[10]

One evening after sundown, we drove in a buggy past old Dorset's house. The kid was in the street, throwing rocks at a kitten on the opposite fence.

"Hey, little boy!" says Bill, "would you like to have a bag of candy and a nice ride?"

The boy catches Bill neatly in the eye with a piece of brick.

"That will cost the old man an extra five hundred dollars," says Bill, climbing over the wheel.

---

8. **bas-relief** (bä´rĭ-lēf´): slightly raised; a kind of sculpture carved so that figures stand out only slightly from the background's flat surface.

9. **brake:** a thick grouping of trees or undergrowth.

10. **provisions** (prə-vĭzh´ənz): supplies.

WORDS TO KNOW
ransom (răn´səm) *n.* a price or a payment demanded in return for the release of property or a person

Pause & Reflect

What do the narrator and his friend plan to do to make money? Check one phrase below. (Clarify)
- ❑ steal a horse
- ❑ kidnap a boy
- ❑ rob a bank
- ❑ kidnap a girl

As the story continues . . .

- The narrator and Bill kidnap a boy.
- The kidnappers take the boy to a cave.

WHAT DOES IT MEAN? *Neatly* means "precisely" or "skillfully."

Pause & Reflect

Circle the phrase below that best describes the boy. **(Clarify)**

sweet and gentle

quiet and sad

playful and violent

obedient and respectful

As the story continues . . .

• The kidnappers and their captive spend the night in the cave.

• "Red Chief" does not behave as expected.

That boy put up a fight like a welterweight cinnamon bear; but, at last, we got him down in the bottom of the buggy and drove away. We took him up to the cave, and I hitched the horse in the cedar brake. After dark I drove the buggy to the little village, three miles away, where we had hired it, and walked back to the mountain.

60 Bill was pasting court plaster[11] over the scratches and bruises on his features.

There was a fire burning behind the big rock at the entrance of the cave, and the boy was watching a pot of boiling coffee, with two buzzard tail feathers stuck in his red hair. He points a stick at me when I come up, and says: "Ha! cursed paleface, do you dare to enter the camp of Red Chief, the terror of the plains?"

"He's all right now," says Bill, rolling up his trousers and examining some bruises on his shins. "We're 70 playing Indian. We're making Buffalo Bill's show look like magic-lantern views[12] of Palestine in the town hall. I'm Old Hank, the Trapper, Red Chief's captive, and I'm to be scalped at daybreak. By Geronimo! that kid can kick hard."

Pause & Reflect

FOCUS

Read to find out how "Red Chief" behaves during his first night as a captive.

MARK IT UP As you read, underline the details that tell you about Red Chief and his behavior.

Yes, sir, that boy seemed to be having the time of his life. The fun of camping out in a cave had made him forget that he was a captive himself. 80 He immediately christened me Snake-eye, the Spy, and

---

11. **court plaster:** adhesive cloth for covering superficial cuts or scratches on the skin, used in the 19th century.

12. **magic-lantern views:** slides. A magic lantern was an early slide projector used to show an enlarged image of a picture; popular in the 19th century.

announced that when his braves returned from the warpath, I was to be broiled at the stake at the rising of the sun.

Then we had supper; and he filled his mouth full of bacon and bread and gravy and began to talk. He made a during-dinner speech something like this:

"I like this fine. I never camped out before; but I had a pet possum once, and I was nine last birthday. I hate to go to school. Rats ate up sixteen of Jimmy Talbot's aunt's speckled hen's eggs. Are there any real Indians in these woods? I want some more gravy. Does the trees moving make the wind blow? We had five puppies. What makes your nose so red, Hank? My father has lots of money. Are the stars hot? I whipped Ed Walker twice, Saturday. I don't like girls. You dassent[13] catch toads unless with a string. Do oxen make any noise? Why are oranges round? Have you got beds to sleep on in this cave? Amos Murray has got six toes. A parrot can talk, but a monkey or a fish can't. How many does it take to make twelve?"

Every few minutes he would remember that he was an Indian, and pick up his stick rifle and tiptoe to the mouth of the cave to search for the scouts of the hated paleface. Now and then he would let out a war whoop that made Old Hank the Trapper shiver. That boy had Bill terrorized from the start.

"Red Chief," says I to the kid, "would you like to go home?"

"Aw, what for?" says he. "I don't have any fun at home. I hate to go to school. I like to camp out. You won't take me back home again, Snake-eye, will you?"

"Not right away," says I. "We'll stay here in the cave awhile."

"All right!" says he. "That'll be fine. I never had such fun in all my life."

---

13. **dassent:** dare not.

Pause & Reflect

How does Red Chief feel about being kidnapped? Check one phrase below. (Infer)

❑ He hates it.
❑ He enjoys it.
❑ He wants to go home.

📝 **As the story continues . . .**

- Red Chief harasses and tortures Bill.
- Sam wonders if the boy's kidnapping has been noticed.

We went to bed about eleven o'clock. We spread down some wide blankets and quilts and put Red Chief between us. We weren't afraid he'd run away. 120 He kept us awake for three hours, jumping up and reaching for his rifle and screeching: "Hist! pard," in mine and Bill's ears, as the fancied crackle of a twig or the rustle of a leaf revealed to his young imagination the stealthy approach of the outlaw band. At last, I fell into a troubled sleep, and dreamed that I had been kidnapped and chained to a tree by a ferocious pirate with red hair.

Pause & Reflect

FOCUS

Read to find out what Red Chief does to Bill in the morning.

Just at daybreak, I was awakened by a series of awful screams from Bill. They weren't 130 yells, or howls, or shouts, or whoops, or yawps, such as you'd expect from a manly set of vocal organs—they were simply indecent, terrifying, humiliating screams, such as women emit when they see caterpillars. It's an awful thing to hear a strong, desperate, fat man scream incontinently[14] in a cave at daybreak.

I jumped up to see what the matter was. Red Chief was sitting on Bill's chest, with one hand twined in Bill's hair. In the other he had the sharp case knife we used for slicing bacon; and he was industriously[15] and realistically 140 trying to take Bill's scalp, according to the sentence that had been pronounced upon him the evening before.

I got the knife away from the kid and made him lie down again. But, from that moment, Bill's spirit was broken. He laid down on his side of the bed, but he never closed an eye again in sleep as long as that boy was with

---

14. **incontinently** (ĭn-kŏn′tə-nənt-lē): uncontrolled.

15. **industriously** (ĭn-dŭs′trē-əs-lē): working hard.

us. I dozed off for a while, but along toward sunup I remembered that Red Chief had said I was to be burned at the stake at the rising of the sun. I wasn't nervous or afraid; but I sat up and leaned against a rock.

150 "What you getting up so soon for, Sam?" asked Bill.

"Me?" says I. "Oh, I got a kind of pain in my shoulder. I thought sitting up would rest it."

"You're a liar!" says Bill. "You're afraid. You was to be burned at sunrise, and you was afraid he'd do it. And he would, too, if he could find a match. Ain't it awful, Sam? Do you think anybody will pay out money to get a little imp like that back home?"

"Sure," said I. "A rowdy kid like that is just the kind that parents dote on. Now, you and the Chief get
160 up and cook breakfast, while I go up on the top of this mountain and reconnoiter."

I went up on the peak of the little mountain and ran my eye over the contiguous[16] vicinity. Over toward Summit I expected to see the sturdy yeomanry of the village armed with scythes and pitchforks beating the countryside for the dastardly kidnappers. But what I saw was a peaceful landscape dotted with one man plowing with a dun mule. Nobody was dragging the creek; no couriers dashed hither and yon, bringing
170 tidings of no news to the distracted parents. There was a sylvan[17] attitude of somnolent[18] sleepiness <u>pervading</u> that section of the external outward surface of Alabama that lay exposed to my view. "Perhaps," says I to myself, "it has not yet been discovered that the wolves have borne away the tender lambkin from the fold. Heaven help the wolves!" says I, and I went down the mountain to breakfast.

16. **contiguous** (kən-tĭg′yōō-əs): sharing an edge or boundary.

17. **sylvan** (sĭl′vən): related to a wood or forest.

18. **somnolent** (sŏm′nə-lənt): drowsy; sleepy.

WORDS TO KNOW
pervade (pər-vād′) *v.* to be spread or to be present throughout

Context Clues
Sometimes the meaning of a word can be understood by studying how it is used in the context of a sentence. Use **context clues** to match the highlighted words with their synonyms (words with almost the same meaning) below.

Words	Synonyms
rowdy	love
dote on	observe
reconnoiter	rough and noisy

WHAT DOES IT MEAN?
Yeomanry means "farmers who work on their own small farms."

the boxed passage. Who is the "tender lambkin" and who are the "wolves"? Why does the narrator say, "Heaven help the wolves"? **(Infer)**

Pause & Reflect

What does Red Chief do to
Bill in the morning?
(Summarize)

As the story continues...

• Red Chief continues to
torment Bill.

• Sam decides that it is time
to send a message to the
boy's father.

MORE ABOUT . . .

(DAVID) In the Bible, David
defeats a giant enemy named
Goliath with a sling and a
stone.

When I got to the cave, I found Bill backed up against
the side of it, breathing hard, and the boy threatening to
180 smash him with a rock half as big as a coconut.

"He put a red-hot boiled potato down my back,"
explained Bill, "and then mashed it with his foot; and I
boxed his ears. Have you got a gun about you, Sam?"

I took the rock away from the boy and kind of
patched up the argument. "I'll fix you," says the kid
to Bill. "No man ever yet struck the Red Chief but he
got paid for it. You better beware!"

Pause & Reflect

FOCUS

Bill continues to suffer at
the hands of Red Chief.
Read to find out what
happens to Bill in this
part.

After breakfast the kid
takes a piece of leather with
190 strings wrapped around it out
of his pocket and goes outside
the cave unwinding it.

"What's he up to now?"
says Bill, anxiously. "You don't think he'll run away,
do you, Sam?"

"No fear of it," says I. "He don't seem to be much of
a homebody. But we've got to fix up some plan about
the ransom. There don't seem to be much excitement
around Summit on account of his disappearance; but
200 maybe they haven't realized yet that he's gone. His folks
may think he's spending the night with Aunt Jane or
one of the neighbors. Anyhow, he'll be missed today.
Tonight we must get a message to his father demanding
the two thousand dollars for his return."

Just then we heard a kind of war whoop, such as
David might have emitted when he knocked out the
champion Goliath. It was a sling that Red Chief had

pulled out of his pocket, and he was whirling it around his head.

210 I dodged, and heard a heavy thud and a kind of a sigh from Bill, like a horse gives out when you take his saddle off. A rock the size of an egg had caught Bill just behind his left ear. He loosened himself all over and fell in the fire across the frying pan of hot water for washing the dishes. I dragged him out and poured cold water on his head for half an hour.

By and by, Bill sits up and feels behind his ear and says: "Sam, do you know who my favorite Biblical character is?"

220 "Take it easy," says I. "You'll come to your senses presently."

"King Herod,"[19] says he. "You won't go away and leave me here alone, will you, Sam?"

I went out and caught that boy and shook him until his freckles rattled.

"If you don't behave," says I, "I'll take you straight home. Now, are you going to be good, or not?"

"I was only funning," says he, sullenly. "I didn't mean to hurt Old Hank. But what did he hit me for? 230 I'll behave, Snake-eye, if you won't send me home and if you'll let me play the Scout today."

"I don't know the game," says I. "That's for you and Mr. Bill to decide. He's your playmate for the day. I'm going away for a while, on business. Now, you come in and make friends with him and say you are sorry for hurting him, or home you go, at once."

Pause & Reflect

English Learner Support
Vocabulary

Idiom *By and by* means "a little later."

WHAT DOES IT MEAN? *Scout* means "person sent to gather information."

Pause & Reflect

REREAD the boxed passage on page 44. Why does Sam want to send a message to the boy's father? Circle one. **(Clarify)**

He wants to reduce the amount of the ransom.

He thinks the boy's family doesn't know he's missing.

He's afraid the boy might run away.

---

19. **King Herod:** Herod ruled Judea from 37 B.C. to 4 B.C., and at one point ordered the execution of all boys in Bethlehem younger than two years old (Matthew 2:16).

- The Kidnappers discuss how much money the boy's father should pay in ransom.

- The Kidnappers write the ransom note.

English Learner Support

Vocabulary

Figure of Speech *Without batting an eye* means "without blinking," or "immediately, without questioning or hesitating."

READING CHECK

How does Bill feel about being left alone with Red Chief?

FOCUS

Sam and Bill write a ransom letter to the boy's father. What do you think it will say?

I made him and Bill shake hands, and then I took Bill aside and told him I was going 240 to Poplar Grove, a little village three miles from the cave, and find out what I could about how the kidnapping had been regarded in Summit. Also, I thought it best to send a peremptory[20] letter to old man Dorset that day, demanding the ransom and dictating how it should be paid.

"You know, Sam," says Bill, "I've stood by you without batting an eye in earthquakes, fire, and flood—in poker games, dynamite outrages,[21] police 250 raids, train robberies, and cyclones. I never lost my nerve yet till we kidnapped that two-legged skyrocket of a kid. He's got me going. You won't leave me long with him, will you, Sam?"

"I'll be back sometime this afternoon," says I. "You must keep the boy amused and quiet till I return. And now we'll write the letter to old Dorset."

Bill and I got paper and pencil and worked on the letter while Red Chief, with a blanket wrapped around him, strutted up and down, guarding the mouth of the 260 cave. Bill begged me tearfully to make the ransom fifteen hundred dollars instead of two thousand. "I ain't attempting," says he, "to decry[22] the celebrated moral aspect of parental affection, but we're dealing with humans, and it ain't human for anybody to give up two thousand dollars for that forty-pound chunk of freckled wildcat. I'm willing to take a chance at fifteen hundred dollars. You can charge the difference up to me."

---

20 **peremptory** (pə-rĕmp′tə-rē): putting an end to all debate or action.

21. **dynamite outrages:** shocking bombings.

22. **decry:** to minimize or make light of.

So, to relieve Bill, I acceded, and we <u>collaborated</u> a letter that ran this way:

270 EBENEZER DORSET, ESQ.:

We have your boy concealed in a place far from Summit. It is useless for you or the most skillful detectives to attempt to find him. Absolutely the only terms on which you can have him restored to you are these: We demand fifteen hundred dollars in large bills for his return; the money to be left at midnight tonight at the same spot and in the same box as your reply— as hereinafter described. If you agree to these terms, send your answer in writing by a solitary messenger

280 tonight at half-past eight o'clock. After crossing Owl Creek on the road to Poplar Grove, there are three large trees about a hundred yards apart, close to the fence of the wheat field on the right-hand side. At the bottom of the fence post, opposite the third tree, will be found a small pasteboard box.

The messenger will place the answer in this box and return immediately to Summit.

If you attempt any treachery[23] or fail to <u>comply</u> with our demand as stated, you will never see your boy again.

290 If you pay the money as demanded, he will be returned to you safe and well within three hours. These terms are final, and if you do not accede[24] to them, no further communication will be attempted.

TWO DESPERATE MEN

Pause & Reflect

WHAT DOES IT MEAN? *Esq.* is an abbreviation for *esquire.* It is a title of honor and dignity.

Pause & Reflect

1. READ ALOUD the boxed passage. Explain how the kidnappers expect to receive a reply to their note. **(Summarize)**

2. Why does Bill want to reduce the ransom from two thousand dollars to fifteen hundred? **(Infer)**

---

23. **treachery** (trĕch′ə-rē): betrayal of trust.

24. **accede** (ăk-sēd′): agree.

WORDS TO KNOW
collaborate (kə-lăb′ə-rāt) *v.* to work together on a project
comply (kəm-plī′) *v.* to act according to a command, request, or order

As the story continues . . .

- Sam leaves Red Chief and Bill alone at the cave while he goes to mail the ransom note.

- Red Chief tricks Bill into playing a new game.

WHAT DOES IT MEAN? *Foil* means "prevent from being successful."

English Learner Support

Vocabulary

Dialect *Hoss* means "horse." *On his all fours* means "on his hands and knees."

What part does Red Chief want Bill to play in his latest game?

FOCUS

Bill stays behind with the boy while Sam mails the ransom letter. Read to find out what the boy persuades Bill to do.

I addressed this letter to Dorset and put it in my pocket. As I was about to start, the kid comes up to me and says:

300   "Aw, Snake-eye, you said I could play the Scout while you was gone."

"Play it, of course," says I. "Mr. Bill will play with you. What kind of a game is it?"

"I'm the Scout," says Red Chief, "and I have to ride to the stockade²⁵ to warn the settlers that the Indians are coming. I'm tired of playing Indian myself. I want to be the Scout."

"All right," says I. "It sounds harmless to me. I guess Mr. Bill will help you foil the enemy."

310   "What am I to do?" asks Bill, looking at the kid suspiciously.

"You are the hoss," says Scout. "Get down on your hands and knees. How can I ride to the stockade without a hoss?"

"You'd better keep him interested," said I, "till we get the scheme going. Loosen up."

Bill gets down on his all fours, and a look comes in his eye like a rabbit's when you catch it in a trap.

"How far is it to the stockade, kid?" he asks, in a
320 husky manner of voice.

"Ninety miles," says the Scout. "And you have to hurry to get there on time. Whoa, now!"

The Scout jumps on Bill's back and digs his heels in his side.

"For Heaven's sake," says Bill, "hurry back, Sam, as soon as you can. I wish we hadn't made the ransom more than a thousand. Say, you quit kicking me or I'll get up and warm you good."

25. **stockade** (stŏ-kād′): a barrier made of wood.

I walked over to Poplar Grove and sat around the
330 post office and store, talking with the chaw-bacons
that came in to trade. One whiskerando says that he
hears Summit is all upset on account of Elder Ebenezer
Dorset's boy having been lost or stolen. That was all I
wanted to know. I referred casually to the price of
black-eyed peas, posted my letter <u>surreptitiously</u>
and came away. The postmaster said the mail carrier
would come by in an hour to take the mail to Summit.

Pause & Reflect

FOCUS

Read to find out what the boy did to Bill while the narrator was away.

MARK IT UP As you read, circle words and phrases that tell you what the boy did to Bill.

When I got back to the cave, Bill and the boy were
340 not to be found. I explored the vicinity[26] of the cave and risked a yodel or two, but there was no response.

So I sat down on a mossy bank to await developments.

In about half an hour I heard the bushes rustle, and Bill wabbled out into the little glade in front of the cave. Behind him was the kid, stepping softly like a scout, with a broad grin on his face. Bill stopped, took
350 off his hat, and wiped his face with a red handkerchief. The kid stopped about eight feet behind him.

"Sam," says Bill, "I suppose you think I'm a renegade, but I couldn't help it. I'm a grown person with masculine proclivities[27] and habits of self-defense,

---

26. **vicinity** (vĭ-sĭn′ĭ-tē): the area nearby.

27. **proclivities** (prō-klĭv′ĭ-tēs): natural tendencies.

WORDS TO KNOW
surreptitiously (sûr′əp-tĭsh′əs-lē) *adv.* in a sneaky way; secretly

Pause & Reflect

Why does the narrator walk to Poplar Grove? Check one phrase below. **(Clarify)**
❑ to pick up the ransom
❑ to visit the police
❑ to see his aunt
❑ to get some information and post the letter

As the story continues . . .

• Sam returns to the cave.
• Bill tells Sam what happened while he was gone.

WHAT DOES IT MEAN? A *yodel* is a loud call. *Wabbled* means "moved unsteadily."

WHAT DOES IT MEAN? A *renegade* is a disloyal person.

English Learner Support
Language

Figure of Speech *There is a time when* means "eventually."

English Learner Support
Vocabulary

Predominance Another word for *predominance* is *superiority*. Bill means that he was not able to control the boy.

READING CHECK

Where does Bill think the boy is now?

but there is a time when all systems of egotism[28] and predominance fail. The boy is gone. I sent him home. All is off. There was martyrs[29] in old times," goes on Bill, "that suffered death rather than give up the particular graft they enjoyed. None of 'em ever was

360 subjugated[30] to such tortures as I have been. I tried to be faithful to our articles of depredation;[31] but there came a limit."

"What's the trouble, Bill?" I asks him.

"I was rode," says Bill, "the ninety miles to the stockade, not barring an inch. Then, when the settlers was rescued, I was given oats. Sand ain't a <u>palatable</u> substitute. And then, for an hour I had to try to explain to him why there was nothin' in holes, how a road can run both ways, and what makes the grass green. I tell

370 you, Sam, a human can only stand so much. I takes him by the neck of his clothes and drags him down the mountain. On the way he kicks my legs black and blue from the knees down; and I've got to have two or three bites on my thumb and hand cauterized.[32]

"But he's gone"—continues Bill—"gone home. I showed him the road to Summit and kicked him about eight feet nearer there at one kick. I'm sorry we lose the ransom; but it was either that or Bill Driscoll to the madhouse."

380 Bill is puffing and blowing, but there is a look of ineffable[33] peace and growing content on his rose-pink features.

---

28. **egotism** (ē′gə-tĭz′əm): an inflated sense of one's own importance.

29. **martyrs** (mär′tərz): people who endure great suffering.

30. **subjugated** (sŭb′jə-gāt′ĭd): enslaved.

31. **depredation** (dĕp′rĭ-dā′shən): robbery or plundering.

32. **cauterized** (kô′tə-rīzd): burned a wound in order to stop the bleeding or to promote healing.

33. **ineffable** (ĭn-ĕf′ə-bəl): unable to be expressed.

WORDS TO KNOW
palatable (păl′ə-tə-bəl) *adj.* acceptable to the taste; able to be eaten

"Bill," says I, "there isn't any heart disease in your family, is there?"

"No," says Bill, "nothing chronic[34] except malaria and accidents. Why?"

"Then you might turn around," says I, "and have a look behind you."

390 Bill turns and sees the boy, and loses his complexion[35] and sits down plump on the ground and begins to pluck aimlessly at grass and little sticks. For an hour I was afraid of his mind. And then I told him that my scheme was to put the whole job through immediately and that we would get the ransom and be off with it by midnight if old Dorset fell in with our <u>proposition</u>. So Bill braced up enough to give the kid a weak sort of a smile and a promise to play the Russian in a Japanese war with him as soon as he felt a little better.

Pause & Reflect

FOCUS

The boy's father sends Sam and Bill a letter with a surprising suggestion. Will the narrator and Bill get their money?

400 I had a scheme for collecting that ransom without danger of being caught by counterplots that ought to <u>commend</u> itself to professional kidnappers. The tree under which the answer was to be left—and the money later on—was close to the road fence, with big, bare fields

---

34. **chronic** (krŏn′ĭk): long-lasting.

35. **complexion** (kəm-plĕk′shən): natural color and appearance of facial skin.

WORDS TO KNOW
proposition (prŏp′ə-zĭsh′ən) *n.* a suggested plan
commend (kə-mĕnd′) *v.* to speak highly of; to praise

WHAT DOES IT MEAN? *Afraid of his mind* means "afraid he had gone crazy."

MORE ABOUT . . .

RUSSO-JAPANESE WAR
Russia and Japan were at war between 1904 and 1905. Russia surrendered after its defeat in a series of attacks.

Pause & Reflect

What does the boy do to Bill while the narrator is away? Check three. **(Summarize)**
❑ rides on his back
❑ asks him puzzling questions
❑ kicks him
❑ gives him a heart attack

As the story ends . . .

• Bill and Sam receive an unexpected reply to their ransom note.

on all sides. If a gang of constables should be watching for anyone to come for the note, they could
410 see him a long way off crossing the fields or in the road. But no, sirree! At half past eight I was up in that tree as well hidden as a tree toad, waiting for the messenger to arrive.

Exactly on time, a half-grown boy rides up the road on a bicycle, locates the pasteboard box at the foot of the fence post, slips a folded piece of paper into it, and pedals away again back toward Summit.

I waited an hour and then concluded the thing was square. I slid down the tree, got the note, slipped
420 along the fence till I struck the woods, and was back at the cave in another half an hour. I opened the note, got near the lantern, and read it to Bill. It was written with a pen in a crabbed hand,[36] and the sum and substance of it was this:

TWO DESPERATE MEN:

Gentlemen: I received your letter today by post, in regard to the ransom you ask for the return of my son. I think you are a little high in your demands, and I hereby make you a counterproposition, which I am inclined to
430 believe you will accept. You bring Johnny home and pay me two hundred and fifty dollars in cash, and I agree to take him off your hands. You had better come at night, for the neighbors believe he is lost, and I couldn't be responsible for what they would do to anybody they saw bringing him back. Very respectfully,

EBENEZER DORSET

"Great Pirates of Penzance," says I; "of all the impudent—"

---

36. **crabbed hand:** handwriting that is difficult to read.

WORDS TO KNOW
impudent (ĭm′pyə-dənt) *adj.* offensively bold and disrespectful

But I glanced at Bill, and hesitated. He had the most
appealing look in his eyes I ever saw on the face of a
dumb or a talking brute.

"Sam," says he, "what's two hundred and fifty
dollars, after all? We've got the money. One more
night of this kid will send me to a bed in Bedlam.[37]
Besides being a thorough gentleman, I think Mr.
Dorset is a spendthrift[38] for making us such a liberal
offer. You ain't going to let the chance go, are you?"

"Tell you the truth, Bill," says I, "this little he-ewe
lamb has somewhat got on my nerves too. We'll take
him home, pay the ransom, and make our getaway."

We took him home that night. We got him to go by
telling him that his father had bought a silver-mounted
rifle and a pair of moccasins for him and we were to
hunt bears the next day.

It was just twelve o'clock when we knocked at
Ebenezer's front door. Just at the moment when I
should have been abstracting the fifteen hundred
dollars from the box under the tree, according to the
original proposition, Bill was counting out two
hundred and fifty dollars into Dorset's hand.

When the kid found out we were going to leave him
at home, he started up a howl like a calliope[39] and
fastened himself as tight as a leech to Bill's leg. His
father peeled him away gradually, like a porous plaster.

"How long can you hold him?" asks Bill.

"I'm not as strong as I used to be," says old Dorset,
"but I think I can promise you ten minutes."

REREAD the boxed text on page 52. Why is Mr. Dorset worried the neighbors might see the kidnappers? (Infer)

READING CHECK How do Sam and Bill finally get rid of Red Chief?

English Learner Support

Language

Simile *As tight as a leech* is a simile that means "very tightly." A *leech* is a bloodsucking worm that clings tightly to its prey.

---

37. **Bedlam:** an insane asylum.

38. **spendthrift** (spĕnd'thrĭft'): a person who spends money wastefully.

39. **calliope** (kə-lī'ə-pē'): an instrument fitted with steam whistles, played by keyboard.

Pause & Reflect

1. When the boy is returned to his father, he is _____. (Check two.) **(Infer)**
   ❏ filled with relief
   ❏ sorry his adventure is over
   ❏ happy to be home
   ❏ exhausted

2. What was your reaction to the ending of the story? **(Connect)**

 What unexpected elements, or twists, did O. Henry weave into this story? Mark passages in the story to support your interpretation. (Analyze)

"Enough," says Bill. "In ten minutes I shall cross the Central, Southern, and Middle Western States and be 470 legging it trippingly for the Canadian border."

And as dark as it was, and as fat as Bill was, and as good a runner as I am, he was a good mile and a half out of Summit before I could catch up with him. ❖

Active Reading SkillBuilder

Predicting

Predicting what will happen in a story is part of the enjoyment of reading. To make predictions you can pay attention to details, think about what the characters say, and look for hints that the narrator gives. Jot down your predictions in the chart below as you read "The Ransom of Red Chief," and then record the actual event. Note whether your prediction was accurate or whether the actual event surprised you.

My Prediction	Actual Event	Surprised?
The boy will be pleased when Bill offers him a bag of candy and a nice ride.	The boy throws a brick at Bill.	yes

Literary Analysis SkillBuilder

Irony

Irony is a contrast or contradiction between what is stated and what is meant or between what is expected and what actually happens. "The Ransom of Red Chief" contains mostly **situational irony,** a contradiction between what happens and what is expected to happen. The story also contains examples of **verbal irony,** when a word or phrase is used to suggest the opposite of its usual meaning. Complete the chart with information from the story and your own experience as a reader.

What We Expect	What Happens	Effect on the Reader
How we expect the kidnappers to behave *They'll be mean and tough.*		
How we expect Red Chief to react to the kidnapping		
How we expect Red Chief's father to react to the kidnapping		

Follow Up: With a partner, look for examples of verbal irony in the story. (Hint: The kidnappers' use of fancy words is sometimes inappropriate.) Also look for places where the definition of a word doesn't quite fit the way the character uses it. For example, think about the contradiction in Sam's statement that "A rowdy kid like that is just the kind that parents dote on."

Words to Know SkillBuilder

Words to Know

collaborate	comply	impudent	pervade	ransom
commend	diatribe	palatable	proposition	surreptitiously

A. Fill in each blank with an **antonym** (or opposite) from the Words to Know list.

1. praise _____

2. polite _____

3. disagreeable _____

4. disapprove _____

5. openly _____

B. Fill in each blank with a **synonym** (or similar-meaning word) from the Words to Know list.

1. cooperate _____

2. permeate _____

3. payment _____

4. suggestion _____

5. obey _____

C. Answer each question by writing one of the Words to Know in the blank.

1. How do the kidnappers examine the town?

_____ (1)

2. What are Bill and Sam expecting from the boy's father?

_____ (2)

3. How does Red Chief act with Bill and Sam?

_____ (3)

4. What do Bill and Sam want Red Chief to do when they give him an order?

_____ (4)

5. How would Red Chief describe the food that he receives?

_____ (5)

Before You Read

Connect to Your Life

In this story, a boy places himself in a dangerous situation in order to perform a good deed. Think about a time when you did a favor for someone. Fill in this chart to show what you did and how other people reacted to your good deed.

Good Deed	How Other People Reacted
I walked my neighbor's dog.	

Key to the Story

WHAT YOU NEED TO KNOW The story takes place in the Klondike, a region in the Yukon Territory of northwestern Canada. In August 1896 gold was discovered in this region. Soon after this event, people began arriving to search for gold in creeks like the Mazy May.

Shade in the Yukon Territory on the map.

The King of Mazy May

by Jack London

PREVIEW In this story, 14-year-old Walt Masters is looking after things while his father is away. When Walt overhears a gang of thieves planning a crime, he is forced to take action.

As the story begins . . .

- Walt Masters lives in Northern Canada where the sun shines at midnight.
- Walt knows how to take care of himself in the wilderness.

Pause & Reflect

1. Review the details you circled as you read. Check the phrase below that best describes Walt. **(Infer)**

   ❑ nasty and rude

   ❑ kind and brave

   ❑ shy and quiet

   ❑ cruel and hateful

2. **MARK IT UP** Underline the phrases that describe Walt's special skills. **(Clarify)**

FOCUS

In this part you will meet Walt Masters, a boy who lives in the Yukon.

MARK IT UP As you read, circle details that help you get to know him. An example is highlighted.

Walt Masters is not a very large boy, but there is manliness in his makeup, and he himself, although he does not know a great deal that most boys know, knows much that other boys do not know. He has never seen a train of cars nor an elevator in his life,

10 and for that matter he has never once looked upon a cornfield, a plow, a cow, or even a chicken. He has never had a pair of shoes on his feet, nor gone to a picnic or a party, nor talked to a girl. But he has seen the sun at midnight, watched the ice jams on one of the mightiest of rivers, and played beneath the northern lights,[1] the one white child in thousands of square miles of frozen wilderness.[2]

Walt has walked all the fourteen years of his life in suntanned, moose-hide moccasins, and he can go to

20 the Indian camps and "talk big" with the men, and trade calico and beads with them for their precious furs. He can make bread without baking powder, yeast, or hops, shoot a moose at three hundred yards, and drive the wild wolf dogs fifty miles a day on the packed trail.

Last of all, he has a good heart, and is not afraid of the darkness and loneliness, of man or beast or thing. His father is a good man, strong and brave, and Walt is growing up like him.

Pause & Reflect

---

1. **northern lights:** bright bands or streamers of light sometimes seen in northern night skies. The lights are believed to be caused by charged particles in the earth's magnetic field.

2. **wilderness** (wĭl′ dər-nĭs): an empty landscape without many human settlers.

FOCUS

Walt and his father have been looking for gold in the Yukon. They are worried about claim-jumpers (thieves).

MARK IT UP As you read, circle the words that describe the crime of "claim-jumping."

30   Walt was born a thousand miles or so down the Yukon,[3] in a trading post below the Ramparts. After his mother died, his father and he came up on the river, step by step, from camp to camp, till now they are settled down on the Mazy May Creek in the Klondike country. Last year they and several others had

40 spent much toil and time on the Mazy May, and endured great hardships: the creek, in turn, was just beginning to show up its richness and to reward them for their heavy labor. But with the news of their discoveries, strange men began to come and go through the short days and long nights, and many unjust things they did to the men who had worked so long upon the creek.

Si Hartman had gone away on a moose hunt, to return and find new stakes driven and his (claim) jumped.[4] George Lukens and his brother had lost their

50 claims in a like manner, having delayed too long on the way to Dawson to record them. In short, it was the old story, and quite a number of the earnest, industrious[5] prospectors had suffered similar losses.

But Walt Masters's father had recorded his claim at the start, so Walt had nothing to fear now that his father had gone on a short trip up the White River prospecting for quartz. Walt was well able to stay by himself in the cabin, cook his three meals a day, and look after things. Not only did he look after his

---

3. **Yukon:** a river flowing from the Yukon Territory of northwest Canada through Alaska to the Bering Sea.

4. **claim jumped:** when a plot of land staked out by a miner is stolen by someone else.

5. **industrious** (ĭn-dŭs′ trē-əs): hard-working.

WORDS TO KNOW
prospector (prŏs′pĕk′tər) *n.* one who explores an area for mineral deposits or oil

As the story continues . . .

• Walt is looking after gold claims while his father is away.

• He sees some strangers who may be thieves.

• Walt's neighbor is old and ill. His claim is in danger.

REREAD the boxed passage. What do the highlighted words, *richness* and *discoveries*, refer to? **(Draw Conclusions)**

MORE ABOUT . . .

GOLD (CLAIMS) When a gold prospector found a piece of land rich with gold, he would drive wooden stakes into the ground to mark the four corners of his claim. Then he would go to the nearest government office to record the claim in his name. He would need to act quickly, however, because claim jumpers might try to steal his claim. They could do this by pulling out the original stakes, putting in new ones, and getting to the government office first to record the claim in their own names.

60 father's claim, but he had agreed to keep an eye on the adjoining one of Loren Hall, who had started for Dawson to record it.

Loren Hall was an old man, and he had no dogs, so he had to travel very slowly. After he had been gone some time, word came up the river that he had broken through the ice at Rosebud Creek and frozen his feet so badly that he would not be able to travel for a couple of weeks. Then Walt Masters received the news that old Loren was nearly all right again, and about to
70 move on foot for Dawson as fast as a weakened man could.

Walt was worried, however; the claim was <u>liable</u> to be jumped at any moment because of this delay, and a fresh <u>stampede</u> had started in on the Mazy May. He did not like the looks of the newcomers, and one day, when five of them came by with crack dog teams and the lightest of camping outfits, he could see that they were prepared to make speed, and resolved to keep an eye on them. So he locked up the cabin and followed
80 them, being at the same time careful to remain hidden.

Pause & Reflect

What might happen to Loren Hall's claim while he is away? (Predict)

As the story continues...

• Walt watches the strangers check the claim for gold.

• He hears them make plans about Loren Hall's claim.

Pause & Reflect

FOCUS

Walt spies on the strangers. What do you think he discovers about their plans? Read to find out.

He had not watched them long before he was sure that they were professional stampeders, bent on[6] jumping all the claims in sight. Walt crept along the snow at the

---

6. **bent on:** planning to.

WORDS TO KNOW
liable (lī′ə-bəl) *adj.* likely
stampede (stăm-pēd′) *n.* a sudden headlong rush or flight of a crowd of people

rim of the creek and saw them change many stakes, destroy old ones, and set up new ones.

90 In the afternoon, with Walt always trailing on their heels, they came back down the creek, unharnessed their dogs, and went into camp within two claims of his cabin. When he saw them make preparations to cook, he hurried home to get something to eat himself, and then hurried back. He crept so close that he could hear them talking quite plainly, and by pushing the underbrush aside he could catch occasional glimpses of them. They had finished eating and were sitting around the fire.

100 "The creek is all right, boys," a large, black-bearded man, evidently the leader, said, "and I think the best thing we can do is to pull out tonight. The dogs can follow the trail; besides, it's going to be moonlight. What say you?"

"But it's going to be beastly cold," objected one of the party. "It's forty below zero now."

"An' sure, can't ye keep warm by jumpin' off the sleds an' runnin' after the dogs?" cried an Irishman. "An' who wouldn't? The creek's as rich as a United States mint! Faith, it's an ilegant chanst to be gettin' a 110 run fer yer money! An' if ye don't run, it's mebbe you'll not get the money at all, at all."

"That's it," said the leader. "If we can get to Dawson and record, we're rich men; and there's no telling who's been sneaking along in our tracks, watching us, and perhaps now off to give the alarm. The thing for us to do is to rest the dogs a bit, and then hit the trail as hard as we can. What do you say?"

Evidently the men had agreed with their leader, for Walt Masters could hear nothing but the rattle of the 120 tin dishes which were being washed. Peering out cautiously, he could see the leader studying a piece of

WORDS TO KNOW
peer (pîr) v. to look intently, searchingly, or with difficulty

paper. Walt knew what it was at a glance—a list of all the unrecorded claims on Mazy May. Any man could get these lists by applying to the gold <u>commissioner</u> at Dawson.

"Thirty-two," the leader said, lifting his face to the men. "Thirty-two isn't recorded, and this is thirty-three. Come on: let's take a look at it. I saw somebody had been working on it when we came up 130 this morning."

Three of the men went with him, leaving one to remain in camp. Walt crept carefully after them till they came to Loren Hall's shaft. One of the men went down and built a fire on the bottom to thaw out the frozen gravel while the others built another fire on the dump and melted water in a couple of gold pans. This they poured into a piece of canvas stretched between two logs, used by Loren Hall in which to wash his gold.

140   In a short time a couple of buckets of dirt were sent up by the man in the shaft, and Walt could see the others grouped anxiously about their leader as he proceeded to wash it. When this was finished, they stared at the broad streak of black sand and yellow gold grains on the bottom of the pan, and one of them called excitedly for the man who had remained in camp to come. Loren Hall had struck it rich and his claim was not yet recorded. It was plain that they were going to jump it.

Pause & Reflect

Pause & Reflect

1. Why do the men decide to jump Loren Hall's claim? **(Cause and Effect)**

2. What do you think Walt will do now that he knows the men's plans? **(Predict)**

WORDS TO KNOW
commissioner (kə-mĭsh'ə-nər) *n.* a person authorized by a commission or special group to perform certain duties

FOCUS

Walt tries to prevent the strangers from jumping Loren Hall's claim. How will he do this?

MARK IT UP As you read, underline the details that help you **visualize**—see, feel, and hear—what he does.

150 Walt lay in the snow, thinking rapidly. He was only a boy, but in the face of the threatened injustice to old lame Loren Hall he felt that he must do something. He waited and watched, with his mind made up, till he saw the men begin to square up new stakes.[7] Then he crawled away till out of hearing, and 160 broke into a run for the camp of the stampeders. Walt's father had taken their own dogs with him prospecting, and the boy knew how impossible it was for him to undertake the seventy miles to Dawson without the aid of dogs.

Gaining the camp, he picked out, with an experienced eye, the easiest running sled and started to harness up the stampeders' dogs. There were three teams of six each, and from these he chose ten of the best. Realizing how necessary it was to have a good head dog, he strove[8] to 170 discover a leader amongst them: but he had little time in which to do it, for he could hear the voices of the returning men. By the time the team was in shape and everything ready, the claim-jumpers came into sight in an open place not more than a hundred yards from the trail, which ran down the bed of the creek. They cried out to Walt, but instead of giving heed to them he grabbed up one of their fur sleeping robes, which lay loosely in the snow, and leaped upon the sled.

"Mush! Hi! Mush on!" he cried to the animals, 180 snapping the keen-lashed whip among them.

As the story continues . . .

• Walt races to the thieves' camp and hooks up ten of their dogs to a sled.

• The claim jumpers try to catch him.

• The race begins.

MORE ABOUT . . .

DOG SLEDS There are no roads or vehicles in this wilderness. The only way to travel is to hitch teams of sled dogs to large sleds. People and supplies can ride on the sleds.

WHAT DOES IT MEAN? *Mush* means "get going!"

---

7. **to square up new stakes:** to make new stakes.
8. **strove:** tried.

REREAD the boxed passage. Circle details that help you **visualize** what Walt is seeing and feeling. For example, you might circle "the sled jerked." Can you see how the sled is moving?

Pause & Reflect

Number the following events in the correct order.
(Sequence of Events)

__ The men return to camp.

__ Walt harnesses the dogs.

__ A man leaps for the sled.

__ Walt reaches the camp.

As the story continues . . .

• Walt races down the frozen Mazy May Creek toward the Yukon River.

• The thieves begin shouting at him.

The dogs sprang against the yoke straps, and the sled jerked under way so suddenly as to almost throw him off. Then it curved into the creek, poising perilously[9] on the runner. He was almost breathless with suspense, when it finally righted with a bound and sprang ahead again. The creek bank was high and he could not see the men, although he could hear their cries and knew they were running to cut him off. He did not dare to think what would happen if they caught him: he just

190 clung to the sled, his heart beating wildly, and watched the snow rim of the bank above him.

Suddenly, over this snow rim came the flying body of the Irishman, who had leaped straight for the sled in a desperate attempt to capture it: but he was an instant too late. Striking on the very rear of it, he was thrown from his feet, backward, into the snow. Yet, with the quickness of a cat, he had clutched the end of the sled with one hand, turned over, and was dragging behind on his breast, swearing at the boy and

200 threatening all kinds of terrible things if he did not stop the dogs; but Walt cracked him sharply across the knuckles with the butt of the dog whip till he let go.

Pause & Reflect

FOCUS

Walt continues his dangerous race along the creek. Will the men catch him before he reaches the Yukon?

It was eight miles from Walt's claim to the Yukon— eight very crooked miles, for the creek wound back and forth like a snake, "tying knots in itself," as George

Lukens said. And because it was so crooked the dogs

210 could not get up their best speed, while the sled

9. **perilously** (pĕr′ ə-ləs′ lē): dangerously.

ground heavily on its side against the curves, now to the right, now to the left.

Travelers who had come up and down the Mazy May on foot, with packs on their backs, had declined to go round all the bends, and instead had made shortcuts across the narrow necks of creek bottom. Two of his pursuers had gone back to harness the remaining dogs, but the others took advantage of these shortcuts, running on foot, and before he knew it they 220 had almost overtaken him.

"Halt!" they cried after him. "Stop, or we'll shoot!"

But Walt only yelled the harder at the dogs, and dashed around the bend with a couple of revolver bullets singing after him. At the next bend they had drawn up closer still, and the bullets struck uncomfortably near him but at this point the Mazy May straightened out and ran for half a mile as the crow flies. Here the dogs stretched out in their long wolf swing, and the stampeders, quickly winded, slowed down and waited 230 for their own sled to come up.

Looking over his shoulder, Walt reasoned that they had not given up the chase for good, and that they would soon be after him again. So he wrapped the fur robe about him to shut out the stinging air, and lay flat on the empty sled, encouraging the dogs, as he well knew how.

At last, twisting abruptly between two river islands, he came upon the mighty Yukon sweeping grandly to the north. He could not see from bank to bank, and in 240 the quick-falling twilight it loomed a great white sea of frozen stillness. There was not a sound, save the breathing of the dogs, and the churn of the steel-shod sled.

 READING TIP Look closely at the description of the chase. Here is a diagram showing how the thieves could get close to Walt even though he is racing away on the dog sled.

The thieves take more direct routes (shortcuts) to chase Walt.

Pause & Reflect

1. What obstacles does Walt overcome to reach the Yukon? Check three phrases below. **(Clarify)**
   - ❏ bitter cold
   - ❏ shots fired at him
   - ❏ lame dogs
   - ❏ a crooked trail

2. **MARK IT UP** Reread the boxed passage. Circle the details that help you imagine what Walt sees and hears. **(Visualize)**

As the story continues...

- It is 40 degrees below zero.
- Walt is in danger of freezing to death.
- The thieves are shooting at him with a rifle.
- Walt's lead dog is a poor leader.

English Learner Support

Language

Pronouns Note the pronouns in blue. The first two pronouns refer to Walt. The last one refers to the head dog.

READING CHECK

What does Walt do to keep from freezing to death?

FOCUS

As the race continues, Walt faces new dangers.

▐▐ **MARK IT UP** ⟩⟩ As you read, circle words that describe these dangers.

No snow had fallen for several weeks, and the traffic had packed the main river trail till it was hard and glassy as glare ice.[10] Over this the sled flew along, and the

250 dogs kept the trail fairly well, although Walt quickly discovered that he had made a mistake in choosing the leader. As they were driven in single file, without reins, he had to guide them by his voice, and it was evident the head dog had never learned the meaning of "gee" and "haw."[11] He hugged the inside of the curves too closely, often forcing his comrades behind him into the soft snow, while several times he thus <u>capsized</u> the sled.

There was no wind, but the speed at which he traveled created a bitter blast, and with the thermometer down to

260 forty below, this bit through fur and flesh to the very bones. Aware that if he remained constantly upon the sled he would freeze to death, and knowing the practice of Arctic travelers, Walt shortened up one of the lashing thongs, and whenever he felt chilled, seized hold of it, jumped off, and ran behind till warmth was restored. Then he would climb on and rest till the process had to be repeated.

Looking back he could see the sled of his pursuers, drawn by eight dogs, rising and falling over the ice

270 hummocks[12] like a boat in a seaway. The Irishman and the black-bearded leader were with it, taking turns in running and riding.

---

10. **glare ice:** ice that reflects light.

11. **"gee" and "haw":** commands to tell an animal to turn to the right or to the left.

12. **hummocks** (hŭm´əks): low mounds of earth.

WORDS TO KNOW

capsize (kăp´sīz) *v.* to overturn or cause to overturn

Night fell, and in the blackness of the first hour or so Walt toiled desperately with his dogs. On account of the poor lead dog, they were continually floundering off the beaten track into the soft snow, and the sled was as often riding on its side or top as it was in the proper way. This work and strain tried his strength sorely. Had he not been in such haste he
280 could have avoided much of it, but he feared the stampeders would creep up in the darkness and overtake him. However, he could hear them yelling to their dogs, and knew from the sounds they were coming up very slowly.

When the moon rose he was off Sixty Mile, and Dawson was only fifty miles away. He was almost exhausted, and breathed a sigh of relief as he climbed on the sled again. Looking back, he saw his enemies had crawled up within four hundred yards. At this
290 space they remained, a black speck of motion on the white river breast. Strive as they would, they could not shorten this distance, and strive as he would, he could not increase it.

Walt had now discovered the proper lead dog, and he knew he could easily run away from them if he could only change the bad leader for the good one. But this was impossible, for a moment's delay, at the speed they were running, would bring the men behind upon him.

300 When he was off the mouth of Rosebud Creek, just as he was topping a rise, the report of a gun[13] and the ping of a bullet on the ice beside him told him that

English Learner Support

Vocabulary

Idiom The words in blue mean that he was near a place called Sixty Mile.

REREAD the boxed passage. Why doesn't Walt change the bad lead dog for the good one? (Question)

---

13. **the report of a gun:** the sound of a gun.

WORDS TO KNOW
flounder (floun'dər) v. to make clumsy attempts to move or regain one's balance

Pause & Reflect

1. Why does Walt's sled often go off track? (Cause and Effect)

2. What do you think is the greatest danger for Walt? (Evaluate)

As the story ends . . .

• Walt's lead dog is killed.

• Walt takes action to save his own life.

• Walt finds Loren Hall.

they were this time shooting at him with a rifle. And from then on, as he cleared the <u>summit</u> of each ice jam, he stretched flat on the leaping sled till the rifle shot from the rear warned him that he was safe till the next ice jam was reached.

Now it is very hard to lie on a moving sled, jumping and plunging and <u>yawing</u> like a boat before the wind, 310 and to shoot through the deceiving moonlight at an object four hundred yards away on another moving sled performing equally wild <u>antics</u>. So it is not to be wondered at that the black-bearded leader did not hit him.

After several hours of this, during which, perhaps, a score of bullets had struck about him, their ammunition began to give out and their fire slackened. They took greater care, and shot at him at the most favorable opportunities. He was also leaving them behind, the 320 distance slowly increasing to six hundred yards.

Pause & Reflect

FOCUS

An accident puts Walt's life in danger. What happens when the stampeders and Walt clash?

Lifting clear on the crest of a great jam off Indian River, Walt Masters met with his first accident. A bullet sang past his ears, and struck the bad lead dog.

The poor brute plunged in a heap, with the rest of the team on top of him.

WORDS TO KNOW
summit (sŭm'ĭt) *n.* the highest point or part; the top
yaw (yô) *v.* to swerve off course momentarily or temporarily
antic (ănt'ĭc) *n.* an odd or extravagant act or gesture; a prank

Like a flash Walt was by the leader. Cutting the
330 traces with his hunting knife, he dragged the dying
animal to one side and straightened out the team.

He glanced back. The other sled was coming up like
an express train. With half the dogs still over their
traces, he cried "Mush on!" and leaped upon the sled
just as the pursuers dashed abreast of him.

WHAT DOES IT MEAN? *The pursuers dashed abreast of him* means that they came up beside him.

The Irishman was preparing to spring for him—they
were so sure they had him that they did not shoot—
when Walt turned fiercely upon them with his whip.

He struck at their faces, and men must save their
340 faces with their hands. So there was no shooting just
then. Before they could recover from the hot rain of
blows, Walt reached out from his sled, catching their
wheel dog by the forelegs in midspring, and throwing
him heavily. This snarled the team, capsizing the sled
and tangling his enemies up beautifully.

READ ALOUD the boxed passage. Vary your voice to express a sense of danger and excitement.

Away Walt flew, the runners of his sled fairly
screaming as they bounded over the frozen surface.
And what had seemed an accident proved to be a
blessing in disguise. The proper lead dog was now to
350 the fore, and he stretched low and whined with joy as
he jerked his comrades along.

READING CHECK Why is Walt now able to go faster?

By the time he reached Ainslie's Creek, seventeen
miles from Dawson, Walt had left his pursuers, a tiny
speck, far behind. At Monte Cristo Island he could no
longer see them. And at Swede Creek, just as daylight
was silvering the pines, he ran plump into the camp of
old Loren Hall.

English Learner Support
Vocabulary
Figure of Speech The words in blue mean that something which at first seemed bad actually turned out to be good.

Almost as quick as it takes to tell it, Loren had his
sleeping furs rolled up, and had joined Walt on the
360 sled. They permitted the dogs to travel more slowly, as
there was no sign of the chase in the rear, and just as

Pause & Reflect

1. Why do the men of the Yukon call Walt "the King of Mazy May"? **(Clarify)**

2. What was your reaction to the story? **(Connect)**

The story is full of suspense. Will Walt get away? Will he be shot? What parts of the story were the most suspenseful? **(Analyze)**

they pulled up at the gold commissioner's office in Dawson, Walt, who had kept his eyes open to the last, fell asleep.

And because of what Walt Masters did on this night, the men of the Yukon have become proud of him, and speak of him now as the King of Mazy May. ❖

Pause & Reflect

MARK IT UP Sketch a diagram of Walt's route as described in the story. Don't forget to include the Mazy May Creek and the Yukon River.

The InterActive Reader PLUS
For English Learners

Active Reading SkillBuilder

Monitoring Your Reading

When you read, you should pause to check, or **monitor,** how well you are understanding the text. The chart below lists strategies you can use to monitor your reading.

Question	Ask questions about the events and characters.
Visualize	Picture characters, events, and settings.
Connect	Note similarities between the selection and your own experiences.
Predict	Predict what might happen next.
Clarify	Pause for a quick review of what you understand so far.
Evaluate	Form opinions about the story.

Read the following passage from "The King of Mazy May" and use the methods above to monitor your reading. Jot down your observations on the lines below.

> Aware that if he remained constantly upon the sled he would freeze to death, and knowing the practice of Arctic travelers, Walt shortened up one of the lashing thongs, and whenever he felt chilled, seized hold of it, jumped off, and ran behind till warmth was restored. Then he would climb on and rest till the process had to be repeated.
>
> Looking back he could see the sled of his pursuers, drawn by eight dogs, rising and falling over the ice hummocks like a boat in a seaway. The Irishman and the black-bearded leader were with it, taking turns in running and riding.

Question: _____

_____

Visualize: _____

_____

Connect: _____

_____

Predict: _____

_____

Clarify: _____

_____

Evaluate: _____

_____

Literary Analysis SkillBuilder

Antagonist and Protagonist

The **protagonist** is the main character or hero of a story. The writer usually wants the reader to like and support this character. The **antagonist** is the protagonist's enemy or opponent. The reader often dislikes a story's antagonist. Use the chart below to record passages from "The King of Mazy May" that influence your opinions about the protagonist and the antagonists.

Passages About Walt	Passages About Claim-Jumpers
Last of all, he has a good heart, and is not afraid of the darkness and loneliness, of man or beast or thing.	

Words to Know SkillBuilder

Words to Know

antic	commissioner	liable	prospector	summit
capsize	flounder	peer	stampede	yaw

A. Complete each sentence with the correct Word to Know.

1. The Klondike attracted many a _____ looking for land during the gold rush.

2. To legalize the sale of land, the _____ in Dawson must sign the official papers.

3. The young boy tried to _____ through the trees to see if he could spy the strangers.

4. A claim was _____ to be jumped if the person delayed registering it in Dawson.

5. The discovery of gold in the Klondike led to a _____ of people hoping to make their fortunes.

6. The boy forced the sled to _____ because he was driving quickly and almost recklessly.

7. The deep snow made the dogs _____ and lose their balance.

8. At the _____ of each hill, the boy had to lie flat on the sled so that the men who were following could not see him.

9. The sled performed one wild _____ after another as it jolted over the rough surface of the ice.

10. The sled began to _____ and swerve like a boat in a storm.

B. Think of a time when you had an outdoor adventure. On a separate sheet of paper, describe the adventure using **five** Words to Know from the list at the top of the page.

Before You Read

Connect to Your Life

What advice would you give to someone younger than you? Use the following chart to show what advice you would give about each subject.

Subject	Advice
homework	It's always best to do your homework as soon as you get home.

Key to the Poems

WHAT TO LISTEN FOR In "Mother to Son" the speaker gives the following advice:

> So boy, don't you turn back.
> Don't you set down on the steps
> 'Cause you finds it's kinder hard.

What makes these words sound like spoken English?

_____

_____

Mother to Son

by Langston Hughes

Speech to the Young
Speech to the Progress-Toward
(Among them Nora and Henry III)

by Gwendolyn Brooks

PREVIEW In "Mother to Son," a mother tells her son how difficult her life has been and gives him advice about how to deal with life's problems. In "Speech to the Young," the speaker also gives advice about life.

📖 **As the poem begins . . .**

• A mother tells her son what her life has been like.

English Learner Support

Language

Dialect This poem is written in dialect, a special way of speaking associated with certain regions. Note the words in blue. The speaker says *ain't* instead of *has not.* The contraction *I'se* means "I have" on line 9 and "I am" on lines 18 and 19. *Set down* means "sit down," and *kinder* means "kind of" or "a little."

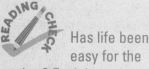 Has life been easy for the mother? Explain.

Pause & Reflect

 the boxed text. What is the mother saying to her son? **(Paraphrase)**

FOCUS

The speaker compares her life to a staircase that she continues to climb.

▯▯▯ **MARK IT UP** ✎ As you read, underline words and phrases that describe a staircase. An example is highlighted.

Mother to Son

by Langston Hughes

Well, son, I'll tell you:
Life for me ain't been no crystal stair.
It's had tacks in it,
And splinters,

5 And boards torn up,
And places with no carpet on the floor—
Bare.
But all the time
I'se been a-climbin' on,

10 And reachin' landin's,
And turnin' corners,
And sometimes goin' in the dark
Where there ain't been no light.
So boy, don't you turn back.

15 Don't you set down on the steps
'Cause you finds it's kinder hard.
Don't you fall now—
For I'se still goin', honey,
I'se still climbin',

20 And life for me ain't been no crystal stair.

Pause & Reflect

FOCUS

In this poem, the speaker tells young people how to develop a good outlook on life.

Speech to the Young
Speech to the
Progress-Toward
(Among them Nora and Henry III)
by Gwendolyn Brooks

Say to them,
say to the down-keepers,
the sun-slappers,
the self-soilers,
5   the harmony-hushers,
"Even if you are not ready for day
it cannot always be night."
You will be right.
For that is the hard home-run.

10   Live not for battles won.
Live not for the-end-of-the-song.
Live in the along.

Pause & Reflect

As the poem begins . . .

• The speaker tells young people what to say to others who have a negative outlook.

English Learner Support
Language

Pronouns Note the pronouns in blue. The first *you* refers to those with a negative outlook. The second *you* refers to young people.

WHAT DOES IT MEAN? *Hard home-run* means that the advice is difficult to follow, but important and true.

 the boxed text. What does the speaker advise? Circle one phrase below. **(Infer)**

to live in the future
to live in the past
to live in the present

 **Pause & Reflect**

Reread lines 6–7. How would you state the speaker's message in your own words? **(Paraphrase)**

Active Reading SkillBuilder

Making Inferences

Inferences are logical ideas that readers form by combining evidence in the text with their own knowledge. Record any inferences you can make about the speakers of these two poems in the charts below. Also write clues from the poems that help you make these inferences.

"Mother to Son"

Clue	Inference
The title is "Mother to Son."	The speaker is a woman.

"Speech to the Young . . ."

Clue	Inference

Literary Analysis SkillBuilder

Speaker

The **speaker** in a poem is the voice that speaks the poem's words. Sometimes the speaker is the poet and sometimes it is a person the poet imagines. Use the diagram below to contrast and compare the speakers in "Mother to Son" and "Speech to the Young . . .".

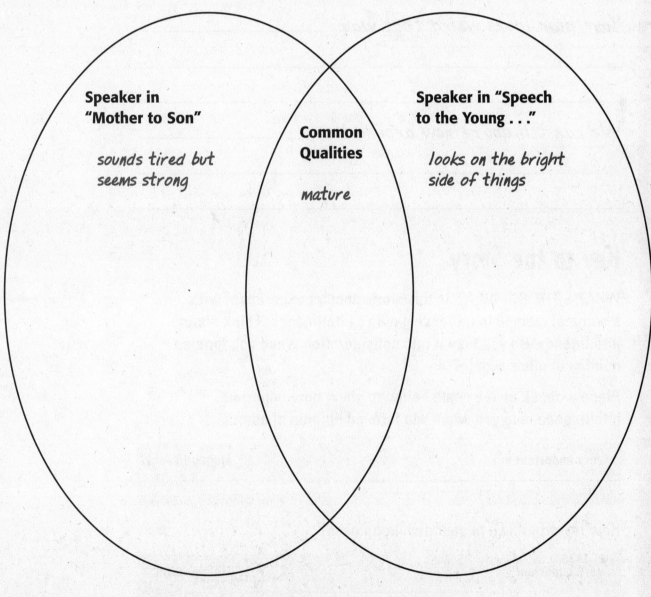

Speaker in "Mother to Son"

sounds tired but seems strong

Common Qualities

mature

Speaker in "Speech to the Young . . ."

looks on the bright side of things

Follow Up: Discuss which advice you would give to your own children.

Before You Read

Connect to Your Life

Everybody is different in some way. Some people speak with a noticeable accent. Others wear unusual clothes. Sometimes people make fun of those who are different. How would you respond to the following statements?

Your hair looks weird that way. _____

_____

_____

We can tell you're new around here. _____

_____

_____

Key to the Story

WHAT'S THE BIG IDEA? In this story, doctors experiment with a surgical method to increase a man's intelligence. Think about intelligence. Do you take it into consideration when you form an opinion of other people?

Place a check on the scale below to show how important intelligence is to you when you form an opinion of others.

Very important	Unimportant

How important is it to your own happiness?

Very important	Unimportant

Flowers for Algernon

by Daniel Keyes

PREVIEW Charlie Gordon is a man with low mental ability. A kind teacher recommends that he undergo an operation that has already tripled the intelligence of a white mouse. Charlie's doctors ask Charlie to write progress reports that should show the changes in his intelligence.

As the story begins . . .

- Charlie Gordon hopes to participate in an experiment that will increase his intelligence.

- Charlie worries he might not be chosen for the experiment because he thinks he failed an inkblot test.

WHAT DOES IT MEAN? In lines 9 and 17, *use me* means "choose me as a candidate for their experiment."

READING TIP Charlie Gordon has low mental ability, which is why he misspells many words and phrases. Try reading these words and phrases aloud; they are often spelled the way they sound.

MARK IT UP **KEEP TRACK**
Remember to use these marks to keep track of your reading.

* This is important.

? I have a question about this.

! This is a surprise.

FOCUS
In this part, you will read the first two progress reports that Charlie writes. He describes how he reacts to an inkblot test.

MARK IT UP As you read, underline details that help you form an impression of Charlie. An example is highlighted.

Progris riport 1—martch 5 1965

Dr. Strauss says I shud rite down what I think and evrey thing that happins to me from now on. I dont know why but he says its importint so they will see if they will use me. I hope they use me. Miss Kinnian says maybe they can make me smart. I want to be smart. My name is Charlie Gordon. I am 37 years old and 2 weeks ago was my brithday. I have nuthing more to rite now so I will close for today.

progris riport 2—martch 6

I had a test today. I think I faled it. and I think that maybe now they wont use me. What happind is a nice young man was in the room and he had some white cards with ink spillled all over them. He sed Charlie what do you see on this card. I was very skared even tho I had my rabits foot in my pockit because when I was a kid I always faled tests in school and I spillled ink to.

I told him I saw a inkblot. He said yes and it made me feel good. I thot that was all but when I got up to go he stopped me. He said now sit down Charlie we are not thru yet. Then I dont remember so good but he wantid me to say what was in the ink. I dint see nuthing in the ink but he said there was picturs there other pepul saw some picturs. I coudnt see any picturs. I reely tryed to see. I held the card close up and then far away. Then I said if I had my glases I coud see better I usally only ware my glases in the movies or TV but I said they are in the closit in the hall. I got them. Then I said let me see that card agen I bet Ill find it now.

I tryed hard but I still coudnt find the picturs I only saw the ink. I told him maybe I need new glases. He rote somthing down on a paper and I got skared of faling the test. I told him it was a very nice inkblot with littel points all around the eges. He looked very sad so that wasnt it. I said please let me try agen. Ill get it in a few minits becaus Im not so fast somtimes. Im a slow reeder too in Miss Kinnians class for slow adults but I'm trying very hard.

He gave me a chance with another card that had 2 kinds of ink spilled on it red and blue.

He was very nice and talked slow like Miss Kinnian does and he explained it to me that it was a *raw shok*.[1] He said pepul see things in the ink. I said show me where. He said think. I told him I think a inkblot but that wasnt rite eather. He said what does it remind you—pretend somthing. I closd my eyes for a long time to pretend. I told him I pretned a fowntan pen with ink leeking all over a table cloth. Then he got up and went out.

I dont think I passd the *raw shok* test.

Pause & Reflect

FOCUS

Charlie is given more tests. Read to find out how he does on these tests.

MARK IT UP As you read, underline details that let you know how Charlie does.

progris report 3—martch 7 Dr Strauss and Dr Nemur say it dont matter about the inkblots. I told them I dint spill the ink on the cards and I coudnt see anything in the ink. They said that maybe they will still use me. I said Miss Kinnian never gave me tests like that one only

1. **raw shok:** Charlie's way of writing *Rorschach* (rôr'shäk'), the name of a test used to analyze people's personalities on the basis of what they see in inkblot designs.

English Learner Support

Vocabulary

Figure of Speech *Slow adults* means "adults for whom learning is difficult."

Pause & Reflect

Circle the phrase below that completes the following sentence: Charlie thinks he has failed the inkblot test because he _____. **(Cause and Effect)**

can't see the inkblot

sees Miss Kinnian

can't see any pictures

As the story continues . . .

- Dr. Strauss and Dr. Nemur tell Charlie they are still considering him for the experiment.
- Charlie takes more tests. In one test, a mouse named Algernon races through a maze while Charlie tries to solve the same maze on paper.

English Learner Support

Language

Contractions *Dint* is an incorrect spelling of the contraction *didn't*, which means "did not."

spelling and reading. They said Miss Kinnian told that I was her bestist pupil in the adult nite scool becaus I tryed the hardist and I reely wantid to lern. They said how come you went to the adult nite scool all by

70 yourself Charlie. How did you find it. I said I askd pepul and sumbody told me where I shud go to lern to read and spell good. They said why did you want to. I told them becaus all my life I wantid to be smart and not dumb. But its very hard to be smart. They said you know it will probly be tempirery. I said yes. Miss Kinnian told me. I dont care if it herts.

Later I had more crazy tests today. The nice lady who gave it me told me the name and I asked her how do you spellit so I can rite it in my progris riport.

80 THEMATIC APPERCEPTION TEST.[2] I dont know the frist 2 words but I know what test means. You got to pass it or you get bad marks. This test lookd easy becaus I coud see the picturs. Only this time she dint want me to tell her the picturs. That mixd me up. I said the man yesterday said I shoud tell him what I saw in the ink she said that dont make no difrence. She said make up storys about the pepul in the picturs.

I told her how can you tell storys about pepul you never met. I said why shud I make up lies. I never tell

90 lies any more becaus I always get caut.

She told me this test and the other one the rawshok was for getting personalty. I laffed so hard. I said how can you get that thing from inkblots and fotos. She got sore and put her picturs away. I dont care. It was sily. I gess I faled that test too.

Later some men in white coats took me to a difernt part of the hospitil and gave me a game to play. It was like a race with a white mouse. They called the mouse Algernon. Algernon was in a box with a lot of twists

---

2. **Thematic Apperception** (thĭ-măt'ĭk ăp'ər-sĕp'shən) **Test:** a test for analyzing people's personalities on the basis of the stories they make up about a series of pictures.

100 and turns like all kinds of walls and they gave me a pencil and a paper with lines and lots of boxes. On one side it said START and on the other end it said FINISH. They said it was *amazed*[3] and that Algernon and me had the same *amazed* to do. I dint see how we could have the same *amazed* if Algernon had a box and I had a paper but I dint say nothing. Anyway there wasnt time because the race started.

One of the men had a watch he was trying to hide so I woudnt see it so I tryed not to look and that made 110 me nervus.

Anyway that test made me feel worser than all the others because they did it over 10 times with difernt *amazeds* and Algernon won every time. I dint know that mice were so smart. Maybe thats because Algernon is a white mouse. Maybe white mice are smarter then other mice.

Pause & Reflect

FOCUS

Charlie hears good news about the experiment. Why is he so excited? Read to find out.

progris riport 4—Mar 8
Their going to use me! Im so exited I can hardly rite. Dr 120 Nemur and Dr Strauss had a argament about it first. Dr Nemur was in the office when Dr Strauss brot me in. Dr Nemur was worryed about using me but Dr Strauss told him Miss Kinnian rekemmended me the best from all the people who she was teaching. I like Miss Kinnian becaus shes a very smart teacher. And she said Charlie your going to have a second chance. If you volenteer for this experament you mite get smart. They dont know if it will

---

3. **amazed:** Charlie's way of writing *a maze*. A *maze* is a complicated and often confusing network of pathways.

be perminint but theirs a chance. Thats why I said ok even when I was scared because she said it was an operashun. She said dont be scared Charlie you done so much with so little I think you deserv it most of all.

So I got scaird when Dr Nemur and Dr Strauss argud about it. Dr Strauss said I had something that was very good. He said I had a good *motor-vation*.[4] I never even knew I had that. I felt proud when he said that not every body with an eye-q[5] of 68 had that thing. I dont know what it is or where I got it but he said Algernon had it too.

Algernons *motor-vation* is the cheese they put in his box. But it cant be that because I didnt eat any cheese this week.

Then he told Dr Nemur something I dint understand so while they were talking I wrote down some of the words.

He said Dr Nemur I know Charlie is not what you had in mind as the first of your new brede of intelek** (coudnt get the word) superman. But most people of his low ment** are host** and uncoop** they are usualy dull apath** and hard to reach. He has a good natcher hes intristed and eager to please.

Dr Nemur said remember he will be the first human beeng ever to have his intelijence trippled by surgicle meens.

Dr Strauss said exakly. Look at how well hes lerned to read and write for his low mentel age its as grate an acheve** as you and I lerning einstines therey of **vity[6] without help. That shows the intenss motor-vation. Its comparat** a tremen** achev** I say we use Charlie.

English Learner Support

Vocabulary

Difficult Words Charlie tries to write down the difficult words used by the doctors. The stars, or asterisks, stand for missing parts of the words. Use the vocabulary list below to understand this passage.

Words	Meanings
intellectual	smart
mentality	mental ability
hostile	not friendly
uncooperative	not willing
apathetic	not interested
achievement	success
comparatively	relatively
tremendous	great

---

4. **motor-vation:** Charlie's way of writing *motivation*, a word referring to the inner drive that makes a person try hard.

5. **eye-q:** Charlie's way of writing *I.Q.* (an abbreviation of *intelligence quotient*), a measurement of a person's mental ability.

6. **einstines therey of **vity:** Charlie's way of writing *Einstein's theory of relativity*, a reference to the scientific theory of space and time developed by Albert Einstein.

160   I dint get all the words and they were talking to fast but it sounded like Dr Strauss was on my side and like the other one wasnt.

    Then Dr Nemur nodded he said all right maybe your right. We will use Charlie. When he said that I got so exited I jumped up and shook his hand for being so good to me. I told him thank you doc you wont be sorry for giving me a second chance. And I mean it like I told him. After the operashun Im gonna try to be smart. Im gonna try awful hard.

Pause & Reflect

FOCUS

Read to find out how Charlie feels before and after the operation.

170 progris ript 5—Mar 10
    Im skared. Lots of people who work here and the nurses and the people who gave me the tests came to bring me candy and wish me luck. I hope I have luck. I got my rabits foot and my lucky penny and my horse shoe. Only a black cat crossed me when I was comming to the hospitil. Dr Strauss says dont be superstitis Charlie this is sience. Anyway Im keeping my rabits foot with me.

180   I asked Dr Strauss if Ill beat Algernon in the race after the operashun and he said maybe. If the operashun works Ill show that mouse I can be as smart as he is. Maybe smarter. Then Ill be abel to read better and spell the words good and know lots of things and be like other people. I want to be smart like other people. If it works perminint they will make everybody smart all over the wurld.

    They dint give me anything to eat this morning. I dont know what that eating has to do with getting
190 smart. Im very hungry and Dr Nemur took away my

Pause & Reflect

Write the number 1, 2, 3, or 4 beside each sentence below to show the order in which the events occur. (**Sequence of Events**)

___ Dr. Strauss praises Charlie's motivation.

___ Charlie is chosen to have the operation.

___ Dr. Nemur and Dr. Strauss argue.

___ Miss Kinnian encourages Charlie.

As the story continues . . .

• Charlie prepares for surgery.

• After the operation, Charlie takes more tests.

English Learner Support

Culture

Superstitions The *rabit's foot*, *lucky penny*, and *horse shoe* are common good luck charms. People sometimes carry a good luck charm or hang it on a wall, hoping it will cause good things to happen. A common symbol of bad luck is a *black cat* crossing your path.

MORE ABOUT . . .

OPERATIONS Before major operations, doctors give patients a drug that causes loss of feeling. Patients are told not to eat because the drug can prevent normal reflexes from working. If undigested food comes up from the stomach, it could go into the lungs and cause serious damage.

Pause & Reflect

1. How does Charlie feel before the operation? Circle two words below. **(Draw Conclusions)**

   cheerful

   frightened

   angry

   superstitious

2. **MARK IT UP** Reread the boxed passage and circle words and phrases that show how Charlie responds to his lab tasks. **(Clarify)**

box of candy. That Dr Nemur is a grouch. Dr Strauss says I can have it back after the operashun. You cant eat befor a operashun. . .

Progress Report 6—Mar 15

The operashun dint hurt. He did it while I was sleeping. They took off the bandijis from my eyes and my head today so I can make a PROGRESS REPORT. Dr Nemur who looked at some of my other ones says I spell PROGRESS wrong and he told me how to spell
200 it and REPORT too. I got to try and remember that.

I have a very bad memary for spelling. Dr Strauss says its ok to tell about all the things that happin to me but he says I shoud tell more about what I feel and what I think. When I told him I dont know how to think he said try. All the time when the bandijis were on my eyes I tryed to think. Nothing happened. I dont know what to think about. Maybe if I ask him he will tell me how I can think now that Im suppose to get smart. What do smart people think about. Fancy things
210 I suppose. I wish I knew some fancy things alredy.

Progress Report 7—mar 19

Nothing is happining. I had lots of tests and different kinds of races with Algernon. I hate that mouse. He always beats me. Dr Strauss said I got to play those games. And he said some time I got to take those tests over again. Those inkblots are stupid. And those pictures are stupid too. I like to draw a picture of a man and a woman but I wont make up lies about people.

I got a headache from trying to think so much. I
220 thot Dr Strauss was my frend but he dont help me. He dont tell me what to think or when Ill get smart. Miss Kinnian dint come to see me. I think writing these progress reports are stupid too.

FOCUS

Charlie writes about his friends at work and about his nights at the lab.

MARK IT UP > Circle details that show you how Charlie's friends treat him.

Progress Report 8—Mar 23

Im going back to work at the factery. They said it was better I shud go back to work but I cant tell anyone what the operashun was for and I

230 have to come to the hospitil for an hour evry night after work. They are gonna pay me mony every month for lerning to be smart.

Im glad Im going back to work because I miss my job and all my frends and all the fun we have there.

Dr Strauss says I shud keep writing things down but I dont have to do it every day just when I think of something or something speshul happins. He says dont get discoridged because it takes time and it happins slow. He says it took a long time with Algernon before

240 he got 3 times smarter then he was before. Thats why Algernon beats me all the time because he had that operashun too. That makes me feel better. I coud probly do that *amazed* faster than a reglar mouse. Maybe some day Ill beat Algernon. Boy that would be something. So far Algernon looks like he mite be smart perminent.

Mar 25 (I dont have to write PROGRESS REPORT on top any more just when I hand it in once a week for Dr Nemur to read. I just have to put the date on.

250 That saves time)

We had a lot of fun at the factery today. Joe Carp said hey look where Charlie had his operashun what did they do Charlie put some brains in. I was going to tell him but I remembered Dr Strauss said no. Then Frank Reilly said what did you do Charlie forget your key and open your door the hard way. That made me laff. Their really my friends and they like me.

As the story continues...

- Charlie goes back to his factory job during the day.
- The doctors give Charlie a machine to help him learn at night.

English Learner Support

Language

Figure of Speech *Boy* is an expression of mild enthusiasm or astonishment. *That would be something* means "that would be remarkable or amazing."

READING CHECK Why would it be good news for Charlie if Algernon were permanently smarter?

READING CHECK What do Joe Carp and Frank Reilly say to Charlie when he returns? Why?

WHAT DOES IT MEAN?

4 man stands for *foreman.* It means "someone who is the boss or in charge of other workers."

English Learner Support

Language

Figure of Speech *For God's sake* is an expression of annoyance or frustration.

MORE ABOUT . . .

SLEEP Some scientists believe that people can learn and remember things even while they are sleeping.

REREAD the boxed passage on this page. What do you think Charlie's friends mean by "pulled a Charlie Gordon"? (Infer)

Sometimes somebody will say hey look at Joe or Frank or George he really pulled a Charlie Gordon. I
260 dont know why they say that but they always laff. This morning Amos Borg who is the 4 man at Donnegans used my name when he shouted at Ernie the office boy. Ernie lost a packige. He said Ernie for godsake what are you trying to be a Charlie Gordon. I dont understand why he said that. I never lost any packiges.

Mar 28 Dr Straus came to my room tonight to see why I dint come in like I was suppose to. I told him I dont like to race with Algernon any more. He said I dont have to for a while but I shud come in. He had a
270 present for me only it wasnt a present but just for lend. I thot it was a little television but it wasnt. He said I got to turn it on when I go to sleep. I said your kidding why shud I turn it on when Im going to sleep. Who ever herd of a thing like that. But he said if I want to get smart I got to do what he says. I told him I dint think I was going to get smart and he put his hand on my sholder and said Charlie you dont know it yet but your getting smarter all the time. You wont notice for a while. I think he was just being nice to
280 make me feel good because I dont look any smarter.

Oh yes I almost forgot. I asked him when I can go back to the class at Miss Kinnians school. He said I wont go their. He said that soon Miss Kinnian will come to the hospitil to start and teach me speshul. I was mad at her for not comming to see me when I got the operashun but I like her so maybe we will be frends again.

Mar 29 That crazy TV kept me up all night. How can I sleep with something yelling crazy things all
290 night in my ears. And the nutty pictures. Wow. I dont know what it says when Im up so how am I going to know when Im sleeping.

Dr Strauss says its ok. He says my brains are lerning when I sleep and that will help me when Miss Kinnian starts my lessons in the hospitl (only I found out it isnt a hospitil its a labatory). I think its all crazy. If you can get smart when your sleeping why do people go to school. That thing I dont think will work. I use to watch the late show and the late late show on TV all the time and it never made me smart. Maybe you have to sleep while you watch it.

Pause & Reflect

FOCUS

Charlie's friends get him in trouble. Read to find out what happens on their night out.

MARK IT UP > As you read, underline details of the events of that night.

PROGRESS REPORT 9—
April 3
Dr Strauss showed me how to keep the TV turned low so now I can sleep. I dont hear a thing. And I still dont understand what it says. A few times I play it over in the morning to find out what I lerned when I was sleeping and I dont think so. Miss Kinnian says Maybe its another langwidge or something. But most times it sounds american. It talks so fast faster than even Miss Gold who was my teacher in 6 grade and I remember she talked so fast I coudnt understand her.

I told Dr Strauss what good is it to get smart in my sleep. I want to be smart when Im awake. He says its the same thing and I have two minds. Theres the *subconscious* and the *conscious* (thats how you spell it). And one dont tell the other one what its doing. They dont even talk to each other. Thats why I dream. And boy have I been having crazy dreams. Wow. Ever since that night TV. The late late late late late show.

Pause & Reflect

1. How do Charlie's friends treat him? (Evaluate)

2. What does Dr. Strauss bring Charlie? Circle the answer below. (Clarify)
   a book
   a TV for sleep-learning
   a tape recorder
   a white mouse

As the story continues...

- Charlie goes out with Joe Carp and Frank Reilly.
- Charlie comes home with a headache and some bruises.

 READING TIP **Word Parts** Look at the word *subconscious* in line 318. It is made up of the prefix *sub-*, meaning "under" or "below," and the word *conscious,* meaning "awareness." *Subconscious* means "below a person's awareness." Breaking long words down into prefixes, roots, and suffixes can help you determine their meanings.

I forgot to ask him if it was only me or if everybody had those two minds.

(I just looked up the word in the dictionary Dr Strauss gave me. The word is *subconscious. adj. Of the nature of mental operations yet not present in consciousness; as, subconscious conflict of desires.*) There's more but I still dont know what it means. This
330 isnt a very good dictionary for dumb people like me.

Anyway the headache is from the party. My frends from the factery Joe Carp and Frank Reilly invited me to go with them to Muggsys Saloon for some drinks. I dont like to drink but they said we will have lots of fun. I had a good time.

> Joe Carp said I shoud show the girls how I mop out the toilet in the factory and he got me a mop. I showed them and everyone laffed when I told that Mr Donnegan said I was the best janiter he ever had
> 340 because I like my job and do it good and never come late or miss a day except for my operashun.

I said Miss Kinnian always said Charlie be proud of your job because you do it good.

Everybody laffed and we had a good time and they gave me lots of drinks and Joe said Charlie is a card when hes potted.[7] I dont know what that means but everybody likes me and we have fun. I cant wait to be smart like my best frends Joe Carp and Frank Reilly.

I dont remember how the party was over but I think
350 I went out to buy a newspaper and coffe for Joe and Frank and when I came back there was no one their. I looked for them all over till late. Then I dont remember so good but I think I got sleepy or sick. A nice cop brot me back home. Thats what my landlady Mrs Flynn says.

But I got a headache and a big lump on my head and black and blue all over. I think maybe I fell but

Cause

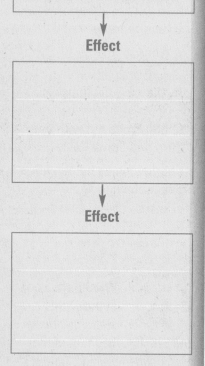

Charlie's friends encourage him to drink at the saloon.

↓

Effect

↓

Effect

English Learner Support

Language

Figure of Speech *Black and blue all over* means having many bruises on different parts of the body.

---

7. **Charlie is a card when hes potted:** Charlie is funny when he's drunk.

Joe Carp says it was the cop they beat up drunks some times. I don't think so. Miss Kinnian says cops are to
360 help people. Anyway I got a bad headache and Im sick and hurt all over. I dont think Ill drink anymore.

Pause & Reflect

FOCUS

Charlie starts to make progress. Read to find out how he feels about Algernon.

April 6 I beat Algernon! I dint even know I beat him until Burt the tester told me. Then the second time I lost because I got so exited I fell off the chair before I finished. But after that I beat him 8 more times. I must be getting smart to beat a smart mouse like Algernon. But I dont *feel* smarter.

370 I wanted to race Algernon some more but Burt said thats enough for one day. They let me hold him for a minit. Hes not so bad. Hes soft like a ball of cotton. He blinks and when he opens his eyes their black and pink on the eges.

I said can I feed him because I felt bad to beat him and I wanted to be nice and make frends. Burt said no Algernon is a very specshul mouse with an operashun like mine, and he was the first of all the animals to stay smart so long. He told me Algernon is so smart
380 that every day he has to solve a test to get his food. Its a thing like a lock on a door that changes every time Algernon goes in to eat so he has to lern something new to get his food. That made me sad because if he coudnt lern he woud be hungry.

I dont think its right to make you pass a test to eat. How woud Dr Nemur like it to have to pass a test

Pause & Reflect

READ ALOUD the boxed text on page 94. Why do the people laugh at Charlie? **(Infer)**

_____

As the story continues . . .

• Charlie beats Algernon for the first time.
• Charlie wants to be friends with Algernon.

READING CHECK How do Charlie's feelings for Algernon change?

Pause & Reflect

Why is it so important for Charlie to beat Algernon? **(Infer)**

📑 **As the story continues . . .**

- Charlie reads a difficult book with Miss Kinnian's help.
- Miss Kinnian tells Charlie that he is learning very fast.

English Learner Support
Vocabulary

Marooned *Merooned* is an incorrect spelling of the word *marooned,* which means "stranded" or "left alone."

WHAT DOES IT MEAN? The words in blue mean that correct spelling is not based on a few simple or logical rules. Words are not always spelled the way they sound.

every time he wants to eat. I think Ill be frends with Algernon.

Pause & Reflect

FOCUS

Read to find out what Charlie learns as he works with Miss Kinnian.

April 9 Tonight after work
390 Miss Kinnian was at the laboratory. She looked like she was glad to see me but scared. I told her dont worry Miss Kinnian Im not smart yet and she laffed. She said I have confidence in you Charlie the way you struggled so hard to read and right better than all the others. At werst you will have it for a littel wile and your doing somthing for sience.

We are reading a very hard book. I never read such a hard book before. Its called *Robinson Crusoe* about
400 a man who gets merooned on a dessert Iland. Hes smart and figers out all kinds of things so he can have a house and food and hes a good swimmer. Only I feel sorry because hes all alone and has no frends. But I think their must be somebody else on the iland because theres a picture with his funny umbrella looking at footprints. I hope he gets a frend and not be lonly.

April 10 Miss Kinnian teaches me to spell better. She says look at a word and close your eyes and say it over and over until you remember. I have lots of truble
410 with *through* that you say *threw* and *enough* and *tough* that you dont say *enew* and *tew*. You got to say *enuff* and *tuff*. Thats how I use to write it before I started to get smart. Im confused but Miss Kinnian says theres no reason in spelling.

Apr 14 Finished *Robinson Crusoe*. I want to find out more about what happens to him but Miss Kinnian says thats all there is. *Why*

Apr 15 Miss Kinnian says Im lerning fast. She read some of the Progress Reports and she looked at me kind of funny. She says Im a fine person and Ill show them all. I asked her why. She said never mind but I shoudnt feel bad if I find out that everybody isnt nice like I think. She said for a person who god gave so little to you done more then a lot of people with brains they never even used. I said all my frends are smart people but there good. They like me and they never did anything that wasnt nice. Then she got something in her eye and she had to run out to the ladys room.

Apr 16 Today, I lerned, the comma, this is a *comma* (,) a period, with a tail, Miss Kinnian, says its important, because, it makes writing, better, she said, somebody, coud lose, a lot of money, if a comma, isnt, in the, right place, I dont have, any money, and I dont see, how a comma, keeps you, from losing it,

But she says, everybody, uses commas, so Ill use, them too,

Apr 17 I used the comma wrong. Its *punctuation*. Miss Kinnian told me to look up long words in the dictionary to lern to spell them. I said whats the difference if you can read it anyway. She said its part of your education so now on Ill look up all the words Im not sure how to spell. It takes a long time to write that way but I think Im remembering. I only have to look up once and after that I get it right. Anyway thats how come I got the word *punctuation* right. (Its that way in the dictionary). Miss Kinnian says a period is punctuation too, and there are lots of other marks to lern. I told her I thot all the periods had to have tails but she said no.

REREAD the boxed passage. Miss Kinnian runs to the ladies' room because she is crying. Why is she crying? **(Infer)**

Pause & Reflect

Charlie finishes reading the book *Robinson Crusoe.* Why is that an important event?
(Draw Conclusions)

As the story continues . . .

- Charlie reads his earlier progress reports and sees an improvement in his writing.

- He realizes what people mean when they say "pull a Charlie Gordon."

WHAT DOES IT MEAN?
Photostated means "photocopied."

450 You got to mix them up, she showed? me" how. to mix! them (up,. and now; I can! mix up all kinds" of punctuation, in! my writing? There, are lots! of rules? to lern; but Im gettin'g them in my head.

One thing I? like about, Dear Miss Kinnian: (thats the way it goes in a business letter if I ever go into business) is she, always gives me' a reason" when—I ask. She's a gen'ius! I wish! I cou'd be smart" like, her; (Punctuation, is; fun!)

Pause & Reflect

FOCUS

460 Charlie begins to see things in a new light. Read to find out what new things he starts to understand.

MARK IT UP Underline the new discoveries Charlie makes.

April 18 What a dope I am! 460 I didn't even understand what she was talking about. I read the grammar book last night and it explanes the whole thing. Then I saw it was the same way as Miss Kinnian was trying to tell me, but I didn't get it. I got up in the middle of the night, and the whole thing straightened out in my mind.

Miss Kinnian said that the TV working in my sleep 470 helped out. She said I reached a plateau. Thats like the flat top of a hill.

After I figgered out how punctuation worked, I read over all my old Progress Reports from the beginning. Boy, did I have crazy spelling and punctuation! I told Miss Kinnian I ought to go over the pages and fix all the mistakes but she said, "No, Charlie, Dr. Nemur wants them just as they are. That's why he let you keep them after they were photostated, to see your own progress. You're coming along fast, Charlie."

480 That made me feel good. After the lesson I went down and played with Algernon. We don't race any more.

April 20 I feel sick inside. Not sick like for a doctor, but inside my chest it feels empty like getting punched and a heartburn at the same time.

I wasn't going to write about it, but I guess I got to, because its important. Today was the first time I ever stayed home from work.

Last night Joe Carp and Frank Reilly invited me to a party. There were lots of girls and some men from the 490 factory. I remembered how sick I got last time I drank too much, so I told Joe I didn't want anything to drink. He gave me a plain coke instead. It tasted funny, but I thought it was just a bad taste in my mouth.

We had a lot of fun for a while. Joe said I should dance with Ellen and she would teach me the steps. I fell a few times and I couldn't understand why because no one else was dancing besides Ellen and me. And all the time I was tripping because somebody's foot was always sticking out.

500 Then when I got up I saw the look on Joe's face and it gave me a funny feeling in my stomack. "He's a scream," one of the girls said. Everybody was laughing.

Frank said, "I ain't laughed so much since we sent him off for the newspaper that night at Muggsy's and ditched him."

"Look at him. His face is red."

"He's blushing. Charlie is blushing."

"Hey, Ellen, what'd you do to Charlie? I never saw 510 him act like that before."

I didn't know what to do or where to turn. Everyone was looking at me and laughing and I felt naked. I wanted to hide myself. I ran out into the street and I threw up. Then I walked home. It's a funny thing I

English Learner Support

Language

Figure of Speech In lines 482–484, Charlie means that he is very unhappy and upset emotionally.

Why did Charlie keep falling when he was dancing with Ellen?

English Learner Support

Vocabulary

Slang *Ditched* means "left without telling."

Pause & Reflect

Review the details you underlined as you read. How does Charlie's view of himself and others change? (Summarize)

As the story continues . . .

- Charlie begins to study more subjects.
- Charlie takes the inkblot test again with different results.

READ ALOUD As you read this passage aloud, try to express the pride Charlie feels as he begins to increase his knowledge and understanding.

never knew that Joe and Frank and the others liked to have me around all the time to make fun of me.

Now I know what it means when they say "to pull a Charlie Gordon."

I'm ashamed.

Pause & Reflect

FOCUS

Charlie is learning quickly. He wonders what an "I.Q." is and retakes the inkblot test.

MARK IT UP As you read, circle details that tell you what Charlie is learning.

520   PROGRESS REPORT 11
April 21 Still didn't go into the factory. I told Mrs. Flynn my landlady to call and tell Mr. Donnegan I was sick. Mrs. Flynn looks at me very funny lately like she's scared of me.

I think it's a good thing about finding out how everybody laughs at me. I thought about it a lot. It's 530 because I'm so dumb and I don't even know when I'm doing something dumb. People think it's funny when a dumb person can't do things the same way they can.

Anyway, now I know I'm getting smarter every day. I know punctuation and I can spell good. I like to look up all the hard words in the dictionary and I remember them. I'm reading a lot now, and Miss Kinnian says I read very fast. Sometimes I even understand what I'm reading about, and it stays in my mind. There are times when I can close my eyes and 540 think of a page and it all comes back like a picture.

Besides history, geography, and arithmetic, Miss Kinnian said I should start to learn a few foreign languages. Dr. Strauss gave me some more tapes to play while I sleep. I still don't understand how that conscious and unconscious mind works, but Dr. Strauss says not to worry yet. He asked me to promise that when I start learning college subjects next week I wouldn't read any books on psychology[8]—that is, until he gives me permission.

550   I feel a lot better today, but I guess I'm still a little angry that all the time people were laughing and making fun of me because I wasn't so smart. When I become intelligent like Dr. Strauss says, with three times my I.Q. of 68, then maybe I'll be like everyone else and people will like me and be friendly.

    I'm not sure what an *I.Q.* is. Dr. Nemur said it was something that measured how intelligent you were— like a scale in the drugstore weighs pounds. But Dr. Strauss had a big arguement with him and said an I.Q.
560 didn't weigh intelligence at all. He said an I.Q. showed how much intelligence you could get, like the numbers on the outside of a measuring cup. You still had to fill the cup up with stuff.

    Then when I asked Burt, who gives me my intelligence tests and works with Algernon, he said that both of them were wrong (only I had to promise not to tell them he said so). Burt says that the I.Q. measures a lot of different things including some of the things you learned already, and it really isn't any
570 good at all.

    So I still don't know what I.Q. is except that mine is going to be over 200 soon. I didn't want to say anything, but I don't see how if they don't know *what* it is, or *where* it is—I don't see how they know *how much* of it you've got.

    Dr. Nemur says I have to take a *Rorshach Test* tomorrow. I wonder what *that* is.

    April 22 I found out what a *Rorshach* is. It's the test I took before the operation—the one with the inkblots

MORE ABOUT . . .

I.Q. An I.Q. score below 70 is considered extremely low, while a score of over 130 is considered exceptionally high. Some people think these tests are not fair because people can show their intelligence in different ways.

English Learner Support
Language

Analogy An analogy is a comparison between two situations or relationships. Dr. Nemur wants to explain how an I.Q. test measures intelligence. So, he makes an analogy to something Charlie knows—a scale that measures weight.

---

8. **psychology** (sī-kŏl′ə-jē): the study of mental processes and behavior.

580 on the pieces of cardboard. The man who gave me the test was the same one.

I was scared to death of those inkblots. I knew he was going to ask me to find the pictures and I knew I wouldn't be able to. I was thinking to myself, if only there was some way of knowing what kind of pictures were hidden there. Maybe there weren't any pictures at all. Maybe it was just a trick to see if I was dumb enough to look for something that wasn't there. Just thinking about that made me sore at him.

590 "All right, Charlie," he said, "you've seen these cards before, remember?"

"Of course I remember."

The way I said it, he knew I was angry, and he looked surprised. "Yes, of course. Now I want you to look at this one. What might this be? What do you see on this card? People see all sorts of things in these inkblots. Tell me what it might be for you—what it makes you think of."

I was shocked. That wasn't what I had expected him 600 to say at all. "You mean there are no pictures hidden in those inkblots?"

He frowned and took off his glasses. "What?"

"Pictures. Hidden in the inkblots. Last time you told me that everyone could see them and you wanted me to find them too."

He explained to me that the last time he had used almost the exact same words he was using now. I didn't believe it, and I still have the suspicion that he misled me at the time just for the fun of it. Unless—I don't 610 know any more—could I have been *that* feeble-minded?

We went through the cards slowly. One of them looked like a pair of bats tugging at something. Another one looked like two men fencing with swords. I imagined all sorts of things. I guess I got carried away. But I didn't trust him any more, and I kept

turning them around and even looking on the back to see if there was anything there I was supposed to catch. While he was making his notes, I peeked out of the corner of my eye to read it. But it was all in code
620 that looked like this:

WF+A DdF-Ad orig. WF–A SF+obj

The test still doesn't make sense to me. It seems to me that anyone could make up lies about things that they didn't really see. How could he know I wasn't making a fool of him by mentioning things that I didn't really imagine? Maybe I'll understand it when Dr. Strauss lets me read up on psychology.

Pause & Reflect

Pause & Reflect

What happens when Charlie takes the inkblot test again? What does he see this time? (Summarize)

FOCUS

Read on to find out what changes take place in Charlie's relationship with the people at work and with Miss Kinnian.

MARK IT UP > As you read, circle details that help you understand how his relationships have changed.

April 25 I figured out a new way to line up the machines in
630 the factory, and Mr. Donnegan says it will save him ten thousand dollars a year in labor and increased production. He gave me a $25 bonus.

I wanted to take Joe Carp and Frank Reilly out to lunch to celebrate, but Joe said he had to buy some things for his wife, and Frank said he was meeting his cousin for lunch. I guess it'll take a
640 little time for them to get used to the changes in me. Everybody seems to be frightened of me. When I went over to Amos Borg and tapped him on the shoulder, he jumped up in the air.

People don't talk to me much any more or kid around the way they used to. It makes the job kind of lonely.

As the story continues . . .

- Charlie's coworkers begin to treat him differently.
- Charlie notices that Miss Kinnian is beautiful.

English Learner Support

Vocabulary

Bonus Money given to a worker in addition to his or her regular paycheck is called a bonus.

English Learner Support
Vocabulary

Idiom To *get up the nerve* is to overcome one's fear of doing something.

READ ALOUD the boxed passage. As you read, note that Charlie sees Dr. Strauss and Dr. Nemur differently. What does the passage tell you about Charlie's ability to understand other people? **(Infer)**

MORE ABOUT . . .

PUBLISHING THE RESULTS

When doctors and research scientists complete an experiment, they may decide to publish, or share, their results. They publish the information by writing articles for medical and scientific journals.

WHAT DOES IT MEAN? The words in lines 667–668 mean "to become famous for what someone else has done."

April 27 I got up the nerve today to ask Miss Kinnian to have dinner with me tomorrow night to celebrate my bonus.

650   At first she wasn't sure it was right, but I asked Dr. Strauss and he said it was okay. Dr. Strauss and Dr. Nemur don't seem to be getting along so well. They're arguing all the time. This evening when I came in to ask Dr. Strauss about having dinner with Miss Kinnian, I heard them shouting. Dr. Nemur was saying that it was *his* experiment and *his* research, and Dr. Strauss was shouting back that he contributed just as much, because he found me through Miss Kinnian and he performed the operation. Dr. Strauss said that someday thousands of neurosurgeons[9] might be using
660   his technique all over the world.

Dr. Nemur wanted to publish the results of the experiment at the end of this month. Dr. Strauss wanted to wait a while longer to be sure. Dr. Strauss said that Dr. Nemur was more interested in the Chair of Psychology at Princeton[10] than he was in the experiment. Dr. Nemur said that Dr. Strauss was nothing but an <u>opportunist</u> who was trying to ride to glory on *his* coattails.

When I left afterwards, I found myself trembling. I
670   don't know why for sure, but it was as if I'd seen both men clearly for the first time. I remember hearing Burt say that Dr. Nemur had a <u>shrew</u> of a wife who was pushing him all the time to get things published so that he could become famous. Burt said that the dream of her life was to have a big shot husband.

---

9. **neurosurgeons** (noŏr′ō-sûr′jənz): doctors who perform operations on the brain and other parts of the nervous system.

10. **Chair of Psychology at Princeton:** the position of head of the Psychology Department at Princeton University.

WORDS TO KNOW
opportunist (ŏp′ər-tōō′nĭst) *n.* a person who takes advantage of any opportunity to achieve a goal, with little regard for moral principles
shrew (shrōō) *n.* a mean, nagging woman

Was Dr. Strauss really trying to ride on his coattails?

April 28 I don't understand why I never noticed how beautiful Miss Kinnian really is. She has brown eyes and feathery brown hair that comes to the top of her
680 neck. She's only thirty-four! I think from the beginning I had the feeling that she was an unreachable genius— and very, very old. Now, every time I see her she grows younger and more lovely.

We had dinner and a long talk. When she said that I was coming along so fast that soon I'd be leaving her behind, I laughed.

"It's true, Charlie. You're already a better reader than I am. You can read a whole page at a glance while I can take in only a few lines at a time. And you
690 remember every single thing you read. I'm lucky if I can recall the main thoughts and the general meaning."

"I don't feel intelligent. There are so many things I don't understand."

She took out a cigarette and I lit it for her. "You've got to be a *little* patient. You're accomplishing in days and weeks what it takes normal people to do in half a lifetime. That's what makes it so amazing. You're like a giant sponge now, soaking things in. Facts, figures, general knowledge. And soon you'll begin to connect
700 them, too. You'll see how the different branches of learning are related. There are many levels, Charlie, like steps on a giant ladder that take you up higher and higher to see more and more of the world around you.

"I can see only a little bit of that, Charlie, and I won't go much higher than I am now, but you'll keep climbing up and up, and see more and more, and each step will open new worlds that you never even knew existed." She frowned. "I hope . . . I just hope to God—"

"What?"

REREAD Notice the descriptive details in the boxed passage that help you **visualize,** or picture, Miss Kinnian. List some below.

MORE ABOUT . . .

PHOTOGRAPHIC MEMORY
Some gifted people can read an entire page at a glance, or by looking at it very briefly. They also can remember everything on the page. This is called having a "photographic memory." It is like having a picture of the page in your mind.

English Learner Support
Language
Figure of Speech In lines 704–705, Miss Kinnian means that she will not be able to increase her level of intelligence much beyond what it is now.

Pause & Reflect

Charlie begins to notice things about other people. Identify the characters in the story that these sentences refer to. **(Clarify)**

They are frightened of him.

They are arguing about him.

He is finding her more attractive.

📖 **As the story continues . . .**

- Charlie's boss shows him a petition signed by most of the workers.
- Charlie talks to Fanny Girden, the one person who did not sign the petition.

710   "Never mind, Charles. I just hope I wasn't wrong to advise you to go into this in the first place."

I laughed. "How could that be? It worked, didn't it? Even Algernon is still smart."

We sat there silently for a while, and I knew what she was thinking about as she watched me toying with the chain of my rabbit's foot and my keys. I didn't want to think of that possibility any more than elderly people want to think of death. I *knew* that this was only the beginning. I knew what she meant about
720 levels because I'd seen some of them already. The thought of leaving her behind made me sad.

I'm in love with Miss Kinnian.

FOCUS

Read to find out what happens to Charlie at work.

PROGRESS REPORT 12
April 30 I've quit my job with Donnegan's Plastic Box Company. Mr. Donnegan insisted that it would be better for all concerned if I left. What did I do to make them hate me so?

The first I knew of it was when Mr. Donnegan
730 showed me the petition. Eight hundred and forty names, everyone connected with the factory, except Fanny Girden. Scanning the list quickly, I saw at once that hers was the only missing name. All the rest demanded that I be fired.

Joe Carp and Frank Reilly wouldn't talk to me about it. No one else would either, except Fanny. She was one of the few people I'd known who set her mind to something and believed it no matter what the rest of the world proved, said, or did—and Fanny did
740 not believe that I should have been fired. She had been

against the petition on principle, and despite the pressure and threats she'd held out.

"Which don't mean to say," she remarked, "that I don't think there's something mighty strange about you, Charlie. Them changes. I don't know. You used to be a good, dependable, ordinary man—not too bright maybe, but honest. Who knows what you done to yourself to get so smart all of a sudden. Like everybody around here's been saying, Charlie, it's not right."

750 "But how can you say that, Fanny? What's wrong with a man becoming intelligent and wanting to acquire knowledge and understanding of the world around him?"

She stared down at her work, and I turned to leave. Without looking at me, she said: "It was evil when Eve listened to the snake and ate from the tree of knowledge. It was evil when she saw that she was naked. If not for that, none of us would ever have to grow old and sick and die."[11]

760 Once again now I have the feeling of shame burning inside me. This intelligence has driven a wedge between me and all the people I once knew and loved. Before, they laughed at me and despised me for my ignorance and dullness; now, they hate me for my knowledge and understanding. What in God's name do they want of me?

They've driven me out of the factory. Now I'm more alone than ever before . . .

Pause & Reflect

English Learner Support

Language

Metaphor A *wedge* is an object that can be pushed between two things to separate them. The sentence in lines 761–762 means that Charlie's intelligence has created a barrier between him and his friends.

Pause & Reflect

1. Why does Charlie quit his job? **(Cause and Effect)**

2. In what way was Charlie's life better or worse before he became smart? **(Evaluate)**

---

11. **It was evil . . . die:** a reference to the biblical story of Adam and Eve (Genesis 2–3). After they ate fruit from the tree of knowledge of good and evil, they were banished from the Garden of Eden, and they and their descendants became subject to illness and death.

As the story continues . . .

- Charlie begins to realize that he knows more than Dr. Nemur and Dr. Strauss.

- Charlie's thinking is so advanced that Miss Kinnian has trouble understanding him.

REREAD As you reread the boxed passage, try to picture this scene. What do you notice about Charlie's vocabulary? **(Draw Conclusions)**

English Learner Support
Vocabulary

Synonyms Another word for *specter* is *shadow*. To be "under the specter" is to be under the control or influence.

English Learner Support
Vocabulary

Idiom *Along these lines* means "with similar results."

FOCUS
Charlie gets smarter and smarter. Read to find out what he realizes about his doctors and Miss Kinnian.

May 15 Dr. Strauss is very angry at me for not having 770 written any progress reports in two weeks. He's justified because the lab is now paying me a regular salary. I told him I was too busy thinking and reading. When I pointed out that writing was such a slow process that it made me impatient with my poor handwriting, he suggested that I learn to type. It's much easier to write now because I can type nearly seventy-five words a minute. Dr. Strauss continually reminds me of the need to 780 speak and write simply so that people will be able to understand me.

I'll try to review all the things that happened to me during the last two weeks. Algernon and I were presented to the American Psychological Association sitting in convention with the World Psychological Association last Tuesday. We created quite a sensation. Dr. Nemur and Dr. Strauss were proud of us.

I suspect that Dr. Nemur, who is sixty—ten years older than Dr. Strauss—finds it necessary to see 790 tangible results of his work. Undoubtedly the result of pressure by Mrs. Nemur.

Contrary to my earlier impressions of him, I realize that Dr. Nemur is not at all a genius. He has a very good mind, but it struggles under the specter of self-doubt. He wants people to take him for a genius. Therefore, it is important for him to feel that his work is accepted by the world. I believe that Dr. Nemur was afraid of further delay because he worried that someone else might make a discovery along these lines 800 and take the credit from him.

WORDS TO KNOW
sensation (sĕn-sā′shən) *n.* a state of great interest and excitement
tangible (tăn′jə-bəl) *adj.* able to be seen or touched; material

Dr. Strauss, on the other hand, might be called a genius, although I feel that his areas of knowledge are too limited. He was educated in the tradition of narrow specialization; the broader aspects of background were neglected far more than necessary—even for a neurosurgeon.

I was shocked to learn that the only ancient languages he could read were Latin, Greek, and Hebrew and that he knows almost nothing of mathematics beyond the
810 elementary levels of the calculus of variations.[12] When he admitted this to me, I found myself almost annoyed. It was as if he'd hidden this part of himself in order to deceive me, pretending—as do many people, I've discovered—to be what he is not. No one I've ever known is what he appears to be on the surface.

Dr. Nemur appears to be uncomfortable around me. Sometimes when I try to talk to him, he just looks at me strangely and turns away. I was angry at first when Dr. Strauss told me I was giving Dr. Nemur an
820 inferiority complex.[13] I thought he was mocking me, and I'm oversensitive at being made fun of.

How was I to know that a highly respected psychoexperimentalist like Nemur was unacquainted with Hindustani[14] and Chinese? It's absurd when you consider the work that is being done in India and China today in the very field of his study.

I asked Dr. Strauss how Nemur could refute Rahajamati's attack on his method and results if Nemur couldn't even read them in the first place. That
830 strange look on Dr. Strauss's face can mean only one of two things. Either he doesn't want to tell Nemur

---

12. **calculus** (kăl′kyə-ləs) **of variations:** a branch of higher mathematics.

13. **inferiority complex:** a psychological condition involving feelings of worthlessness.

14. **Hindustani** (hĭn′dōō-stä′nē): a group of languages used in India.

WORDS TO KNOW
 specialization (spĕsh′ə-lĭ-zā′shən) *n.* a focus on a particular activity or area of study
 absurd (əb-sûrd′) *adj.* ridiculously unreasonable

2. What kind of man has Charlie become? Circle three phrases below. (Infer)

smarter than his doctors

rejected by his fellow workers

aware of his great intelligence

closer to Miss Kinnian

As the story continues . . .

• Charlie witnesses some customers in a diner laughing at a dishwasher who breaks some dishes.

• The incident helps Charlie realize something about himself.

what they're saying in India, or else—and this worries me—Dr. Strauss doesn't know either. I must be careful to speak and write clearly and simply so that people won't laugh.

May 18 I am very disturbed. I saw Miss Kinnian last night for the first time in over a week. I tried to avoid all discussions of intellectual concepts and to keep the conversation on a simple, everyday level, but she just
840 stared at me blankly and asked me what I meant about the mathematical variance equivalent in Dorbermann's Fifth Concerto.

When I tried to explain, she stopped me and laughed. I guess I got angry, but I suspect I'm approaching her on the wrong level. No matter what I try to discuss with her, I am unable to communicate. I must review Vrostadt's equations on levels of semantic progression. I find that I don't communicate with people much any more. Thank God for books and
850 music and things I can think about. I am alone in my apartment at Mrs. Flynn's boarding house most of the time and seldom speak to anyone.

Pause & Reflect

FOCUS

Charlie witnesses an incident at the corner diner. Read to find out how Charlie reacts.

May 20 I would not have noticed the new dishwasher, a boy of about sixteen, at the corner diner where I take my evening meals if not for the incident of the broken dishes. They crashed to the floor, shattering and sending bits of white china under

860 the tables. The boy stood there, dazed and frightened, holding the empty tray in his hand. The whistles and catcalls from the customers (the cries of "Hey, there go the profits! . . ." "*Mazeltov!* . . ." and "Well, *he* didn't work here very long. . . ." which invariably seem to follow the breaking of glass or dishware in a public restaurant) all seemed to confuse him.

When the owner came to see what the excitement was about, the boy cowered as if he expected to be struck and threw up his arms as if to ward off the blow.

870 "All right! All right, you dope," shouted the owner, "don't just stand there! Get the broom and sweep that mess up. A broom . . . a broom, you idiot! It's in the kitchen. Sweep up all the pieces."

The boy saw that he was not going to be punished. His frightened expression disappeared, and he smiled and hummed as he came back with the broom to sweep the floor. A few of the rowdier customers kept up the remarks, amusing themselves at his expense.

"Here, sonny, over here there's a nice piece behind 880 you. . . ."

"C'mon, do it again. . . ."

"He's not so dumb. It's easier to break 'em than to wash 'em. . . ."

As his vacant eyes moved across the crowd of amused onlookers, he slowly mirrored their smiles and finally broke into an uncertain grin at the joke which he obviously did not understand.

I felt sick inside as I looked at his dull, <u>vacuous</u> smile, the wide, bright eyes of a child, uncertain but 890 eager to please. They were laughing at him because he was mentally retarded.

And I had been laughing at him too.

Suddenly, I was furious at myself and all those who were smirking at him. I jumped up and shouted, "Shut

WHAT DOES IT MEAN?

Mazeltov is a Yiddish expression that means "good luck." It is usually spoken after a glass has been broken as part of a celebration. *Invariably* means "always." *Cowered* means "cringed" or "winced."

REREAD the boxed passage. How do you think the boy in the diner feels? (Connect)

English Learner Support
Vocabulary

Context Clues Find context clues that help you understand that *smirking* means "smiling in a mean way."

WORDS TO KNOW
vacuous (văk′yo̅o̅-əs) *adj.* showing a lack of intelligence or thought

up! Leave him alone! It's not his fault he can't understand! He can't help what he is! But for God's sake . . . he's still a human being!"

The room grew silent. I cursed myself for losing control and creating a scene. I tried not to look at the
900 boy as I paid my check and walked out without touching my food. I felt ashamed for both of us.

How strange it is that people of honest feelings and sensibility, who would not take advantage of a man born without arms or legs or eyes—how such people think nothing of abusing a man born with low intelligence. It infuriated[15] me to think that not too long ago, I, like this boy, had foolishly played the clown.

And I had almost forgotten.

910 I'd hidden the picture of the old Charlie Gordon from myself because now that I was intelligent, it was something that had to be pushed out of my mind. But today in looking at that boy, for the first time I saw what I had been. *I was just like him!*

Only a short time ago, I learned that people laughed at me. Now I can see that unknowingly I joined with them in laughing at myself. That hurts most of all.

I have often reread my progress reports and seen the illiteracy, the childish <u>naïveté</u>, the mind of low
920 intelligence peering from a dark room, through the keyhole, at the dazzling light outside. I see that even in my dullness I knew that I was inferior and that other people had something I lacked—something denied me. In my mental blindness, I thought that it was somehow connected with the ability to read and write, and I was sure that if I could get those skills I would automatically have intelligence too.

---

15. **infuriated** (ĭn-fyŏŏr′ē-ā tĭd): angered, enraged.

WORDS TO KNOW
naïveté (nä′ēv-tā′) *n.* a lack of sophistication; simplicity

READING CHECK What similarities does Charlie see between himself and the dishwasher?

REREAD the boxed passage. Charlie says he "can see that unknowingly I joined with them in laughing at myself." What do you think he means? **(Clarify)**

English Learner Support
Language

Imagery In lines 919–921, Charlie uses the image of a dark room to represent his mind before the operation. The dazzling light represents the world that he did not understand and the intelligence that he now possesses.

Even a feeble-minded man wants to be like other men.

A child may not know how to feed itself, or what to
930 eat, yet it knows of hunger.

This, then, is what I was like. I never knew. Even with
my gift of intellectual awareness, I never really knew.

This day was good for me. Seeing the past more
clearly, I have decided to use my knowledge and skills
to work in the field of increasing human intelligence
levels. Who is better equipped for this work? Who else
has lived in both worlds? These are my people. Let me
use my gift to do something for them.

Tomorrow, I will discuss with Dr. Strauss the
940 manner in which I can work in this area. I may be able
to help him work out the problems of widespread use
of the technique which was used on me. I have several
good ideas of my own.

There is so much that might be done with this
technique. If I could be made into a genius, what
about thousands of others like myself? What fantastic
levels might be achieved by using this technique on
normal people? on *geniuses*?

There are so many doors to open. I am impatient to
950 begin.

Pause & Reflect

READING CHECK How does Charlie understand the past more clearly?

Pause & Reflect

1. Circle two words below that describe the boy in the diner. (**Evaluate**)

   scared   defiant

   angry   talkative

   childlike   brave

2. Why does Charlie react so strongly when people laugh at the boy in the diner? (**Infer**)

FOCUS

Charlie notices changes in Algernon's behavior.

MARK IT UP Underline details that describe these changes.

PROGRESS REPORT 13
May 23 It happened today.
Algernon bit me. I visited
the lab to see him, as I do
occasionally, and when I
took him out of his cage, he
snapped at my hand. I put him back and watched him
for a while. He was unusually disturbed and vicious.

As the story continues...

- Algernon begins to act differently.
- Charlie decides to continue the research of Dr. Strauss and Dr. Nemur.
- Charlie writes a letter to Dr. Strauss explaining the "Algernon-Gordon Effect."

WHAT DOES IT MEAN? *The shifting-lock problem* was the test that Algernon took every day to get his food.

READING CHECK Why has time become so important to Charlie?

English Learner Support
Vocabulary

Idiom The words in blue mean "I'm about to discover something or solve a mystery."

English Learner Support
Vocabulary

Context Clues Find context clues that help you define *cram* as "fit" or "squeeze."

May 24 Burt, who is in charge of the experimental animals, tells me that Algernon is changing. He is less cooperative; he refuses to run the maze any more; general motivation has decreased. And he hasn't been eating. Everyone is upset about what this may mean.

May 25 They've been feeding Algernon, who now refuses to work the shifting-lock problem. Everyone identifies me with Algernon. In a way we're both the first of our kind. They're all pretending that Algernon's behavior is not necessarily significant for me. But it's hard to hide the fact that some of the other animals who were used in this experiment are showing strange behavior.

Dr. Strauss and Dr. Nemur have asked me not to come to the lab any more. I know what they're thinking, but I can't accept it. I am going ahead with my plans to carry their research forward. With all due respect to both of these fine scientists, I am well aware of their limitations. If there is an answer, I'll have to find it out for myself. Suddenly, time has become very important to me.

May 29 I have been given a lab of my own and permission to go ahead with the research. I'm onto something. Working day and night. I've had a cot moved into the lab. Most of my writing time is spent on the notes which I keep in a separate folder, but from time to time I feel it necessary to put down my moods and my thoughts out of sheer habit.

I find the calculus of intelligence to be a fascinating study. Here is the place for the application of all the knowledge I have acquired. In a sense it's the problem I've been concerned with all my life.

May 31 Dr. Strauss thinks I'm working too hard. Dr. Nemur says I'm trying to cram a lifetime of research and thought into a few weeks. I know I should rest, but I'm driven on by something inside that won't let me stop. I've got to find the reason for the sharp

regression in Algernon. I've got to know *if* and *when* it will happen to me.

June 4

LETTER TO DR. STRAUSS *(copy)*

Dear Dr. Strauss:

Under separate cover I am sending you a copy of my report entitled "The Algernon-Gordon Effect: A Study of Structure and Function of Increased Intelligence," which I would like to have you read and have published.

As you see, my experiments are completed. I have included in my report all of my formulae,[16] as well as mathematical analysis in the appendix. Of course, these should be verified.[17]

Because of its importance to both you and Dr. Nemur (and need I say to myself, too?) I have checked and rechecked my results a dozen times in the hope of finding an error. I am sorry to say the results must stand. Yet for the sake of science, I am grateful for the little bit that I here add to the knowledge of the function of the human mind and of the laws governing the artificial increase of human intelligence.

I recall your once saying to me that an experimental *failure* or the *disproving* of a theory was as important to the advancement of learning as a success would be. I know now that this is true. I am sorry, however, that my own contribution to the field must rest upon the ashes of the work of two men I regard so highly.

Yours truly,

Charles Gordon

encl.: rept.

READING TIP Notice that Charlie is now using very difficult language. The author does this on purpose to show that Charlie is becoming a genius. Don't worry if you can't understand all the words. Keep reading to get the general idea.

English Learner Support

Vocabulary

Word Origins *Appendix* comes from the Latin word *appendere,* which means "to hang upon." An appendix is additional information that is attached to the end of a book or report.

English Learner Support

Vocabulary

Idiom In line 1011, *stand* means "stay as they are."

WHAT DOES IT MEAN? *Ashes* means "remains." To *regard* is to respect. *Encl.: rept.* stands for "enclosure: report." Charlie has enclosed a report with his letter to Dr. Strauss.

---

16. **formulae** (fôr′myə-lē′): plural of *formula,* a set of symbols in mathematics that expresses a rule or principle.

17. **verified** (vĕr′ə-fīd′): proved the truth of by presentation of evidence or testimony.

WORDS TO KNOW

regression (rĭ-grĕsh′ən) *n.* a return to a less developed condition

June 5 I must not become emotional. The facts and the results of my experiments are clear, and the more sensational aspects of my own rapid climb cannot obscure the fact that the tripling of intelligence by the surgical technique developed by Drs. Strauss and 1030 Nemur must be viewed as having little or no practical applicability (at the present time) to the increase of human intelligence.

As I review the records and data on Algernon, I see that although he is still in his physical infancy, he has regressed mentally. Motor activity[18] is <u>impaired</u>; there is a general reduction of glandular[19] activity; there is an accelerated loss of coordination.

There are also strong indications of progressive amnesia.[20]

As will be seen by my report, these and other 1040 physical and mental deterioration <u>syndromes</u> can be predicted with <u>statistically</u> significant results by the application of my formula.

The surgical stimulus[21] to which we were both subjected has resulted in an intensification and acceleration of all mental processes. The unforeseen development, which I have taken the liberty of calling the Algernon-Gordon effect, is the logical extension of the entire intelligence speedup. The <u>hypothesis</u> here proven may be described simply in the following terms:

---

18. **motor activity:** movement produced by use of the muscles.

19. **glandular** (glăn′jə-lər): affecting a gland—an organ in the body that produces some special substance, such as a hormone or an enzyme.

20. **progressive amnesia** (ăm-nē′zhə): an increasing loss of memory.

21. **stimulus** (stĭm′yə-ləs): something that causes an organ or a body part to change or respond.

WORDS TO KNOW
impair (ĭm-pâr′) *v.* to weaken; damage
syndrome (sĭn′drōm′) *n.* a group of symptoms that characterizes a disease or psychological disorder
statistically (stə-tĭs′tĭ-klē) *adv.* in terms of the principles used to analyze numerical data
hypothesis (hī-pŏth′ĭ-sĭs) *n.* a theory used as a basis for research

READING CHECK

How does Algernon change?

WHAT DOES IT MEAN?
Deterioration means "becoming worse."

English Learner Support
Vocabulary

Word Parts The word *unforeseen* is made from these word parts:

un (not) +
fore (earlier) +
seen = unforeseen (not seen or predicted earlier)

WHAT DOES IT MEAN? *The hypothesis here proven* means that the following sentence is the theory, or idea, that Charlie proves in his research.

1050 Artificially increased intelligence deteriorates at a rate of time directly <u>proportional</u> to the quantity of the increase.

I feel that this, in itself, is an important discovery.

As long as I am able to write, I will continue to record my thoughts in these progress reports. It is one of my few pleasures. However, by all indications, my own mental deterioration will be very rapid.

I have already begun to notice signs of emotional instability[22] and forgetfulness, the first symptoms of the burnout.

Pause & Reflect

FOCUS

Read to find out how Charlie's mental powers are slipping.

▐▐ MARK IT UP ⟩ As you read, underline details that help you understand what is happening to Charlie.

1060 *June 10* Deterioration progressing. I have become absent-minded. Algernon died two days ago. Dissection shows my predictions were right. His brain had decreased in weight, and there was a general smoothing out of cerebral convolutions as well as a deepening and broadening of brain fissures.[23]

1070 I guess the same thing is or will soon be happening to me. Now that it's definite, I don't want it to happen.

I put Algernon's body in a cheese box and buried him in the back yard. I cried.

---

22. **emotional instability:** unsteady, complex feelings.

23. **cerebral convolutions** (sĕr′ə-brəl kŏn′və-lo͞o′shənz) . . . **brain fissures** (fĭsh′ərz): features of the brain. Cerebral convolutions are the ridges or folds on the brain's surface; fissures are grooves that divide the brain into lobes, or sections.

WORDS TO KNOW
proportional (prə-pôr′shə-nəl) *adj.* having a constant relation in degree or number

Pause & Reflect

Review the details you underlined. In the list below, mark a "T" beside the true statements and an "F" beside the false statements. **(Evaluate)**

___ Charlie notices that he is becoming forgetful and emotionally unreliable.

___ Charlie cannot compare his condition to Algernon's.

___ Charlie concludes that the more one's intelligence is increased through surgery, the faster it will decrease.

⟨ As the story continues . . .

• Algernon dies.

• Dr. Strauss tries to visit Charlie, but Charlie does not want to speak to him.

• Charlie forgets things that he had learned.

English Learner Support
Vocabulary

Scientific Term *Dissection* means cutting something open to examine it. After Algernon died, Charlie dissected the mouse's brain to learn why Algernon died.

June 15 Dr. Strauss came to see me again. I wouldn't open the door, and I told him to go away. I want to be left to myself. I have become touchy and irritable. I feel the darkness closing in. It's hard to throw off thoughts of suicide. I keep telling myself how important this <u>introspective</u> journal will be.

1080   It's a strange sensation to pick up a book that you've read and enjoyed just a few months ago and discover that you don't remember it. I remembered how great I thought John Milton was, but when I picked up *Paradise Lost,* I couldn't understand it at all. I got so angry I threw the book across the room.

I've got to try to hold on to some of it. Some of the things I've learned. Oh, God, please don't take it all away.

June 19 Sometimes, at night, I go out for a walk.
1090 Last night I couldn't remember where I lived. A policeman took me home. I have the strange feeling that this has all happened to me before—a long time ago. I keep telling myself I'm the only person in the world who can describe what's happening to me.

June 21 Why can't I remember? I've got to fight. I lie in bed for days, and I don't know who or where I am. Then it all comes back to me in a flash. Fugues[23] of amnesia. Symptoms of senility—second childhood. I can watch them coming on. It's so cruelly logical. I
1100 learned so much and so fast. Now my mind is deteriorating rapidly. I won't let it happen. I'll fight it. I can't help thinking of the boy in the restaurant, the blank expression, the silly smile, the people laughing at him. No—please—not that again . . .

---

24. **fugues** (fyo͞ogz): psychological states in which people seem to be acting consciously, although later they have no memory of the activity.

WORDS TO KNOW

introspective (ĭn'trə-spĕk'tĭv) *adj.* examining one's own thoughts, feelings, and sensations

June 22 I'm forgetting things that I learned recently. It seems to be following the classic pattern—the last things learned are the first things forgotten. Or is that the pattern? I'd better look it up again . . .

I reread my paper on the Algernon-Gordon effect, and I get the strange feeling that it was written by someone else. There are parts I don't even understand.

Motor activity impaired. I keep tripping over things, and it becomes increasingly difficult to type.

June 23 I've given up using the typewriter completely. My coordination is bad. I feel that I'm moving slower and slower. Had a terrible shock today. I picked up a copy of an article I used in my research, Krueger's "Über psychische Ganzheit," to see if it would help me understand what I had done. First I thought there was something wrong with my eyes. Then I realized I could no longer read German. I tested myself in other languages. All gone.

June 30 A week since I dared to write again. It's slipping away like sand through my fingers. Most of the books I have are too hard for me now. I get angry with them because I know that I read and understood them just a few weeks ago.

I keep telling myself I must keep writing these reports so that somebody will know what is happening to me. But it gets harder to form the words and remember spellings. I have to look up even simple words in the dictionary now, and it makes me impatient with myself.

Dr. Strauss comes around almost every day, but I told him I wouldn't see or speak to anybody. He feels guilty. They all do. But I don't blame anyone. I knew what might happen. But how it hurts.

READ ALOUD Charlie describes what is happening to him. As you read aloud the boxed passage, use your voice to express how he feels.

Pause & Reflect

1. How does Charlie know that his mental powers are decreasing? Check three phrases below. **(Infer)**
   - ❏ forgets where he lives
   - ❏ forgets languages that he learned
   - ❏ cannot understand what Miss Kinnian is saying
   - ❏ cannot understand his report on the Algernon-Gordon effect

2. Do you think Charlie can escape Algernon's fate? **(Predict)**

   YES / NO, because

As the story continues . . .

- Charlie stays in bed for days at a time.
- He has no job and no money to pay the rent.
- He does not want to see Miss Kinnian.

FOCUS

Charlie recalls his childhood. Read to find out how he spends his time and how he feels.

MARK IT UP As you read, underline details that help you understand how he feels.

July 7 I don't know where the week went. Todays Sunday 1140 I know because I can see through my window people going to church. I think I stayed in bed all week but I remember Mrs. Flynn bringing food to me a few times. I keep saying over and over Ive got to do something but then I forget or maybe its just easier not to do what I say Im going to do.

I think of my mother and father a lot these days. I 1150 found a picture of them with me taken at a beach. My father has a big ball under his arm and my mother is holding me by the hand. I dont remember them the way they are in the picture. All I remember is my father drunk most of the time and arguing with mom about money.

He never shaved much and he used to scratch my face when he hugged me. My mother said he died but Cousin Miltie said he heard his mom and dad say that my father ran away with another woman. When I asked my mother she slapped my face and said my 1160 father was dead. I dont think I ever found out which was true but I dont care much. (He said he was going to take me to see cows on a farm once but he never did. He never kept his promises . . .)

July 10 My landlady Mrs. Flynn is very worried about me. She says the way I lay around all day and dont do anything I remind her of her son before she threw him out of the house. She said she doesnt like loafers. If Im sick its one thing, but if Im a loafer thats another thing and she wont have it. I told her I think Im sick.

1170 I try to read a little bit every day, mostly stories, but sometimes I have to read the same thing over and over again because I dont know what it means. And its hard

WHAT DOES IT MEAN? *Loafers* means "lazy people."

to write. I know I should look up all the words in the dictionary but its so hard and Im so tired all the time.

Then I got the idea that I would only use the easy words instead of the long hard ones. That saves time. I put flowers on Algernons grave about once a week. Mrs Flynn thinks Im crazy to put flowers on a mouses grave but I told her that Algernon was special.

1180 *July 14* Its sunday again. I dont have anything to do to keep me busy now because my television set is broke and I dont have any money to get it fixed. (I think I lost this months check from the lab. I dont remember)

I get awful headaches and asperin doesnt help me much. Mrs Flynn knows Im really sick and she feels very sorry for me. Shes a wonderful woman whenever someone is sick.

July 22 Mrs Flynn called a strange doctor to see me. She was afraid I was going to die. I told the doctor I
1190 wasnt too sick and that I only forget sometimes. He asked me did I have any friends or relatives and I said no I dont have any. I told him I had a friend called Algernon once but he was a mouse and we used to run races together. He looked at me kind of funny like he thought I was crazy.

He smiled when I told him I used to be a genius. He talked to me like I was a baby and he winked at Mrs Flynn. I got mad and chased him out because he was making fun of me the way they all used to.

1200 *July 24* I have no more money and Mrs Flynn says I got to go to work somewhere and pay the rent because I havent paid for over two months. I dont know any work but the job I used to have at Donnegans Plastic Box Company. I dont want to go back there because they all knew me when I was smart and maybe they'll laugh at me. But I dont know what else to do to get money.

Why does the doctor treat Charlie like a baby and wink at Mrs. Flynn?

Pause & Reflect

1. What does Charlie remember about his childhood? Cross out the sentence that does *not* apply. **(Clarify)**

   His family was wealthy.

   His father drank too much.

   His father disappeared.

2. Why does Charlie send Miss Kinnian away? **(Infer)**

As the story ends . . .

• Charlie goes back to work in the factory.

• He goes to Miss Kinnian's classroom and sits in his old seat.

English Learner Support

Language

Slang *You got guts* means "you have courage."

July 25 I was looking at some of my old progress reports and its very funny but I cant read what I wrote. I can make out some of the words but they 1210 dont make sense.

Miss Kinnian came to the door but I said go away I dont want to see you. She cried and I cried too but I wouldnt let her in because I didnt want her to laugh at me. I told her I didn't like her any more. I told her I didnt want to be smart any more. Thats not true. I still love her and I still want to be smart but I had to say that so shed go away. She gave Mrs. Flynn money to pay the rent. I dont want that. I got to get a job.

Please . . . please let me not forget how to read 1220 and write . . .

Pause & Reflect

FOCUS

Read to find out what happens to Charlie at the end of the story.

MARK IT UP As you read, list his actions in the margin.

July 27 Mr. Donnegan was very nice when I came back and asked him for my old job of janitor. First he was very suspicious but I told him what happened to me then he looked very sad and put his hand on my shoulder and said Charlie Gordon you got guts.

1230 Everybody looked at me when I came downstairs and started working in the toilet sweeping it out like I used to. I told myself Charlie if they make fun of you dont get sore because you remember their not so smart as you once thot they were. And besides they were once your friends and if they laughed at you that doesnt mean anything because they liked you too.

One of the new men who came to work there after I went away made a nasty crack he said hey Charlie I hear your a very smart fella a real quiz kid. Say something intelligent. I felt bad but Joe Carp came over and grabbed him by the shirt and said leave him alone you lousy cracker or Ill break your neck. I didnt expect Joe to take my part so I guess hes really my friend.

Later Frank Reilly came over and said Charlie if anybody bothers you or trys to take advantage you call me or Joe and we will set em straight. I said thanks Frank and I got choked up so I had to turn around and go into the supply room so he wouldnt see me cry. Its good to have friends.

1250 *July 28* I did a dumb thing today I forgot I wasnt in Miss Kinnians class at the adult center any more like I use to be. I went in and sat down in my old seat in the back of the room and she looked at me funny and she said Charles. I dint remember she ever called me that before only Charlie so I said hello Miss Kinnian Im redy for my lesin today only I lost my reader that we was using. She startid to cry and run out of the room and everybody looked at me and I saw they wasnt the same pepul who use to be in my class.

1260 Then all of a suddin I rememberd some things about the operashun and me getting smart and I said holy smoke I reely pulled a Charlie Gordon that time. I went away before she come back to the room.

Thats why Im going away from New York for good. I dont want to do nothing like that agen. I dont want Miss Kinnian to feel sorry for me. Evry body feels sorry at the factery and I dont want that eather so Im going someplace where nobody knows that Charlie Gordon was once a genus and now he cant even reed

1270 a book or rite good.

Im taking a cuple of books along and even if I cant reed them Ill practise hard and maybe I wont forget every

READ ALOUD the boxed passage. Notice how Joe Carp has changed.

English Learner Support
Language
Slang A *nasty crack* is an unkind remark.

WHAT DOES IT MEAN? *Take my part* means "defend me."

English Learner Support
Vocabulary
Idiom *Holy smoke* is an expression of surprise.

READING CHECK Why does Charlie decide to move?

Pause & Reflect

1. Think of how Charlie makes peace with himself. Review the details that you listed in the margin. Then put a check next to the sentences below that reflect a likely **prediction** for the rest of Charlie's life.

❏ Charlie leaves Miss Kinnian.

❏ Charlie knows he'll be a genius again.

❏ Charlie moves to New York.

❏ Charlie feels sad a lot.

2. Do you think Charlie is happier at the end of the story than at the beginning? Explain why or why not. **(Infer)**

Imagine that Charlie had been able to keep his great intelligence. What kind of life would he have had? Discuss your thoughts with a partner. **(Make Judgments)**

thing I lerned. If I try reel hard maybe Ill be a littel bit smarter then I was before the operashun. I got my rabits foot and my luky penny and maybe they will help me.

If you ever reed this Miss Kinnian dont be sorry for me Im glad I got a second chanse to be smart becaus I lerned a lot of things that I never even new were in this world and Im grateful that I saw it all for a littel 1280 bit. I dont know why Im dumb agen or what I did wrong maybe its becaus I dint try hard enuff. But if I try and practis very hard maybe Ill get a littl smarter and know what all the words are. I remember a littel bit how nice I had a feeling with the blue book that has the torn cover when I red it. Thats why Im gonna keep trying to get smart so I can have that feeling agen. Its a good feeling to know things and be smart. I wish I had it rite now if I did I woud sit down and reed all the time. Anyway I bet Im the first dumb 1290 person in the world who ever found out somthing importent for sience. I remember I did somthing but I dont remember what. So I gess its like I did it for all the dumb pepul like me.

Goodbye Miss Kinnian and Dr. Strauss and evreybody. And P.S. please tell Dr Nemur not to be such a grouch when pepul laff at him and he woud have more frends. Its easy to make frends if you let pepul laff at you. Im going to have lots of frends where I go.

P.P.S. Please if you get a chanse put some flowers on 1300 Algernons grave in the bak yard. . . . ❖

Active Reading SkillBuilder

Making Inferences

When readers draw logical conclusions about characters and events in a story they are **making inferences.** Inferences should be based on information in the story and your own experience. In the chart below, jot down clues from "Flowers for Algernon" to help you understand Charlie's character.

Clue from Text	Inference
Charlie's early progress reports are poorly written and show a lack of comprehension of even simple ideas.	Charlie is not very smart.

Literary Analysis SkillBuilder

Characterization

Characterization refers to the techniques used by a writer to build and develop a character. A character may be shown through physical description; through his or her thoughts, speech, or behavior; and through other characters' comments or actions. In the diagram below, note examples of different techniques used by the author to develop Charlie's character. Record in the chart more than one example of each technique.

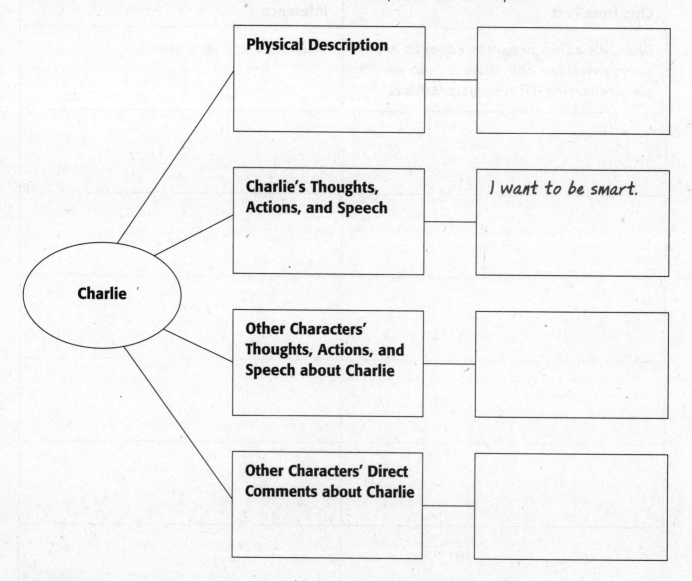

Charlie

Physical Description

Charlie's Thoughts, Actions, and Speech — *I want to be smart.*

Other Characters' Thoughts, Actions, and Speech about Charlie

Other Characters' Direct Comments about Charlie

Follow Up: Discuss what the characterization technique of using Charlie's journal contributes to the effect of the story.

Words to Know SkillBuilder

Words to Know

absurd	introspective	proportional	shrew	syndrome
hypothesis	naïveté	regression	specialization	tangible
impair	opportunist	sensation	statistically	vacuous

A. Fill in each set of blanks with the correct Word to Know. The boxed letters will spell out what Charlie's operation was supposed to affect.

1. This is someone who reminds you of Cinderella's stepmother. __ ☐ __ __ __

2. This is a person who would sell tickets to a neighbor's house fire. __ __ __ __ __ __ __ __ ☐ __ __

3. This describes the idea that the moon is made of green cheese. __ __ ☐ __ __ __

4. This is what you focus on when you narrow your interests to just one. __ __ __ __ ☐ __ __ __ __ __ __ __ __

5. This describes people who "look within" to try to "find" themselves. __ ☐ __ __ __ __ __ __ __ __ __ __

6. This describes anything that can be touched. ☐ __ __ __ __ __ __

7. This is often part of the name of a serious medical condition. __ __ __ __ __ __ ☐ __

8. This refers to how numbers are used to get or present information. __ __ __ __ __ __ __ __ __ ☐ __ __

9. This describes the sales tax on an item in relation to the item's cost. __ __ __ __ __ __ __ __ __ __ ☐

10. This is what the flu might do to a performer's ability to perform. ☐ __ __ __ __ __

11. This is like sliding backward. It's the opposite of progress. __ __ ☐ __ __ __ __ __ __

12. This is an idea—something that may or may not be provable. __ __ __ __ __ __ ☐ __ __ __

13. This is something that causes a big splash and makes everyone talk. __ __ ☐ __ __ __ __ __ __

14. This is a classy word for describing an action that was just plain dumb. __ __ ☐ __ __ __ __

15. This is the opposite of sophistication. __ __ __ __ ☐ __ __

Before You Read

Connect to Your Life

Have you ever felt that a particular situation or
law needed to be changed? Use the following chart
to show what you believe about an important issue.

Issue	What I Believe
the death penalty	The death penalty should be replaced with life imprisonment.

Key to the Story

WHAT DO YOU THINK this sentence from the story might
mean? Think of related words to help you unlock the
meaning of the circled words.

"Don't forget either, you unhappy man, that voluntary

is much heavier than enforced *imprisonment."*

THE BET

by Anton Chekhov

PREVIEW

This story is set in Russia in the late 1800s. A banker and a lawyer make a strange bet to prove a point. This unusual bet leads to a surprising outcome.

As the story begins …

- A banker remembers a party that he hosted 15 years ago.
- He and his guests discuss capital punishment (the death penalty).
- A lawyer says that he would choose life imprisonment over capital punishment.

READING TIP Watch out for time jumps in the story. Use a chart like the one below to keep track of the current action of the story and the events that occurred at an earlier time.

Past Events	Current Action
Guests discuss death penalty	Banker remembers party

FOCUS

A banker recalls a party he gave 15 years ago. Read to find out what the guests at that party think of the death penalty.

It was a dark autumn night. The old banker was pacing from corner to corner of his study, recalling to his mind the party he gave in the autumn fifteen years ago. There were many clever people at the party and much interesting conversation. They talked among other things of capital punishment.[1] The guests, among them 10 not a few scholars and journalists, for the most part disapproved of capital punishment.

They found it <u>obsolete</u> as a means of punishment, and <u>immoral</u>. Some of them thought that capital punishment should be replaced universally by life imprisonment.

"I don't agree with you," said the host. "I myself have experienced neither capital punishment nor life imprisonment, but if one may judge a priori,[2] then in my opinion capital punishment is more moral and 20 more <u>humane</u> than imprisonment. Execution kills instantly; life imprisonment kills by degrees. Who is the more humane executioner, one who kills you in a few seconds or one who draws the life out of you <u>incessantly</u>, for years?"

"They're both equally immoral," remarked one of the guests, "because their purpose is the same, to take away life. The state[3] is not all powerful. It has no right to take away that which it cannot give back, if it should so desire."

---

1. **capital punishment:** the death penalty.
2. **a priori** (ä′prē-ôr′ē): based on a theory rather than on experience.
3. **the state:** the supreme political power; the government.

WORDS TO KNOW
obsolete (ŏb′sə-lēt′) *adj.* out-of-date
immoral (ĭ-môr′əl) *adj.* contrary to what is considered to be correct behavior
humane (hyōō-mān′) *adj.* merciful; showing the best qualities of humans
incessantly (ĭn-sĕs′ənt-lē) *adv.* continually, without interruption

30   Among the company was a lawyer, a young man of about twenty-five. On being asked his opinion, he said:

"Capital punishment and life imprisonment are equally immoral; but if I were offered the choice between them, I would certainly choose the second. It's better to live somehow than not to live at all."

Pause & Reflect

FOCUS

The banker and the lawyer make a bet.

MARK IT UP Circle details that tell you about the bet. An example is highlighted.

    There ensued[4] a lively discussion. The banker, who was then younger and more nervous, suddenly lost his
40 temper, banged his fist on the table, and turning to the young lawyer, cried out:

"It's a lie. I bet you two millions you wouldn't stick in a cell even for five years."

"If you're serious," replied the lawyer, "then I bet I'll stay not five but fifteen."

"Fifteen! Done!" cried the banker. "Gentlemen, I stake two millions."

"Agreed. You stake two millions, I my freedom,"
50 said the lawyer.

    So this wild, ridiculous bet came to pass. The banker, who at that time had too many millions to count, spoiled and <u>capricious</u>, was beside himself with <u>rapture</u>. During supper he said to the lawyer jokingly:

"Come to your senses, young man, before it's too late. Two millions are nothing to me, but you stand to lose three or four of the best years of your life. I say

---

4. **ensued:** followed.

WORDS TO KNOW
capricious (kə-prĭsh′əs) *adj.* unpredictable
rapture (răp′chər) *n.* feeling of ecstasy; great joy

Pause & Reflect

1. MARK IT UP Read aloud the boxed passage on page 130. Underline the sentences that tell why the banker is in favor of the death penalty. **(Clarify)**

2. Imagine that you are a guest at the banker's party. Whose side would you take in the debate? Circle your answer below. **(Connect)**

   the banker's

   the lawyer's

As the story continues . . .

• The banker challenges the lawyer's statement, and the two gentleman make a bet.

• The lawyer agrees to be imprisoned in a part of the banker's house for 15 years.

English Learner Support
Vocabulary

Idiom The idiom *beside himself* means "excited."

 What do the two gentlemen bet?

REREAD the boxed passage. What did the banker think of the bet later? Do you agree with him? **(Make Judgments)**

READING CHECK How will the lawyer communicate with the outside world while in prison?

three or four, because you'll never stick it out any longer. Don't forget either, you unhappy man, that voluntary[5] is
60 much heavier than enforced imprisonment. The idea that you have the right to free yourself at any moment will poison the whole of your life in the cell. I pity you."

And now the banker, pacing from corner to corner, recalled all this and asked himself:

"Why did I make this bet? What's the good? The lawyer loses fifteen years of his life and I throw away two millions. Will it convince people that capital punishment is worse or better than imprisonment for life? No, no! all stuff and rubbish. On my part, it was the caprice[6] of a
70 well-fed man; on the lawyer's, pure greed of gold."

He recollected[7] further what happened after the evening party. It was decided that the lawyer must undergo his imprisonment under the strictest observation, in a garden wing of the banker's house. It was agreed that during the period he would be deprived[8] of the right to cross the threshold,[9] to see living people, to hear human voices, and to receive letters and newspapers. He was permitted to have a musical instrument, to read books and to write letters.
80 By the agreement he could communicate, but only in silence, with the outside world through a little window specially constructed for this purpose. Everything necessary, books, music, he could receive in any quantity by sending a note through the window. The agreement provided for all the minutest[10] details, which made the confinement[11] strictly solitary, and it obliged[12] the lawyer to remain exactly fifteen years

---

5. **voluntary** (vŏl′ ən-tĕr′ ē): chosen.

6. **caprice** (kə-prēs′): sudden decision.

7. **recollected:** remembered.

8. **deprived:** not allowed.

9. **threshold** (thrĕsh′ ōld′): entrance or doorway.

10. **minutest:** smallest.

11. **confinement** (kən-fīn′ mənt): imprisonment.

12. **obliged:** forced.

from twelve o'clock of November 14th, 1870, to twelve o'clock of November 14th, 1885. The least attempt on
90 his part to violate[13] the conditions, to escape if only for two minutes before the time, freed the banker from the obligation to pay him the two millions.

Pause & Reflect

FOCUS

As the years go by, the lawyer finds ways of passing the time while in prison.

MARK IT UP As you read, underline the things the lawyer does in the cell.

During the first year of imprisonment, the lawyer, as far as it was possible to judge from his short notes, suffered terribly from loneliness and boredom. From his wing day and night came the sound of
100 the piano. During the first year, the lawyer was sent books of a light character; novels with a complicated love interest, stories of crime and fantasy, comedies, and so on.

In the second year, the piano was heard no longer and the lawyer asked only for classics. In the fifth year, music was heard again. Those who watched him said that during the whole of that year he was only eating, drinking, and lying on his bed. He yawned often and talked angrily to himself. Books he did not
110 read. Sometimes at night he would sit down to write. He would write for a long time and tear it all up in the morning. More than once he was heard to weep.

In the second half of the sixth year, the prisoner began zealously[14] to study languages, philosophy, and history. He fell on these subjects so hungrily that the banker hardly had time to get books enough for him.

---

13. **violate** (vī′ə-lāt′): disregard.
14. **zealously** (zĕl′ əs-lē): enthusiastically.

Pause & Reflect

Review the details about the bet that you underlined. Then complete the following sentence. (Clarify)

The lawyer will lose

the bet if he

_____

As the story continues . . .

• During his years in prison, the lawyer pursues many different interests.

MORE ABOUT . . .

CLASSICS Classics are works of literature that people have considered important for many centuries. Many of these works come from ancient Greek and Roman times.

English Learner Support
Language

Figure of Speech The words in blue mean that the lawyer was extremely interested in languages, philosophy, and history. He wanted to read many books about these subjects.

READING CHECK

Why were two shots fired in the garden?

MORE ABOUT . . .

THE NEW TESTAMENT The Christian Bible consists of the Old Testament and the New Testament. The New Testament contains stories about the life and teachings of Jesus Christ and the development of the early Christian church.

In the space of four years about six hundred volumes were bought at his request. It was while that passion lasted that the banker received the following letter from the prisoner: "My dear jailer, I am writing these lines in six languages. Show them to experts. Let them read them. If they do not find one single mistake, I beg you to give orders to have a gun fired off in the garden. By the noise I shall know that my efforts have not been in vain. The geniuses of all ages and countries speak in different languages; but in them all burns the same flame. Oh, if you knew my heavenly happiness now that I can understand them!" The prisoner's desire was fulfilled. Two shots were fired in the garden by the banker's order.

Later on, after the tenth year, the lawyer sat immovable[15] before his table and read only the New Testament. The banker found it strange that a man who in four years had mastered six hundred erudite[16] volumes, should have spent nearly a year in reading one book, easy to understand and by no means thick. The New Testament was then replaced by the history of religions and theology.[17]

During the last two years of his confinement the prisoner read an extraordinary amount, quite haphazardly. Now he would apply himself to the natural sciences, then would read Byron[18] or Shakespeare. Notes used to come from him in which he asked to be sent at the same time a book on chemistry, a textbook of medicine, a novel, and some treatise[19] on philosophy or theology. He read as

---

15. **immovable** (ĭ-mŏo′ və-bəl): impossible to move.

16. **erudite** (ĕr′yə-dīt′): scholarly.

17. **theology** (thē-ŏl′ ə-jē): the study of religious truth.

18. **Byron:** George Gordon Byron (1788–1824), a leading English poet of the Romantic movement.

19. **treatise** (trē′ tĭs): written discourse.

WORDS TO KNOW
haphazardly (hăp-hăz′ərd-lē) *adv.* in a random manner

though he were swimming in the sea among broken pieces of wreckage, and in his desire to save his life was eagerly grasping one piece after another.

Pause  Reflect

FOCUS

Fifteen years have passed. Read to find out what the banker decides to do about the prisoner.

The banker recalled all this, 150 and thought:

"Tomorrow at twelve o'clock he receives his freedom. Under the agreement, I shall have to pay him two millions. If I pay, it's all over with me. I am ruined forever. . . ."

Fifteen years before he had too many millions to count, but now he was afraid to ask himself which he had more of, money or debts. Gambling on the (stock) exchange, risky speculation,[20] and the recklessness[21] of 160 which he could not rid himself even in old age, had gradually brought his business to decay; and the fearless, self-confident, proud man of business had become an ordinary banker, trembling at every rise and fall in the market.

"That cursed bet," murmured the old man clutching his head in despair. . . . "Why didn't the man die? He's only forty years old. He will take away my last penny, marry, enjoy life, gamble on the exchange, and I will look on like an envious beggar and hear the same 170 words from him every day: 'I'm obliged to you for the happiness of my life. Let me help you.' No, it's too much! The only escape from bankruptcy and disgrace—is that the man should die."

---

20. **speculation** (spĕk-yə-lā′shən): business investment.
21. **recklessness** (rĕk′lĭs-nĕs): carelessness.

Pause  Reflect

During his 15 years in prison, the lawyer _____. (Check one.) **(Clarify)**
❏ builds clocks
❏ exercises often
❏ learns to paint
❏ reads many books

▣ **As the story continues . . .**

• The banker has lost much of his money since he made the bet.

• He thinks of a way to avoid paying the lawyer.

MORE ABOUT . . .

(STOCK) Investors purchase stocks, or shares of companies, in order to make a profit. The investor earns money if the value of the company increases and loses money if its value decreases. Trading stocks is a form of gambling because the investor cannot know for certain whether a company's value will increase or decrease.

READ ALOUD the boxed passage. Why does the banker want the lawyer to die? **(Cause and Effect)**

English Learner Support
Language

Figure of Speech *Gave the trees no rest* means that the trees were constantly blowing in the wind.

WHAT DOES IT MEAN? *Fulfill my intention* means "carry out my plan."

Pause & Reflect

1. What is the banker planning to do? (Infer)

2. MARK IT UP ▷ Underline details on this page that help you **visualize** what the banker notices that night.

The clock had just struck three. The banker was listening. In the house everyone was asleep, and one could hear only the frozen trees whining outside the windows. Trying to make no sound, he took out of his safe the key of the door which had not been opened for fifteen years, put on his overcoat, and went out of
180 the house. The garden was dark and cold. It was raining. A keen damp wind hovered howling over all the garden and gave the trees no rest. Though he strained his eyes, the banker could see neither the ground, nor the white statues, nor the garden wing, nor the trees. Approaching the place where the garden wing stood, he called the watchman twice. There was no answer. Evidently the watchman had taken shelter from the bad weather and was now asleep somewhere in the kitchen or the greenhouse.
190   "If I have the courage to fulfill my intention," thought the old man, "the suspicion will fall on the watchman first of all."

In the darkness he groped for the stairs and the door and entered the hall of the garden wing, then poked his way into a narrow passage and struck a match. Not a soul was there. Someone's bed, with no bedclothes on it, stood there, and an iron stove was dark in the corner. The seals on the door that led into the prisoner's room were unbroken.
200   When the match went out, the old man, trembling from agitation,[22] peeped into the little window.

Pause & Reflect

_____

22. **agitation** (ăj'i-tā'shən): emotional disturbance.

The banker quietly enters the lawyer's cell. Read to find out what he notices about the prisoner.

MARK IT UP Underline the details that help you picture the prisoner's appearance.

In the prisoner's room a candle was burning dim. The prisoner himself sat by the table. Only his back, the hair on his head, and his hands were visible. On the table, the two chairs, and on the carpet by the table, open 210 books were strewn.

Five minutes passed and the prisoner never once stirred. Fifteen years' confinement had taught him to sit motionless. The banker tapped on the window with his finger, but the prisoner gave no movement in reply. Then the banker cautiously tore the seals from the door and put the key into the lock. The rusty lock gave a hoarse groan and the door creaked. The banker expected instantly to hear a cry of surprise and the sound of steps. Three minutes passed and it was as 220 quiet behind the door as it had been before. He made up his mind to enter.

Before the table sat a man, unlike an ordinary human being. It was a skeleton, with tight-drawn skin, with a woman's long curly hair, and a shaggy beard. The color of his face was yellow, of an earthy shade; the cheeks were sunken, the back long and narrow, and the hand upon which he leaned his hairy head was so lean and skinny that it was painful to look upon. His hair was already silvering with grey, and no one 230 who glanced at the senile emaciation[23] of the face would have believed that he was only forty years old. On the table, before his bent head, lay a sheet of paper on which something was written in a tiny hand.

"Poor fellow," thought the banker, "he's asleep and probably seeing millions in his dreams. I have only to take and throw this half-dead thing on the bed,

As the story continues...

• The banker unlocks the door to the lawyer's cell.
• The lawyer is sitting at a table with a piece of paper in front of him.

English Learner Support
Language
Figure of Speech *It was a skeleton* means that the lawyer had become very thin.

English Learner Support
Vocabulary
Hand In this sentence, the word *hand* means "handwriting." *Written in a tiny hand* means that the handwriting was very small.

---

23. emaciation (ĭ-mā′shē-ā′shən): abnormal thinness, usually caused by starvation.

As the story ends...

- The banker reads the prisoner's letter.
- He locks the letter in his safe.

MORE ABOUT...

ELBRUZ AND MONT BLANC

Elbruz most likely refers to Mount Elbrus, the highest peak in Russia. Mont Blanc, located in the Alps on the French-Italian border, is the highest peak in Europe.

smother him a moment with the pillow, and the most careful examination will find no trace of unnatural death. But, first, let us read what he has written here."

Pause & Reflect

FOCUS

Read to find out about the prisoner's letter and its effect on the banker.

240 The banker took the sheet from the table and read:

"Tomorrow at twelve o'clock midnight, I shall obtain my freedom and the right to mix with people. But before I leave this room and see the sun I think it necessary to say a few words to you. On my own clear conscience, I declare to you that I despise freedom, life, health, and all that your books call the blessings of the world.

"For fifteen years I have diligently[24] studied earthly 250 life. True, I saw neither the earth nor the people, but in your books I sang songs, hunted deer and wild boar in the forests, loved women. . . . And beautiful women, like clouds ethereal,[25] created by the magic of your poets' genius, visited me by night and whispered to me wonderful tales, which made my head spin. In your books I climbed the summits of Elbruz and Mont Blanc and saw from there how the sun rose in the morning, and in the evening overflowed the sky, the ocean and the mountain ridges with a purple gold. 260 From there I saw how above me lightnings glimmered, cleaving the clouds; I saw green forests, fields, rivers, lakes, cities; I heard sirens[26] singing, and the playing of the pipes of Pan. . . .[27] In your books I cast myself into

24. **diligently** (dĭl′ ə-jənt lē): carefully and with much hard work.

25. **ethereal** (ĭ-thîr′ē-əl): delicate; heavenly.

26. **sirens:** from Greek mythology, sea goddesses whose sweet singing lured sailors to their deaths on rocky coasts.

27. **pipes of Pan:** Pan, the Greek god of woods, fields, and flocks, played a flutelike pipe instrument.

bottomless abysses,[28] worked miracles, burned cities to the ground, preached new religions, conquered whole countries. . . .

"Your books gave me wisdom. All that unwearying human thought created in the centuries is compressed to a little lump in my skull. I know that I am more 270 clever than you all.

"And I despise your books, despise all worldly blessings and wisdom. Everything is void, frail, visionary and delusive as a mirage.[29] Though you be proud and wise and beautiful, yet will death wipe you from the face of the earth like the mice underground; and your <u>posterity</u>, your history, and the immortality of your men of genius will be as frozen slag,[30] burnt down together with the terrestrial globe.

"You are mad, and gone the wrong way. You take 280 lie for truth and ugliness for beauty. You would marvel if by certain conditions frogs and lizards should suddenly grow on apple and orange trees, instead of fruit, and if roses should begin to breathe the odor of a sweating horse. So do I marvel at you, who have bartered[31] heaven for earth. I do not want to understand you.

"That I may show you in deed my contempt[32] for that by which you live, I waive[33] the two millions of which I once dreamed of as paradise, and which I now 290 despise. That I may deprive myself of my right to them,

WORDS TO KNOW
posterity (pŏ-stĕr'ĭ-tē) *n.* future generations

WHAT DOES IT MEAN?
Unwearying means "never losing its power."

English Learner Support
Vocabulary

Prefix The prefix *im—* means "not," and the word *mortality* means "the condition of having to die." *Immortality* means "never having to die."

im (not) + mortality (having to die) = immortality (never having to die)

WHAT DOES IT MEAN?
Terrestrial means "earthly." *Marvel* means "wonder" or "be amazed."

 REREAD the boxed passage. What does the lawyer think about the way human beings live their lives? **(Infer)**

WHAT DOES IT MEAN?
Deprive means "deny."

English Learner Support

Vocabulary

Contempt To have *contempt* is to have feelings of disgrace and shame.

Pause & Reflect

1. Why does the lawyer give up the chance of winning the bet? **(Summarize)**

2. Number the following events in the order in which they happen. **(Sequence of Events)**

___ lawyer leaves prison

___ banker plans murder

___ banker finds note

___ lawyer bets with banker

Who do you think changes more in this story, the lawyer or the banker? Underline passages in the story to support your opinion. **(Compare and Contrast)**

I shall come out from here five minutes before the <u>stipulated</u> term, and thus shall violate the agreement."

When he had read, the banker put the sheet on the table, kissed the head of the strange man, and began to weep. He went out of the wing. Never at any other time, not even after his terrible losses on the Exchange, had he felt such contempt for himself as now. Coming home, he lay down on his bed, but agitation and tears kept him long from sleep. . . .

300   The next morning the poor watchman came running to him and told him that they had seen the man who lived in the wing climbing through the window into the garden. He had gone to the gate and disappeared. With his servants the banker went instantly to the wing and established the escape of his prisoner. To avoid unnecessary rumors he took the paper with the <u>renunciation</u> from the table and, on his return, locked it in his safe. ❖

Pause & Reflect

WORDS TO KNOW
stipulated (stĭp′yə-lā′tĭd) *adj.* arranged in an agreement **stipulate** *v.*
renunciation (rĭ-nŭn′sē-ā′shən) *n.* declaration in which something is given up

Active Reading SkillBuilder

Sequence of Events

The **sequence of events** in a story refers to the order in which events happen. While following the sequence of events in "The Bet," pay attention to whether the characters are acting in the present or thinking about something that happened in the past. Use the chart to write down the sequence of major events. Continue the chart on a separate sheet of paper if necessary. An example is shown.

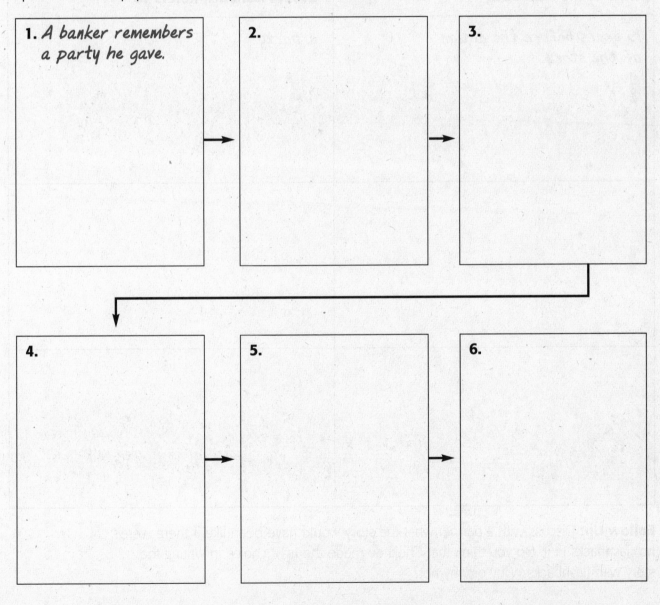

1. *A banker remembers a party he gave.*

2.

3.

4.

5.

6.

Literary Analysis SkillBuilder

Flashback

A scene from an earlier time that interrupts the ongoing action of a story is called a **flashback.** Use the chart below to write down when each flashback in "The Bet" occurs and what it is about.

Time of the Flashback	Event Flashback Refers To
15 years before the action of the story	*a party*

Follow Up: Discuss with a partner what the story would have been like if there were no flashbacks in it. Do you think that Chekhov made the right choice in writing the story with flashbacks? Why or why not?

Words to Know SkillBuilder

Words to Know

capricious	humane	incessantly	posterity	renunciation
haphazardly	immoral	obsolete	rapture	stipulated

A. Write the Word to Know that completes each phrase.

1. _____ weather

2. handed down to _____

3. _____ in the contract

4. wandering _____

5. either cruel or _____

B. Write the Word to Know that completes each sentence.

1. Many people believe that killing in any form should not be allowed because

   it is _____.

2. It's impossible to interrupt him because he talks _____.

3. When Maria heard the good news, she was overcome with

   _____.

4. In 50 years, many of the machines we use today will be

   _____.

5. The government issued a _____, in which it gave up its

   claim to the island.

C. On a separate sheet of paper, write three descriptive sentences about
"The Bet," using at least **one** of the Words to Know in each sentence.

Before You Read

Connect to Your Life

How do you feel when you see homeless people? Is there anything you can do to help solve the problem of homelessness? On the word web, write down ideas for helping the homeless.

Helping the Homeless

collect blankets

Key to the Story

WHAT'S THE BIG IDEA? What is a treasure? Think of two words related to treasure. Write them in the boxes. Then write each word in a separate sentence.

1. treasure

_____

2.

_____

3.

_____

The Treasure of Lemon Brown

by Walter Dean Myers

PREVIEW When Greg Ridley wanders into an empty apartment building, he meets Lemon Brown, a homeless man who reveals that he has a treasure. What will Greg and Lemon Brown do when thieves come searching for the treasure?

As the story begins . . .

- Greg Ridley wants to play for a basketball team called the Scorpions.

- Greg is upset because his father might not allow him to play.

- Greg enters an abandoned building during a storm.

 REREAD the boxed passage. Why doesn't Greg's father want him to play for the Scorpions? **(Infer)**

WHAT DOES IT MEAN? *Knitted* means "furrowed" or "wrinkled."

English Learner Support

Vocabulary

Idiom *Hit those books* means "study."

FOCUS

Greg, a 14-year-old boy, is angry and upset. Read to find out why and what he decides to do.

The dark sky, filled with angry, swirling clouds, reflected Greg Ridley's mood as he sat on the stoop[1] of his building. His father's voice came to him again, first reading the letter the principal had sent to the house, then lecturing endlessly about his poor efforts in math.

"I had to leave school when I was thirteen," his father had said. "That's a year younger than you are now. If I'd had half the chances that you have, I'd . . ."

Greg had sat in the small, pale green kitchen listening, knowing the lecture would end with his father saying he couldn't play ball with the Scorpions. He had asked his father the week before, and his father had said it depended on his next report card. It wasn't often the Scorpions took on new players, especially 14-year-olds, and this was a chance of a lifetime for Greg. He hadn't been allowed to play high school ball, which he had really wanted to do, but playing for the community center team was the next best thing. Report cards were due in a week, and Greg had been hoping for the best. But the principal had ended the suspense early when she sent that letter saying Greg would probably fail math if he didn't spend more time studying.

"And you want to play *basketball?*" His father's brows knitted over deep brown eyes. "That must be some kind of a joke. Now you just get into your room and hit those books."

That had been two nights before. His father's words, like the distant thunder that now echoed through the streets of Harlem,[2] still rumbled softly in his ears.

It was beginning to cool. Gusts of wind made bits of paper dance between the parked cars. There was a

---

1. **stoop:** small porch or staircase at the entrance of a building.

2. **Harlem:** section of New York City; since about 1910, it has been one of the largest African-American communities in the United States.

flash of nearby lightning, and soon large drops of rain splashed onto his jeans. He stood to go upstairs, thought of the lecture that probably awaited him if he did anything except shut himself in his room with his math book, and started walking down the street

40 instead. Down the block there was an old tenement[3] that had been abandoned[4] for some months. Some of the guys had held an <u>impromptu</u> checker tournament there the week before, and Greg had noticed that the door, once boarded over, had been slightly <u>ajar.</u>

Pulling his collar up as high as he could, he checked for traffic and made a dash across the street. He reached the house just as another flash of lightning changed the night to day for an instant, then returned the (graffiti)-scarred building to the grim shadows. He

50 <u>vaulted</u> over the outer stairs and pushed <u>tentatively</u> on the door. It was open, and he let himself in.

Pause (&) Reflect

FOCUS

Greg enters a room in a vacant apartment building. Read to find out what he notices there.

⫴ **MARK IT UP** ⧁ As you read, underline details about the building. An example is highlighted.

The inside of the building was dark except for the dim light that filtered through the dirty windows from the street lamps. There was a room a few feet from the door, and from where he stood at the entrance, Greg could see a squarish patch

60 of light on the floor. He

---

3. **tenement** (tĕn′ ə-mənt): a run-down, low-rental apartment building.

4. **abandoned** (ə-băn′ dənd): deserted, left empty.

WORDS TO KNOW
impromptu (ĭm-prŏmp′tōō) *adj.* done on the spur of the moment; unplanned
ajar (ə-jär′) *adj.* partially open
vault (vôlt) *v.* jump or leap
tentatively (tĕn′tə-tĭv-lē) *adv.* with uncertainty or hesitation

English Learner Support
Culture

Games Checkers is a board game for two people. A *checker tournament* is a series of games that eliminates players until there is one winner.

MORE ABOUT . . .

(GRAFFITI) Graffiti are designs or writings made on a wall or other surface.

Pause (&) Reflect

⫴ **MARK IT UP** ⧁ Circle the sentence on this page that tells you why Greg walks away from his home. (**Clarify**)

⟮As⟯ the story continues . . .

• Greg enters a room that has a musty smell.

• He realizes that someone else is in the room.

WHAT DOES IT MEAN? A
parlor is a formal living room
for entertaining guests.

REREAD the boxed passage.
Why do Greg's
thoughts shift
back and forth between the
Scorpions and his father?
(Infer)

MORE ABOUT . . .
POSTAL WORKERS Workers
must pass a test in order to
qualify for a job with the
United States Postal Service.

WHAT DOES IT MEAN?
Intently means "closely."

WHAT DOES IT MEAN?
Tensing means "becoming
nervous."

entered the room, frowning at the musty smell. It was
a large room that might have been someone's parlor at
one time. Squinting, Greg could see an old table on its
side against one wall, what looked like a pile of rags
or a torn mattress in the corner, and a couch, with one
side broken, in front of the window.

He went to the couch. The side that wasn't broken
was comfortable enough, though a little creaky. From
this spot he could see the blinking neon sign over the
70 bodega⁵ on the corner. He sat awhile, watching the
sign blink first green, then red, allowing his mind to
drift to the Scorpions, then to his father. His father
had been a postal worker for all Greg's life and was
proud of it, often telling Greg how hard he had
worked to pass the test. Greg had heard the story too
many times to be interested now.

For a moment Greg thought he heard something
that sounded like a scraping against the wall. He
listened carefully, but it was gone.

80 Outside, the wind had picked up, sending the rain
against the window with a force that shook the glass
in its frame. A car passed, its tires hissing over the wet
street and its red taillights glowing in the darkness.

Greg thought he heard the noise again. His stomach
tightened as he held himself still and listened intently.
There weren't any more scraping noises, but he was sure
he had heard something in the darkness—something
breathing!

He tried to figure out just where the breathing was
90 coming from; he knew it was in the room with him.
Slowly he stood, tensing. As he turned, a flash of
lightning lit up the room, frightening him with its
sudden brilliance. He saw nothing, just the overturned
table, the pile of rags, and an old newspaper on the
floor. Could he have been imagining the sounds? He

5. **bodega** (bō-dā′gə): a small grocery store.

continued listening but heard nothing and thought that it might have just been rats. Still, he thought, as soon as the rain let up he would leave. He went to the window and was about to look out when he heard a
100 voice behind him.

"Don't try nothin' 'cause I got a razor here sharp enough to cut a week into nine days!"

Greg, except for an involuntary <u>tremor</u> in his knees, stood stock-still. The voice was high and brittle, like dry twigs being broken, surely not one he had ever heard before. There was a shuffling sound as the person who had been speaking moved a step closer. Greg turned, holding his breath, his eyes straining to see in the dark room.

Pause & Reflect

FOCUS

Greg meets Lemon Brown, the figure in the darkness. Read to find out what he is like.

MARK IT UP As you read, underline details that tell you about Lemon Brown.

110 The upper part of the figure before him was still in darkness. The lower half was in the dim rectangle of light that fell unevenly from the window. There were two feet, in cracked, dirty shoes from which rose legs that were wrapped in rags.

"Who are you?" Greg hardly recognized his own
120 voice.

"I'm Lemon Brown," came the answer. "Who're you?"

"Greg Ridley."

"What you doing here?" The figure shuffled forward again, and Greg took a small step backward.

English Learner Support
Language

Dialect Lemon Brown speaks in dialect—he does not follow all the rules of written English. The words in blue mean "Do not try anything because I have a razor that is very sharp."

Pause & Reflect

When Greg enters the room, he sees _____. (Check one.)
(Visualize)
❑ a broken couch
❑ a man sitting alone
❑ many people
❑ his father

As the story continues . . .

• Greg enters a room that has a musty smell.

• He realizes that someone else is in the room.

WORDS TO KNOW
tremor (trĕm′ər) *n.* shaking or vibrating movement; nervous trembling or quivering

MARK IT UP Underline the words and phrases in the boxed passage that help you **visualize** Lemon Brown.

"It's raining," Greg said.

"I can see that," the figure said.

The person who called himself Lemon Brown peered forward, and Greg could see him clearly. He was an old man. His black, heavily wrinkled face was surrounded
130 by a halo of crinkly white hair and whiskers that seemed to separate his head from the layers of dirty coats piled on his smallish frame. His pants were bagged to the knee, where they were met with rags that went down to the old shoes. The rags were held on with strings, and there was a rope around his middle. Greg relaxed. He had seen the man before, picking through the trash on the corner and pulling clothes out of a Salvation Army box. There was no sign of the razor that could "cut a week into nine days."

140 "What are you doing here?" Greg asked.

"This is where I'm staying," Lemon Brown said. "What you here for?"

"Told you it was raining out," Greg said, leaning against the back of the couch until he felt it give slightly.

"Ain't you got no home?"

"I got a home," Greg answered.

"You ain't one of them bad boys looking for my treasure, is you?" Lemon Brown cocked his head to one side and squinted one eye. "Because I told you I
150 got me a razor."

"I'm not looking for your treasure," Greg answered, smiling. "*If* you have one."

"What you mean, *if* I have one," Lemon Brown said. "Every man got a treasure. You don't know that, you must be a fool!"

"Sure," Greg said as he sat on the sofa and put one leg over the back. "What do you have, gold coins?"

"Don't worry none about what I got," Lemon Brown said. "You know who I am?"

MORE ABOUT . . .

SALVATION ARMY The Salvation Army is a religious organization that provides food and clothing to the poor.

English Learner Support

Language

Dialect Use the list below to understand the dialect on this page.

Dialect	Meaning
what you	what are you
told you	I told you
ain't you got no	do you not have a
you ain't one of them	you are not one of those
is you	are you
I got me	I have

160 "You told me your name was orange or lemon or something like that."

"Lemon Brown," the old man said, pulling back his shoulders as he did so. "They used to call me Sweet Lemon Brown."

"Sweet Lemon?" Greg asked.

"Yessir. Sweet Lemon Brown. They used to say I sung the blues[6] so sweet that if I sang at a funeral, the dead would commence to rocking with the beat. Used to travel all over Mississippi and as far as Monroe, 170 Louisiana, and east on over to Macon, Georgia. You mean you ain't never heard of Sweet Lemon Brown?"

"Afraid not," Greg said. "What . . . what happened to you?"

"Hard times, boy. Hard times always after a poor man. One day I got tired, sat down to rest a spell, and felt a tap on my shoulder. Hard times caught up with me."

"Sorry about that."

"What you doing here? How come you didn't go on 180 home when the rain come? Rain don't bother you young folks none."

"Just didn't." Greg looked away.

"I used to have a knotty-headed boy just like you." Lemon Brown had half walked, half shuffled back to the corner and sat down against the wall. "Had them big eyes like you got. I used to call them moon eyes. Look into them moon eyes and see anything you want."

"How come you gave up singing the blues?" Greg asked.

190 "Didn't give it up," Lemon Brown said. "You don't give up the blues; they give you up. After a while you do

---

6. **blues:** a style of music developed from southern African-American songs, characterized by a slow tempo and flattened notes that seem to conflict with the melody.

WORDS TO KNOW
commence (kə-mĕns′) v. begin; start

English Learner Support
Language

Metaphor Reread the words in blue. Lemon Brown expresses the idea that his singing is very powerful by using the image of bodies rising from the dead to dance to his music.

Personification The practice of applying human qualities to nonhuman objects or ideas is called personification. Lemon Brown uses the image of a person chasing him to describe hard times, or a difficult period. Lemon Brown was a successful blues singer until hard times finally "caught" him.

READ ALOUD the boxed passage. What connection is Lemon Brown making between Greg and his own son? (Compare and Contrast)

Pause & Reflect

What was your impression of
Lemon Brown when he first
appeared in the story?
(Connect)

As the story continues . . .

- Three men enter the
  building looking for Lemon
  Brown.
- Greg and Lemon Brown
  hide on the stairs.

WHAT DOES IT MEAN? *Thugs*
are criminals.

English Learner Support
Language

Slang The thugs are
showing disrespect by
calling Lemon Brown *rag
man*. The rags are the
cloths in which his legs
are wrapped.

good for yourself, and it ain't nothing but foolishness
singing about how hard you got it. Ain't that right?"

"I guess so."

"What's that noise?" Lemon Brown asked, suddenly
sitting upright.

Pause & Reflect

FOCUS

Three men come looking
for Lemon Brown. Read
to find out why.

Greg listened, and he heard
a noise outside. He looked at
Lemon Brown and saw the
200 old man was pointing toward
the window.

Greg went to the window and saw three men,
neighborhood thugs, on the stoop. One was carrying a
length of pipe. Greg looked back toward Lemon Brown,
who moved quietly across the room to the window.
The old man looked out, then <u>beckoned</u> frantically for
Greg to follow him. For a moment Greg couldn't move.
Then he found himself following Lemon Brown into
the hallway and up darkened stairs. Greg followed as
210 closely as he could. They reached the top of the stairs,
and Greg felt Lemon Brown's hand, first lying on his
shoulder, then <u>probing</u> down his arm until he finally
took Greg's hand into his own as they crouched in the
darkness.

"They's bad men," Lemon Brown whispered. His
breath was warm against Greg's skin.

"Hey! Rag man!" a voice called. "We know you in
here. What you got up under them rags? You got any
money?"

220 Silence.

WORDS TO KNOW
beckon (bĕk′ən) *v.* signal to come by nodding or waving
probe (prōb) *v.* investigate or explore by touch; search

"We don't want to have to come in and hurt you, old man, but we don't mind if we have to."

Lemon Brown squeezed Greg's hand in his own hard, <u>gnarled</u> fist.

There was a banging downstairs and a light as the men entered. They banged around noisily, calling for the rag man.

"We heard you talking about your treasure." The voice was slurred. "We just want to see it, that's all."

230 "You sure he's here?" One voice seemed to come from the room with the sofa.

"Yeah, he stays here every night."

"There's another room over there; I'm going to take a look. You got that flashlight?"

"Yeah, here, take the pipe too."

Greg opened his mouth to quiet the sound of his breath as he sucked it in uneasily. A beam of light hit the wall a few feet opposite him, then went out.

"Ain't nobody in that room," a voice said. "You 240 think he gone or something?"

"I don't know," came the answer. "All I know is that I heard him talking about some kind of treasure. You know they found that shopping-bag lady with that money in her bags."

"Yeah. You think he's upstairs?"

"HEY, OLD MAN, ARE YOU UP THERE?"
Silence.

"Watch my back. I'm going up."

There was a footstep on the stairs, and the beam 250 from the flashlight danced crazily along the peeling wallpaper. Greg held his breath. There was another step and a loud crashing noise as the man banged the pipe against the wooden banister. Greg could feel his temples throb as the man slowly neared them. Greg

READING CHECK Why are the men trying to find Lemon Brown?

READ ALOUD the boxed passage with a partner. Let your voice express the danger in the scene.

English Learner Support
Language
Figurative Language
Danced crazily means "moved quickly and irregularly."

WHAT DOES IT MEAN?
Temples are the flat areas along either side of the forehead. *Throb* means "beat" or "pound."

WORDS TO KNOW
gnarled (närld) *adj.* rugged and roughened, as from old age or work

What do you think the three
men will do to Greg if they
find him with Lemon Brown?
(Predict)

As the story continues . . .

- The men see Lemon Brown.
- Lemon Brown jumps from
  the stairs.

WHAT DOES IT MEAN? *Eerie*
means "ghostly" or
"mysterious."

English Learner Support
Vocabulary

Hurl Another word for *hurl*
is *throw*.

thought about the pipe, wondering what he would do
when the man reached them—what he *could* do.

Pause & Reflect

FOCUS

The thief gets closer and
closer to Lemon Brown
and Greg. Read on to find
out what happens next.

Then Lemon Brown released
his hand and moved toward
the top of the stairs. Greg
260 looked around and saw stairs
going up to the next floor. He
tried waving to Lemon Brown, hoping the old man
would see him in the dim light and follow him to the
next floor. Maybe, Greg thought, the man wouldn't
follow them up there. Suddenly, though, Lemon Brown
stood at the top of the stairs, both arms raised high
above his head.

"There he is!" a voice cried from below.

"Throw down your money, old man, so I won't
270 have to bash your head in!"

Lemon Brown didn't move. Greg felt himself near
panic. The steps came closer, and still Lemon Brown
didn't move. He was an eerie sight, a bundle of rags
standing at the top of the stairs, his shadow on the
wall looming over him. Maybe, the thought came to
Greg, the scene could be even eerier.

Greg wet his lips, put his hands to his mouth, and tried
to make a sound. Nothing came out. He swallowed hard,
wet his lips once more, and howled as evenly as he could.

280 *"What's that?"*

As Greg howled, the light moved away from Lemon
Brown, but not before Greg saw him hurl his body
down the stairs at the men who had come to take his
treasure. There was a crashing noise and then footsteps.

A rush of warm air came in as the downstairs door opened, then there was only an <u>ominous</u> silence.

Greg stood on the landing. He listened, and after a while there was another sound on the staircase.

"Mr. Brown?" he called.

290 "Yeah, it's me," came the answer. "I got their flashlight."

Greg exhaled in relief as Lemon Brown made his way slowly back up the stairs.

"You O.K.?"

"Few bumps and bruises," Lemon Brown said.

"I think I'd better be going," Greg said, his breath returning to normal. "You'd better leave, too, before they come back."

"They may hang around outside for a while,"
300 Lemon Brown said, "but they ain't getting their nerve up to come in here again. Not with crazy old rag men and howling spooks. Best you stay awhile till the coast is clear. I'm heading out west tomorrow, out to East St. Louis."[7]

"They were talking about treasures," Greg said. "You *really* have a treasure?"

"What I tell you? Didn't I tell you every man got a treasure?" Lemon Brown said. "You want to see mine?"

"If you want to show it to me," Greg shrugged.

310 "Let's look out the window first, see what them scoundrels[8] be doing," Lemon Brown said.

They followed the oval beam of the flashlight into one of the rooms and looked out the window. They saw the men who had tried to take the treasure sitting on the curb near the corner. One of them had his pants leg up, looking at his knee.

---

7. **East St. Louis:** a city in southwestern Illinois, across the Mississippi River from St. Louis, Missouri.

8. **scoundrels** (skoun'drəlz): bad people, villains.

WORDS TO KNOW
ominous (ŏm'ə-nəs) *adj.* menacing; threatening

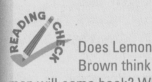

Does Lemon Brown think the men will come back? Why or why not?

English Learner Support
Vocabulary
Idiom *Till the coast is clear* means "until there are no signs of danger or surprise."

Pause & Reflect

How does Greg feel about Lemon Brown at this point in the story? (Infer)

_____

_____

As the story ends . . .

- Lemon Brown shows his treasure to Greg.
- He tells Greg about his son, Jesse.

MORE ABOUT . . .

HARMONICA A harmonica is a musical instrument. It has a small, rectangular shape and a row of air holes in it. Each hole produces a different tone when a person breathes into it.

English Learner Support

Vocabulary

Headliner *Headliner* means "main performer of a show." The clipping says that Lemon Brown's performance was the most popular, although he was not the headliner.

"You sure you're not hurt?" Greg asked Lemon Brown.

"Nothing that ain't been hurt before," Lemon 320 Brown said. "When you get as old as me, all you say when something hurts is 'Howdy, Mr. Pain, sees you back again.' Then when Mr. Pain see he can't worry you none, he go on mess with somebody else."

Greg smiled.

Pause & Reflect

FOCUS

Lemon Brown shows Greg his treasure. What will it be?

MARK IT UP > As you read, circle details that tell you about the treasure 330 and its importance to Lemon Brown.

"Here, you hold this." Lemon Brown gave Greg the flashlight.

He sat on the floor near Greg and carefully untied the strings that held the rags on his right leg. When he took the rags away, Greg saw a piece of plastic. The old man carefully took off the plastic and unfolded it. He revealed some yellowed newspaper clippings and a battered harmonica.

"There it be," he said, nodding his head. "There it be."

Greg looked at the old man, saw the distant look in his eye, then turned to the clippings. They told of Sweet Lemon Brown, a blues singer and harmonica 340 player who was appearing at different theaters in the South. One of the clippings said he had been the hit of the show, although not the headliner. All of the clippings were reviews of shows Lemon Brown had been in more than 50 years ago. Greg looked at the harmonica. It was dented badly on one side, with the reed holes on one end nearly closed.

"I used to travel around and make money for to feed my wife and Jesse—that's my boy's name. Used to feed them good, too. Then his mama died, and he stayed with his mama's sister. He growed up to be a man, and when the war come, he saw fit to go off and fight in it. I didn't have nothing to give him except these things that told him who I was and what he come from. If you know your pappy did something, you know you can do something too.

"Anyway, he went off to war, and I went off still playing and singing. 'Course by then I wasn't as much as I used to be, not without somebody to make it worth the while. You know what I mean?"

"Yeah," Greg nodded, not quite really knowing.

"I traveled around, and one time I come home, and there was this letter saying Jesse got killed in the war. Broke my heart, it truly did.

"They sent back what he had with him over there, and what it was is this old mouth fiddle and these clippings. Him carrying it around with him like that told me it meant something to him. That was my treasure, and when I give it to him, he treated it just like that, a treasure. Ain't that something?"

"Yeah, I *guess* so," Greg said.

"You guess so?" Lemon Brown's voice rose an octave as he started to put his treasure back into the plastic. "Well, you got to guess 'cause you sure don't know nothing. Don't know enough to get home when it's raining."

"I guess . . . I mean, you're right."

"You O.K. for a youngster," the old man said as he tied the strings around his leg, "better than those scalawags[9] what come here looking for my treasure. That's for sure."

9. **scalawags** (skăl'ə-wăgz'): rascals; shameless people.

Family Names Children often call their fathers *Pappy.*

READING CHECK

What did Lemon Brown give to his son?

REREAD the boxed passage. Why does Lemon Brown call these things his "treasure"? (**Infer**)

WHAT DOES IT MEAN? The words in blue mean that Lemon's voice had a higher pitch because he was surprised or annoyed.

WHAT DOES IT MEAN?

'Cepting means "except."

English Learner Support

Language

Dialect The word *foolishest* is not standard English. Lemon Brown creates this word by adding the suffix *–est* ("most") to the word *foolish*. He means "most foolish."

Pause & Reflect

1. How does Lemon Brown feel about his son, Jesse? **(Infer)**

2. REREAD the boxed sentence. How do you feel about this ending? **(Connect)**

How can Greg's experience with Lemon Brown help him in his relationship with his father? Mark passages in the story to support your ideas. **(Draw Conclusions)**

"You really think that treasure of yours was worth fighting for?" Greg asked. "Against a pipe?"

"What else a man got 'cepting what he can pass on to his son, or his daughter if she be his oldest?" Lemon Brown said. "For a bigheaded boy you sure do ask the foolishest questions."

Lemon Brown got up after patting his rags in place and looked out the window again.

"Looks like they're gone. You get on out of here 390 and get yourself home. I'll be watching from the window so you'll be all right."

Lemon Brown went down the stairs behind Greg. When they reached the front door, the old man looked out first, saw the street was clear, and told Greg to scoot on home.

"You sure you'll be O.K.?" Greg asked.

"Now didn't I tell you I was going to East St. Louis in the morning?" Lemon Brown asked. "Don't that sound O.K. to you?"

400 "Sure it does," Greg said. "Sure it does. And you take care of that treasure of yours."

"That I'll do," Lemon said, the wrinkles about his eyes suggesting a smile. "That I'll do."

The night had warmed, and the rain had stopped, leaving puddles at the curbs. Greg didn't even want to think how late it was. He thought ahead of what his father would say and wondered if he should tell him about Lemon Brown. He thought about it until he reached his stoop, and decided against it. Lemon 410 Brown would be O.K., Greg thought, with his memories and his treasure.

Greg pushed the button over the bell marked Ridley, thought of the lecture he knew his father would give him, and smiled. ❖

Pause & Reflect

Active Reading SkillBuilder

Connecting

When what you read reminds you of what you already know or have experienced, you are making connections. **Connecting** helps you identify with what characters experience in a story. Use the diagram to list events or situations from "The Treasure of Lemon Brown" and related events from your own life.

Event from the Story	Event from My Life
Greg's father wants him to do better in math.	My parents want me to do better in math.

Literary Analysis SkillBuilder

Dynamic and Static Characters

Characters in stories are usually either dynamic or static. A **dynamic** character changes during a story. Dynamic characters may develop emotionally or discover something new about themselves. A **static** character does not change during a story. Review "The Treasure of Lemon Brown" and use the chart to record what Lemon and Greg were like at the beginning and at the end of the story.

Character	Beginning of Story	End of Story	Static/Dynamic
Lemon Brown	homeless person who cares about his treasure more than anything else		
Greg			

Follow Up: Once you've identified the dynamic character in this story, write a brief summary of the changes this character experiences. Discuss how these changes might affect the character's future actions.

_____

_____

Words to Know SkillBuilder

Words to Know

ajar	commence	impromptu	probe	tremor
beckon	gnarled	ominous	tentatively	vault

Decide which Word to Know belongs in each numbered blank. Then write the word on the blank to the right.

I didn't get to school 'til ten.
My teacher said, "You're late again!
If you can speak in your defense,
I would suggest that you (1)!"
I said, with doubt, "I *think* I can."

So, (2), I began.
"You can't blame me, it was not my choice,"
I said, with a (3) in my voice.
"I took a shortcut and met some creatures
with some terrifying features!
They were (4) for sure
And made me feel quite insecure!
Their hair was long and badly snarled.
Their hands were rough, their fingers (5).
With those same fingers, they did (6),

So I ran—a mile, I reckon!
I ran so fast, and oh, so far,
But couldn't find one gate (7).
So then I did what made most sense:
I tried to (8) across a fence.
But then I fell and hit my head!
It's just a wonder I'm not dead!"

"Stop," my teacher said (to (9) me more),
"Don't you know what an excuse is for?
It has to have one small restriction:
Your excuse *cannot* be fiction."
I said, "Whew! It's *hard* to romp through
Any story that (10)."

_____
(1)

_____
(2)

_____
(3)

_____
(4)

_____
(5)

_____
(6)

_____
(7)

_____
(8)

_____
(9)

_____
(10)

Before You Read

Connect to Your Life

What words and phrases come to mind when you hear the word *snow?* Write them down on this word web.

Key to the Poem

WHAT TO LISTEN FOR Many poems are based on a rhythm of stressed and unstressed words or syllables. Read the following lines from "Stopping by Woods on a Snowy Evening." Notice that each stressed word or syllable has been underlined.

> Whose <u>woods</u> these <u>are</u> I <u>think</u> I <u>know</u>.
> His <u>house</u> is <u>in</u> the <u>village</u> <u>though</u>;

Now underline the stressed words and syllables in the following line:

> He will not see me stopping here.

Stopping by Woods on a Snowy Evening

BY ROBERT FROST

PREVIEW This poem is set in the country. The speaker is riding alone in the woods one snowy evening and pauses to behold and to admire the world.

WHAT DOES IT MEAN? *Queer* means "odd" or "strange."

MORE ABOUT . . .

WINTER "The (darkest) (evening) of the year" is a reference to the winter solstice, the shortest day and longest night of the year. It usually occurs on or about December 21.

 READING CHECK Why does the horse shake his harness bells?

English Learner Support

| Language |

Imagery The words in blue (lines 11–12) refer to the sound of a gentle wind and falling snow.

FOCUS

The speaker of this poem pauses briefly to take in the beautiful landscape.

MARK IT UP > As you read, underline the words that describe what the speaker sees and hears. An example is highlighted.

Stopping by Woods on a Snowy Evening
by Robert Frost

Whose woods these are I think I know.
His house is in the village though;
He will not see me stopping here
To watch his woods fill up with snow.

5   My little horse must think it queer
To stop without a farmhouse near
Between the woods and frozen lake
The darkest evening of the year.

He gives his harness bells a shake
10   To ask if there is some mistake.
The only other sound's the sweep
Of easy wind and downy flake.

The woods are lovely, dark and deep,
But I have promises to keep,
15   And miles to go before I sleep,
And miles to go before I sleep.

MARK IT UP What images do you see when you read the poem? In the space below, draw a sketch of the landscape described in "Stopping by Woods on a Snowy Evening."

1. Check the word below that tells how the speaker feels about the woods. (Infer)

❑ afraid

❑ sad

❑ attracted

❑ angry

2. **READ ALOUD** the boxed passage, lines 13–16. How does the speaker feel about moving on? (Question)

3. What words or phrases from this poem linger in your mind? How do these words and phrases make you feel? (Connect)

Active Reading SkillBuilder

Questioning

Asking questions about a poem or work of literature as you read is one way to understand the selection better. Use the five W's—*who, what, where, when, why*—to help you ask your questions. In the chart below, record questions and the answers you discover while reading Robert Frost's poem "Stopping by Woods on a Snowy Evening."

"Stopping by Woods on a Snowy Evening"	
Who *is the speaker?*	*a thoughtful person*
What	
Where	
When	
Why	

Literary Analysis SkillBuilder

Rhyme

Rhyme is a repetition of sounds at the end of words. For example, the word *flame* rhymes with *tame*. The pattern of rhymes in a poem is the poem's **rhyme scheme.** A rhyme scheme can be shown by using a different letter to represent each rhyming sound. For example, look at the rhyme scheme of the first stanza of "Stopping by Woods on a Snowy Evening."

Whose woods these are I think I know.	(a)
His house is in the village though;	(a)
He will not see me stopping here	(b)
To watch his woods fill up with snow.	(a)

Now show the rhyme scheme for the remaining stanzas.

My little horse must think it <u>queer</u>	_____
To stop without a farmhouse <u>near</u>	_____
Between the woods and frozen <u>lake</u>	_____
The darkest evening of the <u>year</u>.	_____
He gives his harness bells a <u>shake</u>	_____
To ask if there is some <u>mistake</u>.	_____
The only other sound's the <u>sweep</u>	_____
Of easy wind and downy <u>flake</u>.	_____
The woods are lovely, dark and <u>deep</u>,	_____
But I have promises to <u>keep</u>,	_____
And miles to go before I <u>sleep</u>,	_____
And miles to go before I <u>sleep</u>.	_____

Follow Up: Discuss your answers to the following questions: Why do you think Frost repeats the last line? What is the effect of changing the rhyme pattern of the last stanza?

Before You Read

Connect to Your Life

How often do your friends or family members ask you to do things for them? Do you ever feel torn between what you want to do and what other people want you to do? In the charts, list the things you do for yourself and the things you do for others.

Things I Do for Myself
play soccer

Things I Do for Others
carry groceries

Key to the Poems

WHAT DO YOU THINK? In "the drum" Nikki Giovanni uses a musical instrument as a symbol of independence.

i'm gonna beat
out my own rhythm

If you were writing about independence, what objects or animals might represent your ideas? Write the names of some symbols of independence in the box below.

Legacies

by NIKKI GIOVANNI

the drum

by NIKKI GIOVANNI

Choices

by NIKKI GIOVANNI

PREVIEW The poems you are about to read look simple but are highly original. The speakers of these poems describe tense moments and deep emotions.

As the poem begins . . .

- A grandmother wants to teach her granddaughter how to make rolls.

- The granddaughter does not want to learn.

 READING TIP These poems have no capital letters, periods, or commas. The words flow along as they would in spoken English. Try reading the poems aloud, and listen for the natural pauses.

English Learner Support

Language

Dialect *Chu* means "you."

 READING CHECK Why does the little girl refuse to make rolls?

Pause & Reflect

What can you conclude about the little girl? Check one. **(Infer)**

❏ She hates her grandmother.

❏ She is very obedient.

❏ She can't say what she really feels.

FOCUS

A little girl and her grandmother disagree about something. Read to find out why.

Legacies

by Nikki Giovanni

her grandmother called her from the playground
  "yes, ma'am" said the little girl
  "i want chu to learn how to make rolls" said
    the old
woman proudly
5 but the little girl didn't want
to learn how because she knew
even if she couldn't say it that
that would mean when the old one died she
  would be less
10 dependent on her spirit so
  the little girl said
  "i don't want to know how to make no rolls"
with her lips poked out
and the old woman wiped her hands on
15 her apron saying "lord
  these children"
and neither of them ever
said what they meant
and i guess nobody ever does

Pause & Reflect

---

1. **legacies** (lĕg' ə-sēz): things that are handed down from one generation to the next.

FOCUS

What do you think the speaker of this poem is like?

the drum

by Nikki Giovanni

daddy says the world is
a drum tight and hard
and i told him
i'm gonna beat
5 out my own rhythm

As the poem begins . . .

- A father tells his child what the world is like.
- The child replies.

English Learner Support

Language

Slang *Gonna* means "going to."

READING CHECK

What does the speaker's father say about the world? How does the speaker reply?

Pause & Reflect

1. How would you describe the speaker of this poem? Check one word below. **(Infer)**

   ❏ timid

   ❏ worried

   ❏ confident

2. What do you think the speaker wants from life? Check one. **(Infer)**

   ❏ independence

   ❏ music lessons

   ❏ a close family

READING CHECK What is the speaker's attitude toward doing what she does not want to do?

REREAD the boxed passage. How does the speaker feel about not getting what she wants? (Paraphrase)

Choices

by Nikki Giovanni

> if i can't do
> what i want to do
> then my job is to not
> do what i don't want
> 5 to do
>
> it's not the same thing
> but it's the best i can
> do
>
> if i can't have
> 10 what i want   then
> my job is to want
> what i've got
> and be satisfied
> that at least there
> 15 is something more
> to want

since i can't go
where i need
to go   then i must   go
20 where the signs point
though always understanding
parallel[1] movement
isn't lateral[2]

when i can't express
25 what i really feel
i practice feeling
what i can express
and none of it is equal
i know
30 but that's why mankind
alone among the mammals
learns to cry

Pause & Reflect

WHAT DOES IT MEAN? Lines 21–23 mean that even though the speaker is unable to move directly toward her goal, she is still able to make progress in her life.

Pause & Reflect

1. **MARK IT UP** Which of the speaker's choices would you make? Place a star next to that choice. **(Connect)**

2. How do you think the speaker feels at the end of the poem? Check two words below. **(Infer)**
   ❏ happy   ❏ sad
   ❏ frustrated   ❏ playful

3. Why do you think Nikki Giovanni wrote this poem? Check your answer(s) below. **(Author's Purpose)**
   __ to inform
   __ to entertain
   __ to express an opinion
   __ to persuade
   __ to _____

 Which poem did you like best? What is the **theme,** or main message, of your favorite poem? Underline passages in the poem to support your opinion. **(Analyze)**

1. **parallel:** in the same direction
2. **lateral:** to the side; sideways.

Active Reading SkillBuilder

Identifying the Author's Purpose

Poetry is written for a **purpose,** such as to inform, to entertain, to express an opinion, or to persuade. Some poems have only one purpose, while others may have two or more. After you read the three poems by Nikki Giovanni, place one or more check marks in the chart below to show the purpose or purposes of each poem. Use the lines below the chart to explain some of your choices. An example is provided.

| Poem | Author's Purpose | | | |
	To Entertain	To Inform	To Express an Opinion	To Persuade
"Legacies"	✔		✔	
"the drum"				
"Choices"				

<u>In "Legacies" the author entertains the reader by describing a very interesting</u>
<u>conversation. The author also expresses the opinion that people often don't say</u>
<u>what they mean.</u>

Literary Analysis SkillBuilder

Lyric Poetry

A **lyric poem** is usually short and expresses the personal thoughts and opinions of a single speaker. Working with a partner, rewrite either "Legacies" or "Choices" as a very short dialogue. Your dialogue should express the main idea of the lyric poem. Build your dialogue using the charts below. Examples are provided. Add extra lines to the charts if necessary.

"Legacies"
Grandmother: *"Granddaughter, come into the kitchen for a minute."*
Little Girl:
Grandmother:
Little Girl:
Grandmother:

"Choices"
Speaker: *"I can't do what I want to do."*
Friend:
Speaker:
Friend:
Speaker:

Before You Read

Connect to Your Life

In this drama, Anne Frank tells her friend Peter:

> "We have problems that no other
> people our age have ever had."

What are some problems that people your age have today? List two
or three. Circle any that teenagers have never had before.

Violence on television and in the movies

_____

_____

_____

Key to the Drama

WHAT YOU NEED TO KNOW Anne Frank and her family were
victims of the Nazis during World War II. World War II began over
60 years ago when Nazi Germany invaded Poland in 1939.
Germany was part of the Axis powers,
which also included Italy
and Japan. On the other
side were the Allies, which
included the United States,
France, Great Britain,
and the Soviet Union.

from
The Diary of
Anne
Frank

Drama by FRANCES GOODRICH AND ALBERT HACKETT
Based on the book *Anne Frank: The Diary of a Young Girl*

Before You Read

PREVIEW WHO WAS ANNE FRANK?

*The drama you are about to read is based on the book
Anne Frank: The Diary of a Young Girl. During World War II,
Anne Frank's family spent more than two years living
in hiding.*

BORN INTO DANGER Annelies Marie Frank was born in
Frankfurt, Germany, on June 12, 1929. Although the
Franks were German citizens, as Jews they faced
persecution—cruel treatment—in their own country.
The group persecuting them was the National Socialist
German Workers Party, or Nazis, as they were called.

Led by Adolf Hitler, the Nazis rose to power after
Germany's defeat in World War I. Hitler and the Nazis
blamed Germany's problems on people whom they
regarded as inferior, such as Jews and Gypsies.

THE NAZIS IN POWER At first, few people paid attention
to Hitler and his followers. Then a great depression hit
Germany and many other countries. In 1932, about 30
percent of Germany's work force had no jobs. Many
people wanted someone to blame for their troubles.
Hitler turned their anger on the Jewish population.

By 1933, the Nazis controlled German life. Jews were
singled out for especially cruel treatment. Soon they
had no rights under the law. Nazi gangs burned and
looted Jewish homes and businesses. Later, Hitler tried
to do away with Jewish people completely. Millions
of Jews were herded into special prisons known as
concentration camps. There they were worked to
death or murdered. Many died from disease. This horrible
destruction of human life is now known as the Holocaust.

MAIN IDEA Why was
Anne "born into danger"?

She was _____

_____

MAIN IDEA What group
of people did Hitler and
the Nazis blame when a
depression hit Germany
in the early 1930s?

Hitler blamed _____

_____

_____

for the depression.

TRAPPED IN HOLLAND In 1933, Otto Frank moved to Amsterdam in Holland (now called the Netherlands). By February 1934, the rest of his family had joined him. Believing they would be safe, they settled into a new life. However, in 1940, Germany invaded Holland. The Franks were trapped.

A LIFE IN HIDING On July 6, 1942, Anne and her family moved into the "Secret Annex," a small attic area hidden above Otto Frank's office. Soon after, they were joined by Otto Frank's business partner, his wife, and their 16-year-old son, Peter. Later, Mr. Dussel joined the group.

In her diary, Anne describes the group's life in hiding and their constant fear of discovery. For over two years, the group lived invisibly, in the hope that victory by Allied forces would end their nightmare.

DISCOVERY AND DEATH As Allied armies began liberating Europe, it seemed only a matter of time before Anne, her family, and friends could come out of hiding. However, on August 4, 1944, the Nazis discovered the Secret Annex and arrested the residents. All were sent to the Auschwitz-Birkenau concentration camp in Poland, where members of the group were separated. Anne was moved to the Bergen-Belsen camp in Germany. There she tragically died only weeks before the camp was set free by Allied forces. Of the eight residents of the Secret Annex, only Otto Frank survived.

ANNE'S DIARY In the confusion and terror of her family's arrest, Anne left her diary behind. Later, Otto Frank read his daughter's account of the war, along with her fears and hopes for the future. He decided to share Anne's diary with the world. Since its publication in 1947, Anne's diary has been read by millions.

MAIN IDEA What happened in Holland in 1940?

_____

_____

MAIN IDEA Where did the Franks hide for over two years?

They hid in

_____

_____

MAIN IDEA What happened to the inhabitants of the Secret Annex?

Except for Mr.

Frank, all

_____

READ ALOUD the names of the play's characters. Notice that eight of the characters live in the Secret Annex. What are the names of the two people who do not live in the Secret Annex? What do these two people do? **(Question)**

As the play begins...

- The setting is in an annex, or extension, of an office building.
- A bookcase hides the door to the annex.

English Learner Support

Vocabulary

Compound Word
wares (goods) + house = warehouse (building where goods are stored)

WHAT DOES IT MEAN? A *belfry* is the part of a steeple where bells are hung.

Characters

Secret Annex Residents

Anne Frank

Margot Frank

Mr. Frank

Mrs. Frank

Peter Van Daan

Mr. Van Daan

Mrs. Van Daan

Mr. Dussel

Workers in Mr. Frank's Business

Miep Gies [mēp gēs]

Mr. Kraler [krä′lər]

The Time

July 1942–August 1944

November 1945

The Place

Amsterdam, the Netherlands

FOCUS

This part describes the play's setting.

MARK IT UP Underline details that help you picture where the play takes place. An example is highlighted.

The scene remains the same throughout the play. It is the top floor of a warehouse and office building in Amsterdam, Holland. The sharply peaked roof of the building is outlined against a sea of other rooftops, stretching away into the distance. Nearby is the belfry of
10 a church tower, the Westertoren, whose carillon[1] rings out the hours. Occasionally faint sounds float up from below: the voices of children playing in the street, the tramp of marching feet, a boat whistle from the canal.

The three rooms of the top floor and a small attic space above are exposed to our view. The largest of the rooms is in the center, with two small rooms, slightly raised, on either side. On the right is a bathroom, out of sight. A narrow steep flight of stairs at the back leads up to the attic. The rooms are sparsely furnished
20 with a few chairs, cots, a table or two. The windows are painted over, or covered with makeshift blackout

---

1. **carillon** (kăr′ ə-lŏn′): a set of tuned bells.

curtains. In the main room there is a sink, a gas ring for cooking, and a wood-burning stove for warmth.

The room on the left is hardly more than a closet. There is a skylight in the sloping ceiling. Directly under this room is a small steep stairwell, with steps leading down to a door. This is the only entrance from the building below. When the door is opened we see that it has been concealed on the outer side by
30 a bookcase attached to it.

Pause & Reflect

Pause & Reflect

 the highlighted text on page 180. In your own words, describe where the play takes place. (Paraphrase)

FOCUS

In this part, you meet Anne's father, Otto Frank. He has returned to the place where he and his family hid from the Nazis. Read to find out how he discovers Anne's diary.

Act 1

Scene 1

The curtain rises on an empty stage. It is late afternoon November, 1945.

The rooms are dusty, the curtains in rags. Chairs and tables are overturned.

The door at the foot of the small stairwell swings open. Mr. Frank comes up the steps into view. He is a gentle, cultured European in his middle years. There
40 *is still a trace of a German accent in his speech.*

He stands looking slowly around, making a supreme effort at self-control. He is weak, ill. His clothes are threadbare.

After a second he drops his rucksack on the couch and moves slowly about. He opens the door to one of the smaller rooms, and then abruptly closes it again, turning away. He goes to the window at the back,

As the play continues . . .

- Mr. Frank looks around the annex where he and his family hid from the Nazis.
- Miep has saved some of the Frank family's belongings.
- Mr. Frank reads from his daughter Anne's diary.

 READING TIP The stage directions appear in *italicized* type. Stage directions describe the action of the play. They also tell how the characters feel. As you read, underline important actions and feelings named in the stage directions.

WHAT DOES IT MEAN? A *rucksack* is another word for a backpack or knapsack.

looking off at the Westertoren as its carillon strikes the hour of six, then he moves restlessly on.

50 *From the street below we hear the sound of a barrel organ and children's voices at play. There is a many-colored scarf hanging from a nail. Mr. Frank takes it, putting it around his neck. As he starts back for his rucksack, his eye is caught by something lying on the floor. It is a woman's white glove. He holds it in his hand and suddenly all of his self-control is gone. He* breaks down, *crying.*

We hear footsteps on the stairs. Miep Gies comes up, looking for Mr. Frank. Miep is a Dutch girl of about 60 *twenty-two. She wears a coat and hat, ready to go home. She is pregnant. Her attitude toward Mr. Frank is protective, compassionate.*

Miep. Are you all right, Mr. Frank?

Mr. Frank (*Quickly controlling himself*). Yes, Miep, yes.

Miep. Everyone in the office has gone home . . . It's after six. (*Then pleading*) Don't stay up here, Mr. Frank. What's the use of torturing yourself like this?

Mr. Frank. I've come to say good-bye . . . I'm leaving here, Miep.

70 **Miep.** What do you mean? Where are you going? Where?

Mr. Frank. I don't know yet. I haven't decided.

Miep. Mr. Frank, you can't leave here! This is your home! Amsterdam is your home. Your business is here, waiting for you . . . You're needed here . . . Now that the war is over, there are things that . . .

Mr. Frank. I can't stay in Amsterdam, Miep. It has too many memories for me. Everywhere there's something . . . the house we lived in . . . the school . . . that street organ playing out there . . . 80 I'm not the person you used to know, Miep. I'm a

Why has Mr. Frank decided to leave Amsterdam?

bitter old man. (*Breaking off*) Forgive me. I shouldn't speak to you like this . . . after all that you did for us . . . the suffering . . .

Miep. No. No. It wasn't suffering. You can't say we suffered. (*As she speaks, she straightens a chair which is overturned.*)

Mr. Frank. I know what you went through, you and Mr. Kraler. I'll remember it as long as I live. (*He gives one last look around.*) Come, Miep.

90 (*He starts for the steps, then remembers his rucksack, going back to get it.*)

Miep (*Hurrying up to a cupboard*). Mr. Frank, did you see? There are some of your papers here. (*She brings a bundle of papers to him.*) We found them in a heap of rubbish on the floor after . . . after you left.

Mr. Frank. Burn them.

(*He opens his rucksack to put the glove in it.*)

Miep. But, Mr. Frank, there are letters, notes . . .

Mr. Frank. Burn them. All of them.

100 **Miep.** Burn this?

(*She hands him a paperbound notebook.*)

Mr. Frank (*Quietly*). Anne's diary. (*He opens the diary and begins to read.*) "Monday, the sixth of July, nineteen forty-two." (*To Miep*) Nineteen forty-two. Is it possible, Miep? . . . Only three years ago. (*As he continues his reading, he sits down on the couch.*) "Dear Diary, since you and I are going to be great friends, I will start by telling you about myself. My name is Anne Frank. I am

110 thirteen years old. I was born in Germany the twelfth of June, nineteen twenty-nine. As my family is Jewish, we emigrated to Holland when Hitler came to power."

English Learner Support

Language

Adverbs The verb *break* can be followed by various adverbs, such as *down* or *off*, to change its meaning. *Breaking off* means "stopping."

Punctuation Note the ellipses (. . .) in blue. An ellipsis is used to show a pause or to show that words are missing. The ellipses on this page indicate pauses in speech as Miep and Mr. Frank recall horrifying events. In line 95, instead of referring to the Nazis' discovery and arrest of the Franks, Miep pauses and says, "after you left."

REREAD the boxed text. What is the date of the diary entry that Mr. Frank begins to read? How many years earlier is this date? (**Clarify**)

Pause & Reflect

Imagine you are in Mr. Frank's situation. How do you think you would feel as you read Anne's diary? (Connect)

─ As the play continues . . .

- Anne's voice joins in as Mr. Frank reads her diary.
- Time travels back to 1942, when Germany controlled Holland.
- Mr. Frank tells Anne that their family will go into hiding.

MORE ABOUT . . .

DUTCH CAPITULATION
Germany invaded Holland in the spring of 1940. Within a week, the Dutch army was defeated, and Germany gained control of Holland.

MORE ABOUT . . .

YELLOW STARS By the 19th century, the Star of David had become the official symbol of Judaism. The Nazis forced all Jews to wear the stars so they could be easily identified and punished.

(As Mr. Frank reads on, another voice joins his, as if coming from the air. It is Anne's voice.)

Pause & Reflect

FOCUS

As Mr. Frank reads Anne's diary, the years slip away to a day three years earlier. Read to find out how things changed for Anne and her family when the Nazis came to power in Holland.

▌ MARK IT UP ⟩ As you read, circle details that help you understand these changes.

Mr. Frank and Anne's voice.
"My father started a business, importing spices and herbs. Things went well
120 for us until nineteen forty. Then the war came, and the Dutch capitulation,[2] followed by the arrival of the Germans. Then things got very bad for the Jews."

(Mr. Frank's voice dies out. Anne's voice continues alone. The lights dim slowly to darkness. The curtain falls on the scene.)

130 **Anne's Voice.** You could not do this and you could not do that. They forced Father out of his business. We had to wear yellow stars.[3] I had to turn in my bike. I couldn't go to a Dutch school any more. I couldn't go to the movies, or ride in an automobile, or even on a streetcar, and a million other things. But somehow we children still managed to have fun. Yesterday Father told me we were going into hiding. Where, he wouldn't say. At five o'clock this morning Mother woke me and told me to hurry
140 and get dressed. I was to put on as many clothes as I could. It would look too suspicious if we walked

─────────

2. **capitulation** (kə-pǐch′ōō-lā′shən): the act of surrendering.

3. **yellow stars:** the six-pointed Stars of David that the Nazis ordered all Jews to wear for identification.

along carrying suitcases. It wasn't until we were on our way that I learned where we were going. Our hiding place was to be upstairs in the building where Father used to have his business. Three other people were coming in with us . . . the Van Daans and their son Peter . . . Father knew the Van Daans but we had never met them . . .

(*During the last lines the curtain rises on the scene.* 150 *The lights dim on. Anne's voice fades out.*)

Pause & Reflect

FOCUS

Read to find out about the Van Daan family and the Frank family.

|||MARK IT UP⟩ In the margin, make notes about each member of the household.

Scene 2

It is early morning, July 1942. The rooms are bare, as before, but they are now clean and orderly.

Mr. Van Daan, a tall, portly man in his late forties, is in the main room, pacing up and down, nervously smoking a cigarette. His clothes and overcoat are expensive and well cut.

10 *Mrs. Van Daan sits on the couch, clutching her possessions, a hatbox, bags, etc. She is a pretty woman in her early forties. She wears a fur coat over her other clothes.*

Peter Van Daan is standing at the window of the room on the right, looking down at the street below. He is a shy, awkward boy of sixteen. He wears a cap, a raincoat, and long Dutch trousers, like "plus fours."[4] *At his feet is a black case, a carrier for his cat.*

---

4. **plus fours:** short, loose trousers gathered at the knees; knickers.

Pause & Reflect

REREAD the boxed text on page 184. Describe the effects of the Nazis' rise to power in Holland on the Jews. **(Cause and Effect)**

Cause
The Nazis came to power in Holland.

↓

Effect

As the play continues . . .

• The Franks and the Van Daans arrive at their hiding place.

• Mr. Frank tells everyone the rules of the Secret Annex.

The yellow Star of David is <u>conspicuous</u> on all of
20 their clothes.

Mrs. Van Daan (*Rising, nervous, excited*).
Something's happened to them! I know it!

Mr. Van Daan. Now, Kerli!

Mrs. Van Daan. Mr. Frank said they'd be here at
seven o'clock. He said . . .

Mr. Van Daan. They have two miles to walk. You
can't expect . . .

Mrs. Van Daan. They've been picked up. That's
what's happened. They've been taken . . .

30 (Mr. Van Daan *indicates that he hears someone coming.*)

Mr. Van Daan. You see?

(Peter *takes up his carrier and his schoolbag, etc.,
and goes into the main room as* Mr. Frank *comes up
the stairwell from below.* Mr. Frank *looks much
younger now. His movements are brisk, his manner
confident. He wears an overcoat and carries his hat
and a small cardboard box. He crosses to the Van
Daans,* shaking hands with each of them.)

Mr. Frank. Mrs. Van Daan, Mr. Van Daan, Peter.
40 (*Then, in explanation of their lateness*) There were
too many of the Green Police⁵ on the streets . . . we
had to take the long way around.

(Up the steps come Margot Frank, Mrs. Frank, Miep
(not pregnant now), and Mr. Kraler. All of them carry
bags, packages, and so forth. The Star of David is
conspicuous on all of the Franks' clothing. Margot is
eighteen, beautiful, quiet, shy. Mrs. Frank is a young
mother, gently bred, reserved. She, like Mr. Frank,
has a slight German accent. Mr. Kraler is a
50 Dutchman, dependable, kindly.

---

5. **Green Police:** the Nazi police who wore green uniforms.

WORDS TO KNOW
conspicuous (kən-spĭk′ yōo-əs) *adj.* easy to notice; obvious

English Learner Support
Vocabulary

Idiom The words in blue
are a way of saying "They
have been caught by the
police."

Why are the
Franks late?

MORE ABOUT . . .
THE GREEN POLICE It was
important for Jews to avoid
being noticed by the Nazi
police. If Jews were arrested
by the police, they could end
up being sent to labor or
concentration camps.

As Mr. Kraler *and* Miep *go* upstage *to put down their parcels,* Mrs. Frank *turns back to call* Anne.)

Mrs. Frank. Anne?

(Anne *comes running up the stairs. She is thirteen, quick in her movements, interested in everything, mercurial*[6] *in her emotions. She wears a cape and long wool socks and carries a schoolbag.)*

Mr. Frank (*Introducing them*). My wife, Edith. Mr. and Mrs. Van Daan (Mrs. Frank *hurries over, shaking hands with them.*) . . . their son, Peter . . . my daughters, Margot and Anne.

(Anne *gives a polite little curtsy as she shakes* Mr. Van Daan's *hand. Then she immediately starts off on a tour of investigation of her new home, going upstairs to the attic room.* Miep *and* Mr. Kraler *are putting the various things they have brought on the shelves.)*

Mr. Kraler. I'm sorry there is still so much confusion.

Mr. Frank. Please. Don't think of it. After all, we'll have plenty of leisure to arrange everything ourselves.

Miep (*To* Mrs. Frank). We put the stores of food you sent in here. Your drugs are here . . . soap, linen here.

Mrs. Frank. Thank you, Miep.

Miep. I made up the beds . . . the way Mr. Frank and Mr. Kraler said. (*She starts out.*) Forgive me. I have to hurry. I've got to go to the other side of town to get some ration books[7] for you.

Mrs. Van Daan. Ration books? If they see our names on ration books, they'll know we're here.

Mr. Kraler. There isn't anything . . .

Miep. Don't worry. Your names won't be on them. (*As she hurries out*) I'll be up later.

WHAT DOES IT MEAN? When Miep says *drugs*, she means "medicines."

English Learner Support
Vocabulary

Idiom *Made up* has several meanings. In the sentence in blue, it means "put sheets and blankets on a bed."

---

6. **mercurial** (mər-kyŏor′ē-əl): changing quickly and unpredictably.

7. **ration books:** books of stamps or coupons issued by the government in wartime. With these coupons, people could purchase scarce items, such as food, clothing, and gasoline.

MORE ABOUT . . .

THE BLACK MARKET A black market is the illegal buying or selling of goods. A black market often exists when a nation is at war and goods are limited. Black market sellers want to make a profit. They obtain goods or extra ration stamps and sell them to anyone who can pay a high price.

English Learner Support

Vocabulary

Idiom The words in blue mean "the door needs a bolt on the inside so that you can lock it yourself."

What will Miep and Mr. Kraler be doing for the people in the Secret Annex?

Mr. Frank. Thank you, Miep.

Mrs. Frank (*To Mr. Kraler*). It's illegal, then, the ration books? We've never done anything illegal.

Mr. Frank. We won't be living here exactly according to regulations. (*As Mr. Kraler reassures Mrs. Frank, he takes various small things, such as matches, soap, etc., from his pockets, handing them to her.*)

Mr. Kraler. This isn't the black market,[8] Mrs. Frank.
90 This is what we call the white market . . . helping all of the hundreds and hundreds who are hiding out in Amsterdam.

(*The carillon is heard playing the quarter-hour before eight. Mr. Kraler looks at his watch. Anne stops at the window as she comes down the stairs.*)

Anne. It's the Westertoren!

Mr. Kraler. I must go. I must be out of here and downstairs in the office before the workmen get here. (*He starts for the stairs leading out.*) Miep or I, or
100 both of us, will be up each day to bring you food and news and find out what your needs are. Tomorrow I'll get you a better bolt for the door at the foot of the stairs. It needs a bolt that you can throw yourself and open only at our signal. (*To Mr. Frank*) Oh . . . You'll tell them about the noise?

Mr. Frank. I'll tell them.

Mr. Kraler. Good-bye then for the moment. I'll come up again, after the workmen leave.

Mr. Frank. Good-bye, Mr. Kraler.

110 **Mrs. Frank** (*Shaking his hand*). How can we thank you? (*The others murmur their good-byes.*)

Mr. Kraler. I never thought I'd live to see the day when a man like Mr. Frank would have to go into

---

8. **black market:** a system for selling goods illegally, in violation of rationing or other restrictions.

hiding. When you think—(*He breaks off, going out. Mr. Frank follows him down the steps, bolting the door after him. In the interval before he returns, Peter goes over to Margot, shaking hands with her. As Mr. Frank comes back up the steps, Mrs. Frank questions him anxiously.*)

120 **Mrs. Frank.** What did he mean, about the noise?

Mr. Frank. First let us take off some of these clothes. (*They all start to take off garment after garment. On each of their coats, sweaters, blouses, suits, dresses, is another yellow Star of David. Mr. and Mrs. Frank are underdressed quite simply. The others wear several things, sweaters, extra dresses, bathrobes, aprons, nightgowns, etc.*)

Mr. Van Daan. It's a wonder we weren't arrested, walking along the streets . . . Petronella with a fur
130 coat in July . . . and that cat of Peter's crying all the way.

Anne (*As she is removing a pair of panties*). A cat?

Mrs. Frank (*Shocked*). Anne, please!

Anne. It's all right. I've got on three more. (*She pulls off two more. Finally, as they have all removed their surplus clothes, they look to Mr. Frank, waiting for him to speak.*)

Mr. Frank. Now. About the noise. While the men are in the building below, we must have complete quiet.
140 Every sound can be heard down there, not only in the workrooms, but in the offices, too. The men come at about eight-thirty, and leave at about five-thirty. So, to be perfectly safe, from eight in the morning until six in the evening we must move only when it is necessary, and then in stockinged feet. We must not speak above a whisper. We must not run any water. We cannot use the sink, or even, forgive

READING CHECK Why is Mr. Van Daan amazed that his family wasn't arrested?

REREAD the boxed text. What do you think would be most difficult about living in hiding? (Evaluate)

me, the w.c.[9] The pipes go down through the workrooms. It would be heard. No trash . . .

150 (Mr. Frank *stops abruptly as he hears the sound of marching feet from the street below. Everyone is motionless, paralyzed with fear. Mr. Frank goes quietly into the room on the right to look down out of the window. Anne runs after him, peering out with him. The tramping feet pass without stopping. The tension is relieved. Mr. Frank, followed by Anne, returns to the main room and resumes his instructions to the group*) . . . No trash must ever be thrown out which might reveal that someone is

160 living up here . . . not even a potato paring. We must burn everything in the stove at night. This is the way we must live until it is over, if we are to survive.

(*There is silence for a second.*)

Mrs. Frank. Until it is over.

Mr. Frank. (*Reassuringly*). After six we can move about . . . we can talk and laugh and have our supper and read and play games . . . just as we would at home. (*He looks at his watch.*) And now I think it would be wise if we all went to our rooms, and were

170 settled before eight o'clock. Mrs. Van Daan, you and your husband will be upstairs. I regret that there's no place up there for Peter. But he will be here, near us. This will be our common room, where we'll meet to talk and eat and read, like one family.

Pause & Reflect

---

9. **w.c.**: water closet; toilet.

FOCUS

As the families settle in to their new home, Peter and Anne get to know each other. Read to find out what they have in common.

Mr. Van Daan. And where do you and Mrs. Frank sleep?

Mr. Frank. This room is also our bedroom.

Mrs. Van Daan. That isn't 180 right. We'll sleep here and you take the room upstairs.

Mr. Van Daan. It's your place.

Mr. Frank. Please. I've thought this out for weeks. It's the best arrangement. The only arrangement.

Mrs. Van Daan (*To* Mr. Frank). Never, never can we thank you. (*Then to* Mrs. Frank) I don't know what would have happened to us, if it hadn't been for Mr. Frank.

190 **Mr. Frank.** You don't know how your husband helped me when I came to this country . . . knowing no one . . . not able to speak the language. I can never repay him for that. (*Going to* Mr. Van Daan) May I help you with your things?

Mr. Van Daan. No. No. (*To* Mrs. Van Daan) Come along, liefje.[10]

Mrs. Van Daan. You'll be all right, Peter? You're not afraid?

Peter (*Embarrassed*). Please, Mother.

(*They start up the stairs to the attic room above.* 200 Mr. Frank *turns to* Mrs. Frank.)

Mr. Frank. You too must have some rest, Edith. You didn't close your eyes last night. Nor you, Margot.

Anne. I slept, Father. Wasn't that funny? I knew it was the last night in my own bed, and yet I slept soundly.

As the play continues . . .

• Mr. and Mrs. Van Daan take their things to the attic room.

• The Franks and Peter settle into the other three rooms.

 READING CHECK Why did Mr. Frank invite the Van Daans to share the hiding place with his family?

English Learner Support
Vocabulary

Idioms Many phrases are made from the verb *come* plus an adverb, such as *along* or *over*. The phrase *come along* means "hurry." *Come over* (see page 193) means "visit."

WHAT DOES IT MEAN? *I slept soundly* means she slept well.

10. **liefje** (lēf'yə) *Dutch:* little darling.

English Learner Support

Vocabulary

Context Clues Use the stage directions in lines 209–210 and your knowledge of what is happening in the play to figure out the meaning of the words in blue.

Mr. Frank. I'm glad, Anne. Now you'll be able to help me straighten things in here. (*To* Mrs. Frank *and* Margot) Come with me . . . You and Margot rest in this room for the time being. (*He picks up their* 210 *clothes, starting for the room on the right.*)

Mrs. Frank. You're sure . . . ? I could help . . . And Anne hasn't had her milk . . .

Mr. Frank. I'll give it to her. (*To* Anne *and* Peter) Anne, Peter . . . it's best that you take off your shoes now, before you forget. (*He leads the way to the room, followed by* Margot.)

Mrs. Frank. You're sure you're not tired, Anne?

Anne. I feel fine. I'm going to help Father.

Mrs. Frank. Peter, I'm glad you are to be with us.

220 **Peter.** Yes, Mrs. Frank.

(Mrs. Frank *goes to join* Mr. Frank *and* Margot.)

(*During the following scene* Mr. Frank *helps* Margot *and* Mrs. Frank *to hang up their clothes. Then he persuades them both to lie down and rest. The* Van Daans *in their room above settle themselves. In the main room* Anne *and* Peter *remove their shoes.* Peter *takes his cat out of the carrier.*)

Anne. What's your cat's name?

Peter. Mouschi.[11]

READ ALOUD the boxed text. What are your impressions of Anne? (Connect)

230 **Anne.** Mouschi! Mouschi! Mouschi! (*She picks up the cat, walking away with it. To* Peter) I love cats. I have one . . . a darling little cat. But they made me leave her behind. I left some food and a note for the neighbors to take care of her . . . I'm going to miss her terribly. What is yours? A him or a her?

Peter. He's a tom. He doesn't like strangers. (*He takes the cat from her, putting it back in its carrier.*)

WHAT DOES IT MEAN? The word *tom* is short for *tomcat,* a male cat.

---

11. **Mouschi** (moo'shē).

Anne (*Unabashed*). Then I'll have to stop being a stranger, won't I? Is he fixed?

240 **Peter** (*Startled*). Huh?

Anne. Did you have him fixed?

Peter. No.

Anne. Oh, you ought to have him fixed—to keep him from—you know, fighting. Where did you go to school?

Peter. Jewish Secondary.

Anne. But that's where Margot and I go! I never saw you around.

Peter. I used to see you . . . sometimes . . .

250 **Anne.** You did?

Peter . . . in the school yard. You were always in the middle of a bunch of kids. (*He takes a penknife from his pocket.*)

Anne. Why didn't you ever come over?

Peter. I'm sort of a lone wolf. (*He starts to rip off his Star of David.*)

Anne. What are you doing?

Peter. Taking it off.

Anne. But you can't do that. They'll arrest you if you
260 go out without your star.

(*He tosses his knife on the table.*)

Peter. Who's going out?

Anne. Why, of course! You're right! Of course we don't need them any more. (*She picks up his knife and starts to take her star off.*) I wonder what our friends will think when we don't show up today?

Peter. I didn't have any dates with anyone.

Why does Peter take off his Star of David?

How did the Franks make it appear that they had been called away suddenly?

REREAD the boxed text. Which of the following statements describes Anne's attitude toward the yellow Star of David that the Nazis have made all Jews wear? Circle one. **(Infer)**

She wants to throw it away because it stands for oppression.

She cannot throw it away because it is a symbol of Judaism.

Anne. Oh, I did. I had a date with Jopie to go and play ping-pong at her house. Do you know Jopie de Waal?[12]

Peter. No.

Anne. Jopie's my best friend. I wonder what she'll think when she telephones and there's no answer? . . . Probably she'll go over to the house . . . I wonder what she'll think . . . we left everything as if we'd suddenly been called away . . . breakfast dishes in the sink . . . beds not made . . . (*As she pulls off her star, the cloth underneath shows clearly the color and form of the star.*) Look! It's still there! (*Peter goes over to the stove with his star.*) What're you going to do with yours?

Peter. Burn it.

Anne (*She starts to throw hers in, and cannot.*) It's funny, I can't throw mine away. I don't know why.

Peter. You can't throw . . . ? Something they branded you with . . . ? That they made you wear so they could spit on you?

Anne. I know. I know. But after all, it is the Star of David, isn't it?

(*In the bedroom, right,* Margot *and* Mrs. Frank *are lying down.* Mr. Frank *starts quietly out.*)

Peter. Maybe it's different for a girl.

(Mr. Frank *comes into the main room.*)

Mr. Frank. Forgive me, Peter. Now let me see. We must find a bed for your cat. (*He goes to a cupboard.*) I'm glad you brought your cat. Annie was feeling so badly about hers. (*Getting a used small washtub*) Here we are. Will it be comfortable in that?

Peter (*Gathering up his things*). Thanks.

12. **Jopie de Waal** (yō′pē də väl′).

Mr. Frank (*Opening the door of the room on the left*).
300 And here is your room. But I warn you, Peter, you
can't grow any more. Not an inch, or you'll have to
sleep with your feet out of the skylight. Are you
hungry?

Peter. No.

Mr. Frank. We have some bread and butter.

Peter. No, thank you.

Mr. Frank. You can have it for luncheon then. And
tonight we will have a real supper . . . our first
310 supper together.

Peter. Thanks. Thanks.

(*He goes into his room. During the following scene
he arranges his possessions in his new room.*)

Mr. Frank. That's a nice boy, Peter.

Anne. He's awfully shy, isn't he?

Mr. Frank. You'll like him, I know.

Anne. I certainly hope so, since he's the only boy I'm
likely to see for months and months.

(*Mr. Frank sits down, taking off his shoes.*)

As the play continues . . .

- Mr. Frank gives Anne a diary.
- Anne realizes what it means to be in hiding.

FOCUS

Anne loves and trusts her father. How does he help her feel less afraid?

MARK IT UP As you read, underline what Mr. Frank says and does to comfort Anne.

320 **Mr. Frank.** Annele,[13] there's a
box there. Will you open it?
(*He indicates a carton on the
couch.* Anne *brings it to the
center table. In the street
below there is the sound of
children playing.*)

Pause & Reflect

1. Anne and Peter both went to the same school. Who was more popular with the other students? (**Compare and Contrast**)

2. Do you think that Anne and Peter will become friends? (**Predict**)
YES / NO, because

---

13. **Annele/Anneke** (än'ə-lə) (än'ə-kə): nicknames for Anne.

MORE ABOUT . . .

QUEEN WILHELMINA She was queen of the Netherlands from 1890 to 1948. When the Germans invaded Holland, she took the Dutch government to London. She kept the hope of her people alive by broadcasting to them over the radio throughout the war.

REREAD the boxed passage. How would you say this in your own words? (Paraphrase)

Anne (*As she opens the carton*). You know the way I'm going to think of it here? I'm going to think of it as a boardinghouse. A very peculiar summer
330 boardinghouse, like the one that we—(*She breaks off as she pulls out some photographs.*) Father! My movie stars! I was wondering where they were! I was looking for them this morning . . . and Queen Wilhelmina! How wonderful!

Mr. Frank. There's something more. Go on. Look further. (*He goes over to the sink, pouring a glass of milk from a thermos bottle.*)

Anne (*Pulling out a pasteboard-bound book*). A diary! (*She throws her arms around her father.*) I've
340 never had a diary. And I've always longed for one. (*She looks around the room.*) Pencil, pencil, pencil, pencil. (*She starts down the stairs.*) I'm going down to the office to get a pencil.

Mr. Frank. Anne! No! (*He goes after her, catching her by the arm and pulling her back.*)

Anne (*Startled*). But there's no one in the building now.

Mr. Frank. It doesn't matter. I don't want you ever to go beyond that door.

Anne (*Sobered*). Never . . . ? Not even at nighttime,
350 when everyone is gone? Or on Sundays? Can't I go down to listen to the radio?

Mr. Frank. Never. I am sorry, Anneke. It isn't safe. No, you must never go beyond that door.

(*For the first time Anne realizes what "going into hiding" means.*)

Anne. I see.

Mr. Frank. It'll be hard, I know. But always remember this, Anneke. There are no walls, there are no bolts, no locks that anyone can put on your mind. Miep
360 will bring us books. We will read history, poetry,

mythology. (*He gives her the glass of milk.*) Here's your milk. (*With his arm about her, they go over to the couch, sitting down side by side.*) As a matter of fact, between us, Anne, being here has certain advantages for you. For instance, you remember the battle you had with your mother the other day on the subject of overshoes? But in the end you had to wear them? Well now, you see, for as long as we are here you will never have to wear overshoes! Isn't

370 that good? And the coat that you inherited from Margot, you won't have to wear that any more. And the piano! You won't have to practice on the piano. I tell you, this is going to be a fine life for you!

(*Anne's panic is gone.* Peter *appears in the doorway of his room, with a saucer in his hand. He is carrying his cat.*)

Peter. I . . . I . . . I thought I'd better get some water for Mouschi before . . .

Mr. Frank. Of course.

380 (*As he starts toward the sink the carillon begins to chime the hour of eight. He tiptoes to the window at the back and looks down at the street below. He turns to* Peter, *indicating in pantomime that it is too late.* Peter *starts back for his room. He steps on a creaking board. The three of them are frozen for a minute in fear. As* Peter *starts away again,* Anne *tiptoes over to him and pours some of the milk from her glass into the saucer for the cat.* Peter *squats on the floor, putting the milk before the cat.* Mr. Frank *gives* Anne

390 *his fountain pen, and then goes into the room at the right. For a second* Anne *watches the cat, then she goes over to the center table, and opens her diary.*

In the room at the right, Mrs. Frank *has sat up quickly at the sound of the carillon.* Mr. Frank *comes*

WHAT DOES IT MEAN? *In pantomime* means "by using a signal, without speaking."

What are the reactions of Mr. Frank, Peter, and Anne after Peter steps on a creaking board? Why do they react this way?

in and sits down beside her on the settee, his arm comfortingly around her.

Upstairs, in the attic room, Mr. and Mrs. Van Daan have hung their clothes in the closet and are now seated on the iron bed. Mrs. Van Daan leans back 400 *exhausted. Mr. Van Daan fans her with a newspaper.*

Anne starts to write in her diary. The lights dim out, the curtain falls.

In the darkness Anne's voice comes to us again, faintly at first, and then with growing strength.)

Anne's Voice. I expect I should be describing what it feels like to go into hiding. But I really don't know yet myself. I only know it's funny never to be able to go outdoors . . . never to breathe fresh air . . . never to run and shout and jump. It's the silence in 410 the nights that frightens me most. Every time I hear a creak in the house, or a step on the street outside, I'm sure they're coming for us. The days aren't so bad. At least we know that Miep and Mr. Kraler are down there below us in the office. Our protectors, we call them. I asked Father what would happen to them if the Nazis found out they were hiding us. Pim[14] said that they would suffer the same fate that we would . . . Imagine! They know this, and yet when they come up here, they're always cheerful 420 and gay as if there were nothing in the world to bother them . . . Friday, the twenty-first of August, nineteen forty-two. Today I'm going to tell you our general news. Mother is unbearable. She insists on treating me like a baby, which I <u>loathe</u>. Otherwise things are going better. The weather is . . .

---

14. **Pim:** Anne's nickname for her father.

The InterActive Reader PLUS
198 For English Learners

WORDS TO KNOW
   loathe (lōth) *v.* to hate; to dislike someone or something greatly

What would happen to Miep and Mr. Kraler if they were discovered to be helping the Franks?

(As Anne's voice is fading out, the curtain rises on the scene.)

Pause & Reflect

Pause & Reflect

READ ALOUD the boxed text on page 198. How does Anne feel about living in hiding? Circle words and phrases that show her feelings. **(Infer)**

FOCUS

In Scene 3, you get to know Anne better.

▨ **MARK IT UP** ▷ As you read, underline passages that reveal Anne's personality.

Scene 3

It is a little after six o'clock in the evening, two months later.

Margot is in the bedroom at the right, studying. Mr. Van Daan is lying down in the attic room above.

The rest of the "family" is in the main room. Anne and Peter sit opposite each other at the center table, where they have been doing their lessons. Mrs. Frank
10 *is on the couch. Mrs. Van Daan is seated with her fur coat, on which she has been sewing, in her lap. None of them are wearing their shoes.*

Their eyes are on Mr. Frank, waiting for him to give them the signal which will release them from their day-long quiet. Mr. Frank, his shoes in his hand, stands looking down out of the window at the back, watching to be sure that all of the workmen have left the building below.

After a few seconds of motionless silence, Mr. Frank
20 *turns from the window.*

Mr. Frank (*Quietly, to the group*). It's safe now. The last workman has left. (*There is an immediate stir of relief.*)

Anne (*Her pent-up energy explodes*). WHEE!

Mrs. Frank (*Startled, amused*). Anne!

▨ **As the play continues . . .**

• Two months have passed since the Franks and the Van Daans moved to the Secret Annex.

• Anne tries to have fun by teasing Peter.

English Learner Support

Language

Onomatopoeia The use of words to imitate sounds is called onomatopoeia. Practice saying *whee* aloud. It sounds like what it means—a way to show excitement.

Mrs. Van Daan. I'm first for the w.c. (*She hurries off to the bathroom. Mrs. Frank puts on her shoes and starts up to the sink to prepare supper. Anne sneaks Peter's shoes from under the table and hides them* 30 *behind her back. Mr. Frank goes into Margot's room.*)

Mr. Frank (*To Margot*). Six o'clock. School's over.

(*Margot gets up, stretching. Mr. Frank sits down to put on his shoes. In the main room Peter tries to find his.*)

Peter (*To Anne*). Have you seen my shoes?

Anne (*Innocently*). Your shoes?

Peter. You've taken them, haven't you?

Anne. I don't know what you're talking about.

40 **Peter.** You're going to be sorry!

Anne. Am I? (*Peter goes after her. Anne, with his shoes in her hand, runs from him, dodging behind her mother.*)

Mrs. Frank (*Protesting*). Anne, dear!

Peter. Wait till I get you!

Anne. I'm waiting! (*Peter makes a lunge for her. They both fall to the floor. Peter pins her down, wrestling with her to get the shoes.*) Don't! Don't! Peter, stop it. Ouch!

50 **Mrs. Frank.** Anne! . . . Peter!

(*Suddenly Peter becomes self-conscious. He grabs his shoes roughly and starts for his room.*)

Anne (*Following him*). Peter, where are you going? Come dance with me.

Peter. I tell you I don't know how.

Anne. I'll teach you.

Peter. I'm going to give Mouschi his dinner.

Anne. Can I watch?

Peter. He doesn't like people around while he eats.

60 **Anne.** Peter, please.

Peter. No! (*He goes into his room. Anne slams his door after him.*)

Mrs. Frank. Anne, dear, I think you shouldn't play like that with Peter. It's not dignified.

Anne. Who cares if it's dignified? I don't want to be dignified.

(Mr. Frank *and* Margot *come from the room on the right.* Margot *goes to help her mother.* Mr. Frank *starts for the center table to correct* Margot's *school papers.*)

70 **Mrs. Frank** (*To Anne*). You complain that I don't treat you like a grown-up. But when I do, you resent it.

Anne. I only want some fun . . . someone to laugh and clown with . . . After you've sat still all day and hardly moved, you've got to have some fun. I don't know what's the matter with that boy.

Mr. Frank. He isn't used to girls. Give him a little time.

Anne. Time? Isn't two months time? I could cry. (*Catching hold of* Margot) Come on, Margot . . . dance with me. Come on, please.

80 **Margot.** I have to help with supper.

Anne. You know we're going to forget how to dance . . . When we get out we won't remember a thing.

(*She starts to sing and dance by herself.* Mr. Frank *takes her in his arms, waltzing with her.* Mrs. Van Daan *comes in from the bathroom.*)

Mrs. Van Daan. Next? (*She looks around as she starts putting on her shoes.*) Where's Peter?

Anne (*As they are dancing*). Where would he be!

READING CHECK

What is Anne afraid will happen if she is in hiding for too long?

English Learner Support

Vocabulary

Idiom The phrase in blue means that Peter's father will be angry at him; it does not mean that he will harm Peter physically.

90 **Mrs. Van Daan.** He hasn't finished his lessons, has he? His father'll kill him if he catches him in there with that cat and his work not done. (*Mr. Frank and Anne finish their dance. They bow to each other with extravagant formality.*) Anne, get him out of there, will you?

Anne (*At Peter's door*). Peter? Peter?

Peter (*Opening the door a crack*). What is it?

Anne. Your mother says to come out.

Peter. I'm giving Mouschi his dinner.

100 **Mrs. Van Daan.** You know what your father says. (*She sits on the couch, sewing on the lining of her fur coat.*)

Peter. For heaven's sake, I haven't even looked at him since lunch.

Mrs. Van Daan. I'm just telling you, that's all.

Anne. I'll feed him.

Peter. I don't want you in there.

Mrs. Van Daan. Peter!

Peter (*To Anne*). Then give him his dinner and come right out, you hear? (*He comes back to the table.*

110 Anne *shuts the door of* Peter's *room after her and disappears behind the curtain covering his closet.*)

Mrs. Van Daan (*To Peter*). Now is that any way to talk to your little girl friend?

Peter. Mother . . . for heaven's sake . . . will you please stop saying that?

Mrs. Van Daan. Look at him blush! Look at him!

Peter. Please! I'm not . . . anyway . . . let me alone, will you?

Mrs. Van Daan. He acts like it was something to be
120 ashamed of. It's nothing to be ashamed of, to have a little girl friend.

Why does Peter blush?

Peter. You're crazy. She's only thirteen.

Mrs. Van Daan. So what? And you're sixteen. Just perfect. Your father's ten years older than I am. (*To Mr. Frank*) I warn you, Mr. Frank, if this war lasts much longer, we're going to be related and then . . .

Mr. Frank. Mazel tov![15]

Mrs. Frank (*Deliberately changing the conversation*). I wonder where Miep is. She's usually so prompt.

130 (*Suddenly everything else is forgotten as they hear the sound of an automobile coming to a screeching stop in the street below. They are tense, motionless in their terror. The car starts away. A wave of relief sweeps over them. They pick up their occupations again.* Anne *flings open the door of* Peter's *room, making a dramatic entrance. She is dressed in* Peter's *clothes.* Peter *looks at her in fury. The others are amused.*)

Anne. Good evening, everyone. Forgive me if I don't stay. (*She jumps up on a chair.*) I have a friend
140 waiting for me in there. My friend Tom. Tom Cat. Some people say that we look alike. But Tom has the most beautiful whiskers, and I have only a little fuzz. I am hoping . . . in time . . .

Peter. All right, Mrs. Quack Quack!

Anne (*Outraged—jumping down*). Peter!

Peter. I heard about you . . . How you talked so much in class they called you Mrs. Quack Quack. How Mr. Smitter made you write a composition . . . "'Quack, quack,' said Mrs. Quack Quack."

150 **Anne.** Well, go on. Tell them the rest. How it was so good he read it out loud to the class and then read it to all his other classes!

Peter. Quack! Quack! Quack . . . Quack . . . Quack . . .

(Anne *pulls off the coat and trousers.*)

---

15. **mazel tov** (mä′zəl tôf′) *Hebrew:* good luck.

REREAD the boxed stage directions. Notice that everything stops whenever the family members are reminded of the danger in which they live. What do you think it would be like to live this way? How might you behave? **(Connect)**

READ ALOUD the boxed text. Let your voice express the way in which Peter teases Anne. Is this the way young people today behave? **(Connect)**

Pause & Reflect

As the play continues . . .

- Daily life becomes more and more difficult for the residents of the Secret Annex.
- Mrs. Frank is worried about Anne.

 Why would illness be a serious problem for the people in the Secret Annex?

Anne. You are the most intolerable, <u>insufferable</u> boy I've ever met!

(*She throws the clothes down the stairwell. Peter goes down after them.*)

Peter. Quack, quack, quack!

160 **Mrs. Van Daan** (*To Anne*). That's right, Anneke! Give it to him!

Anne. With all the boys in the world . . . Why I had to get locked up with one like you! . . .

Peter. Quack, quack, quack, and from now on stay out of my room!

(*As Peter passes her, Anne puts out her foot, tripping him. He picks himself up, and goes on into his room.*)

Pause & Reflect

FOCUS

Living in hiding is difficult for Anne and Peter. It is also difficult for their parents. Read to find out about their parents' concerns.

Mrs. Frank (*Quietly*). Anne, dear . . . your hair. (*She feels* 170 Anne's *forehead.*) You're warm. Are you feeling all right?

Anne. Please, Mother. (*She goes over to the center table, slipping into her shoes.*)

Mrs. Frank (*Following her*). You haven't a fever, have you?

Anne (*Pulling away*). No. No.

Mrs. Frank. You know we can't call a doctor here, ever. There's only one thing to do . . . watch 180 carefully. Prevent an illness before it comes. Let me see your tongue.

WORDS TO KNOW
insufferable (ĭn-sŭf′ər-ə-bəl) *adj.* unbearable

Anne. Mother, this is perfectly absurd.

Mrs. Frank. Anne, dear, don't be such a baby. Let me see your tongue. (*As Anne refuses, Mrs. Frank appeals to Mr. Frank.*) Otto . . . ?

Mr. Frank. You hear your mother, Anne. (*Anne flicks out her tongue for a second, then turns away.*)

Mrs. Frank. Come on—open up! (*As Anne opens her mouth very wide*) You seem all right . . . but perhaps an aspirin . . .

Mrs. Van Daan. For heaven's sake, don't give that child any pills. I waited for fifteen minutes this morning for her to come out of the w.c.

Anne. I was washing my hair!

Mr. Frank. I think there's nothing the matter with our Anne that a ride on her bike, or a visit with her friend Jopie de Waal wouldn't cure. Isn't that so, Anne?

(*Mr. Van Daan comes down into the room. From outside we hear faint sounds of bombers going over and a burst of ack-ack.*)

Mr. Van Daan. Miep not come yet?

Mrs. Van Daan. The workmen just left, a little while ago.

Mr. Van Daan. What's for dinner tonight?

Mrs. Van Daan. Beans.

Mr. Van Daan. Not again!

Mrs. Van Daan. Poor Putti! I know. But what can we do? That's all that Miep brought us.

(*Mr. Van Daan starts to pace, his hands behind his back. Anne follows behind him, imitating him.*)

Anne. We are now in what is known as the "bean cycle." Beans boiled, beans en casserole, beans with strings, beans without strings . . .

READING CHECK What does Mr. Frank suggest is wrong with Anne?

(Peter *has come out of his room. He slides into his place at the table, becoming immediately absorbed in his studies.*)

Mr. Van Daan (*To* Peter). I saw you . . . in there, playing with your cat.

220 **Mrs. Van Daan.** He just went in for a second, putting his coat away. He's been out here all the time, doing his lessons.

Mr. Frank (*Looking up from the papers*). Anne, you got an excellent in your history paper today . . . and very good in Latin.

Anne (*Sitting beside him*). How about algebra?

Mr. Frank. I'll have to make a confession. Up until now I've managed to stay ahead of you in algebra. Today you caught up with me. We'll leave it to
230 Margot to correct.

Anne. Isn't algebra <u>vile</u>, Pim!

Mr. Frank. Vile!

Margot (*To* Mr. Frank). How did I do?

Anne (*Getting up*). Excellent, excellent, excellent, excellent!

Mr. Frank (*To* Margot). You should have used the subjunctive here . . .

Margot. Should I? . . . I thought . . . look here . . . I didn't use it here . . . (*The two become absorbed in*
240 *the papers.*)

Pause & Reflect

1. How does Anne feel about the way her mother treats her? **(Infer)**

2. Who do you think is a better father, Mr. Frank or Mr. Van Daan? Explain. **(Evaluate)**

WORDS TO KNOW
vile (vīl) *adj.* disgusting; hateful; unpleasant

FOCUS

People in the Secret Annex are starting to get on one another's nerves. Read to find out about the quarrels that break out and how Anne reacts to them.

Anne. Mrs. Van Daan, may I try on your coat?

Mrs. Frank. No, Anne.

Mrs. Van Daan (*Giving it to* Anne). It's all right . . . but careful with it. (Anne *puts it on and struts with it.*)

My father gave me that the year before he died. He always bought the best that money could buy.

250 **Anne.** Mrs. Van Daan, did you have a lot of boy friends before you were married?

Mrs. Frank. Anne, that's a personal question. It's not courteous to ask personal questions.

Mrs. Van Daan. Oh I don't mind. (*To* Anne) Our house was always swarming with boys. When I was a girl we had . . .

Mr. Van Daan. Oh, God. Not again!

Mrs. Van Daan (*Good-humored*). Shut up! (*Without a pause, to* Anne. Mr. Van Daan *mimics* Mrs. Van
260 Daan, *speaking the first few words in unison with her.*) One summer we had a big house in Hilversum. The boys came buzzing round like bees around a jam pot. And when I was sixteen! . . . We were wearing our skirts very short those days and I had good-looking legs. (*She pulls up her skirt, going to* Mr. Frank.) I still have 'em. I may not be as pretty as I used to be, but I still have my legs. How about it, Mr. Frank?

Mr. Van Daan. All right. All right. We see them.

270 **Mrs. Van Daan.** I'm not asking you. I'm asking Mr. Frank.

Peter. Mother, for heaven's sake.

As the play continues . . .

- The residents of the Secret Annex become annoyed with each other.
- Mrs. Van Daan, Mr. Van Daan, and Anne argue.

READING CHECK Why does Mrs. Van Daan ask Anne to be careful with her coat?

MORE ABOUT . . .

HILVERSUM Hilversum is a city in northern Holland. It is located about 15 miles southeast of Amsterdam.

English Learner Support

Language

Simile Draw the picture that the words in blue create in your mind. Mrs. Van Daan uses this comparison to show how popular she was with boys when she was younger.

Idioms To *get fresh* is to behave badly or be disrespectful. *So-and-So* is an unspecified person—it could refer to any young man who "got fresh" with Mrs. Van Daan.

Mrs. Van Daan. Oh, I embarrass you, do I? Well, I just hope the girl you marry has as good. (*Then to* Anne) My father used to worry about me, with so many boys hanging round. He told me, if any of them gets fresh, you say to him . . . "Remember, Mr. So-and-So, remember I'm a lady."

280 **Anne.** "Remember, Mr. So-and-So, remember I'm a lady." (*She gives* Mrs. Van Daan *her coat.*)

Mr. Van Daan. Look at you, talking that way in front of her! Don't you know she puts it all down in that diary?

Mrs. Van Daan. So, if she does? I'm only telling the truth!

(Anne *stretches out, putting her ear to the floor, listening to what is going on below. The sound of the bombers fades away.*)

Mrs. Frank (*Setting the table*). Would you mind,
290 Peter, if I moved you over to the couch?

Anne (*Listening*). Miep must have the radio on.

(Peter *picks up his papers, going over to the couch beside* Mrs. Van Daan.)

Mr. Van Daan (*Accusingly, to* Peter). Haven't you finished yet?

Peter. No.

Mr. Van Daan. You ought to be ashamed of yourself.

WHAT DOES IT MEAN? A *dunce* is someone who is not very smart.

Peter. All right. All right. I'm a dunce. I'm a hopeless case. Why do I go on?

300 **Mrs. Van Daan.** You're not hopeless. Don't talk that way. It's just that you haven't anyone to help you, like the girls have. (*To* Mr. Frank) Maybe you could help him, Mr. Frank?

Mr. Frank. I'm sure that his father . . . ?

Why is Mr. Van Daan angry at Peter?

Mr. Van Daan. Not me. I can't do anything with him. He won't listen to me. You go ahead . . . if you want.

Mr. Frank (*Going to* Peter). What about it, Peter? Shall we make our school coeducational?

Mrs. Van Daan (*Kissing* Mr. Frank). You're an angel, Mr. Frank. An angel. I don't know why I didn't meet you before I met that one there. Here, sit down, Mr. Frank . . . (*She forces him down on the couch beside* Peter.) Now, Peter, you listen to Mr. Frank.

Mr. Frank. It might be better for us to go into Peter's room. (Peter *jumps up eagerly, leading the way.*)

Mrs. Van Daan. That's right. You go in there, Peter. You listen to Mr. Frank. Mr. Frank is a highly educated man. (*As* Mr. Frank *is about to follow* Peter *into his room,* Mrs. Frank *stops him and wipes the lipstick from his lips. Then she closes the door after them.*)

Anne (*On the floor, listening*). Shh! I can hear a man's voice talking.

Mr. Van Daan (*To* Anne). Isn't it bad enough here without your sprawling all over the place? (Anne *sits up.*)

Mrs. Van Daan (*To* Mr. Van Daan). If you didn't smoke so much, you wouldn't be so bad-tempered.

Mr. Van Daan. Am I smoking? Do you see me smoking?

Mrs. Van Daan. Don't tell me you've used up all those cigarettes.

Mr. Van Daan. One package. Miep only brought me one package.

Mrs. Van Daan. It's a filthy habit anyway. It's a good time to break yourself.

Mr. Van Daan. Oh, stop it, please.

WHAT DOES IT MEAN?
Coeducational means "for both males and females."

English Learner Support
Vocabulary
Idiom *You're an angel* means "you are a very good person."

WHAT DOES IT MEAN?
Sprawling means "spreading out" or "taking up a lot of space."

English Learner Support
Vocabulary
Idiom *Break yourself* means "stop yourself" or "cure yourself." Mr. Van Daan needs to stop himself from smoking.

Mrs. Van Daan. Will you shut up? (*During this,* Mrs.
Frank *and* Margot *have studiously kept their eyes*
340 *down. But* Anne, *seated on the floor, has been*
following the discussion interestedly. Mr. Van Daan
turns to see her staring up at him.) And what are
you staring at?

Anne. I never heard grown-ups quarrel before. I
thought only children quarreled.

Mr. Van Daan. This isn't a quarrel! It's a discussion.
And I never heard children so rude before.

Anne (*Rising,* <u>*indignantly*</u>). I, rude!

Mr. Van Daan. Yes!

350 **Mrs. Frank** (*Quickly*). Anne, will you get me my
knitting? (Anne *goes to get it.*) I must remember,
when Miep comes, to ask her to bring me some
more wool.

Margot (*Going to her room*). I need some hairpins
and some soap. I made a list. (*She goes into her*
bedroom to get the list.)

Mrs. Frank (*To* Anne) Have you some library books
for Miep when she comes?

Anne. It's a wonder that Miep has a life of her own,
360 the way we make her run errands for us. Please,
Miep, get me some starch. Please take my hair out
and have it cut. Tell me all the latest news, Miep.
(*She goes over, kneeling on the couch beside* Mrs.
Van Daan.) Did you know she was engaged? His
name is Dirk, and Miep's afraid the Nazis will ship
him off to Germany to work in one of their war
plants. That's what they're doing with some of the
young Dutchmen . . . they pick them up off the
streets—

WORDS TO KNOW
indignantly (ĭn-dĭg′ nənt-lē) *adv.* angrily aroused by something mean,
unjust, or unworthy

370 **Mr. Van Daan** (*Interrupting*). Don't you ever get tired of talking? Suppose you try keeping still for five minutes. Just five minutes. (*He starts to pace again. Again* Anne *follows him,* mimicking *him.* Mrs. Frank *jumps up and takes her by the arm up to the sink, and gives her a glass of milk.*)

Mrs. Frank. Come here, Anne. It's time for your glass of milk.

Mr. Van Daan. Talk, talk, talk. I never heard such a child. Where is my . . . ? Every evening it's the same, **380** talk, talk, talk. (*He looks around.*) Where is my . . . ?

Mrs. Van Daan. What're you looking for?

Mr. Van Daan. My pipe. Have you seen my pipe?

Mrs. Van Daan. What good's a pipe? You haven't got any tobacco.

Mr. Van Daan. At least I'll have something to hold in my mouth! (*Opening* Margot's *bedroom door*) Margot, have you seen my pipe?

Margot. It was on the table last night. (Anne *puts her glass of milk on the table and picks up his pipe,* **390** *hiding it behind her back.*)

Mr. Van Daan. I know. I know. Anne, did you see my pipe? . . . Anne!

Mrs. Frank. Anne, Mr. Van Daan is speaking to you.

Anne. Am I allowed to talk now?

Mr. Van Daan. You're the most aggravating . . . The trouble with you is, you've been spoiled. What you need is a good old-fashioned spanking.

Anne (*Mimicking* Mrs. Van Daan). "Remember, Mr. So-and-So, remember I'm a lady." (*She thrusts the* **400** *pipe into his mouth, then picks up her glass of milk.*)

Mr. Van Daan (*Restraining himself with difficulty*). Why aren't you nice and quiet like your sister

READING CHECK

Why does Anne ask if she is allowed to talk now?

WHAT DOES IT MEAN?

Scoffingly means "in a mocking and disrespectful way."

Pause & Reflect

1. Earlier in the play, Mr. Frank said there was nothing wrong with Anne that a little fresh air could not cure. Do you think this advice applies to other family members? **(Infer)**

   YES / NO, because

   _____

   _____

   _____

2. **REREAD** the boxed text. Anne wants to be a singer or a dancer when she grows up. Do you think those would be good careers for her? **(Evaluate)**

   _____

   _____

   _____

   _____

Margot? Why do you have to show off all the time? Let me give you a little advice, young lady. Men don't like that kind of thing in a girl. You know that? A man likes a girl who'll listen to him once in a while . . . a domestic girl, who'll keep her house shining for her husband . . . who loves to cook and sew and . . .

410 **Anne.** I'd cut my throat first! I'd open my veins! I'm going to be remarkable! I'm going to Paris . . .

Mr. Van Daan (*Scoffingly*). Paris!

Anne. . . . to study music and art.

Mr. Van Daan. Yeah! Yeah!

Anne. I'm going to be a famous dancer or singer . . . or something wonderful. (*She makes a wide gesture, spilling the glass of milk on the fur coat in* Mrs. Van Daan's *lap.* Margot *rushes quickly over with a towel.* Anne *tries to brush the milk off with her skirt.*)

420 **Mrs. Van Daan.** Now look what you've done . . . you clumsy little fool! My beautiful fur coat my father gave me . . .

Anne. I'm so sorry.

Mrs. Van Daan. What do you care? It isn't yours . . . So go on, ruin it! Do you know what that coat cost? Do you? And now look at it! Look at it!

Anne. I'm very, very sorry.

Mrs. Van Daan. I could kill you for this. I could just kill you! (Mrs. Van Daan *goes up the stairs,*
430 *clutching the coat.* Mr. Van Daan *starts after her.*)

Mr. Van Daan. Petronella . . . liefje! Liefje! . . . Come back . . . the supper . . . come back!

FOCUS

Anne's conflict with her mother gets worse. Read to find out why mother and daughter quarrel.

Mrs. Frank. Anne, you must not behave in that way.

Anne. It was an accident. Anyone can have an accident.

Mrs. Frank. I don't mean that. I mean the answering back. You must not answer back. They are our guests. We must always show the greatest courtesy to them. We're all living under terrible tension. (*She stops as* Margot *indicates that* Van Daan *can hear. When he is gone, she continues.*) That's why we must control ourselves . . . You don't hear Margot getting into arguments with them, do you? Watch Margot. She's always courteous with them. Never familiar. She keeps her distance. And they respect her for it. Try to be like Margot.

Anne. And have them walk all over me, the way they do her? No, thanks!

Mrs. Frank. I'm not afraid that anyone is going to walk all over you, Anne. I'm afraid for other people, that you'll walk on them. I don't know what happens to you, Anne. You are wild, self-willed. If I had ever talked to my mother as you talk to me . . .

Anne. Things have changed. People aren't like that any more. "Yes, Mother." "No, Mother." "Anything you say, Mother." I've got to fight things out for myself! Make something of myself!

Mrs. Frank. It isn't necessary to fight to do it. Margot doesn't fight, and isn't she . . . ?

Anne (*Violently rebellious*). Margot! Margot! Margot! That's all I hear from everyone . . . how wonderful Margot is . . . "Why aren't you like Margot?"

Margot (*Protesting*). Oh, come on, Anne, don't be so . . .

440

450

460

Anne (*Paying no attention*). Everything she does is right, and everything I do is wrong! I'm the goat around here! . . . You're all against me! . . . And you worst of all!

470 (*She rushes off into her room and throws herself down on the settee, stifling her sobs. Mrs. Frank sighs and starts toward the stove.*)

Mrs. Frank (*To Margot*). Let's put the soup on the stove . . . if there's anyone who cares to eat. Margot, will you take the bread out? (Margot *gets the bread from the cupboard.*) I don't know how we can go on living this way . . . I can't say a word to Anne . . . she flies at me . . .

Margot. You know Anne. In half an hour she'll be
480 out here, laughing and joking.

Mrs. Frank. And . . . (*She makes a motion upwards, indicating the* Van Daans.) . . . I told your father it wouldn't work . . . but no . . . no . . . he had to ask them, he said . . . he owed it to him, he said. Well, he knows now that I was right! These quarrels! . . . This bickering!

Margot (*With a warning look*). Shush. Shush.

(*The buzzer for the door sounds.* Mrs. Frank *gasps, startled.*)

490 **Mrs. Frank.** Every time I hear that sound, my heart stops!

Margot (*Starting for* Peter's *door*). It's Miep. (*She knocks at the door.*) Father?

(Mr. Frank *comes quickly from* Peter's *room.*)

Mr. Frank. Thank you, Margot. (*As he goes down the steps to open the outer door*) Has everyone his list?

Margot. I'll get my books. (*Giving her mother a list.*) Here's your list. (Margot *goes into her and* Anne's

English Learner Support

Vocabulary

Idiom The words in blue express the idea that Anne gets angry at her mother.

bedroom on the right. Anne *sits up, hiding her*
500 *tears, as* Margot *comes in.*) Miep's here.

(Margot *picks up her books and goes back.* Anne
hurries over to the mirror, smoothing her hair.)

Mr. Van Daan (*Coming down the stairs*). Is it Miep?

Margot. Yes. Father's gone down to let her in.

Mr. Van Daan. At last I'll have some cigarettes!

Mrs. Frank (*To Mr. Van Daan*). I can't tell you how
unhappy I am about Mrs. Van Daan's coat. Anne
should never have touched it.

Mr. Van Daan. She'll be all right.

510 **Mrs. Frank.** Is there anything I can do?

Mr. Van Daan. Don't worry.

(*He turns to meet* Miep. *But it is not* Miep *who
comes up the steps. It is* Mr. Kraler, *followed by* Mr.
Frank. *Their faces are grave.* Anne *comes from the
bedroom.* Peter *comes from his room.*)

Pause & Reflect

1. Do you think Anne's mother treats her fairly? (**Evaluate**)

YES / NO, because

_____

_____

_____

_____

2. How would you **contrast** Anne with her sister, Margot? What are their major differences?

_____

_____

_____

_____

_____

FOCUS

Mr. Kraler arrives with news to tell the families. Mr. Frank then makes an important decision. Read to find out what his decision is and how the others react to it.

Mrs. Frank. Mr. Kraler!

Mr. Van Daan. How are you, Mr. Kraler?

Margot. This is a surprise.

520 **Mrs. Frank.** When Mr. Kraler comes, the sun begins to shine.

Mr. Van Daan. Miep is coming?

Mr. Kraler. Not tonight.

(Kraler *goes to* Margot *and* Mrs. Frank *and* Anne,
shaking hands with them.)

As the play continues . . .

• Mr. Kraler tells the Franks that Miep knows someone who is in trouble.

• Mr. Kraler introduces Mr. Dussel to the Franks.

English Learner Support

Language

Figure of Speech The words in blue mean "the day seems better and brighter."

Verb Phrase When the adverb *over* is used with the verb *talk*, the verb phrase *talk over* is created. *To talk over* means "to discuss."

From whom must the Jewish dentist hide?

the boxed text. What does Mr. Frank's answer tell you about him? (Draw Conclusions)

Mrs. Frank. Wouldn't you like a cup of coffee? . . . Or, better still, will you have supper with us?

Mr. Frank. Mr. Kraler has something to talk over with
530 us. Something has happened, he says, which demands an immediate decision.

Mrs. Frank (*Fearful*). What is it?

(Mr. Kraler *sits down on the couch. As he talks he takes bread, cabbages, milk, etc., from his briefcase, giving them to* Margot *and* Anne *to put away.*)

Mr. Kraler. Usually, when I come up here, I try to bring you some bit of good news. What's the use of telling you the bad news when there's nothing that you can do about it? But today something has
540 happened . . . Dirk . . . Miep's Dirk, you know, came to me just now. He tells me that he has a Jewish friend living near him. A dentist. He says he's in trouble. He begged me, could I do anything for this man? Could I find him a hiding place? . . . So I've come to you . . . I know it's a terrible thing to ask of you, living as you are, but would you take him in with you?

Mr. Frank. Of course we will.

Mr. Kraler (*Rising*). It'll be just for a night or two . . .
550 until I find some other place. This happened so suddenly that I didn't know where to turn.

Mr. Frank. Where is he?

Mr. Kraler. Downstairs in the office.

Mr. Frank. Good. Bring him up.

Mr. Kraler. His name is Dussel . . . Jan Dussel.

Mr. Frank. Dussel . . . I think I know him.

Mr. Kraler. I'll get him. (*He goes quickly down the steps and out.* Mr. Frank *suddenly becomes conscious of the others.*)

Mr. Frank. Forgive me. I spoke without consulting
you. But I knew you'd feel as I do.

> **Mr. Van Daan.** There's no reason for you to consult
> anyone. This is your place. You have a right to do
> exactly as you please. The only thing I feel . . .
> there's so little food as it is . . . and to take in
> another person . . .

(Peter *turns away, ashamed of his father.*)

Mr. Frank. We can stretch the food a little. It's only
for a few days.

Mr. Van Daan. You want to make a bet?

Mrs. Frank. I think it's fine to have him. But, Otto,
where are you going to put him? Where?

Peter. He can have my bed. I can sleep on the floor. I
wouldn't mind.

Mr. Frank. That's good of you, Peter. But your room's
too small . . . even for *you.*

Anne. I have a much better idea. I'll come in here with
you and Mother, and Margot can take Peter's room
and Peter can go in our room with Mr. Dussel.

Margot. That's right. We could do that.

Mr. Frank. No, Margot. You mustn't sleep in that
room . . . neither you nor Anne. Mouschi has caught
some rats in there. Peter's brave. He doesn't mind.

Anne. Then how about *this?* I'll come in here with
you and Mother, and Mr. Dussel can have my bed.

Mrs. Frank. No. No. *No!* Margot will come in here
with us and he can have her bed. It's the only way.
Margot, bring your things in here. Help her, Anne.

(Margot *hurries into her room to get her things.*)

Anne (*To her mother*). Why Margot? Why can't I
come in here?

REREAD the boxed text.
What does Mr. Van
Daan say about
Mr. Frank's decision to take in
Mr. Dussel? What do you
think Mr. Van Daan really
means? **(Infer)**

What Mr. Van Daan says:

What Mr. Van Daan means:

READING CHECK
Why can't one of
the girls have
Peter's room?

Mrs. Frank. Because it wouldn't be proper for Margot to sleep with a . . . Please, Anne. Don't argue. Please. (Anne *starts slowly away.*)

Mr. Frank (*To* Anne). You don't mind sharing your room with Mr. Dussel, do you, Anne?

Anne. No. No, of course not.

Mr. Frank. Good. (Anne *goes off into her bedroom, helping* Margot. Mr. Frank *starts to search in the*
600 *cupboards.*) Where's the cognac?

Mrs. Frank. It's there. But, Otto, I was saving it in case of illness.

Mr. Frank. I think we couldn't find a better time to use it. Peter, will you get five glasses for me?

(Peter *goes for the glasses.* Margot *comes out of her bedroom, carrying her possessions, which she hangs behind a curtain in the main room.* Mr. Frank *finds the cognac and pours it into the five glasses that* Peter *brings him.* Mr. Van Daan *stands looking on* sourly.
610 Mrs. Van Daan *comes downstairs and looks around at all the bustle.*)

Mrs. Van Daan. What's happening? What's going on?

Mr. Van Daan. Someone's moving in with us.

Mrs. Van Daan. In here? You're joking.

Margot. It's only for a night or two . . . until Mr. Kraler finds him another place.

Mr. Van Daan. Yeah! Yeah!

(Mr. Frank *hurries over as* Mr. Kraler *and* Dussel *come up.* Dussel *is a man in his late fifties,* meticulous,
620 *finicky . . .* bewildered *now. He wears a raincoat. He carries a briefcase, stuffed full, and a small medicine case.*)

Mr. Frank. Come in, Mr. Dussel.

Mr. Kraler. This is Mr. Frank.

Dussel. Mr. Otto Frank?

Mr. Frank. Yes. Let me take your things. (*He takes the hat and briefcase, but* Dussel *clings to his medicine case.*) This is my wife Edith . . . Mr. and Mrs. Van Daan . . . their son, Peter . . . and my daughters, Margot and Anne.

630

(Dussel *shakes hands with everyone.*)

Mr. Kraler. Thank you, Mr. Frank. Thank you all. Mr. Dussel, I leave you in good hands. Oh . . . Dirk's coat.

(Dussel *hurriedly takes off the raincoat, giving it to* Mr. Kraler. *Underneath is his white dentist's jacket, with a yellow Star of David on it.*)

Dussel (*To* Mr. Kraler). What can I say to thank you . . . ?

640 **Mrs. Frank** (*To* Dussel). Mr. Kraler and Miep . . . They're our lifeline. Without them we couldn't live.

Mr. Kraler. Please. Please. You make us seem very heroic. It isn't that at all. We simply don't like the Nazis. (*To* Mr. Frank, *who offers him a drink*) No, thanks. (*Then, going on*) We don't like their methods. We don't like . . .

Mr. Frank (*Smiling*). I know. I know. "No one's going to tell us Dutchmen what to do with our damn Jews!"

650 **Mr. Kraler** (*To* Dussel). Pay no attention to Mr. Frank. I'll be up tomorrow to see that they're treating you right. (*To* Mr. Frank) Don't trouble to come down again. Peter will bolt the door after me, won't you, Peter?

Peter. Yes, sir.

Mr. Frank. Thank you, Peter. I'll do it.

Mr. Kraler. Good night. Good night.

English Learner Support
Vocabulary

Context Clues Mrs. Frank has just praised Mr. Kraler, but Mr Kraler says that he is not a hero. This helps you understand that by *Please. Please,* Mr. Kraler means "stop" or "that's enough."

READING CHECK What is the reason Mr. Kraler and Miep help people like the Franks?

Pause & Reflect

Do you agree with Mr. Frank's decision to take in Mr. Dussel? **(Evaluate)**

YES / NO, because

_____

_____

_____

_____

📑 **As the play ends . . .**

• Mr. Dussel says that hundreds of Jews are being taken away from Amsterdam every day.

• Anne helps Mr. Dussel move into his new room.

▶ **MORE ABOUT . . .**

ZURICH Zurich is a city in Switzerland. Unlike Holland, Switzerland was not controlled by the Nazis during World War II.

READING CHECK Why does Mr. Frank want the adults to have a glass of cognac?

Group. Good night, Mr. Kraler. We'll see you tomorrow, (*etc., etc.*)

660 (Mr. Kraler *goes out with* Mr. Frank. Mrs. Frank *gives each one of the "grown-ups" a glass of cognac.*)

Pause & Reflect

FOCUS

Mr. Dussel tells the families what is going on in the outside world.

▥ **MARK IT UP** ⟩ As you read, circle details that tell you about what is happening to the Jews in Holland.

Mrs. Frank. Please, Mr. Dussel, sit down.

(Mr. Dussel *sinks into a chair.* Mrs. Frank *gives him a glass of cognac.*)

Dussel. I'm dreaming. I know it. I can't believe my eyes. Mr. Otto Frank here! (*To*

670 Mrs. Frank) You're not in Switzerland then? A woman told me . . . She said she'd gone to your house . . . the door was open, everything was in disorder, dishes in the sink. She said she found a piece of paper in the wastebasket with an address scribbled on it . . . an address in Zurich. She said you must have escaped to Zurich.

Anne. Father put that there purposely . . . just so people would think that very thing!

Dussel. And you've been here all the time?

680 **Mrs. Frank.** All the time . . . ever since July.

(Anne *speaks to her father as he comes back.*)

Anne. It worked, Pim . . . the address you left! Mr. Dussel says that people believe we escaped to Switzerland.

Mr. Frank. I'm glad . . . And now let's have a little drink to welcome Mr. Dussel. (*Before they can* *drink*, Mr. Dussel *bolts his drink*. Mr. Frank *smiles and raises his glass*.) To Mr. Dussel. Welcome. We're very honored to have you with us.

690 **Mrs. Frank.** To Mr. Dussel, welcome.

(*The* Van Daans *murmur a welcome. The "grown-ups" drink.*)

Mrs. Van Daan. Um. That was good.

Mr. Van Daan. Did Mr. Kraler warn you that you won't get much to eat here? You can imagine . . . three ration books among the seven of us . . . and now you make eight.

(Peter *walks away, humiliated. Outside a street organ is heard dimly.*)

700 **Dussel** (*Rising*). Mr. Van Daan, you don't realize what is happening outside that you should warn me of a thing like that. You don't realize what's going on . . . (As Mr. Van Daan *starts his characteristic pacing*, Dussel *turns to speak to the others*.) Right here in Amsterdam every day hundreds of Jews disappear . . . They surround a block and search house by house. Children come home from school to find their parents gone. Hundreds are being deported . . . people that you and I know . . . the
710 Hallensteins . . . the Wessels . . .

Mrs. Frank (*In tears*). Oh, no. No!

Dussel. They get their call-up notice . . . come to the Jewish theatre on such and such a day and hour . . . bring only what you can carry in a rucksack. And if you refuse the call-up notice, then they come and drag you from your home and ship you off to Mauthausen.[16] The death camp!

Mrs. Frank. We didn't know that things had got so much worse.

16. **Mauthausen** (mout′hou′zən): a Nazi concentration camp in Austria.

English Learner Support

Vocabulary

Idiom The words in blue mean "swallows his drink in one big sip."

REREAD the boxed passage. Why does Peter feel ashamed of his father? (**Infer**)

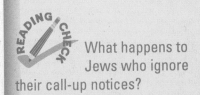
READING CHECK What happens to Jews who ignore their call-up notices?

Why does Mr. Frank suggest that they stop asking Mr. Dussel questions until another time?

720 **Dussel.** Forgive me for speaking so.

Anne (*Coming to* Dussel). Do you know the de Waals? . . . What's become of them? Their daughter Jopie and I are in the same class. Jopie's my best friend.

Dussel. They are gone.

Anne. Gone?

Dussel. With all the others.

Anne. Oh, no. Not Jopie!

(*She turns away, in tears.* Mrs. Frank *motions to*
730 Margot *to comfort her.* Margot *goes to* Anne, *putting her arms comfortingly around her.*)

Mrs. Van Daan. There were some people called Wagner. They lived near us . . . ?

Mr. Frank (*Interrupting, with a glance at* Anne). I think we should put this off until later. We all have many questions we want to ask . . . But I'm sure that Mr. Dussel would like to get settled before supper.

Dussel. Thank you. I would. I brought very little with me.

740 **Mr. Frank** (*Giving him his hat and briefcase*). I'm sorry we can't give you a room alone. But I hope you won't be too uncomfortable. We've had to make strict rules here . . . a schedule of hours . . . We'll tell you after supper. Anne, would you like to take Mr. Dussel to his room?

Anne (*Controlling her tears*). If you'll come with me, Mr. Dussel? (*She starts for her room.*)

Dussel (*Shaking hands with each in turn*). Forgive me if I haven't really expressed my gratitude to all of
750 you. This has been such a shock to me. I'd always thought of myself as Dutch. I was born in Holland.

My father was born in Holland, and my grandfather. And now . . . after all these years . . . (*He breaks off*). If you'll excuse me.

(Dussel *gives a little bow and hurries off after* Anne. Mr. Frank *and the others are subdued.*)

Anne (*Turning on the light*). Well, here we are.

(Dussel *looks around the room. In the main room* Margot *speaks to her mother.*)

760 **Margot.** The news sounds pretty bad, doesn't it? It's so different from what Mr. Kraler tells us. Mr. Kraler says things are improving.

Mr. Van Daan. I like it better the way Kraler tells it.

(*They resume their occupations, quietly.* Peter *goes off into his room. In* Anne's *room,* Anne *turns to* Dussel.)

Anne. You're going to share the room with me.

Dussel. I'm a man who's always lived alone. I haven't had to adjust myself to others. I hope you'll bear with me until I learn.

770 **Anne.** Let me help you. (*She takes his briefcase.*) Do you always live all alone? Have you no family at all?

Dussel. No one. (*He opens his medicine case and spreads his bottles on the dressing table.*)

Anne. How dreadful. You must be terribly lonely.

Dussel. I'm used to it.

Anne. I don't think I could ever get used to it. Didn't you even have a pet? A cat, or a dog?

Dussel. I have an allergy for fur-bearing animals. They give me asthma.

780 **Anne.** Oh, dear. Peter has a cat.

Dussel. Here? He has it here?

READING CHECK Why is Mr. Dussel shocked by what has happened to him?

English Learner Support
Vocabulary
Idiom The words in blue mean "be patient with me."

Word Parts
fortis (strong) +
fy (make) =
fortify (make strong)

What does Anne say is the best thing about their room?

REREAD the boxed text. Do you think Anne and Mr. Dussel will become friends? **(Predict)**

YES / NO, because

Anne. Yes. But we hardly ever see it. He keeps it in his room all the time. I'm sure it will be all right.

Dussel. Let us hope so.

(*He takes some pills to* fortify *himself.*)

Anne. That's Margot's bed, where you're going to sleep. I sleep on the sofa there. (*Indicating the clothes hooks on the wall*) We cleared these off for your things. (*She goes over to the window.*) The best part
790 about this room . . . you can look down and see a bit of the street and the canal. There's a houseboat . . . you can see the end of it . . . a bargeman lives there with his family . . . They have a baby and he's just beginning to walk and I'm so afraid he's going to fall into the canal some day. I watch him . . .

Dussel (*Interrupting*). Your father spoke of a schedule.

Anne (*Coming away from the window*). Oh, yes. It's mostly about the times we have to be quiet. And
800 times for the w.c. You can use it now if you like.

Dussel (*Stiffly*). No, thank you.

Anne. I suppose you think it's awful, my talking about a thing like that. But you don't know how important it can get to be, especially when you're frightened . . . About this room, the way Margot and I did . . . she had it to herself in the afternoons for studying, reading . . . lessons, you know . . . and I took the mornings. Would that be all right with you?

Dussel. I'm not at my best in the morning.

810 **Anne.** You stay here in the mornings then. I'll take the room in the afternoons.

Dussel. Tell me, when you're in here, what happens to me? Where am I spending my time? In there, with all the people?

Anne. Yes.

Dussel. I see. I see.

Anne. We have supper at half past six.

Dussel (*Going over to the sofa*). Then, if you don't mind . . . I like to lie down quietly for ten minutes before eating. I find it helps the digestion.

Anne. Of course. I hope I'm not going to be too much of a bother to you. I seem to be able to get everyone's back up.

(Dussel *lies down on the sofa, curled up, his back to her.*)

Dussel. I always get along very well with children. My patients all bring their children to me, because they know I get on well with them. So don't you worry about that.

(Anne *leans over him, taking his hand and shaking it gratefully.*)

Anne. Thank you. Thank you, Mr. Dussel.

(*The lights dim to darkness. The curtain falls on the scene. Anne's voice comes to us faintly at first, and then with increasing power.*)

Anne's Voice. . . . And yesterday I finished Cissy Van Marxvelt's latest book. I think she is a first-class writer. I shall definitely let my children read her. Monday the twenty-first of September, nineteen forty-two. Mr. Dussel and I had another battle yesterday. Yes, Mr. Dussel! According to him, nothing, I repeat . . . nothing, is right about me . . . my appearance, my character, my manners. While he was going on at me I thought . . . sometime I'll give you such a smack that you'll fly right up to the ceiling! Why is it that every grown-up thinks he

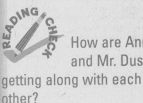

READING CHECK How are Anne and Mr. Dussel getting along with each other?

Pause & Reflect

Review the details you circled. Which statement best summarizes the news that Mr. Dussel tells the families? Check one. (**Summarize**)

❏ Conditions on the outside have become much worse.

❏ Conditions on the outside have improved.

❏ Conditions on the outside have stayed the same.

Even before Mr. Dussel's arrival, tension among family members has increased. What do you think will happen now that an additional person has joined the group? (**Predict**)

Moving On

You can check your prediction by reading the rest of the play—which consists of Scenes 4 and 5 of Act One and Act Two. If you have a copy of *The Language of Literature,* turn to page 476 for Act One, Scene 4. You can also find *The Diary of Anne Frank* by Frances Goodrich and Albert Hackett in most libraries.

knows the way to bring up children? Particularly the grown-ups that never had any. I keep wishing that Peter was a girl instead of a boy. Then I would have someone to talk to. Margot's a darling, but she takes everything too seriously. To pause for a moment on the subject of Mrs. Van Daan. I must tell you that her attempts to flirt with father are getting her nowhere. Pim, thank goodness, won't play.

(*As she is saying the last lines, the curtain rises on the darkened scene. Anne's voice fades out.*)

Active Reading SkillBuilder

Story Mapping

When you read a work of fiction, especially a long piece such as a play, creating a **story map** will help you keep track of elements of the story. As you read the first three scenes of Act One, complete a story map for each scene to show the characters, the setting, and the most important events.

Scene One

Characters: *Otto Frank, Miep Gies*	
Setting:	
Main Events:	

Scene Two

Characters:	
Setting:	
Main Events:	

Scene Three

Characters:	
Setting:	
Main Events:	

Literary Analysis SkillBuilder

Flashback

In a literary work, a **flashback** is an interruption of the action to present events that took place at an earlier time. In *The Diary of Anne Frank,* most of the action is presented as a flashback. As you read the play, look for clues that signal a flashback. These clues may be visual, such as a change in the setting or in the age of the characters. Sometimes music or other sound effects (auditory) introduce changes. Use the following chart to list the flashback clues.

Auditory
Anne's voice joins her father's as he reads her diary.

Flashback Clues

Visual

Dialogue

Words to Know SkillBuilder

Words to Know

conspicuous   indignantly   insufferable   loathe   vile

A. Write the letter of the best answer.

1. You would most likely respond **indignantly** if someone _____ .
   a. praised you   b. hired you   c. insulted you

2. Something is **conspicuous** if it is easy to _____ .
   a. get angry at   b. lose   c. see

3. If I **loathe** you, I _____ .
   a. hate you   b. love you   c. miss you

4. A person is **vile** if he or she is _____ .
   a. lovable   b. hateful   c. angry

5. An **insufferable** silence would be _____ .
   a. unbearable   b. pleasant   c. quiet

B. Complete each sentence with a Word to Know.

1. Anne and her family hated the _____ war; it was hateful and caused them endless suffering.

2. Sometimes Anne became irritated with Peter and thought that his behavior was _____ .

3. The door to the secret attic was not _____; it was carefully hidden.

4. Like Anne, I _____ war because of the suffering that it causes.

5. Anne often responded _____ when someone insulted her.

Before You Read

Connect to Your Life

Think of a time when you made an important decision. What were your choices? How did you finally make your decision? Use the following chart to describe the process.

Choices	How I Decided
Try out for the swim team or get an after-school job.	Talked with swimming coach and my parents. Talked with Heather, who baby-sits after school.

Key to the Story

WHAT YOU NEED TO KNOW
The unusual system of justice in this story brings to mind the gladiator games of ancient Rome. In a large arena known as the Colosseum, cheering crowds watched in horror and fascination as gladiators fought to the death or condemned criminals battled with wild animals.

In the Colosseum, chambers below the floor housed wild animals.

The Lady, or the Tiger?

BY FRANK R. STOCKTON

PREVIEW The story you are about to read takes place long ago in the time of the Roman Empire. A strange king uses a public arena to reward the innocent and punish the guilty. Life or death depends on one difficult decision.

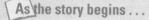

As the story begins . . .

- There is a mighty king who lives in an ancient time.

- The king has strong opinions and demands that everything be done his way.

WHAT DOES IT MEAN? *Fancy* means "imagination."

English Learner Support

Language

Figurative Language The words in lines 19–20 mean "correct problems."

Pause & Reflect

How does the king react to problems? **(Draw Conclusions)**

As the story begins . . .

- Under the king's system of justice, an accused person must open one of two doors in the public arena.

FOCUS

Read to find out about a king who lived long, long ago. The king is described as "semibarbaric," that is, somewhat crude and wild.

MARK IT UP As you read, underline words and phrases that tell you about the king. An example is highlighted.

In the very olden time, there lived a semibarbaric king, whose ideas, though somewhat polished and sharpened by the progressiveness of distant Latin neighbors,[1] were still large, florid, and untrammeled,[2] as became the half of him which was barbaric. He was a man of
10 exuberant fancy, and, withal, of an authority so irresistible that, at his will, he turned his varied fancies into facts. He was greatly given to self-communing; and, when he and himself agreed upon anything, the thing was done. When every member of his domestic and political systems moved smoothly in its appointed course, his nature was bland and genial; but whenever there was a little hitch and some of his orbs got out of their orbits, he was blander and more genial still, for nothing pleased him so much as to make the
20 crooked straight and crush down uneven places.

Pause & Reflect

FOCUS

The king has created an unusual system of justice. Read to find out how he decides if a person is guilty or innocent.

Among the borrowed notions by which his barbarism had become semifixed was that of the public arena, in which, by

---

1. **sharpened by the progressiveness . . . Latin neighbors:** more civilized, less wild, because of the influence of other peoples living in the Roman Empire.

2. **whose ideas . . . were still large, florid, and untrammeled:** ideas that were wild and not carefully thought through.

WORDS TO KNOW
   exuberant (ĭg-zōō'bər-ənt) *adj.* vigorous and unrestrained

exhibitions of manly and beastly <u>valor</u>, the minds of his subjects were refined and cultured.

But even here the exuberant and barbaric fancy <u>asserted</u> itself. The arena of the king was built, not to give the people an opportunity of hearing the rhapsodies of dying gladiators, nor to enable them to view the inevitable conclusion of a conflict between religious opinions and hungry jaws, but for purposes far better adapted to widen and develop the mental energies of the people. This vast amphitheater, with its encircling galleries, its mysterious vaults, and its unseen passages, was an agent of poetic justice,[3] in which crime was punished or virtue rewarded by the <u>decrees</u> of an impartial and incorruptible chance.

When a subject was accused of a crime of sufficient importance to interest the king, public notice was given that on an appointed day the fate of the accused person would be decided in the king's arena, a structure which well deserved its name. Although its form and plan were borrowed from afar, its purpose emanated solely from the brain of this man, who, every barleycorn a king,[4] knew no tradition to which he owed more allegiance than pleased his fancy and who ingrafted on every adopted form of human thought and action the rich growth of his barbaric idealism.

When all the people had assembled in the galleries and the king, surrounded by his court, sat high up on his throne of royal state on one side of the arena, he gave a signal, a door beneath him opened, and the

English Learner Support
Culture

Architecture Arenas or amphitheaters are round or oval open-roofed structures. Many people can sit in seats surrounding a center field or space.

English Learner Support
Vocabulary

Synonyms Another word for *chance* is *luck.* Luck, which cannot be controlled, decides the outcome of the king's trials.

WHAT DOES IT MEAN?
Emanated means "originated" or "came." *Ingrafted on* means "added to."

READING TIP If a difficult word is not footnoted, try to figure it out from context clues.

---

3. **poetic justice:** an outcome in which everyone gets what he or she deserves, with goodness being rewarded and evil being punished.

4. **every barleycorn a king:** a playful exaggeration of the expression "every inch a king," meaning "thoroughly kingly." (Grains of barley were formerly used as units of measurement.)

WORDS TO KNOW
valor (văl′ər) *n.* courage; bravery
assert (ə-sûrt′) *v.* to put forward in a forceful or insistent way
decree (dĭ-krē′) *n.* an official order

MARK IT UP Underline the words in the boxed text that describe what an accused person faces when he first enters the arena. **(Clarify)**

READING TIP Notice that the difficult words give the story a legal or royal tone. Focus on the words you already know in order to get the general meaning.

WHAT DOES IT MEAN?

Wended means "walked." *Merited so dire a fate* means "deserved such a terrible consequence."

READING CHECK What happens if the accused person already has a wife when he opens the door to the beautiful lady?

accused subject stepped out into the amphitheater. Directly opposite him, on the other side of the enclosed space, were two doors, exactly alike and side by side. It was the duty and the privilege of the person
60 on trial to walk directly to these doors and open one of them. He could open either door he pleased; he was subject to no guidance or influence but that of the aforementioned impartial and incorruptible chance. If he opened the one, there came out of it a hungry tiger, the fiercest and most cruel that could be <u>procured</u>, which immediately sprang upon him and tore him to pieces, as a punishment for his guilt. The moment that the case of the criminal was thus decided, <u>doleful</u> iron bells were clanged, great wails went up
70 from the hired mourners posted on the outer rim of the arena, and the vast audience, with bowed heads and downcast hearts, wended slowly their homeward way, mourning greatly that one so young and fair, or so old and respected, should have merited so dire a fate.

But if the accused person opened the other door, there came forth from it a lady, the most suitable to his years and station[5] that his majesty could select among his fair subjects; and to this lady he was immediately married, as a reward for his innocence. It
80 mattered not that he might already possess a wife and family or that his affections might be engaged upon an object of his own selection. The king allowed no such <u>subordinate</u> arrangements to interfere with his great scheme of <u>retribution</u> and reward. The exercises, as in the other instance, took place immediately and in the arena. Another door opened beneath the king, and a

---

5. **station:** social position; rank.

WORDS TO KNOW
procure (prō-kyŏŏr') *v.* to obtain; acquire
doleful (dōl'fəl) *adj.* sad; mournful
subordinate (sə-bôr'dn-ĭt) *adj.* less important or lower in rank; secondary
retribution (rĕt'rə-byōō'shən) *n.* punishment for bad behavior

priest, followed by a band of choristers and dancing maidens blowing joyous airs on golden horns and treading an epithalamic measure,[6] advanced to where
90 the pair stood, side by side, and the wedding was promptly and cheerily solemnized. Then the gay brass bells rang forth their merry peals, the people shouted glad hurrahs, and the innocent man, preceded by children strewing flowers on his path, led his bride to his home.

Pause & Reflect

FOCUS

The king and his people are very pleased with his system of justice. Read to find out why.

This was the king's semibarbaric method of administering justice. Its perfect fairness is obvious.
100 The criminal could not know out of which door would come the lady. He opened either he pleased, without having the slightest idea whether, in the next instant, he was to be devoured or married. On some occasions the tiger came out of one door and on some out of the other. The decisions of this tribunal[7] were not only fair, they were positively determinate.[8] The accused person was instantly punished if he found himself guilty, and, if innocent, he was rewarded on the spot, whether he liked it or
110 not. There was no escape from the judgments of the king's arena.

The institution was a very popular one. When the people gathered together on one of the great trial days, they never knew whether they were to witness a bloody slaughter or a hilarious wedding. This element

---

6. **treading an epithalamic** (ĕp′ə-thə-lăm′ĭk) **measure:** dancing to wedding music.

7. **tribunal** (trī-byōō′nəl): court of justice.

8. **determinate** (dĭ-tûr′mə-nĭt): final.

Pause & Reflect

What **questions** do you have at this point? Write one question in the space below. See if it is answered as you read.

📖 **As the story continues . . .**

- The spectators find the trials entertaining.

- People think the system is fair because the accused person chooses which door to open.

REREAD the boxed text. What conclusion would the king draw if the accused chose the tiger? What if he chose the lady? Complete the chart. **(Draw Conclusions)**

If	Then
the door of the tiger	he must be _____
the door of the lady	he must be _____

The system of justice is popular in the kingdom because people never know whether they will

witness a _____

or a _____.

(Summarize)

📄 **As the story continues . . .**

• The king discovers his daughter's love affair with a common man.

• The kingdom prepares for an important trial.

English Learner Support

Vocabulary

Idiom The words in lines 127–128 mean "his favorite."

MORE ABOUT . . .

(LOWNESS OF STATION) In societies like the Roman Empire, a person's social status was determined by several factors, including family background and wealth. Laws kept the classes separate from one another, often forbidding marriage between people in different classes.

of uncertainty lent an interest to the occasion which it could not otherwise have attained. Thus, the masses were entertained and pleased, and the thinking part of the community could bring no charge of unfairness
120 against this plan; for did not the accused person have the whole matter in his own hands?

Pause & Reflect

FOCUS

Read to find out what happens when the king learns that his daughter is in love.

▌▌ **MARK IT UP** ✎ As you read, circle details that help you get to know the king's daughter.

This semibarbaric king had a daughter as blooming as his most florid fancies and with a soul as fervent and <u>imperious</u> as his own. As is usual in such cases, she was the apple of his eye and was loved by him above all humanity.

130 Among his courtiers[9] was a young man of that fineness of blood and (lowness of station) common to the conventional heroes of romance who love royal maidens. This royal maiden was well satisfied with her lover, for he was handsome and brave to a degree unsurpassed in all this kingdom, and she loved him with an ardor that had enough of barbarism in it to make it exceedingly warm and strong. This love affair moved on happily for many months, until one day the king happened to discover its existence. He did not
140 hesitate nor waver in regard to his duty in the premises. The youth was immediately cast into prison, and a day was appointed for his trial in the king's arena. This, of course, was an especially important

9. **courtiers** (kôr′tē-ərz): royal attendants.

WORDS TO KNOW
imperious (ĭm-pîr′ē-əs) *adj.* proud; overbearing

occasion, and his majesty, as well as all the people, was greatly interested in the workings and development of this trial. Never before had such a case occurred; never before had a subject dared to love the daughter of a king. In after-years such things became commonplace enough, but then they were, in no slight

150 degree, novel and startling.

The tiger cages of the kingdom were searched for the most savage and relentless beasts, from which the fiercest monster might be selected for the arena, and the ranks of maiden youth and beauty throughout the land were carefully surveyed by competent judges, in order that the young man might have a fitting bride in case fate did not determine for him a different destiny. Of course, everybody knew that the deed with which the accused was charged had been done. He had loved

160 the princess, and neither he, she, nor anyone else thought of denying the fact, but the king would not think of allowing any fact of this kind to interfere with the workings of the tribunal, in which he took such great delight and satisfaction. No matter how the affair turned out, the youth would be disposed of, and the king would take an aesthetic pleasure in watching the course of events, which would determine whether or not the young man had done wrong in allowing himself to love the princess.

170 The appointed day arrived. From far and near the people gathered and thronged the great galleries of the arena, and crowds, unable to gain admittance, massed themselves against its outside walls. The king and his court were in their places opposite the twin doors— those fateful portals so terrible in their similarity.

All was ready. The signal was given. A door beneath the royal party opened, and the lover of the princess walked into the arena. Tall, beautiful, fair, his

WHAT DOES IT MEAN? *Novel* means "new" or "different."

WHAT DOES IT MEAN? *Tribunal* means "court."

 REREAD the boxed text. Why will the king be pleased no matter how the affair turns out? (Draw Conclusions)

 READING CHECK What will the trial of the young man decide?

Check the words below that describe ways in which the princess and the king are alike. (Compare and Contrast)

❏ proud
❏ kind and merciful
❏ semibarbaric
❏ gentle

As the story continues . . .

- The young man enters the arena.
- He looks at the princess and their eyes meet.

English Learner Support

Vocabulary

Multiple Meanings In line 200, *possessed of* means "having." In line 203, the phrase in blue means "she had learned."

MARK IT UP > Reread the boxed text. Underline the words that explain what the princess has found out. (Clarify)

appearance was greeted with a low hum of admiration
180 and anxiety. Half the audience had not known so grand a youth had lived among them. No wonder the princess loved him! What a terrible thing for him to be there!

Pause & Reflect

FOCUS

The youth is about to meet his fate. His eyes are on the princess. Read to find out what she alone knows.

As the youth advanced into the arena, he turned, as the custom was, to bow to the king, but he did not think at all of that royal personage; his eyes were fixed upon the
190 princess who sat to the right of her father. Had it not been for the moiety[10] of barbarism in her nature, it is probable that lady would not have been there, but her intense and fervid soul would not allow her to be absent on an occasion in which she was so terribly interested.

From the moment that the decree had gone forth, that her lover should decide his fate in the king's arena, she had thought of nothing, night or day, but this great event and the various subjects connected
200 with it. Possessed of more power, influence, and force of character than anyone who had ever before been interested in such a case, she had done what no other person had done—she had possessed herself of the secret of the doors. She knew in which of the two rooms that lay behind those doors stood the cage of the tiger, with its open front, and in which waited the lady. Through these thick doors, heavily curtained with skins on the inside, it was impossible that any

---

10. **moiety** (moi′ĭ-tē): half; portion.

noise or suggestion should come from within to the person who should approach to raise the latch of one of them; but gold and the power of a woman's will had brought the secret to the princess.

And not only did she know in which room stood the lady ready to emerge, all blushing and radiant, should her door be opened, but she knew who the lady was. It was one of the fairest and loveliest of the damsels[11] of the court who had been selected as the reward of the accused youth should he be proved innocent of the crime of aspiring to one so far above him, and the princess hated her. Often had she seen, or imagined that she had seen, this fair creature throwing glances of admiration upon the person of her lover, and sometimes she thought these glances were perceived and even returned. Now and then she had seen them talking together; it was but for a moment or two, but much can be said in a brief space. It may have been on most unimportant topics, but how could she know that? The girl was lovely, but she had dared to raise her eyes to the loved one of the princess; and, with all the intensity of the savage blood transmitted to her through long lines of wholly barbaric ancestors, she hated the woman who blushed and trembled behind that silent door.

When her lover turned and looked at her, and his eyes met hers as she sat there paler and whiter than anyone in the vast ocean of anxious faces about her, he saw, by that power of quick perception which is given to those whose souls are one, that she knew behind which door crouched the tiger and behind which stood the lady. He had expected her to know it. He understood her nature, and his soul was assured that she would never rest until she had made plain to herself this thing, hidden to all other lookers-on, even

---

11. **damsels** (dăm'zəlz): young women; maidens.

English Learner Support
Vocabulary

Idiom To *throw a glance* is to look quickly and then look away.

REREAD the boxed text. Why does the princess hate the woman behind the door? **(Infer)**

WHAT DOES IT MEAN? The words in blue mean "the savage qualities the princess has inherited from her family."

READING CHECK Is the young man surprised that the princess knows the secret of the doors? Why or why not?

Which phrase below describes the princess? Check one. **(Evaluate)**

❏ jealous and quick to anger
❏ calm and just

As the story ends . . .

- The princess quickly points to the door on the right.
- Her lover opens the door.

 the boxed text. Judging from the young man's actions, which of the following can you infer? Circle one. **(Infer)**

He doubts the princess.

He loves the lady behind the door.

He trusts the princess.

He knows the king will save him.

to the king. The only hope for the youth in which there was any element of certainty was based upon the success of the princess in discovering this mystery, and the moment he looked upon her, he saw she had succeeded, as in his soul he knew she would succeed.

Pause & Reflect

FOCUS

The princess knows what is behind each door. Will she save the young man's life or let the tiger eat him?

250 Then it was that his quick and anxious glance asked the question: "Which?" It was as plain to her as if he shouted it from where he stood. There was not an instant to be lost. The question was asked in a flash; it must be answered in another.

Her right arm lay on the cushioned parapet[12] before her. She raised her hand and made a slight, quick movement toward the right. No one but her lover saw 260 her. Every eye but his was fixed on the man in the arena.

He turned, and with a firm and rapid step he walked across the empty space. Every heart stopped beating, every breath was held, every eye was fixed immovably upon that man. Without the slightest hesitation, he went to the door on the right and opened it.

Now, the point of the story is this: Did the tiger come out of that door, or did the lady?

270 The more we reflect upon this question, the harder it is to answer. It involves a study of the human heart which leads us through devious mazes of passion, out

---

12. **parapet** (păr′ə-pĭt): a low wall or railing along the edge of a roof or balcony.

of which it is difficult to find our way. Think of it, fair reader, not as if the decision of the question depended upon yourself, but upon that hot-blooded, semibarbaric princess, her soul at a white heat beneath the combined fires of despair and jealousy. She had lost him, but who should have him?

280 How often, in her waking hours and in her dreams, had she started in wild horror and covered her face with her hands as she thought of her lover opening the door on the other side of which waited the cruel fangs of the tiger!

But how much oftener had she seen him at the other door! How in her grievous reveries[13] had she gnashed her teeth and torn her hair, when she saw his start of rapturous[14] delight as he opened the door of the lady! How her soul had burned in agony when she had seen him rush to meet that woman, with her flushing cheek 290 and sparkling eye of triumph; when she had seen him lead her forth, his whole frame kindled with the joy of recovered life; when she had heard the glad shouts from the multitude, and the wild ringing of the happy bells; when she had seen the priest, with his joyous followers, advance to the couple and make them man and wife before her very eyes; and when she had seen them walk away together upon their path of flowers, followed by the tremendous shouts of the hilarious multitude, in which her one despairing shriek was lost 300 and drowned!

Would it not be better for him to die at once and go to wait for her in the blessed regions of semibarbaric futurity?

And yet, that awful tiger, those shrieks, that blood!

Her decision had been indicated in an instant, but it had been made after days and nights of anguished

READING TIP The princess has faced a difficult decision. Use the chart below to record reasons she might want to send her lover to the lady and reasons she might want to send him to the tiger.

It would be best to send him to the LADY because

It would be best to send him to the TIGER because

---

13. **reveries** (rĕv′ər-ēz): daydreams.

14. **rapturous** (răp′chər-əs): filled with great pleasure.

Pause & Reflect

1. Which do you think came
out—the lady or the tiger?
Why? **(Draw Conclusions)**

I think the

came out, because

2. Were any of your **questions**
about the story answered?
If so, write the answer.
If not, write another
question.

Do you think it is
fair for the author
to end the story
the way he did? Why or why
not? Discuss your answer in a
small group. **(Evaluate)**

deliberation. She had known she would be asked, she
had decided what she would answer, and, without the
slightest hesitation, she had moved her hand to the
310 right.

The question of her decision is one not to be lightly
considered, and it is not for me to presume to set
myself up as the one person able to answer it. And so I
leave it with all of you: Which came out of the opened
door—the lady, or the tiger? ❖

Pause & Reflect

MARK IT UP In the space below, draw a picture of
which creature you think comes out. **(Visualize)**

Active Reading SkillBuilder

Drawing Conclusions

When you **draw conclusions,** you combine clues from a text with information from your own experiences to figure out something that is not directly stated. In this story, you have to draw some conclusions about the princess. Complete the following chart. Your conclusion should state the decision you think the princess makes based on the information in your chart.

Stated Facts She was beautiful, but had a "fervent and imperious" soul.
Inferred Facts She was obsessed with jealousy about her lover.
My Knowledge Princesses are often spoiled and used to getting their own way.
Conclusion (What the Princess Decides)

Literary Analysis SkillBuilder

Surprise Ending

In this story, the author builds suspense as the ending nears. We aren't sure whether the princess will tell the man to choose the door with the tiger or the one with the lady. However, the actual ending is a **surprise ending,** because the author leaves this decision up to the reader. There are many clues given in the story to sway the reader one way or the other. Complete the chart below to help you think about the possible endings of the story.

Clues to Surprise Ending	
Clues Leading to the Lady's Door	**Clues Leading to the Tiger's Door**
The princess was very happy with her young man.	The princess is as proud and spoiled as her father.

Words to Know SkillBuilder

Words to Know

assert	destiny	exuberant	procure	subordinate
decree	doleful	imperious	retribution	valor

A. Decide which Word to Know belongs in each numbered blank. Then write the word on the corresponding line on the right.

In her (1) way, without humility,

The princess chose a boyfriend who lacked nobility.

She knew her father would object, but felt it was her (2)

To love this man, and so she did, and never would have guessed any

Tragic ending would result. Her love was handsome and full of (3),

Unlike so many princes, with their royal, sickly pallor.

The girl would not acknowledge that she was (4)

To the will of any other, and she would not budge one bit.

But while the princess did (5) her right to choose her mate,

When her father learned what she had done, he planned a different fate.

The king was very angry and he made a harsh (6).

The poor young man was caught before he had a chance to flee.

Now the princess felt so (7)—so gloomy and so sad—

That she worked to find an answer that would save her favorite lad.

She did (8) the information that could turn the big event

From a tiger's bloody dinner to a dance (9).

Finally arrived the day for the young man's (10).

What took place in the arena? That's the reader's contribution!

_____ (1)

_____ (2)

_____ (3)

_____ (4)

_____ (5)

_____ (6)

_____ (7)

_____ (8)

_____ (9)

_____ (10)

Before You Read

Connect to Your Life

What do you think makes a good horror story? Is it an evil character, a creepy mood, or a surprise ending? Write your ideas below.

> A good horror story should
>
> 1. be filled with suspense.
>
> 2.
>
> 3.
>
> 4.
>
> 5.

Key to the Story

WHAT TO LISTEN FOR Here is how the narrator of "The Tell-Tale Heart" introduces himself:

True!—nervous—very, very dreadfully nervous I had been and am! but why will you say that I am mad?

Read the lines aloud a few times. As you read, notice that the narrator's voice sounds jumpy and unsteady, while claiming to be sane. The dashes and short phrases add to the jittery tone. Think about an extremely nervous person. What words and phrases might describe such a person? Write the words and phrases in the space below.

A nervous person is_____.

The Tell-Tale Heart

PREVIEW Edgar Allan Poe wrote horror stories. "The Tell-Tale Heart" is one of his best. In "The Tell-Tale Heart" the narrator tells you what happened when he tried to commit the perfect crime.

- The narrator says that he is nervous but not crazy.
- The narrator is disturbed by an old man's eye.
- The narrator thinks of a plan.

English Learner Support

Punctuation Note the dashes (—) in blue. A dash is used to show a sudden stop or change in a sentence. The dashes on this page also show the narrator's nervousness and excitement.

English Learner Support

Idiom *My blood ran cold* means the narrator felt great fear.

Pause & Reflect

What does the narrator decide to do? Why does he decide to do it? (Cause and Effect)

He decides to

because

FOCUS
The narrator of this story wants you to believe that he is sane. Is he?

MARK IT UP As you read, underline details that reveal the narrator's state of mind. An example is highlighted.

True!—nervous—very, very dreadfully nervous I had been and am! but why *will* you say that I am mad? The disease had sharpened my senses—not destroyed—not dulled them. Above all was the sense of hearing acute. I
10 heard all things in the heaven and in the earth. I heard many things in hell. How, then, am I mad? Hearken![1] and observe how healthily—how calmly I can tell you the whole story.

It is impossible to say how first the idea entered my brain; but once conceived, it haunted me day and night. Object there was none. Passion there was none. I loved the old man. He had never wronged me. He had never given me insult. For his gold I had no desire. I think it was his eye! yes, it was this! He had the eye of a vulture—a pale blue eye, with a film over
20 it. Whenever it fell upon me, my blood ran cold; and so by degrees—very gradually—I made up my mind to take the life of the old man, and thus rid myself of the eye forever.

Now this is the point. You fancy me mad. Madmen know nothing. But you should have seen *me*. You should have seen how wisely I proceeded—with what caution—with what foresight—with what dissimulation[2] I went to work!

Pause & Reflect

---

1. **Hearken** (här′kən): pay close attention to.
2. **dissimulation:** a hiding of one's true feelings.

WORDS TO KNOW
acute (ə-kyo͞ot′) *adj.* sharp; keen
conceived (kən-sēvd′) *adj.* thought of **conceive** *v.*

FOCUS

Read to find out what the narrator does at midnight for seven nights and what happens on the eighth night.

MARK IT UP As you read, circle details that tell you about the narrator's actions.

I was never kinder to the
30 old man than during the
whole week before I killed
him. And every night, about
midnight, I turned the latch of
his door and opened it—oh,
so gently! And then, when I
had made an opening
sufficient for my head, I put
in a dark lantern, all closed, closed, so that no light
shone out, and then I thrust in my head. Oh, you
40 would have laughed to see how cunningly I thrust it
in! I moved it slowly—very, very slowly, so that I
might not disturb the old man's sleep. It took me an
hour to place my whole head within the opening so far
that I could see him as he lay upon his bed. Ha!—
would a madman have been so wise as this? And then,
when my head was well in the room, I undid the
lantern cautiously—oh, so cautiously—cautiously (for
the hinges creaked)—I undid it just so much that a
single thin ray fell upon the vulture eye. And this I did
50 for seven long nights—every night just at midnight—
but I found the eye always closed; and so it was
impossible to do the work; for it was not the old man
who <u>vexed</u> me, but his Evil Eye. And every morning,
when the day broke, I went boldly into the chamber,
and spoke courageously to him, calling him by name
in a hearty tone, and inquiring how he had passed the
night. So you see he would have been a very profound[3]
old man, indeed, to suspect that every night, just at
twelve, I looked in upon him while he slept.

---

3. **profound:** having great knowledge.

WORDS TO KNOW
vex (věks) *v.* to disturb; to annoy

As the story continues . . .

- For seven nights, the narrator tries to carry out his plan.

- He does not succeed because the old man's eye remains closed.

REREAD the boxed text. What does the narrator do for seven nights? **(Clarify)**

MORE ABOUT . . .

EVIL EYE Many cultures believed that someone with an evil eye could harm others simply by looking at them.

English Learner Support
Vocabulary

Idiom *Passed the night* means "slept."

READING CHECK How does the narrator act toward the old man each morning?

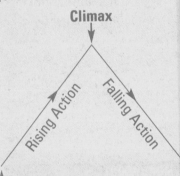

60   Upon the eighth night I was more than usually cautious in opening the door. A watch's minute hand moves more quickly than did mine. Never before that night had I *felt* the extent of my own powers—of my sagacity.[4] I could scarcely contain my feelings of triumph. To think that there I was, opening the door, little by little, and he not even to dream of my secret deeds or thoughts. I fairly chuckled at the idea; and perhaps he heard me; for he moved on the bed suddenly, as if startled. Now you may think that I

70 drew back—but no. His room was as black as pitch with the thick darkness (for the shutters were close fastened, through fear of robbers), and so I knew that he could not see the opening of the door, and I kept pushing it on steadily, steadily.

>   I had my head in, and was about to open the lantern, when my thumb slipped upon the tin fastening, and the old man sprang up in the bed, crying out—"Who's there?"

  I kept quite still and said nothing. For a whole hour
80 I did not move a muscle, and in the meantime I did not hear him lie down. He was still sitting up in the bed listening—just as I have done, night after night, hearkening to the death watches[5] in the wall.

  Presently I heard a slight groan, and I knew it was the groan of mortal terror. It was not a groan of pain or grief—oh, no!—it was the low, <u>stifled</u> sound that arises from the bottom of the soul when overcharged with awe. I knew the sound well. Many a night, just at midnight, when all the world slept, it has welled up from

---

4. **sagacity:** sound judgment; intelligence.

5. **death watches:** deathwatch beetles—wood-burrowing insects that make a tapping sound with their heads.

WORDS TO KNOW
stifled (stī′fəld) *adj.* smothered **stifle** *v.*

90 my own bosom, deepening, with its dreadful echo, the
terrors that distracted me. I say I knew it well. I knew
what the old man felt, and pitied him, although I
chuckled at heart. I knew that he had been lying awake
ever since the first slight noise, when he had turned in
the bed. His fears had been ever since growing upon him.
He had been trying to fancy them causeless, but could
not. He had been saying to himself—"It is nothing but
the wind in the chimney—it is only a mouse crossing the
floor," or "it is merely a cricket which has made a single
100 chirp." Yes, he has been trying to comfort himself with
these suppositions; but he had found all in vain.

All in vain; because Death, in approaching him, had
stalked with his black shadow before him, and
enveloped the victim. And it was the mournful influence
of the unperceived shadow that caused him to *feel*—
although he neither saw nor heard—to feel the presence
of my head within the room.

Pause & Reflect

FOCUS

The old man senses that
someone is in his room.
What does the narrator
hear in the dark?

When I had waited a long
time, very patiently, without
110 hearing him lie down, I
resolved to open a little—a
very, very little <u>crevice</u> in the
lantern. So I opened it—you cannot imagine how
<u>stealthily</u>, stealthily—until, at length, a single dim ray,
like the thread of the spider, shot from out the crevice
and fell full upon the vulture eye.

WORDS TO KNOW
crevice (krĕv'ĭs) *n.* a crack
stealthily (stĕl'thĭ-lē) *adv.* cautiously; secretly

English Learner Support
Language

Word Parts The words
dreadful and *causeless* are
made up of these parts:

dread (fear) +
ful (full of) =
dreadful (full of
fear)

cause + less
(without) = causeless
(without cause)

WHAT DOES IT MEAN? *All in
vain* means that it was all
useless or no good.
Enveloped means
"surrounded."

Pause & Reflect

MARK IT UP Reread
the boxed text on this
page. Underline all the
"suppositions" or ideas that
the narrator imagines the old
man has. (Clarify)

As the story continues...

• The narrator becomes
furious at the sight of the
old man's eye.

• He hears a sound that
bothers him.

It was open—wide, wide open—and I grew furious as I gazed upon it. I saw it with perfect distinctness—all a dull blue, with a hideous veil over it that chilled the
120 very marrow in my bones; but I could see nothing else of the old man's face or person: for I had directed the ray as if by instinct, precisely upon the damned spot.

And now have I not told you that what you mistake for madness is but over-acuteness of the senses?—now, I say, there came to my ears a low, dull, quick sound, such as a watch makes when enveloped in cotton. I knew *that* sound well too. It was the beating of the old man's heart. It increased my fury, as the beating of a drum stimulates the soldier into courage.

130 But even yet I refrained and kept still. I scarcely breathed. I held the lantern motionless. I tried how steadily I could maintain the ray upon the eye. Meantime the hellish tattoo[6] of the heart increased. It grew quicker and quicker, and louder and louder every instant. The old man's terror *must* have been extreme! It grew louder, I say, louder every moment!—do you mark me well? I have told you that I am nervous: so I am. And now at the dead hour of the night, amid the dreadful silence of that old house, so strange a noise
140 as this excited me to uncontrollable terror. Yet, for some minutes longer I refrained and stood still. But the beating grew louder, louder! I thought the heart must burst. And now a new anxiety seized me—the sound would be heard by a neighbor! The old man's hour had come! With a loud yell, I threw open the lantern and leaped into the room. He shrieked once— once only. In an instant I dragged him to the floor, and pulled the heavy bed over him. I then smiled gaily, to find the deed so far done. But, for many minutes, the

---

6. **hellish tattoo:** awful drumming.

150 heart beat on with a muffled sound. This, however, did not vex me; it would not be heard through the wall. At length it ceased. The old man was dead. I removed the bed and examined the corpse. Yes, he was stone, stone dead. I placed my hand upon the heart and held it there many minutes. There was no pulsation. He was stone dead. His eye would trouble me no more.

Pause & Reflect

FOCUS

Read to find out what the narrator does with the dead man's body and how he reacts to the police officers.

If still you think me mad, you will think so no longer when I describe the wise
160 precautions I took for the concealment[7] of the body. The night waned,[8] and I worked hastily, but in silence. First of all I dismembered[9] the corpse. I cut off the head and the arms and the legs.

I then took up three planks from the flooring of the chamber, and deposited all between the scantlings.[10] I then replaced the boards so cleverly, so cunningly, that no human eye—not even *his*—could have detected anything wrong. There was nothing to wash out—no
170 stain of any kind—no blood-spot whatever. I had been too wary for that. A tub had caught all—ha! ha!

When I made an end of these labors, it was four o'clock—still dark as midnight. As the bell sounded the hour, there came a knocking at the street door. I went down to open it with a light heart,—for what had I *now* to fear? There entered three men, who

---

7. **concealment:** hiding.

8. **waned:** approached its end.

9. **dismembered:** cut to pieces.

10. **scantlings:** small wooden beams supporting the floor.

English Learner Support

Vocabulary

Stone Used as an adjective, *stone* means "completely."

Pause & Reflect

MARK IT UP To what two things does the narrator compare the beating of the old man's heart? Circle the answers on page 252.

As the story continues . . .

• The narrator hides the evidence of his crime.

• Three police officers arrive to search the house.

REREAD the boxed text. Do you agree with the narrator that his actions are those of a sane man? Why or why not? (Evaluate)

WHAT DOES IT MEAN? *Wary* is another word for careful. *Light heart* means "a carefree or fearless feeling."

Pause & Reflect

1. What does the narrator do with the dead body? (Summarize)

2. What does the narrator do when the police officers come to the house? (Clarify)

As the story ends . . .

- The narrator becomes more and more upset by a noise he hears in the room.
- He thinks the police are pretending to ignore the sound.

introduced themselves, with perfect suavity,[11] as officers of the police. A shriek had been heard by a neighbor during the night: suspicion of foul play had 180 been aroused; information had been lodged at the police office, and they (the officers) had been deputed[12] to search the premises.

I smiled,—for *what* had I to fear? I bade the gentlemen welcome. The shriek, I said, was my own in a dream. The old man, I mentioned, was absent in the country. I took my visitors all over the house. I bade them search—search *well*. I led them, at length, to *his* chamber. I showed them his treasures, secure, undisturbed. In the enthusiasm of my confidence, I 190 brought chairs into the room, and desired them *here* to rest from their fatigues,[13] while I myself, in the wild <u>audacity</u> of my perfect triumph, placed my own seat upon the very spot beneath which reposed[14] the corpse of the victim.

Pause & Reflect

FOCUS

Read to find out what happens to the narrator at the end of the story.

The officers were satisfied. My *manner* had convinced them. I was singularly at ease. They sat, and while I answered cheerily, they chatted of familiar things. But, ere long, I 200 felt myself getting pale and wished them gone. My head ached, and I fancied a ringing in my ears: but still they

---

11. **suavity** (swäv′ĭ-tē): smooth courteousness.

12. **deputed**: chosen.

13. **fatigues** (fǝ-tēgz′): hard work, labor.

14. **reposed**: rested.

WORDS TO KNOW
   audacity (ô-dăs′ĭ-tē) *n.* shameless daring or boldness

sat and still chatted. The ringing became more distinct:—it continued and became more distinct; I talked more freely to get rid of the feeling: but it continued and gained definitiveness—until, at length, I found that the noise was *not* within my ears.

No doubt I now grew *very* pale;—but I talked more fluently,[15] and with a heightened voice. Yet the sound increased—and what could I do? It was *a low, dull,*
210 *quick sound—much such a sound as a watch makes when enveloped in cotton.* I gasped for breath—and yet the officers heard it not. I talked more quickly— more <u>vehemently</u>; but the noise steadily increased. I arose and argued about trifles,[16] in a high key and with violent gesticulations,[17] but the noise steadily increased. Why *would* they not be gone? I paced the floor to and fro with heavy strides, as if excited to fury by the observations of the men—but the noise steadily increased. What *could* I do? I foamed—I raved—I
220 swore. I swung the chair upon which I had been sitting, and grated it upon the boards, but the noise arose over all and continually increased. It grew louder—louder—*louder!* And still the men chatted pleasantly, and smiled. Was it possible they heard not? Almighty God!—no, no! They heard!—they suspected!—they *knew!*—they were making a *mockery* of my horror!—this I thought, and this I think. But any thing was better than this agony! Any thing was more tolerable than this <u>derision</u>! I could bear those

READ ALOUD As you read this passage aloud, try to express the narrator's mood. Circle the word below that describes the narrator's behavior as the noise increases. **(Draw Conclusions)**

calm

frantic

thoughtful

READING TIP Be sure to complete your plot diagram with details of the story's ending.

---

15. **fluently** (flōo′ənt-lē) smoothly, without effort.

16. **trifles** (trī′fəlz): unimportant matters.

17. **gesticulations** (jĕ-stĭk′yə-lā′shənz): energetic gestures of the hands or arms.

WORDS TO KNOW
vehemently (vē′ə-mənt-lē) *adv.* with intense emotion
derision (dĭ-rĭzh′ən) *n.* ridicule

hypocritical smiles no longer! I felt that I must scream or die—and now—again!—hark! louder! louder!! *louder!*—

"Villains!" I shrieked, "dissemble[18] no more! I admit the deed!—tear up the planks—here, here!—it is the beating of his hideous heart!" ❖

Pause & Reflect

Pause & Reflect

1. How does the story end? Check one. **(Clarify)**

❑ The narrator confesses because he thinks that the police can hear the beating of the old man's heart.

❑ The police dig up the body and accuse the narrator of murder.

❑ The narrator gets away with the murder.

2. Why do you think the narrator hears the beating of the old man's heart after the old man is dead? **(Infer)**

_____

_____

_____

_____

CHALLENGE What might have happened if the narrator had not confessed to the police? Would he have gotten away with his crime? Would he have run away? Discuss your answer with a partner. **(Analyze)**

✏️ **MARK IT UP** ⟩ The narrator compares the beating of the heart to many things. Which comparison is most chilling? Draw it here. Write the words from the story beneath your sketch.

---

18. **dissemble:** pretend.

WORDS TO KNOW
hypocritical (hĭp′ə-krĭt′ĭ-kəl) *adj.* false or deceptive, like a person who is pretending to be what he or she is not

Active Reading SkillBuilder

Visualizing

The process of forming a mental picture based on a written description is called **visualizing.** Readers use details of sight, sound, touch, taste, and smell to visualize characters, settings, and events. In the chart below, write details from the text of "The Tell-Tale Heart" that help you form mental images of the narrator, the old man, and the setting. Then draw or describe your visualization of each one.

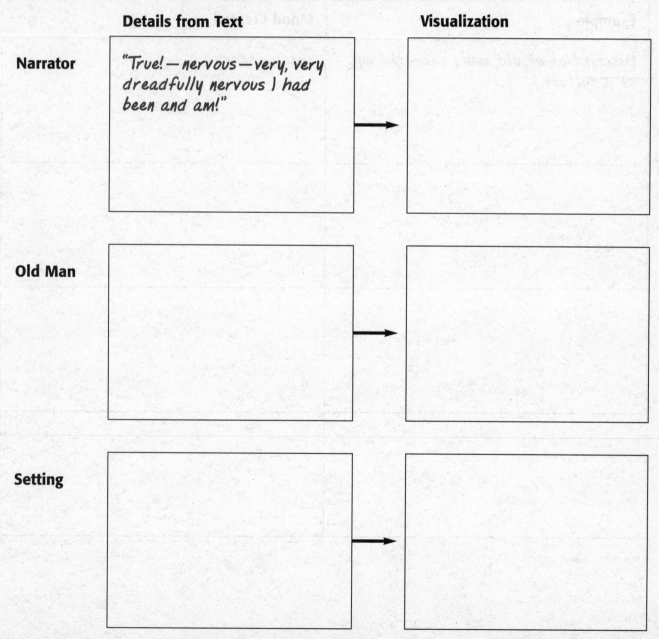

	Details from Text	**Visualization**
Narrator	"True!—nervous—very, very dreadfully nervous I had been and am!"	
Old Man		
Setting		

Literary Analysis SkillBuilder

Mood

Mood is the feeling that a story conveys to its readers. Descriptive words and phrases contribute to the mood of a work. Complete the chart below with examples from the text that help create different moods. Look for descriptive words, interesting sentence structures, and intriguing plot twists. Identify the mood created by each example.

Example	Mood Created
Description of old man's eye—the eye of a vulture	creepy, scary

Words to Know SkillBuilder

Words to Know

acute	conceived	derision	stealthily	vehemently
audacity	crevice	hypocritical	stifled	vex

A. Fill in each blank with the correct Word to Know.

1. Your ability to be bold is your capacity for _____.

2. A goal must be imagined in the mind before it can be met; that is, it must be _____ to be achieved.

3. A crook who ran for office using a "Get tough on crime" campaign slogan would be both political and _____.

4. A bloodhound, which can follow a scent that's ten days old, might be said to have an amazingly _____ snoot.

5. If you do something just to annoy a former sweetheart, you are trying to _____ your ex.

B. Fill in each set of blanks with the correct Word to Know. The boxed letters will spell out what bothered the narrator about the old man.

1. In sneakers, you can move this way. __ __ __ __ __ __ [ ] __ __ __

2. This could be a crack or a canyon. __ __ __ __ [ ] __ __

3. A snicker is this kind of laugh. [ ] __ __ __ __ __ __

4. Screams are uttered this way. __ __ __ [ ] __ __ __ __ [ ]

5. Scornful laughter expresses this. __ [ ] __ __ __ __ __

Before You Read

Connect to Your Life

Have you ever wanted to change an event or a situation in your life? In the chart below, describe what you would like to change and how this change might affect your life.

Event or situation that I would like to change:	How this change might affect my life:

Key to the Story

WHAT'S THE BIG IDEA? Have you ever read a horror story or seen a horror film? Think of some scary movies that you have seen. List the names of these movies in the chart below and explain what made each movie so scary.

Title of Movie	What Made the Movie Scary?

The MONKEY'S PAW

by W. W. Jacobs

PREVIEW The story you are about to read is a classic horror story. It may send chills down your spine. It may also make you think about how much control people have over their lives.

- The Whites are spending an evening at home on a rainy night.
- Father and son are playing chess, and Mrs. White is knitting by the fire.

English Learner Support

Vocabulary

Context Clues Find context clues that help you understand that *without* means "outside" and *hark at* means "listen to."

MORE ABOUT . . .

CHESS The object of the game of chess is to trap the opponent's king. When a player says "check," it signals that the opponent's king is in danger of being captured. When the player says "checkmate" or "mate," it signals that the opponent's king is trapped and the game is over.

WHAT DOES IT MEAN?

Bawled means "shouted."

 REREAD the boxed text. Underline the words and phrases that help you **visualize** the Whites' neighborhood.

FOCUS

One rainy night, Mr. and Mrs. White and their son are at home, waiting for a visitor. Read to find out about this family.

MARK IT UP As you read, underline details that help you visualize the White family. An example is highlighted.

Without, the night was cold and wet, but in the small parlor of Laburnum Villa the blinds were drawn and the fire burned brightly. Father and son were at chess; the former, who possessed ideas about the game involving radical changes, putting his king into such sharp
10 and unnecessary perils that it even provoked comment from the white-haired old lady knitting placidly by the fire.

"Hark at the wind," said Mr. White, who, having seen a fatal mistake after it was too late, was amiably desirous[1] of preventing his son from seeing it.

"I'm listening," said the latter, grimly surveying the board as he stretched out his hand. "Check."

"I should hardly think that he'd come tonight," said his father, with his hand poised over the board.
20 "Mate," replied the son.

"That's the worst of living so far out," bawled Mr. White, with sudden and unlooked-for violence; "of all the beastly, slushy, out-of-the-way places to live in, this is the worst. Pathway's a bog,[2] and the road's a torrent.[3] I don't know what people are thinking about. I suppose because only two houses in the road are let,[4] they think it doesn't matter."

"Never mind, dear," said his wife soothingly; "perhaps you'll win the next one."

---

1. **amiably desirous:** hoping in a pleasant, friendly way.

2. **bog:** swamp.

3. **torrent** (tôr′ənt): swift-flowing stream.

4. **let:** rented.

WORDS TO KNOW

peril (pĕr′əl) *n.* danger

surveying (sər-vā′ ĭng) *adj.* looking over carefully; inspecting **survey** *v.*

30 Mr. White looked up sharply, just in time to intercept[5] a knowing glance between mother and son. The words died away on his lips, and he hid a guilty grin in his thin gray beard.

"There he is," said Herbert White, as the gate banged loudly and heavy footsteps came toward the door.

Pause & Reflect

The White family lives in a neighborhood that is _____. (Check one.) **(Clarify)**

❏ lively and busy

❏ incredibly rich

❏ isolated and lonely

FOCUS

The visitor arrives. Read to find out about him and the strange object he has with him.

MARK IT UP As you read, underline details that tell you about this object.

The old man rose with hospitable haste, and opening the door, was heard condoling[6] with the new arrival. The new 40 arrival also condoled with himself, so that Mrs. White said, "Tut, tut!" and coughed gently as her husband entered the room, followed by a tall, burly man, beady of eye and rubicund of visage.[7]

"Sergeant-Major Morris," he said, introducing him.

The sergeant-major shook hands, and taking the proffered seat by the fire, watched contentedly while his host brought out drinks and stood a small copper 50 kettle on the fire.

He began to talk, the little family circle regarding with eager interest this visitor from distant parts, as he squared his broad shoulders in the chair and spoke of wild scenes and doughty[8] deeds; of wars and plagues and strange peoples.

As the story continues . . .

• Sergeant-Major Morris arrives.

• He tells the Whites about his travels and explains the magical power of the object he has brought.

WHAT DOES IT MEAN?

Hospitable haste means "in a hurry to welcome someone." Someone who is *burly* is big and strong-looking. *Proffered* means "offered."

---

5. **intercept** (ĭn′ tər-sĕpt′): catch.

6. **condoling** (kən-dō′lĭng): expressing sympathy (in this case, about the visitor's journey through bad weather).

7. **rubicund** (rōō′bĭ-kənd) **of visage** (vĭz′ĭj): with a red face.

8. **doughty** (dou′tē): brave.

WHAT DOES IT MEAN? *Slip of a youth* means a small, thin young person.

English Learner Support
Language

Dialect Mrs. White's incorrect use of *don't* instead of *doesn't* was the way many people spoke at the time of the story.

MORE ABOUT . . .

FAKIRS This term has come to refer to Hindu holy men who have special powers, such as the ability to walk over fire.

WHAT DOES IT MEAN?

Off-handedly means "casually" or "informally."

What does the paw look like?

"Twenty-one years of it," said Mr. White, nodding at his wife and son. "When he went away, he was a slip of a youth in the warehouse. Now look at him."

"He don't look to have taken much harm," said
60 Mrs. White politely.

"I'd like to go to India myself," said the old man, "just to look round a bit, you know."

"Better where you are," said the sergeant-major, shaking his head. He put down the empty glass, and sighing softly, shook it again.

"I should like to see those old temples and fakirs[9] and jugglers," said the old man. "What was that you started telling me the other day about a monkey's paw or something, Morris?"

70 "Nothing," said the soldier hastily. "Leastways nothing worth hearing."

"Monkey's paw?" said Mrs. White curiously.

"Well, it's just a bit of what you might call magic, perhaps," said the sergeant-major off-handedly.

His three listeners leaned forward eagerly. The visitor absent-mindedly put his empty glass to his lips and then set it down again. His host filled it for him.

"To look at," said the sergeant-major, fumbling in his pocket, "it's just an ordinary little paw, dried to a
80 mummy."

He took something out of his pocket and proffered it. Mrs. White drew back with a grimace, but her son, taking it, examined it curiously.

"And what is there special about it?" inquired Mr. White as he took it from his son, and having examined it, placed it upon the table.

---

9. **fakir** (fə-kîr′): Hindu holy man.

WORDS TO KNOW
grimace (grĭm′ ĭs) *n.* a facial expression of pain or disgust

"It had a spell put on it by an old fakir," said the sergeant-major, "a very holy man. He wanted to show that <u>fate</u> ruled people's lives, and that those who interfered with it did so to their sorrow. He put a spell on it so that three separate men could each have three wishes from it."

His manner was so impressive that his hearers were conscious that their light laughter jarred somewhat.

"Well, why don't you have three, sir?" said Herbert White cleverly.

The soldier regarded him in the way that middle age is wont to regard presumptuous youth.[10] "I have," he said quietly, and his blotchy face whitened.

"And did you really have the three wishes granted?" asked Mrs. White.

"I did," said the sergeant-major, and his glass tapped against his strong teeth.

"And has anybody else wished?" persisted the old lady.

"The first man had his three wishes. Yes," was the reply, "I don't know what the first two were, but the third was for death. That's how I got the paw."

His tones were so grave that a hush fell upon the group.

"If you've had your three wishes, it's no good to you now, then, Morris," said the old man at last. "What do you keep it for?"

The soldier shook his head. "Fancy,[11] I suppose," he said slowly. "I did have some idea of selling it, but I don't think I will. It has caused enough mischief already. Besides, people won't buy. They think it's a fairy tale, some of them; and those who do think

---

10. **middle age is wont to regard presumptuous youth:** how middle-aged people usually look at young people who show no respect.

11. **fancy** (făn′ sē): whim, humor.

WHAT DOES IT MEAN?
The words in blue mean that their reaction of laughing didn't fit the mood.

 READ ALOUD the boxed text. How did the sergeant-major get the paw? **(Infer)**

WHAT DOES IT MEAN? *Grave* means "very serious."

English Learner Support
Language

Contractions In a contraction, an apostrophe (′) shows where one or more letters are left out.

that's	=	that is
you've	=	you have
it's	=	it is

Check three phrases below that apply to the monkey's paw. **(Clarify)**

❑ has a spell on it

❑ brings only happiness to its owner

❑ looks ordinary

❑ grants three wishes

As the story continues . . .

- The Whites keep the paw even though the sergeant-major advises against it.

- They imagine how the paw will change their lives.

Why does the sergeant-major tell Mr. White to throw the paw back on the fire?

WHAT DOES IT MEAN? In line 144, Mrs. White means that she could do more things at the same time with four pairs of hands.

MORE ABOUT . . .

TALISMAN A talisman can be something from nature or man-made. It is supposed to protect or bring good luck to the person who carries it.

anything of it want to try it first and pay me
120 afterward."

"If you could have another three wishes," said the old man, eyeing him keenly, "would you have them?"

"I don't know," said the other. "I don't know."

Pause & Reflect

FOCUS

Read to find out about Morris's attitude toward the monkey's paw.

He took the paw, and dangling it between his forefinger and thumb, suddenly threw it upon the fire. White, with a slight cry, stooped down and snatched it off.

130 "Better let it burn," said the soldier solemnly.

"If you don't want it, Morris," said the other, "give it to me."

"I won't," said his friend doggedly. "I threw it on the fire. If you keep it, don't blame me for what happens. Pitch it on the fire again like a sensible man."

The other shook his head and examined his new possession closely. "How do you do it?" he inquired.

"Hold it up in your right hand and wish aloud,"
140 said the sergeant-major, "but I warn you of the consequences."

"Sounds like the *Arabian Nights*,"[12] said Mrs. White, as she rose and began to set the supper. "Don't you think you might wish for four pairs of hands for me?"

Her husband drew the talisman[13] from his pocket, and then all three burst into laughter as the sergeant-

---

12. *Arabian Nights:* a famous collection of stories that feature magical events.

13. **talisman** (tăl′ĭs-mən): an object thought to have magical powers.

major, with a look of alarm on his face, caught him by
the arm.

150   "If you must wish," he said gruffly, "wish for
something sensible."

    Mr. White dropped it back in his pocket, and
placing chairs, motioned his friend to the table. In the
business of supper the talisman was partly forgotten,
and afterward the three sat listening in an enthralled[14]
fashion to a second installment of the soldier's
adventures in India.

    "If the tale about the monkey's paw is not more
truthful than those he has been telling us," said
160 Herbert, as the door closed behind their guest, just in
time for him to catch the last train, "we shan't make
much out of it."

    "Did you give him anything for it, Father?" inquired
Mrs. White, regarding her husband closely.

    "A trifle,"[15] said he, coloring slightly. "He didn't
want it, but I made him take it. And he pressed me
again to throw it away."

    "Likely," said Herbert, with pretended horror.
"Why, we're going to be rich, and famous, and happy.
170 Wish to be an emperor, Father, to begin with; then you
can't be henpecked."

    He darted round the table, pursued by the
maligned[16] Mrs. White armed with an antimacassar.[17]

Pause & Reflect

English Learner Support
Vocabulary
Idiom *Shan't make
much out of it* expresses
Herbert's doubt that the
paw has any power.
Slang *Henpecked* refers to
someone who is bossed
around by his wife.

Pause & Reflect

1. How does the sergeant-
major's attitude toward the
paw differ from the Whites'
attitude? (**Compare and
Contrast**)

2. Do you think that the
monkey's paw will bring Mr.
White happiness? (**Predict**)
YES / NO, because

---

14. **enthralled** (ĕn-thrôld'): fascinated.

15. **A trifle** (trī' fəl): a small amount.

16. **maligned** (mə-līnd'): insulted.

17. **antimacassar** (ăn'tē-mə-kăs'ər): a cloth placed over a chair to keep it clean.

As the story continues . . .

• Mr. White makes his first wish on the paw.

WHAT DOES IT MEAN?
Shamefacedly means "with embarrassment." *Marred* means "ruined" or "spoiled."

REREAD the boxed text. What is the family's feeling about the paw's power? **(Infer)**

What does Mr. White wish for? Why?

FOCUS
Read to find out what Mr. White does with the monkey's paw.

Mr. White took the paw from his pocket and eyed it dubiously.[18] "I don't know what to wish for, and that's a fact," he said slowly. "It seems to me I've got all I want."

180 "If you only cleared the house,[19] you'd be quite happy, wouldn't you?" said Herbert, with his hand on his shoulder. "Well, wish for two hundred pounds,[20] then; that'll just do it."

His father, smiling shamefacedly at his own credulity, held up the talisman, as his son, with a solemn face, somewhat marred by a wink at his mother, sat down at the piano and struck a few impressive chords.

"I wish for two hundred pounds," said the old man
190 distinctly.

A fine crash from the piano greeted the words, interrupted by a shuddering cry from the old man. His wife and son ran toward him.

"It moved," he cried, with a glance of disgust at the object as it lay on the floor. "As I wished, it twisted in my hand like a snake."

"Well, I don't see the money," said his son, as he picked it up and placed it on the table, "and I bet I never shall."

200 "It must have been your fancy, Father," said his wife, regarding him anxiously.

He shook his head. "Never mind, though; there's no harm done, but it gave me a shock all the same."

---

18. **dubiously** (dōō′ bē-əs lē): with doubt.

19. **cleared the house:** paid off the debt on the house.

20. **two hundred pounds:** sum of British money worth about 1,000 U.S. dollars at the time this story was written.

WORDS TO KNOW
credulity (krĭ-dōō′lĭ-tē) *n.* tendency to believe too easily; gullibility

They sat down by the fire again. Outside, the wind was higher than ever, and the old man started nervously at the sound of a door banging upstairs. A silence unusual and depressing settled upon all three, which lasted until the old couple rose to retire for the night.

210 "I expect you'll find the cash tied up in a big bag in the middle of your bed," said Herbert, as he bade them good-night, "and something horrible squatting up on top of the wardrobe[21] watching you as you pocket your ill-gotten gains."

He sat alone in the darkness, gazing at the dying fire, and seeing faces in it. The last face was so horrible and so simian[22] that he gazed at it in amazement. It got so vivid that, with a little uneasy laugh, he felt on the table for a glass containing a little 220 water to throw over it. His hand grasped the monkey's paw, and with a little shiver he wiped his hand on his coat and went up to bed.

Pause & Reflect

FOCUS

Mr. and Mrs. White react differently to the monkey's paw. Read to find out about their reactions.

In the brightness of the wintry sun next morning as it streamed over the breakfast table he laughed at his fears. There was an air of prosaic[23] wholesomeness about the room which it had lacked on the previous night, and 230 the dirty, shriveled little paw was pitched on the

---

21. **wardrobe:** a tall piece of furniture that serves as a closet.
22. **simian** (sĭm′ē-ən): monkey-like.
23. **prosaic** (prō-zā′ĭk): ordinary; commonplace.

Pause & Reflect

How does the family's mood change after Mr. White makes a wish? **(Compare and Contrast)**

As the story continues . . .

- Mrs. White and Herbert joke about their wish of the night before.
- Herbert leaves for work.

WHAT DOES IT MEAN?

Wholesomeness is another word for innocence or purity.

sideboard[24] with a carelessness which betokened no great belief in its virtues.[25]

"I suppose all old soldiers are the same," said Mrs. White. "The idea of our listening to such nonsense! How could wishes be granted in these days? And if they could, how could two hundred pounds hurt you, Father?"

"Might drop on his head from the sky," said the frivolous[26] Herbert.

240 "Morris said the things happened so naturally," said his father, "that you might if you so wished attribute it to coincidence."

"Well, don't break into the money before I come back," said Herbert as he rose from the table. "I'm afraid it'll turn you into a mean, avaricious[27] man, and we shall have to disown[28] you."

His mother laughed, and following him to the door, watched him down the road; and returning to the breakfast table, was very happy at the expense of her husband's credulity. All of which did not prevent her
250 from scurrying to the door at the postman's knock, when she found that the post brought a tailor's bill.

"Herbert will have some more of his funny remarks, I expect, when he comes home," she said, as they sat at dinner.

"I dare say," said Mr. White, "but for all that, the thing moved in my hand; that I'll swear to."

"You thought it did," said the old lady soothingly.

"I say it did," replied the other. "There was no thought about it; I had just—What's the matter?"

Pause & Reflect

---

24. **sideboard:** a piece of furniture used to store tablecloths and dishes.

25. **virtues:** powers.

26. **frivolous** (frĭv′ ə-ləs): silly.

27. **avaricious** (ăv′ə-rĭsh′əs): greedy.

28. **disown** (dĭs-ōn′): to refuse to accept as one's own; to reject.

WHAT DOES IT MEAN?
Attribute it to coincidence means "think it happened by chance."

English Learner Support
Vocabulary
Idiom To *break into the money* is to begin spending it.

Pause & Reflect

1. How does Mr. White's reaction to the monkey's paw differ from his wife's? (Compare and Contrast)

2. Mr. White is afraid of the paw because it _____. (Check one.) (Clarify)
   ❑ frightened Morris
   ❑ comes from far away
   ❑ scratched him
   ❑ moved in his hand

FOCUS

A strange man arrives at the house. Read to find out about him and his message.

MARK IT UP As you read, underline the words that help you understand the man's message.

260 His wife made no reply. She was watching the mysterious movements of a man outside, who, peering in an undecided fashion at the house, appeared to be trying to make up his mind to enter. In mental connection with the two hundred pounds, she noticed that the stranger was well dressed and wore a silk hat of glossy newness. Three

270 times he paused at the gate, and then walked on again. The fourth time he stood with his hand upon it, and then with sudden resolution flung it open and walked up the path. Mrs. White at the same moment placed her hands behind her, and hurriedly unfastening the strings of her apron, put that useful article of apparel beneath the cushion of her chair.

She brought the stranger, who seemed ill at ease, into the room. He gazed at her furtively,[29] and listened in a preoccupied fashion as the old lady apologized for

280 the appearance of the room, and her husband's coat, a garment which he usually reserved for the garden. She waited patiently for him to broach his business, but he was at first strangely silent.

"I—was asked to call," he said at last, and stooped and picked a piece of cotton from his trousers. "I come from Maw and Meggins."

The old lady started. "Is anything the matter?" she asked breathlessly. "Has anything happened to Herbert? What is it? What is it?"

290 Her husband interposed.[30] "There, there, Mother," he said hastily. "Sit down, and don't jump to conclusions. You've not brought bad news, I'm sure, sir;" and he eyed the other wistfully.[31]

---

29. **furtively** (fûr′ tĭv-lē): in a sly way.

30. **interposed** (ĭn′ tər-pōzd′): interrupted.

31. **wistfully** (wĭst′ fə lē): full of wishful yearning.

As the story continues...

• A well-dressed man from Herbert's workplace visits the Whites.

• He brings a horrifying message.

WHAT DOES IT MEAN?
Resolution means "determination."

MARK IT UP Reread the boxed passage. Underline the words and phrases that describe the messenger's behavior. (Visualize)

WHAT DOES IT MEAN?
Preoccupied means "distracted." *Broach his business* means "explain why he is there."

English Learner Support
Vocabulary

Idiom *Jump to conclusions* means "guess the outcome."

"I'm sorry—" began the visitor.

"Is he hurt?" demanded the mother wildly.

The visitor bowed in assent.[32] "Badly hurt," he said quietly, "but he is not in any pain."

"Oh!" said the old woman, clasping her hands. "Thank goodness for that! Thank—"

300 She broke off suddenly as the sinister meaning of the assurance dawned upon her and she saw the awful confirmation of her fears in the other's averted[33] face. She caught her breath, and turning to her slower-witted husband, laid her trembling old hand upon his. There was a long silence.

"He was caught in the machinery," said the visitor at length in a low voice.

"Caught in the machinery," repeated Mr. White, in a dazed fashion, "yes."

310 He sat staring blankly out at the window, and taking his wife's hand between his own, pressed it as he had been wont to do in their old courting days nearly forty years before.

"He was the only one left to us," he said, turning gently to the visitor. "It is hard."

The other coughed, and rising, walked slowly to the window. "The firm wished me to convey their sincere sympathy with you in your great loss," he said, without looking round. "I beg that you will understand 320 I am only their servant and merely obeying orders."

There was no reply; the old woman's face was white, her eyes staring, and her breath inaudible; on the husband's face was a look such as his friend the sergeant might have carried into his first action.

"I was to say that Maw and Meggins disclaim all responsibility," continued the other. "They admit no liability at all, but in consideration of your son's

---

English Learner Support

Language

Dialect *As he had been wont to do* means "as he had been in the habit of doing" or "as he used to do." *In their old courting days* means "when they first started dating."

WHAT DOES IT MEAN?

Inaudible means "very quiet" or "unable to be heard." *They admit no liability at all* means that Herbert's employers take no responsibility for causing the accident.

---

32. **assent** (ə-sĕnt´): agreement.
33. **averted** (ə-vûr´ tĭd): turned away.

services, they wish to present you with a certain sum as compensation."[34]

> 330 Mr. White dropped his wife's hand, and rising to his feet, gazed with a look of horror at his visitor. His dry lips shaped the words, "How much?"
>
> "Two hundred pounds," was the answer.
>
> Unconscious of his wife's shriek, the old man smiled faintly, put out his hands like a sightless man, and dropped, a senseless heap, to the floor.

Pause & Reflect

FOCUS

Mr. and Mrs. White mourn their dead son. Suddenly, Mrs. White has an idea. What do you think she tells her husband to do?

MARK IT UP As you read, underline her command to her husband.

In the huge new cemetery, some two miles distant, the old people buried their dead, 340 and came back to a house steeped in shadow and silence. It was all over so quickly that at first they could hardly realize it, and remained in a state of expectation as though of something else to happen— something else which was to lighten this load, too heavy for old hearts to bear. But the days passed, and expectation gave place to resignation[35]—the hopeless 350 resignation of the old, sometimes miscalled apathy.[36] Sometimes they hardly exchanged a word, for now they had nothing to talk about, and their days were long to weariness.

---

34. **compensation** (kŏm′ pən-sā′ shən): payment for a loss.

35. **resignation** (rĕz′ ĭg-nā′ shən): acceptance of a difficult situation.

36. **apathy** (ăp′ ə thē): a lack of feeling or interest.

Pause & Reflect

READ ALOUD the boxed passage. Why do Mr. and Mrs. White react so strongly to the news that they will receive two hundred pounds? (Draw Conclusions)

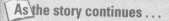

As the story continues . . .

- Without Herbert, the Whites' days are dreary and long.
- Mrs. White remembers that they have two wishes left.
- Mr. White makes another wish.

READING TIP The Whites' first wish did not turn out the way they expected. Use a chart like the one below to compare and contrast their expectations with the actual results.

Expectations	Results

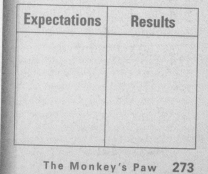

It was about a week after that the old man, waking suddenly in the night, stretched out his hand and found himself alone. The room was in darkness, and the sound of subdued weeping came from the window. He raised himself in bed and listened.

"Come back," he said tenderly. "You will be cold."

360 "It is colder for my son," said the old woman, and wept afresh.

The sound of her sobs died away on his ears. The bed was warm, and his eyes heavy with sleep. He dozed fitfully, and then slept until a sudden wild cry from his wife awoke him with a start.

"*The paw!*" she cried wildly. "The monkey's paw!"

He started up in alarm. "Where? Where is it? What's the matter?"

She came stumbling across the room toward him. "I
370 want it," she said quietly. "You've not destroyed it?"

"It's in the parlor, on the bracket," he replied, marveling. "Why?"

She cried and laughed together, and bending over, kissed his cheek.

"I only just thought of it," she said hysterically. "Why didn't I think of it before? Why didn't *you* think of it?"

"Think of what?" he questioned.

"The other two wishes," she replied rapidly. "We've
380 only had one."

"Was not that enough?" he demanded fiercely.

"No," she cried triumphantly; "we'll have one more. Go down and get it quickly, and wish our boy alive."

The man sat up in bed and flung the bedclothes from his quaking limbs. "You are mad!" he cried, aghast.

"Get it," she panted; "get it quickly, and wish—Oh, my boy, my boy!"

390 Her husband struck a match and lit the candle. "Get back to bed," he said unsteadily. "You don't know what you are saying."

"We had the first wish granted," said the old woman feverishly; "why not the second?"

"A coincidence," stammered the old man.

"Go and get it and wish," cried his wife, quivering with excitement.

He went down in the darkness, and felt his way to the parlor, and then to the mantelpiece. The talisman 400 was in its place, and a horrible fear that the unspoken wish might bring his mutilated[37] son before him ere he could escape from the room seized upon him, and he caught his breath as he found that he had lost the direction of the door. His brow cold with sweat, he felt his way round the table, and groped along the wall until he found himself in the small passage with the unwholesome thing in his hand.

Even his wife's face seemed changed as he entered the room. It was white and expectant, and to his fears 410 seemed to have an unnatural look upon it. He was afraid of her.

"*Wish!*" she cried, in a strong voice.

"It is foolish and wicked," he faltered.

"*Wish!*" repeated his wife.

He raised his hand. "I wish my son alive again."

Pause & Reflect

English Learner Support
Vocabulary
Context Clues Find context clues that help you figure out that *struck* means "ignited" or "lit."

English Learner Support
Language
Dialect *Before* means "in front of." *Ere* means "sooner than."

Pause & Reflect

1. Mrs. White tells her husband to _____. (Check one.) **(Clarify)**
   ❏ destroy the paw
   ❏ return to the cemetery
   ❏ sell the paw
   ❏ wish for Herbert to be alive again

2. the boxed text on this page. What is Mr. White afraid of? **(Summarize)**

37. **mutilated** (myo͞ot′ l-ā′tĭd): badly injured; disfigured.

As the story ends . . .

- Mr. and Mrs. White wait for their second wish to be granted.

- After several hours there is a knock on the door.

How does Mr. White feel when it appears the wish won't come true?

WHAT DOES IT MEAN?

Apathetically means "unemotionally." *Oppressive* means "heavy."

WHAT DOES IT MEAN?

Audible means "capable of being heard." *Suspended* means "stopped."

FOCUS

Read to find out what happens after Mr. White makes his wish.

420

The talisman fell to the floor, and he regarded it fearfully. Then he sank trembling into a chair as the old woman, with burning eyes, walked to the window and raised the blind.

He sat until he was chilled with the cold, glancing occasionally at the figure of the old woman peering through the window. The candle-end, which had burned below the rim of the china candlestick, was throwing pulsating shadows on the ceiling and walls, until, with a flicker larger than the rest, it expired. The old man, with an unspeakable sense of relief at the failure of the talisman, crept back to his bed, and a minute or two afterward the old woman came silently and apathetically beside him.

Neither spoke, but lay silently listening to the ticking of the clock. A stair creaked, and a squeaky mouse scurried noisily through the wall. The darkness was oppressive, and after lying for some time gathering up his courage, he took the box of matches, and striking one, went downstairs for a candle.

At the foot of the stairs the match went out, and he paused to strike another; and at the same moment a knock, so quiet and stealthy as to be scarcely audible, sounded on the front door.

The matches fell from his hand. He stood motionless, his breath suspended until the knock was repeated. Then he turned and fled swiftly back to his room, and closed the door behind him. A third knock sounded through the house.

"*What's that?*" cried the old woman, starting up.

"A rat," said the old man in shaking tones— "a rat. It passed me on the stairs."

430

440

⁴⁵⁰ His wife sat up in bed listening. A loud knock resounded through the house.

"It's Herbert!" she screamed. "It's Herbert!"

She ran to the door, but her husband was before her, and catching her by the arm, held her tightly.

"What are you going to do?" he whispered hoarsely.

"It's my boy; it's Herbert!" she cried, struggling mechanically. "I forgot it was two miles away. What are you holding me for? Let go. I must open the door."

⁴⁶⁰ "Don't let it in," cried the old man, trembling.

"You're afraid of your own son," she cried, struggling. "Let me go. I'm coming, Herbert; I'm coming."

There was another knock, and another. The old woman with a sudden wrench³⁸ broke free and ran from the room. Her husband followed to the landing, and called after her appealingly as she hurried downstairs. He heard the chain rattle back and the bottom bolt drawn slowly and stiffly from the socket.
⁴⁷⁰ Then the old woman's voice, strained and panting.

"The bolt," she cried loudly. "Come down. I can't reach it."

But her husband was on his hands and knees groping wildly on the floor in search of the paw. If he could only find it before the thing outside got in. A perfect fusillade³⁹ of knocks reverberated through the house, and he heard the scraping of a chair as his wife put it down in the passage against the door. He heard the creaking of the bolt as it came slowly back, and at
⁴⁸⁰ the same moment, he found the monkey's paw and frantically breathed his third and last wish.

REREAD the boxed text. What does Mrs. White mean by "I forgot it was two miles away"? (Infer)

WHAT DOES IT MEAN?
Reverberated means "echoed."

READING CHECK What does Mr. White do before his wife can open the door?

---

38. **wrench** (rǝnch): a sharp, forcible twist or turn.

39. **fusillade** (fyo͞oʹsǝ-läd'): a rapid series of loud noises.

Pause & Reflect

1. Did you want Mrs. White to open the door? Explain your answer. (Connect)

2. What is Mr. White's final wish? (Infer)

![Challenge icon] The Indian fakir put a spell on the paw "to show that fate ruled people's lives, and that those who interfered with it did so to their sorrow." How does this message apply to the White family? (Analyze)

The knocking ceased suddenly, although the echoes of it were still in the house. He heard the chair drawn back, and the door opened.

A cold wind rushed up the staircase, and a long loud wail of disappointment and misery from his wife gave him courage to run down to her side, and then to the gate beyond. The streetlamp flickering opposite shone on a quiet and deserted road. ❖

Pause & Reflect

Active Reading SkillBuilder

Clarify

When you **clarify,** you are making something clearer, either to yourself or to others. As you read, it is important to stop often and clarify things you do not understand. You can do this by rereading and thinking about what the author is trying to say. Clarify the following passages from "The Monkey's Paw." An example is shown.

Passage	Passage Clarified
He began to talk, the little family circle regarding with eager interest this visitor from distant parts, as he squared his broad shoulders in the chair and spoke of wild scenes and doughty deeds; of wars and plagues and strange peoples.	*The visitor tells the White family about his strange adventures in a faraway place.*
"If the tale about the monkey's paw is not more truthful than those he has been telling us," said Herbert, as the door closed behind their guest, just in time for him to catch the last train, "we shan't make much out of it."	
Unconscious of his wife's shriek, the old man smiled faintly, put out his hands like a sightless man, and dropped, a senseless heap, to the floor.	

Literary Analysis SkillBuilder

Plot

The order in which events occur within a work of fiction is called the **plot.** There are several stages of the plot: the exposition, the development of the conflict, the rising action, the climax, and the falling action. Writers structure their plots to create certain effects. To keep his readers in suspense, W. W. Jacobs develops the characters and setting of the story before revealing the result of the first wish. Analyze each part of the plot of "The Monkey's Paw" with the help of the questions below.

"The Monkey's Paw"

Exposition
 	
   Setting
 	
   Mood
 	
   Characters
	a house in England during the late 1800s
	
	sinister
	
	Mr. and Mrs. White and their son Herbert; Sergeant-Major Morris

Conflict Which event sets up the major conflict? What is the major conflict? What other conflicts result from the major conflict?	
Rising Action What happens to increase the tension leading up to the climax?	
Climax What is the climax? Why is this event a turning point?	
Falling Action Are all conflicts resolved?	

Words to Know SkillBuilder

Words to Know

credulity   fate   grimace   peril   surveying

A. Complete each analogy with one of the Words to Know. In an **analogy,** the last two words must be related in the same way that the first two are related.

1. SLIPPING : SLIDING : : glancing : _____

2. SORROW : JOY : : safety : _____

3. GIFT : PRESENT : : destiny : _____

4. DOUBT : UNCERTAINTY : : belief : _____

5. PLEASURE : SMILE : : disgust : _____

B. Write the letter of the word that is the best synonym for each underlined word.

_____ 1. a frightening situation puts us in peril

      A. opportunity   B. danger   C. safety   D. panic

_____ 2. obvious grimace of pain

      A. smile   B. scowl   C. gasp   D. groan

_____ 3. surveying the restaurant menu

      A. measuring   B. touring   C. inspecting   D. ignoring

_____ 4. the credulity of the small child

      A. gullibility   B. crankiness   C. cleverness   D. doubt

_____ 5. the twists and turns of fate

      A. life   B. plans   C. destiny   D. circumstance

C. Imagine that one of Mr. White's friends wants the monkey's paw. Write the warning that Mr. White might give to him. Use at least **three** Words to Know.

Before You Read

Connect to Your Life

Do you think that patriotism is an old-fashioned idea, or is it a concept that will never go out of fashion? Use the word web to show what the word *patriotism* means to you.

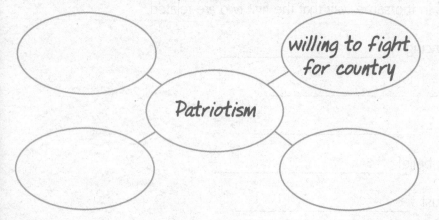

willing to fight for country

Patriotism

Key to the Poem

WHAT YOU NEED TO KNOW In 1770, colonial Boston lived under British rule. The people of Boston had no vote in making British laws that forced them to pay heavy taxes. British King George III had troops and warships stationed in the colonies. In 1774 he sealed off Boston and placed it under military rule. The colonists began to train a ragged, angry army.

When British General Gage heard of this, he ordered his troops to march from Boston to Concord to seize colonial weapons. It was the job of Paul Revere, William Dawes, and Samuel Prescott to warn the colonists when and how the British would strike.

During the winter of 1774–1775 the Minutemen, New England's citizen army, practiced drills and built up stores of weapons.

Paul Revere's Ride

by Henry Wadsworth Longfellow

PREVIEW On the evening of April 18, 1775, Paul Revere, a patriot of Boston, awaits a signal that will tell him whether the British are going to advance by land or by sea. Once he receives the signal, he will ride through the countryside to warn the colonists.

FOCUS

Paul Revere is preparing to warn the colonists that British troops are advancing. Read to find out about his plan.

Listen, my children, and you shall hear
Of the midnight ride of Paul Revere,
On the eighteenth of April, in Seventy-five;
Hardly a man is now alive
5 Who remembers that famous day and year.

He said to his friend, "If the British march
By land or sea from the town to-night,
Hang a lantern aloft in the belfry arch
Of the North Church tower as a signal light,—
10 One if by land, and two if by sea;
And I on the opposite shore will be,
Ready to ride and spread the alarm
Through every Middlesex village and farm,
For the country folk to be up and to arm."

15 Then he said, "Good-night!" and with muffled oar
Silently rowed to the Charlestown shore,
Just as the moon rose over the bay,
Where swinging wide at her moorings lay
The *Somerset*, British man-of-war;
20 A phantom ship, with each mast and spar
Across the moon like a prison bar,
And a huge black hulk, that was magnified
By its own reflection in the tide.

Pause & Reflect

Use this guide for help with unfamiliar words and difficult passages.

4–5 Hardly a man is now alive / Who remembers that famous day and year: Longfellow was born in 1807, 32 years after the events of the poem.

8 belfry (bĕl'frē) **arch:** a curved opening in a bell tower.

13 Middlesex: a county of eastern Massachusetts—the setting of the first battle of the Revolutionary War on April 19, 1775.

18 moorings: anchors and chains.

19 man-of-war: warship.

20 spar: a pole supporting a ship's sail.

As the poem begins . . .

- Paul Revere gives instructions to his friend.
- Revere rows to Charlestown to wait for his friend's signal.

English Learner Support

Vocabulary

Difficult Words and Phrases *To be up* means "to get out of bed." *To arm* means "to get weapons ready." *Muffled oar* means the oars are wrapped in material where they attach to the boat to keep them quiet. *Swinging wide* means moving from side to side. *Hulk* is the body or the frame of the ship.

Pause & Reflect

1. **MARK IT UP** Revere tells his friend to give him a signal if the British troops are on the move. How many lanterns mean that the British are moving by sea? Circle the correct phrase on page 284. **(Clarify)**

2. **READ ALOUD** the boxed lines, which describe the British warship. Cross out the word below that does *not* describe the ship. **(Draw Conclusions)**

threatening

large

cheerful

sinister

FOCUS

Now it is up to Revere's unnamed
friend to listen for the British with
"eager ears."

⃓⃓⃓ **MARK IT UP** ⟩ As you read,
underline details that describe what
he hears and sees.

Meanwhile, his friend, through alley and street
25 Wanders and watches, with eager ears,
Till in the silence around him he hears
The muster of men at the barrack door,
The sound of arms, and the tramp of feet,
And the measured tread of the grenadiers,
30 Marching down to their boats on the shore.

Then he climbed the tower of the Old North Church,
By the wooden stairs, with stealthy tread,
To the belfry chamber overhead,
And startled the pigeons from their perch
35 On the somber rafters, that round him made
Masses and moving shapes of shade,—
By the trembling ladder, steep and tall,
To the highest window in the wall,
Where he paused to listen and look down
40 A moment on the roofs of the town
And the moonlight flowing over all.

Beneath, in the churchyard, lay the dead,
In their night encampment on the hill,
Wrapped in silence so deep and still
45 That he could hear, like a sentinel's tread,
The watchful night-wind, as it went
Creeping along from tent to tent,
And seeming to whisper, "All is well!"

- Revere's friend hears the British soldiers.
- He climbs the tower of the Old North Church.

READING TIP "Paul Revere's Ride" is a narrative poem—it tells a story. As you read, refer to the diagram below to help you keep track of key events in the plot.

27–30 The muster of men . . . And the measured tread of the grenadiers, / Marching down to their boats on the shore: The friend hears the British soldiers (grenadiers) marching onto their ship.

32 stealthy tread: quiet footsteps.

34–36 And startled the pigeons . . . that round him made / Masses and moving shapes of shade: The friend startles a flock of pigeons who look like ghostly shapes in the night.

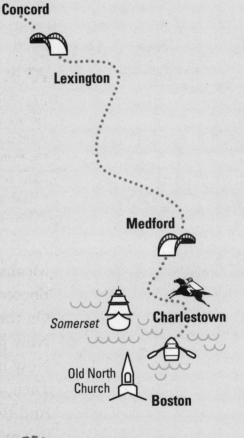

Concord

Lexington

Medford

Charlestown

Somerset

Old North Church

Boston

45 sentinel's: belonging to a guard or sentry.

REREAD the boxed text. Circle three words below that describe the mood in these lines. **(Analyze)**

tense   suspenseful

victorious   eerie

A moment only he feels the spell
50 Of the place and the hour, and the secret dread
Of the lonely belfry and the dead;
For suddenly all his thoughts are bent
On a shadowy something far away,
Where the river widens to meet the bay,—
55 A line of black that bends and floats
On the rising tide like a bridge of boats.

Pause & Reflect

FOCUS

Paul Revere waits on the shore for his friend's signal. Read to find out what Revere does before and after receiving the signal.

MARK IT UP As you read, circle details that help you **visualize** Paul Revere's actions.

Meanwhile, impatient to mount and ride,
Booted and spurred, with a heavy stride
On the opposite shore walked Paul Revere.
60 Now he patted his horse's side,
Now he gazed at the landscape far and near,
Then, impetuous, stamped the earth,
And turned and tightened his saddle girth;
But mostly he watched with eager search
65 The belfry tower of the Old North Church,
As it rose above the graves on the hill,
Lonely and spectral and somber and still.
And lo! as he looks, on the belfry's height
A glimmer, and then a gleam of light!

Pause & Reflect

1. What does Revere's friend hear or see? Check three phrases. **(Clarify)**

❏ the tramp of feet

❏ a graveyard

❏ startled pigeons

❏ troops on horseback

2. How do you think the British will advance? Check one. **(Predict)**

❏ by land

❏ by sea

📖 **As the poem continues . . .**

• Revere sees his friend's signal.

• Revere mounts his horse and sets out on his journey.

WHAT DOES IT MEAN? *Spurred* means wearing spurs—small spiked wheels that attach to a rider's boots. A rider kicks the side of a horse with spurs to make the horse move more quickly. *Somber* means "dark" or "dismal." *Lo* is an old-fashioned word for "see."

| **English Learner Support** |
| **Vocabulary** |

Synonyms *Glimmer* and *gleam* both mean "weak or faint light." The word *then* in line 69, however, tells you that in this poem *gleam* means a stronger, brighter light than *glimmer*.

62 impetuous (ĭm-pĕch'ōō-əs): acting suddenly, on impulse.

63 saddle girth: the strap attaching a saddle to a horse's body.

67 spectral: ghostly.

Paul Revere's Ride   289

70 He springs to the saddle, the bridle he turns,
But lingers and gazes, till full on his sight
A second lamp in the belfry burns.

A hurry of hoofs in a village street,
A shape in the moonlight, a bulk in the dark,
75 And beneath, from the pebbles, in passing, a spark
Struck out by a steed flying fearless and fleet;
That was all! And yet, through the gloom and the light,
The fate of a nation was riding that night;
And the spark struck out by that steed, in his flight,
80 Kindled the land into flame with its heat.

He has left the village and mounted the steep,
And beneath him, tranquil and broad and deep,
Is the Mystic, meeting the ocean tides;
And under the alders that skirt its edge,
85 Now soft on the sand, now loud on the ledge,
Is heard the tramp of his steed as he rides.

Pause & Reflect

FOCUS

Revere rides through the peaceful
countryside and sleeping towns.
Read to find out what he sees,
hears, and feels on his ride.

It was twelve by the village clock,
When he crossed the bridge into Medford town.
He heard the crowing of the cock,
90 And the barking of the farmer's dog,
And felt the damp of the river fog,
That rises after the sun goes down.
It was one by the village clock,

79–80 **And the spark . . . Kindled the land into flame with its heat:** Paul Revere's ride was the spark that started the Revolutionary War.

83 **the Mystic:** a short river flowing into Boston Harbor.

84 **alders:** trees of the birch family.

Pause & Reflect

1. **REREAD** the boxed text. What is the best way to **paraphrase** line 78? Check one.

   ❑ Revere sounded the alarm that started the Revolutionary War.

   ❑ Revere's ride marked the end of the British Empire.

   ❑ Revere was going to become the leader of a new nation.

2. Write the numbers 1, 2, and 3 to show the order in which the events occur in the poem. **(Sequence of Events)**

   ___ Revere's friend hangs two lanterns in the tower.

   ___ Revere begins his ride to warn the colonists.

   ___ Revere rows to the Charlestown shore to await the signal.

As the poem continues . . .

• Revere crosses a bridge into Medford at midnight.

• He rides through Lexington and into Concord.

When he galloped into (Lexington.)
95 He saw the gilded weathercock
Swim in the moonlight as he passed,
And the meeting-house windows, blank and bare,
Gaze at him with a spectral glare,
As if they already stood aghast
100 At the bloody work they would look upon.

It was two by the village clock,
When he came to the bridge in (Concord) town.
He heard the bleating of the flock,
And the twitter of birds among the trees,
105 And felt the breath of the morning breeze
Blowing over the meadow brown.
And one was safe and asleep in his bed
Who at the bridge would be first to fall,
Who that day would be lying dead,
110 Pierced by a British musket-ball.

Pause & Reflect

FOCUS

The poet now tells you that you know
the ending of the story. Do you?

MARK IT UP As you read,
underline the words and phrases
that tell what happens the next day.

You know the rest. In the books you have read
How the British Regulars fired and fled,—

95 gilded weathercock: a golden weather vane in the shape of a rooster.

99 aghast (ə-găst'): terrified.

103 bleating: the crying of sheep.

112 British Regulars: soldiers in Great Britain's standing army.

MORE ABOUT . . .

(LEXINGTON AND CONCORD) The first battles of the Revolutionary War were fought at Lexington and Concord. The colonists were unable to stop the invading British at Lexington. At Concord bridge, however, the British were forced to retreat.

English Learner Support

Culture

History When the action described in this poem took place, *musket-balls* were the lead bullets used in rifles, or muskets (a kind of gun).

Pause & Reflect

1. Circle any phrases below that describe what Revere saw or heard on his ride. **(Visualize)**

   meeting house windows

   the barking of a dog

   a dead soldier

   the songs of birds

   the bleating of sheep

2. ⫼ **MARK IT UP** ✎ Reread the boxed text on page 292. Circle the words and phrases that foreshadow, or hint at, the war that is about to begin. **(Analyze)**

   📄 As the poem ends . . .

• Farmers fight the British soldiers.

• Revere's warning helps the colonists.

How the farmers gave them ball for ball,
From behind each fence and farmyard wall,
115 Chasing the redcoats down the lane,
Then crossing the fields to emerge again
Under the trees at the turn of the road,
And only pausing to fire and load.

So through the night rode Paul Revere;
120 And so through the night went his cry of alarm
To every Middlesex village and farm,—
A cry of defiance, and not of fear,
A voice in the darkness, a knock at the door,
And a word that shall echo forevermore!
125 For, borne on the night-wind of the Past,
Through all our history, to the last,
In the hour of darkness and peril and need,
The people will waken and listen to hear
The hurrying hoof-beats of that steed,
130 And the midnight message of Paul Revere. ❖

Pause & Reflect

127 **peril:** danger.

Pause & Reflect

1. What happens the next day?
   (Cause and Effect)

Cause
Revere warns the colonists.

Effect
The colonists

2. What part of the poem did you find most exciting? **Paraphrase**—or put in your own words—an exciting scene from the poem.

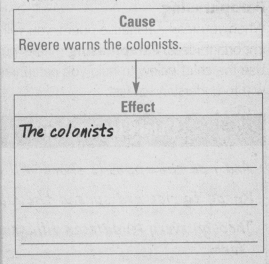

Although this poem is based on historical events, Revere's ride did not occur exactly as Longfellow describes. For example, Revere was captured as he left Lexington, and another patriot, Samual Presscott, completed the journey to Concord. Do you think such inaccuracies make this a bad poem? Discuss your opinion with a group. (Evaluate)

Active Reading SkillBuilder

Paraphrasing

When you read a narrative poem, you will find it easier to follow if you paraphrase important ideas. **Paraphrasing** means putting the writer's ideas into your own words. Use the chart below to help you paraphrase parts of the poem that are difficult for you to understand at first.

Lines from Poem	Paraphrase
And I on the opposite shore will be, Ready to ride and spread the alarm Through every Middlesex village and farm, For the country folk to be up and to arm.	I'll wait on the other side of the river, ready to ride out and warn everyone in the countryside to get up and to arm themselves.

Literary Analysis SkillBuilder

Narrative Poetry

A narrative poem is a story that is told in poetic form. In many ways it is like prose fiction, because it contains similar elements: a setting, characters, and a plot. The plot contains **rising action,** or the events that develop the conflict; a **climax,** or turning point; and **falling action,** when the conflict is resolved. To keep track of the events that make up the plot of "Paul Revere's Ride," fill in the story map below.

Setting: *April 18, 1775, in Massachusetts*
Characters: *Paul Revere; Revere's friend*
Plot—Rising Action
Event: *Revere tells his friend to hang a lantern if the British march.*
Event: *Revere rows to Charlestown to await the signal to begin his ride.*
Event: _____
Event: _____
Event: _____
Plot—Climax
Event: _____
Plot—Falling Action
Event: _____

Before You Read

Connect to Your Life

In this selection, Harriet Tubman, an ex-slave, leads other slaves to freedom. What does the word *freedom* mean to you? Write your ideas in the word web.

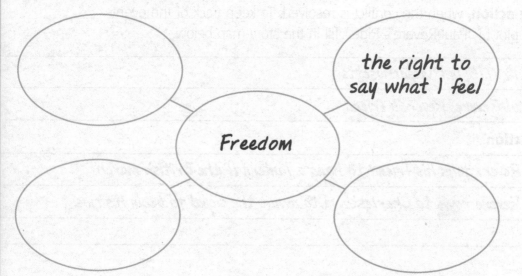

the right to say what I feel

Freedom

Key to the Biography

WHAT YOU NEED TO KNOW In the period before and during the Civil War, many enslaved people fled to freedom using a secret network of escape routes known as the Underground Railroad. The "conductors" on the Underground Railroad were brave men and women. They provided the escapees with food, hid them in tunnels and false cupboards, and guided them to the next "station." Harriet Tubman was one of the most famous of these conductors.

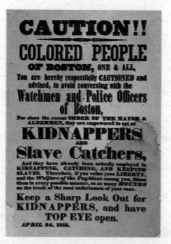

This poster warns fugitives, those who escaped from slavery, of the dangers they face.

from

Harriet Tubman:
Conductor on the Underground Railroad
by Ann Petry

PREVIEW You are about to read part of a biography about Harriet Tubman. In this part the author describes how Tubman led a group of runaway slaves on a long and dangerous journey to freedom. What challenges did she face? What qualities helped her meet these challenges?

- Maryland plantation owners hear rumors about a person named Moses.

- No one has seen Moses, but someone has been helping enslaved people escape from plantations.

MORE ABOUT . . .

(MOSES) The original Moses was a Hebrew leader and prophet in the 13th century B.C. He led the Israelites out of slavery in Egypt.

WHAT DOES IT MEAN?

Whereabouts means "location." An *overseer* is someone who supervises workers. A *whippoorwill* is a bird that comes out at night. *Intervals* are pauses.

English Learner Support
Vocabulary

Idiom The expression *had taken to their heels* means "had run away."

FOCUS

In this part the author takes you into the minds of plantation owners, or masters. Read to find out why they are worried.

Along the Eastern Shore of Maryland, in Dorchester County, in Caroline County, the masters kept hearing whispers about the man named (Moses,) who was running off slaves. At first they did not believe in his existence. The stories about him were fantastic, unbelievable. Yet they watched for him. They offered
10 rewards for his capture.

They never saw him. Now and then they heard whispered rumors to the effect that he was in the neighborhood. The woods were searched. The roads were watched. There was never anything to indicate his whereabouts. But a few days afterward, a goodly number of slaves would be gone from the plantation. Neither the master nor the overseer had heard or seen anything unusual in the quarter.[1] Sometimes one or the other would vaguely remember having heard a
20 whippoorwill call somewhere in the woods, close by, late at night. Though it was the wrong season for whippoorwills.

Sometimes the masters thought they had heard the cry of a hoot owl, repeated, and would remember having thought that the intervals between the low, moaning cry were wrong, that it had been repeated four times in succession instead of three. There was never anything more than that to suggest that all was not well in the quarter. Yet when morning came, they
30 invariably discovered that a group of the finest slaves had taken to their heels.

Unfortunately, the discovery was almost always made on a Sunday. Thus a whole day was lost before

1. **quarter:** the area in which slaves lived.

the machinery of pursuit could be set in motion. The posters offering rewards for the fugitives could not be printed until Monday. The men who made a living hunting for runaway slaves were out of reach, off in the woods with their dogs and their guns, in pursuit of four-footed game, or they were in camp meetings

40 saying their prayers with their wives and families beside them.

Harriet Tubman could have told them that there was far more involved in this matter of running off slaves than signaling the would-be runaways by imitating the call of a whippoorwill or a hoot owl, far more involved than a matter of waiting for a clear night when the North Star was visible.

Pause & Reflect

FOCUS

In December 1851, Tubman plans to lead escaped slaves to Canada. Read to find out what she does before and after setting out.

MARK IT UP ⟩ Underline details that tell you about her actions. An example is highlighted.

In December 1851, when she started out with the band

50 of fugitives that she planned to take to Canada, she had been in the vicinity of the plantation for days, planning the trip, carefully selecting the slaves that she would take with her.

She had announced her arrival in the quarter by singing the forbidden spiritual—"Go down, Moses, 'way down to Egypt

60 Land"[2]—singing it softly outside the door of a slave cabin late at night. The husky voice was beautiful

----

2. **"Go down, Moses, 'way down to Egypt Land"**: a line from a well-known African-American folk song about Moses leading the enslaved Israelites out of Egypt.

MORE ABOUT . . .

THE NORTH STAR This bright star above the North Pole was used by night travelers to guide them north.

Pause & Reflect

What was the real name of the person known as Moses? **(Clarify)**

As the biography continues . . .

- Harriet Tubman plans the escape of the largest group she has ever led to freedom.
- After three nights of walking, the group reaches their first stop.

WHAT DOES IT MEAN?

Fugitives are people running from danger or the law. *Vicinity* means "area."

English Learner Support

Culture

History Enslaved people were not allowed to sing religious songs, or *spirituals*, about freedom.

even when it was barely more than a murmur <u>borne</u> on the wind.

Once she had made her presence known, word of her coming spread from cabin to cabin. The slaves whispered to each other, ear to mouth, mouth to ear, "Moses is here." "Moses has come." "Get ready. Moses is back again." The ones who had agreed to go north with her put ashcake and salt herring in an old
70 bandanna, hastily tied it into a bundle, and then waited patiently for the signal that meant it was time to start.

There were eleven in this party, including one of her brothers and his wife. It was the largest group that she had ever conducted, but she was determined that more and more slaves should know what freedom was like.

She had to take them all the way to Canada. The Fugitive Slave Law[3] was no longer a great many incomprehensible words written down on the
80 country's law books. The new law had become a reality. It was Thomas Sims, a boy, picked up on the streets of Boston at night and shipped back to Georgia. It was Jerry and Shadrach, arrested and jailed with no warning.

She had never been in Canada. The route beyond Philadelphia was strange to her. But she could not let the runaways who accompanied her know this. As they walked along, she told them stories of her own first flight; she kept painting vivid word pictures of
90 what it would be like to be free.

But there were so many of them this time. She knew moments of doubt when she was half-afraid and kept

---

3. **Fugitive Slave Law:** a law passed in 1850, allowing slave owners to recover escaped slaves even if they had reached free states.

WORDS TO KNOW
borne (bôrn) adj. carried bear v.

Ashcake is cornmeal bread, baked in the ashes of the fire. A *herring* is a type of fish. A *bandanna* is a big handkerchief or scarf.

REREAD the boxed text and the footnote. Why did Harriet Tubman have to take the escaped slaves all the way to Canada? **(Cause and Effect)**

WHAT DOES IT MEAN?
Incomprehensible means "not able to be understood."

READING TIP Use a Venn diagram to compare and contrast this trip with Tubman's previous trips. Write the similarities in the middle and the differences in each outer ring.

Other Trips   This Trip

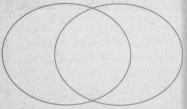

looking back over her shoulder, imagining that she heard the sound of pursuit. They would certainly be pursued. Eleven of them. Eleven thousand dollars' worth of flesh and bone and muscle that belonged to Maryland planters. If they were caught, the eleven runaways would be whipped and sold south, but she— she would probably be hanged.

100 They tried to sleep during the day, but they never could wholly relax into sleep. She could tell by the positions they assumed, by their restless movements. And they walked at night. Their progress was slow. It took them three nights of walking to reach the first stop. She had told them about the place where they would stay, promising warmth and good food, holding these things out to them as an incentive⁴ to keep going.

Pause & Reflect

FOCUS

Finally the slaves, led by Tubman, reach their first stop. Do they find comfort and shelter? Read to find out.

When she knocked on the door of a farmhouse, a place
110 where she and her parties of runaways had always been welcome, always been given shelter and plenty to eat, there was no answer. She knocked again, softly. A voice from within said, "Who is it?" There was fear in the voice.

She knew instantly from the sound of the voice that there was something wrong. She said, "A friend with friends," the password on the Underground
120 Railroad.

---

4. **incentive** (ĭn-sĕn′tĭv): something that prompts action or effort.

Pause & Reflect

1. Tubman had led other groups to freedom. Why was this trip to Canada especially dangerous? **(Draw Conclusions)**

2. ⬛ **MARK IT UP** ▷ What would happen to Tubman if she were caught with the runaways? Find and circle the sentence on this page that tells the answer. **(Cause and Effect)**

As the biography continues . . .

- Tubman knocks on the door of a farmhouse.
- Tubman and the fugitives face an unexpected problem.

English Learner Support

Vocabulary

Context Clues Recall what you have read about the need for secrecy on the Underground Railroad. This helps you figure out that a *password* is a secret code people use to communicate.

English Learner Support
Language

Figurative Language
Feed them on means
"encourage them with."

Pause & Reflect

READ ALOUD the boxed text on this page. In your own words, describe what happened at the first rest stop. **(Paraphrase)**

The door opened, slowly. The man who stood in the doorway looked at her coldly, looked with unconcealed astonishment and fear at the eleven <u>disheveled</u> runaways who were standing near her. Then he shouted, "Too many, too many. It's not safe. My place was searched last week. It's not safe!" and slammed the door in her face.

She turned away from the house, frowning. She had promised her passengers food and rest and warmth, 130 and instead of that there would be hunger and cold and more walking over the frozen ground. Somehow she would have to <u>instill</u> courage into these eleven people, most of them strangers, would have to feed them on hope and bright dreams of freedom instead of the fried pork and corn bread and milk she had promised them.

Pause & Reflect

As the biography continues . . .

- Tubman encourages the runaways to keep moving.
- She tells them about Thomas Garrett.

English Learner Support
Language

Figurative Language *Half-dead* means "very tired." To *paint wondrous word pictures* is to tell stories that bring vivid images to mind.

FOCUS

Turned away, the fugitives feel desperate and alone. It is up to Tubman to urge them on.

▌▌▌ **MARK IT UP** > As you read, underline passages that describe how Tubman encourages them to continue.

They stumbled along behind her, half-dead for sleep, and she urged them on, 140 though she was as tired and as discouraged as they were. She had never been in Canada, but she kept painting wondrous word pictures of what it would be like. She managed to <u>dispel</u> their fear of pursuit so that they would not become hysterical, panic-stricken. Then she had to bring some of the fear back so that they would

WORDS TO KNOW
disheveled (dĭ-shĕv′əld) *adj.* messy; untidy
instill (ĭn-stĭl′) *v.* to supply gradually
dispel (dĭ-spĕl′) *v.* to drive away

stay awake and keep walking though they drooped
150 with sleep.

> Yet during the day, when they lay down deep in a
> thicket, they never really slept, because if a twig
> snapped or the wind sighed in the branches of a pine
> tree, they jumped to their feet, afraid of their own
> shadows, shivering and shaking. It was very cold, but
> they dared not make fires because someone would see
> the smoke and wonder about it.

She kept thinking, Eleven of them. Eleven thousand
dollars' worth of slaves. And she had to take them all
160 the way to Canada. Sometimes she told them about
Thomas Garrett, in Wilmington. She said he was their
friend even though he did not know them. He was the
friend of all fugitives. He called them God's poor. He
was a (Quaker)[5] and his speech was a little different
from that of other people. His clothing was different,
too. He wore the wide-brimmed hat that the Quakers
wear.

She said that he had thick white hair, soft, almost
like a baby's, and the kindest eyes she had ever seen.
170 He was a big man and strong, but he had never used
his strength to harm anyone, always to help people.
He would give all of them a new pair of shoes.
Everybody. He always did. Once they reached his
house in Wilmington, they would be safe. He would
see to it that they were.

She described the house where he lived, told them
about the store where he sold shoes. She said he kept a
pail of milk and a loaf of bread in the drawer of his
desk so that he would have food ready at hand for any
180 of God's poor who should suddenly appear before
him, fainting with hunger. There was a hidden room in
the store. A whole wall swung open, and behind it was
a room where he could hide fugitives. On the wall

REREAD the boxed text. What do you think was the hardest part of being a runaway? (Evaluate)

MORE ABOUT . . .

(QUAKERS) A Quaker is a member of the Christian group called the Society of Friends. Friends were called Quakers ("people who shake or tremble") because they thought people should tremble at the word of God. Quakers believed in honesty, simplicity, and equality. Many Quakers were against slavery and worked on the Underground Railroad.

English Learner Support
Vocabulary
Idiom *See to it* means "make sure."

READING CHECK What did Tubman tell the fugitives about Thomas Garrett? Why?

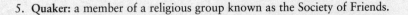

5. **Quaker:** a member of a religious group known as the Society of Friends.

Pause & Reflect

How did Tubman motivate the runaways to continue? (Summarize)

- Tubman knocks on the door of a rest stop.

- The group becomes unhappy when they leave the second house.

English Learner Support

Vocabulary

Idioms In lines 202 and 203, Tubman thinks to herself, "God, I am putting my faith in you, and you must help me."

WHAT DOES IT MEAN?

A *guttural voice* is one produced in the back of the throat.

there were shelves filled with small boxes—boxes of shoes—so that you would never guess that the wall actually opened.

While she talked, she kept watching them. They did not believe her. She could tell by their expressions. They were thinking, New shoes, Thomas Garrett, 190 Quaker, Wilmington—what foolishness was this? Who knew if she told the truth? Where was she taking them anyway?

Pause & Reflect

FOCUS

Once again, the group comes to a rest stop. Tubman silently prays that they will be taken in. Read to find out how they spend the night.

That night they reached the next stop—a farm that belonged to a German. She made the runaways take shelter behind trees at the edge of the fields before she knocked at the door. She

200 hesitated before she approached the door, thinking, Suppose that he, too, should refuse shelter, suppose— Then she thought, Lord, I'm going to hold steady on to You, and You've got to see me through—and knocked softly.

She heard the familiar guttural voice say, "Who's there?"

She answered quickly, "A friend with friends."

He opened the door and greeted her warmly. "How many this time?" he asked.

210 "Eleven," she said and waited, doubting, wondering.

He said, "Good. Bring them in."

He and his wife fed them in the lamp-lit kitchen, their faces glowing as they offered food and more food, urging them to eat, saying there was plenty for everybody, have more milk, have more bread, have more meat.

They spent the night in the warm kitchen. They really slept, all that night and until dusk the next day. When
220 they left, it was with reluctance. They had all been warm and safe and well-fed. It was hard to exchange the security offered by that clean, warm kitchen for the darkness and the cold of a December night.

Harriet had found it hard to leave the warmth and friendliness, too. But she urged them on. For a while, as they walked, they seemed to carry in them a measure of contentment; some of the serenity and the cleanliness of that big, warm kitchen lingered on inside them. But as they walked farther and farther
230 away from the warmth and the light, the cold and the darkness entered into them. They fell silent, <u>sullen</u>, suspicious. She waited for the moment when some one of them would turn <u>mutinous</u>. It did not happen that night.

Pause & Reflect

FOCUS

On the road again, Tubman tells stories about escaped slaves. Read to find out about these stories and about her problems with the runaways.

Two nights later she was aware that the feet behind her were moving slower and slower. She heard the irritability in their voices,
240 knew that soon someone would refuse to go on.

She started talking about William Still and the Philadelphia Vigilance

WORDS TO KNOW
sullen (sŭl'ən) *adj.* showing silent resentment; sulky
mutinous (myōōt'n-əs) *adj.* rebelling against a leader

WHAT DOES IT MEAN?
Reluctance means "unwillingness." *Serenity* means "peacefulness."

Pause & Reflect

1. ▌**MARK IT UP** ⟩ How did the German farmer and his wife treat the runaways? Circle details on pages 306 and 307 that tell the answer. (**Summarize**)

2. What do you think will happen next? (**Predict**)

As the biography continues . . .

• One of the runaways wants to return to slavery.
• Tubman tells the runaways they must keep going or die.

WILLIAM STILL He was the son of former slaves and the chairman of the society that helped fugitives passing through Philadelphia. His house was a stop for runaway slaves.

REREAD the boxed text. Why do you suppose no one responded to Tubman's story of William and Ellen Craft? **(Draw Conclusions)**

WHAT DOES IT MEAN?

Rheumatism is a condition that causes pain in the joints or muscles. *Vain* means "useless." *Evoking* means "recalling" or "bringing back." *Despair* is a loss of hope.

Compound Word A compound word is made from two smaller words. You can use your knowledge of *foot* and *sore* to figure out that *footsore* means "having painful feet from walking."

foot + sore = footsore

Committee.[6] No one commented. No one asked any questions. She told them the story of William and Ellen Craft and how they escaped from Georgia. Ellen was so fair that she looked as though she were white, and so she dressed up in a man's clothing, and she looked like a wealthy young planter. Her husband, 250 William, who was dark, played the role of her slave. Thus they traveled from Macon, Georgia, to Philadelphia, riding on the trains, staying at the finest hotels. Ellen pretended to be very ill—her right arm was in a sling, and her right hand was bandaged, because she was supposed to have rheumatism. Thus she avoided having to sign the register at the hotels, for she could not read or write. They finally arrived safely in Philadelphia and then went on to Boston.

No one said anything. Not one of them seemed to 260 have heard her.

She told them about Frederick Douglass,[7] the most famous of the escaped slaves, of his <u>eloquence</u>, of his magnificent appearance. Then she told them of her own first, vain effort at running away, evoking the memory of that miserable life she had led as a child, reliving it for a moment in the telling.

But they had been tired too long, hungry too long, afraid too long, footsore too long. One of them suddenly cried out in despair, "Let me go back. It is 270 better to be a slave than to suffer like this in order to be free."

She carried a gun with her on these trips. She had never used it—except as a threat. Now as she aimed it,

---

6. **Philadelphia Vigilance Committee:** a fund-raising organization set up before the Civil War to help slaves escaping from the South.

7. **Frederick Douglass:** an African-American leader of the 1800s who worked for the end of slavery in the United States.

WORDS TO KNOW
eloquence (ĕl′ə-kwəns) *n.* an ability to speak forcefully and persuasively

she experienced a feeling of guilt, remembering that time, years ago, when she had prayed for the death of Edward Brodas, the Master, and then not too long afterward had heard that great wailing cry that came from the throats of the field hands, and knew from the sound that the Master was dead.

280 One of the runaways said, again, "Let me go back. Let me go back," and stood still and then turned around and said, over his shoulder, "I am going back."

She lifted the gun, aimed it at the despairing slave. She said, "Go on with us or die." The husky, low-pitched voice was grim.

He hesitated for a moment, and then he joined the others. They started walking again. She tried to explain to them why none of them could go back to 290 the plantation. If a runaway returned, he would turn traitor; the master and the overseer would force him to turn traitor. The returned slave would disclose the stopping places, the hiding places, the corn stacks they had used with the full knowledge of the owner of the farm, the name of the German farmer who had fed them and sheltered them. These people who had risked their own security to help runaways would be ruined, fined, imprisoned.

She said, "We got to go free or die. And freedom's 300 not bought with dust."

This time she told them about the long agony of the Middle Passage[8] on the old slave ships, about the black horror of the holds, about the chains and the whips. They too knew these stories. But she wanted to

---

English Learner Support
Culture

History The *master* owned the slaves and the plantation (a large farm). *Field hands* were farm laborers.

READ ALOUD the boxed text. What do you think motivated Tubman to use a gun as a threat? **(Infer)**

WHAT DOES IT MEAN? *Turn traitor* means "become someone who tells secrets."

English Learner Support
Culture

History Captives were chained below the decks of ships in storage areas called *holds*. Many did not survive the journey from Africa to the Americas.

---

8. **Middle Passage:** the sea route along which African slaves were transported across the Atlantic Ocean to the Americas.

remind them of the long, hard way they had come, about the long, hard way they had yet to go. She told them about Thomas Sims, the boy picked up on the streets of Boston and sent back to Georgia. She said when they got him back to Savannah, got him in prison there, they whipped him until a doctor who was standing by watching said, "You will kill him if you strike him again!" His master said, "Let him die!"

Thus she forced them to go on. Sometimes she thought she had become nothing but a voice speaking in the darkness, <u>cajoling</u>, urging, threatening. Sometimes she told them things to make them laugh; sometimes she sang to them and heard the eleven voices behind her blending softly with hers, and then she knew that for the moment all was well with them.

She gave the impression of being a short, muscular, <u>indomitable</u> woman who could never be defeated. Yet at any moment she was liable to be seized by one of those curious fits of sleep,[9] which might last for a few minutes or for hours.

Even on this trip, she suddenly fell asleep in the woods. The runaways, ragged, dirty, hungry, cold, did not steal the gun, as they might have, and set off by themselves or turn back. They sat on the ground near her and waited patiently until she awakened. They had come to trust her implicitly, totally. They, too, had come to believe her repeated statement, "We got to go free or die." She was leading them into freedom, and so they waited until she was ready to go on.

Finally, they reached Thomas Garrett's house in Wilmington, Delaware. Just as Harriet had promised,

READING CHECK What happened to Thomas Sims as a result of the Fugitive Slave Law?

WHAT DOES IT MEAN? *Liable* means "likely" or "apt." *Implicitly* means "completely."

REREAD the boxed text. How did the attitude of the runaways toward Tubman change? How do you know? (Question)

---

9. **curious fits of sleep:** mysterious spells of dizziness or unconsciousness experienced by Harriet Tubman.

WORDS TO KNOW
cajoling (kə-jō′lĭng) *adj.* urging gently; coaxing **cajole** *v.*
indomitable (ĭn-dŏm′ĭ-tə-bəl) *adj.* unable to be conquered

Garrett gave them all new shoes and provided carriages to take them on to the next stop.

Pause & Reflect

FOCUS

Read to find out about Tubman's other stops on the journey to Canada.

MARK IT UP As you read, underline the names of people who help Tubman and the eleven runaways.

By slow stages they reached Philadelphia, where William
340 Still hastily recorded their names and the plantations whence they had come and something of the life they had led in slavery. Then he carefully hid what he had written, for fear it might be discovered. In 1872 he published this record in book form and called it *The Underground Railroad*. In the foreword to his book he said: "While I knew the danger of keeping strict
350 records, and while I did not then dream that in my day slavery would be blotted out, or that the time would come when I could publish these records, it used to afford me great satisfaction to take them down, fresh from the lips of fugitives on the way to freedom, and to preserve them as they had given them."

William Still, who was familiar with all the station stops on the Underground Railroad, supplied Harriet with money and sent her and her eleven fugitives on to
360 Burlington, New Jersey.

Harriet felt safer now, though there were danger spots ahead. But the biggest part of her job was over. As they went farther and farther north, it grew colder; she was aware of the wind on the Jersey ferry and

Pause & Reflect

Why couldn't Tubman let any of the runaways return to slavery? (**Main Idea**)

_____

_____

_____

As the biography continues . . .

• Tubman and the fugitives make several stops.

• Each stop is farther north and colder than the one before.

English Learner Support
Vocabulary

Multiple Meanings The word *record* (ree-CORD) means "to write down" in line 340. In line 347, however, *record* (REH-cord) means "a piece of writing."

WHAT DOES IT MEAN? *In my day* means "during my lifetime." *Blotted out* means "destroyed completely."

English Learner Support
Vocabulary

Idiom *Under my roof* is an expression that means "in my house."

Pause & Reflect

1. Write the numbers 1, 2, 3, and 4 to list in order the places the runaways visited. **(Sequence of Events)**

   __ Philadelphia, where William Still recorded their names

   __ St. Catharines, Canada

   __ Syracuse, New York, where Tubman met "Jarm" Loguen

   __ Rochester, New York, where they probably stayed with Frederick Douglass

2. **MARK IT UP** How long did the trip to Canada take? Circle the answer on this page. **(Clarify)**

aware of the cold damp in New York. From New York they went on to Syracuse, where the temperature was even lower.

In Syracuse she met the Reverend J. W. Loguen, known as "Jarm" Loguen. This was the beginning of a
370 lifelong friendship. Both Harriet and Jarm Loguen were to become friends and supporters of Old John Brown.[10]

From Syracuse they went north again, into a colder, snowier city—Rochester. Here they almost certainly stayed with Frederick Douglass, for he wrote in his autobiography: "On one occasion I had eleven fugitives at the same time under my roof, and it was necessary for them to remain with me until I could collect sufficient money to get them to Canada. It was
380 the largest number I ever had at any one time, and I had some difficulty in providing so many with food and shelter, but, as may well be imagined, they were not very <u>fastidious</u> in either direction, and were well content with very plain food, and a strip of carpet on the floor for a bed, or a place on the straw in the barn loft."

Late in December 1851, Harriet arrived in St. Catharines, Canada West (now Ontario), with the eleven fugitives. It had taken almost a month to
390 complete this journey; most of the time had been spent getting out of Maryland.

Pause & Reflect

---

10. **Old John Brown:** an antislavery leader executed for leading a raid on the federal arsenal at Harpers Ferry, Virginia, in 1859.

WORDS TO KNOW

fastidious (fă-stĭd′ē-əs) *adj.* difficult to please

FOCUS

At last, the runaways are safe in Canada. Read to find out what Tubman does when they settle there.

That first winter in St. Catharines was a terrible one. Canada was a strange, frozen land, snow everywhere, ice everywhere, and a bone-biting cold the like of which none of them had ever experienced before. Harriet rented a small frame house in the town and set to work to

400 make a home. The fugitives boarded with her. They worked in the forests, felling trees, and so did she. Sometimes she took other jobs, cooking or cleaning house for people in the town. She cheered on these newly arrived fugitives, working herself, finding work for them, praying for them, sometimes begging for them.

Often she found herself thinking of the beauty of Maryland, the mellowness of the soil, the richness of the plant life there. The climate itself made for an ease

410 of living that could never be duplicated in this bleak, barren countryside.

In spite of the severe cold, the hard work, she came to love St. Catharines and the other towns and cities in Canada where black men lived. She discovered that freedom meant more than the right to change jobs at will, more than the right to keep the money that one earned. It was the right to vote and to sit on juries. It was the right to be elected to office. In Canada there were black men who were county officials and

420 members of school boards. St. Catharines had a large colony of ex-slaves, and they owned their own homes, kept them neat and clean and in good repair. They lived in whatever part of town they chose and sent their children to the schools.

As the biography ends . . .

- The fugitives and Tubman settle in St. Catharines.
- Tubman continues to lead slaves to freedom.

English Learner Support

Culture

Buildings A *frame house* is built of wood.

English Learner Support

Language

Context Clues Examine the words around a verb to help determine its meaning. *Boarded* followed by *with her* means "lived." *Felling* followed by *trees* means "cutting down."

WHAT DOES IT MEAN?

Mellowness of the soil is its richness or ability to support life. Another word for *barren* is *unproductive*.

READING CHECK What did Tubman discover about freedom?

1. What did Tubman do for the runaways after they reached Canada? (Clarify)

2. What impressed you the most about Harriet Tubman? (Connect)

Tubman tells the runaways that "freedom's not bought with dust." What are some of the "costs" of freedom for the eleven slaves who escape? Mark passages to support your views. (Analyze)

When spring came, she decided that she would make this small Canadian city her home—as much as any place could be said to be home to a woman who traveled from Canada to the Eastern Shore of Maryland as often as she did.

430   In the spring of 1852, she went back to Cape May, New Jersey. She spent the summer there, cooking in a hotel. That fall she returned, as usual, to Dorchester County and brought out nine more slaves, conducting them all the way to St. Catharines, in Canada West, to the bone-biting cold, the snow-covered forests—and freedom.

She continued to live in this fashion, spending the winter in Canada and the spring and summer working in Cape May, New Jersey, or in Philadelphia. She
440 made two trips a year into slave territory, one in the fall and another in the spring. She now had a definite, crystallized purpose, and in carrying it out, her life fell into a pattern which remained unchanged for the next six years. ❖

Pause & Reflect

Active Reading SkillBuilder

Questioning

You will understand what you read better if you ask yourself questions as you go along. When reading a biography, you might ask yourself questions about the person's actions, ideas, and motivations. As you read *Harriet Tubman: Conductor on the Underground Railroad,* use the chart to write down questions that you ask yourself about Tubman. Write the answers to your questions as you discover them.

Questions	Answers
Why did Tubman make this trip several times, even though it was dangerous?	Tubman was a woman of strong convictions. She was determined to help other slaves escape to freedom, regardless of the risk.

Literary Analysis SkillBuilder

Biography

In a **biography,** a writer tells the story of someone else's life. Biographers often choose exceptional people to write about. These people have not only ordinary qualities but they also have some extraordinary ones as well. As you read the selection, use the chart to jot down some of Harriet Tubman's ordinary and extraordinary qualities.

Ordinary Qualities	Extraordinary Qualities
"She knew moments of doubt when she was half-afraid and kept looking back over her shoulder . . ."	"She had never been in Canada, but she kept painting wondrous word pictures of what it would be like."

Words to Know SkillBuilder

Words to Know

borne	disheveled	eloquence	indomitable	mutinous
cajoling	dispel	fastidious	instill	sullen

A. For each phrase in the first column, find the phrase in the second column that is closest in meaning. Write the letter of that phrase in the blank.

_____ 1. fussy children

_____ 2. **borne** by breezes

_____ 3. totally **indomitable**

_____ 4. childishly rebelling

_____ 5. blow away the odor

_____ 6. **sullen,** distrustful ones

_____ 7. **disheveled** before Saturday

A. **dispel** the smell

B. carried on air

C. untidy by Friday

D. pouting doubters

E. **fastidious** kiddies

F. youthfully **mutinous**

G. completely unbeatable

B. Fill in each blank with the correct Word to Know.

1. A strong wind can _____ fog.

2. Children may become _____ when they are playing.

3. A _____ person insists that everything be "just so."

4. A _____ action is a revolt or uprising.

5. Parents often try to _____ confidence in their children by using encouragement and praise.

6. A team that is _____ never gives up.

7. Martin Luther King, Jr., was known for his _____ when he spoke.

8. A _____ request may work better than a demand.

Before You Read

Connect to Your Life

Have you ever had a job or chore that you enjoyed? What kind of work do you like least? In the chart below list both the jobs you have loved and those you have hated. Explain why you feel the way you do.

Jobs/Chores I Have Loved	Why I Feel This Way
delivering newspapers	It was good exercise.
Jobs/Chores I Have Hated	

Key to the Essay

WHAT'S THE BIG IDEA? In this humorous essay, the narrator tells an exaggerated tale of trying out different jobs. Fill in the word web with the names of different jobs, or vocations. Try to think of professions that seem adventurous, strange, or amusing.

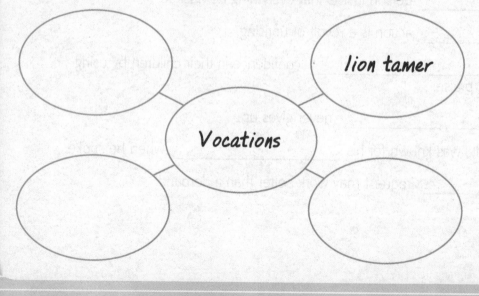

Vocations

lion tamer

318

from

ROUGHING IT

BY
MARK TWAIN

PREVIEW The narrator is not very eager to look for a job. He has tried many different kinds of jobs and has not been very successful at any of them. However, when a newspaper editor offers him a writing job, he finds a quick and easy way to success.

FOCUS

The narrator realizes he must find a job.

⫼ **MARK IT UP** ⟩ As you read, underline the words that describe the narrator's attitude toward work.

Wit to do next? It was a momentous question. I had gone out into the world to shift for myself, at the age of thirteen (for my father had indorsed for friends, and although he left us a sumptuous legacy of pride in his fine Virginian stock and its national distinction, I

10 presently found that I could not live on that alone without occasional bread to wash it down with). I had gained a livelihood in various vocations, but had not dazzled anybody with my successes; still the list was before me, and the amplest liberty in the matter of choosing, provided I wanted to work—which I did not, after being so wealthy.

Pause & Reflect

FOCUS

The narrator describes the jobs he has had.

⫼ **MARK IT UP** ⟩ As you read, underline the jobs that the narrator has tried to do.

I had once been a grocery clerk, for one day, but had consumed so much sugar in

20 that time that I was relieved from further duty by the proprietor; said he wanted me outside, so that he could have my custom. I had studied law an entire week, and then given it up because it was so prosy and tiresome. I had engaged briefly in the study of blacksmithing, but wasted so much time trying to fix the bellows so that it would blow itself, that the master turned me adrift in disgrace, and told me I would come to no good. I had

WORDS TO KNOW
vocation (vō-kā′shən) *n.* job; profession
proprietor (prə-prī′ ĭ-tər) *n.* the owner of a business

Use this guide for help with unfamiliar words and passages.

2 momentous (mō-měn′təs): important.

5–7 my father had indorsed for friends: lent his money to friends.

8–9 sumptuous legacy of pride in his fine Virginian stock: Twain's father left him only a sense of pride in his ancestors.

14 amplest: greatest.

23–24 he could have my custom: he could have me as a customer.

As the essay begins . . .

- The narrator has had many jobs since he began working at age thirteen, when his father died.
- The narrator tries to decide what to do next.

Pause & Reflect

How does the narrator feel about work? (Infer)

_____

_____

_____

_____

As the essay continues . . .

- The narrator describes his past jobs.
- He has been unsuccessful at his jobs.

 READING TIP Use a chart like the one below to keep track of the narrator's work history.

Job	What Happened?
grocery clerk	fired for eating too much while working

WHAT DOES IT MEAN? _Prosy and tiresome_ means "dull and boring." _Bellows_ are pipes used to blow air into a fire.

30 been a bookseller's clerk for a while, but the customers bothered me so much I could not read with any comfort, and so the proprietor gave me a furlough and forgot to put a limit to it. I had clerked in a drug store part of a summer, but my prescriptions were unlucky, and we appeared to sell more (stomach-pumps) than soda-water. So I had to go. I had made of myself a tolerable printer, under the impression that I would be another (Franklin) some day, but somehow had missed the connection thus far. There was no berth open in

40 the Esmeralda *Union,* and besides I had always been such a slow compositor that I looked with envy upon the achievements of apprentices of two years' standing; and when I took a "take," foremen were in the habit of suggesting that it would be wanted "some time during the year." I was a good average St. Louis and New Orleans pilot and by no means ashamed of my abilities in that line; wages were two hundred and fifty dollars a month and no <u>board</u> to pay, and I did long to stand behind a wheel again and never roam

50 any more—but I had been making such a fool of myself lately in grandiloquent letters home about my (blind lead) and my European excursion that I did what many and many a poor disappointed miner had done before; said, "It is all over with me now, and I will never go back home to be pitied—and snubbed." I had been a private secretary, a silver-miner and a silver-mill operative, and amounted to less than nothing in each, and now—

What to do next?

Pause & Reflect

WORDS TO KNOW
board (bôrd) *n.* food and lodging

32 furlough (fûr´ lō): leave of absence; vacation.

41 compositor (kəm-pŏz´ ĭ-tər): a person who sets written material into type.
42 apprentices (ə-prĕn´ tĭ səz): those working to learn a trade.

51 grandiloquent (grăn-dĭl´ ə-kwənt): filled with self-importance.
52 excursion: pleasure trip.

MORE ABOUT . . .
STOMACH PUMPS A stomach pump is used to empty the stomach when a person has been poisoned.

MORE ABOUT . . .
FRANKLIN Benjamin Franklin was a very successful printer who lived in the 1700s.

WHAT DOES IT MEAN? A *berth* is a job. *"Take"* is the written material that is given to the typesetter. *Foremen* means "supervisors." A *pilot* is a riverboat driver.

English Learner Support
Language
Part of Speech In line 49, *long* is a verb meaning "want" or "wish."

MORE ABOUT . . .
BLIND LEAD A blind lead is a deposit of ore, such as silver, that does not show above the ground. The narrator had found a lead and thought he was rich, but it did not work out.

Pause & Reflect

Check the jobs that the narrator has held.
(Clarify)

❑ grocery clerk　　❑ dancer
❑ blacksmith　　❑ compositor

FOCUS

He tries to be a miner—
and fails. Read to find out
which job he takes next
and why.

60   I yielded to Higbie's appeals and consented to try the mining once more. We climbed far up on the mountainside and went to work on a little rubbishy claim of ours that had a shaft on it eight feet deep. Higbie descended into it and worked bravely with his pick till he had loosened up a deal of rock and dirt, and then I went down with a long-handled shovel (the most awkward invention yet <u>contrived</u> by man) to throw it 70 out. You must brace the shovel forward with the side of your knee till it is full, and then, with a skillful toss, throw it backward over your left shoulder. I made the toss, and landed the mess just on the edge of the shaft and it all came back on my head and down the back of my neck. I never said a word, but climbed out and walked home. I inwardly resolved that I would starve before I would make a target of myself and shoot rubbish at it with a long-handled shovel. I sat down, in the cabin, and gave myself up to solid misery—so to speak. Now in 80 pleasanter days I had amused myself with writing letters to the chief paper of the territory, the Virginia *Daily Territorial Enterprise,* and had always been surprised when they appeared in print. My good opinion of the editors had steadily declined; for it seemed to me that they might have found something better to fill up with than my literature. I had found a letter in the post-office as I came home from the hillside, and finally I opened it. Eureka! [I never did know what Eureka meant, but it seems to be as proper a word to heave in as any when no 90 other that sounds pretty offers.] It was a deliberate offer to me of Twenty-five Dollars a week to come up to Virginia and be city editor of the *Enterprise.*

I would have challenged the publisher in the "blind lead" days—I wanted to fall down and worship him,

WORDS TO KNOW
contrive (kən-trīv′) *v.* to invent

61 consented (kən-sĕn′tĭd): agreed.

76 resolved (rĭ-zŏlvd′): decided.

92 Virginia: Virginia City, Nevada.

📖 **As the essay continues . . .**

- The narrator and his partner try mining.
- The narrator is offered a job.

WHAT DOES IT MEAN? A *claim* is a piece of land of which someone has declared ownership. Once miners have a claim, they can profit from any minerals found in the soil. A *shaft* is the vertical opening into a mine.

Why does the narrator get out of the hole and go home?

REREAD the boxed passage. Why does the narrator's opinion of the editors "decline," or drop, when they publish his letters? **(Infer)**

_____

_____

_____

WHAT DOES IT MEAN? *Eureka* is an exclamation that means "I have it!" In lines 93–94, the words in blue mean that he would have asked for more money when he was rich. Now that he is poor, he will take whatever the publisher offers.

now. Twenty-five Dollars a week—it looked like bloated luxury—a fortune, a sinful and <u>lavish</u> waste of money. But my transports cooled when I thought of my inexperience and consequent unfitness for the position—and straightway, on top of this, my long array of failures
100 rose up before me. Yet if I refused this place I must presently become dependent upon somebody for my bread, a thing necessarily distasteful to a man who had never experienced such a humiliation since he was thirteen years old. Not much to be proud of, since it is so common—but then it was all I had to be proud of. So I was scared into being a city editor. I would have declined, otherwise. Necessity is the mother of "taking chances." I do not doubt that if, at that time, I had been offered a salary to translate the Talmud from the
110 original Hebrew, I would have accepted—albeit with diffidence and some misgivings—and thrown as much variety into it as I could for the money.

Pause & Reflect

FOCUS

Read to find out about the narrator's first day on his new job.

|||| MARK IT UP ⟩ As you read, underline the chief editor's advice.

I went up to Virginia and entered upon my new vocation. I was a rusty-looking city editor, I am free to confess—coatless, slouch hat, blue woolen shirt, pantaloons stuffed into boot-
120 tops, whiskered half down to the waist, and the universal navy revolver slung to my belt. But I secured a more conservative costume and discarded the revolver. I had never had occasion to kill anybody, nor

WORDS TO KNOW
lavish (lăv′ ĭsh) *adj.* exceedingly generous; extravagant

97 transports: enthusiasm.

99 array (ə-rā'): large number; list.

109 Talmud (täl'mŏŏd): a collection of ancient writings setting forth the basic traditions of Judaism.
110 albeit (ôl-bē'ĭt): although.
111 diffidence (dĭf'ĭ-dəns): shyness.

119 pantaloons (pān' tə-lōŏnz'): wide trousers.

English Learner Support

Language

Figurative Language Words and phrases don't always mean exactly what they say. *Cooled* in line 97 means "lessened." *Rose up* means "appeared." *Bread* means "livelihood." The sentence in line 107 means that because the narrator had no other choices, he was forced to take a risk.

Pause & Reflect

1. **MARK IT UP** Underline the job the narrator is offered on page 324. **(Clarify)**

2. **REREAD** the boxed passage. Why does the narrator take a job he knows nothing about? **(Infer)**

_____

_____

_____

As the essay continues . . .

- The narrator starts his new job.
- The chief editor gives the narrator some advice about reporting.

WHAT DOES IT MEAN? *I secured a more conservative costume* means that the narrator found a more respectable outfit to wear to work. He *discarded,* or got rid of, his gun.

ever felt a desire to do so, but had worn the thing in deference to popular sentiment, and in order that I might not, by its absence, be offensively conspicuous, and a subject of remark. But the other editors, and all the printers, carried revolvers. I asked the chief editor and proprietor (Mr. Goodman, I will call him, since it describes him as well as any name could do) for some instructions with regard to my duties, and he told me to go all over town and ask all sorts of people all sorts of questions, make notes of the information gained, and write them out for publication. And he added:

"Never say 'We learn' so-and-so, or 'It is reported,' or 'It is rumored,' or 'We understand' so-and-so, but go to headquarters and get the absolute facts, and then speak out and say 'It is so-and-so.' Otherwise, people will not put confidence in your news. Unassailable certainty is the thing that gives a newspaper the firmest and most valuable reputation."

It was the whole thing in a nutshell; and to this day, when I find a reporter commencing his article with "We understand," I gather a suspicion that he has not taken as much pains to inform himself as he ought to have done. I moralize well, but I did not always practise well when I was a city editor; I let fancy get the upper hand of fact too often when there was a dearth of news. I can never forget my first day's experience as a reporter. I wandered about town questioning everybody, boring everybody, and finding out that nobody knew anything.

Pause & Reflect

125 deference (děf′ ər-əns): submission.

126 conspicuous (kən-spĭk′ yōō-əs): obvious.

139 unassailable (ŭn′ə-sā′lə-bəl): impossible to dispute or attack.

149 dearth (dûrth): shortage.

What are the narrator's duties in his new job?

WHAT DOES IT MEAN? *Commencing* means "beginning." To *moralize* is to preach or lecture. *Fancy* means "imagination."

Pause & Reflect

How would you **paraphrase**, or put in your own words, the chief editor's advice?

_____

_____

_____

_____

FOCUS

The narrator finds "news" to write about.

[▌▌ MARK IT UP ⟩] In the margins, list the subjects of his stories.

At the end of five hours my note-book was still <u>barren</u>. I spoke to Mr. Goodman. He said:

"Dan used to make a good thing out of the hay-wagons in a dry time when there were no fires or inquests. Are there no hay-wagons in from the Truckee? If there are, you might speak of the renewed activity and all that sort of thing, in the hay business, you know. It isn't sensational or exciting, but it fills up and looks business-like."

I canvassed the city again and found one wretched old hay-truck dragging in from the country. But I made <u>affluent</u> use of it. I multiplied it by sixteen, brought it into town from sixteen different directions, made sixteen separate items of it, and got up such another sweat about hay as Virginia City had never seen in the world before.

This was encouraging. Two nonpareil columns had to be filled, and I was getting along. Presently, when things began to look dismal again, a desperado killed a man in a saloon and joy returned once more. I never was so glad over any mere trifle before in my life. I said to the murderer:

"Sir, you are a stranger to me, but you have done me a kindness this day which I can never forget. If whole years of gratitude can be to you any slight compensation, they shall be yours. I was in trouble and you have relieved me nobly and at a time when all seemed dark and drear. Count me your friend from this time forth, for I am not a man to forget a favor."

WORDS TO KNOW
barren (băr′ən) *adj.* empty
affluent (ăf′lo̅o̅-ənt) *adj.* abundant; rich

The InterActive Reader PLUS
330 For English Learners

As the essay ends . . .

- The narrator searches the town for news.
- By using his imagination as well as some facts, he fills his two columns.

WHAT DOES IT MEAN? *Inquests* means "investigations." *Wretched* means "miserable" or "broken-down."

163 **sensational** (sĕn-sā' shə-nəl): arousing strong interest.

165 **canvassed:** conducted a survey throughout.

English Learner Support

Vocabulary

Idioms In line 159, *in a dry time* means "during a time when little is happening." *Got up such another sweat* means "stirred up excitement." *Getting along* is making progress.

172 **nonpareil** (nŏn′pə-rĕl′) **columns:** columns of small print.

174 **dismal** (dĭz′ məl): depressing.

174 **desperado** (dĕs′ pə-rä′ dō): a bold or desperate outlaw.

 the boxed passage. What is unusual about the narrator's reaction to the murder? **(Infer)**

WHAT DOES IT MEAN? *Slight* means "small." *Compensation* means "payment" or "reward."

If I did not really say that to him I at least felt a sort of itching desire to do it. I wrote up the murder with a hungry attention to details, and when it was finished experienced but one regret—namely, that they had not hanged my benefactor on the spot, so that I could
190 work him up too.

Next I discovered some emigrant-wagons going into camp on the plaza and found that they had lately come through the hostile Indian country and had fared rather roughly. I made the best of the item that the circumstances permitted, and felt that if I were not confined within rigid limits by the presence of the reporters of the other papers I could add particulars that would make the article much more interesting. However, I found one wagon that was going on to
200 California, and made some judicious inquiries of the proprietor. When I learned, through his short and surly answers to my cross-questioning, that he was certainly going on and would not be in the city next day to make trouble, I got ahead of the other papers, for I took down his list of names and added his party to the killed and wounded. Having more scope here, I put this wagon through an Indian fight that to this day has no parallel in history.

My two columns were filled. When I read them over
210 in the morning I felt that I had found my legitimate occupation at last. I reasoned within myself that news, and stirring news, too, was what a paper needed, and I felt that I was peculiarly endowed with the ability to furnish it. Mr. Goodman said that I was as good a

WORDS TO KNOW
emigrant (ĕm′ ĭ-grənt) *n.* a person who leaves one country or region to settle in another
legitimate (lə-jĭt′ ə-mĭt) *adj.* logical; genuine
endow (ĕn-dou′) *v.* to supply; provide

189 benefactor (bĕn′ ə-făk′ tər): person who gives aid.

200 judicious (jōō-dĭsh′ əs): showing good judgment, sensible.

MORE ABOUT . . .

INDIAN COUNTRY Relations were not always friendly between settlers moving west and Native Americans who lived on the land the settlers crossed.

English Learner Support

Vocabulary

Context Clues Use what you learn from the sentences around unknown words or phrases to figure out their meanings. To *work him up* means to write a story about him. *Made the best of* means "did as well as possible with." *Particulars* are details.

REREAD the boxed passage. Why does the narrator think he cannot make the story more interesting? (Infer)

WHAT DOES IT MEAN? *Surly* means "irritable." *Scope* means "room for exaggeration or imagination."

READING CHECK How does the narrator feel when he reads his columns the next morning?

reporter as Dan. I desired no higher commendation. With encouragement like that, I felt that I could take my pen and murder all the immigrants on the plains if need be, and the interests of the paper demanded it. ❖

Pause & Reflect

Pause & Reflect

1. Which items described by the narrator are true? Check each true item. **(Make Judgments)**

❑ A hay-truck came into town.

❑ Sixteen hay-trucks came into town.

❑ A desperado murdered a man.

❑ A wagon train arrived from "Indian country."

❑ The travelers in the wagon were murdered.

2. Does the narrator do the right thing by inventing the news? Explain. **(Evaluate)**

_____

_____

_____

_____

3. What is the funniest part of Twain's narrative? **(Connect)**

_____

_____

_____

 Review the details of the city editor's first big articles. Write your own version of the news he has witnessed. **(Paraphrase)**

Active Reading SkillBuilder

Making Inferences about the Narrator

Readers make **inferences**—logical ideas based on what they're reading and what they know. See what you can infer about the narrator as you read this selection. Use the ovals in the web to note inferences about the narrator. Write the clue that supports each inference in the appropriate box.

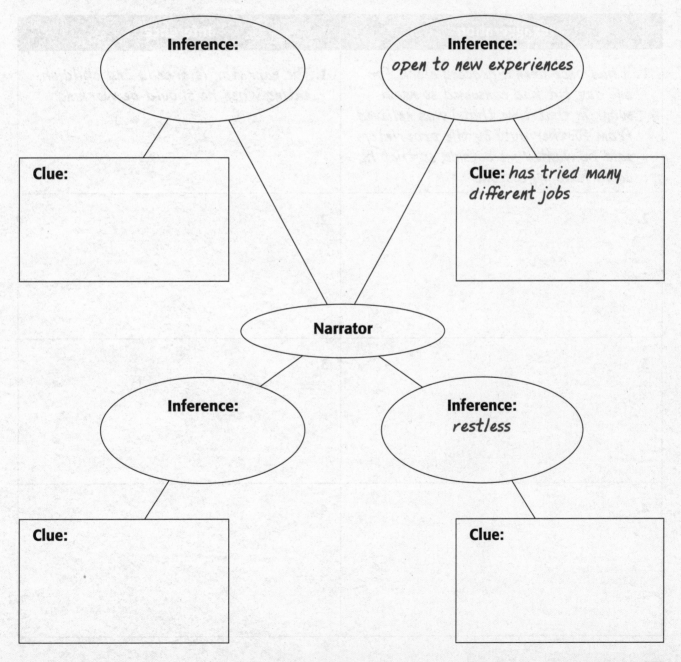

Inference:

Clue:

Inference:
open to new experiences

Clue: *has tried many different jobs*

Narrator

Inference:

Clue:

Inference:
restless

Clue:

Literary Analysis SkillBuilder

Exaggeration

Authors use **exaggeration,** or the overstating of an idea, for humor. Use the chart to record examples of exaggeration you find in the selection. Think about what each exaggeration reveals about the narrator. Beside each exaggeration, describe the inference that can be drawn about the narrator.

Exaggeration	Inference
1. "I had once been a grocery clerk, for one day, but had consumed so much sugar in that time that I was relieved from further duty by the proprietor; said he wanted me outside, so that he could have my custom."	1. The narrator is greedy and childish, eating when he should be working.
2.	2.
3.	3.
4.	4.

Words to Know SkillBuilder

Words to Know

affluent	board	emigrant	lavish	proprietor
barren	contrive	endow	legitimate	vocation

A. Complete the puzzle using the Words to Know.

Across
1. opposite of *frugal*
4. to invent
6. rich
8. food and lodging
9. person leaving a country or region

Down
1. reasonable, genuine
2. profession, calling
3. business owner
5. empty
7. supply, provide

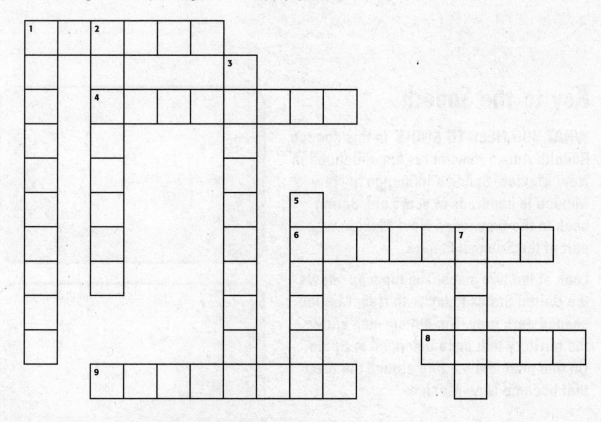

B. On a separate sheet of paper, write a paragraph describing an adventure of your own, real or imagined. Use **five** of the Words to Know.

Before You Read

Connect to Your Life

Some people read a lot of books, while others prefer to read magazines or newspapers. What do you like to read? Write your answers in the web below.

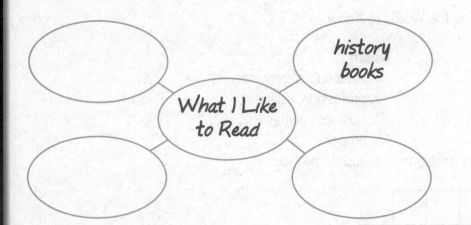

What I Like to Read

history books

Key to the Speech

WHAT YOU NEED TO KNOW In this speech, Rudolfo Anaya remembers his childhood in New Mexico. Spanish influence in New Mexico is hundreds of years old, dating back to the time when New Mexico was part of the Spanish Empire.

Look at the two maps. The top map shows the United States today with New Mexico shaded dark gray. The bottom map shows the territory that once belonged to Spain. On that map, draw a line around the area that became New Mexico.

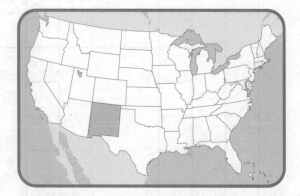

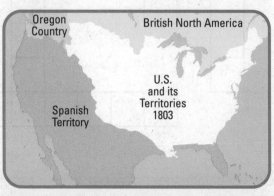

Oregon Country

British North America

U.S. and its Territories 1803

Spanish Territory

ONE MILLION VOLUMES

by Rudolfo Anaya

PREVIEW In this speech, Rudolfo Anaya celebrates a special event—the purchase by the University of New Mexico Library of its one-millionth volume. Anaya recalls his own experiences growing up Hispanic in New Mexico. He describes how he came to know the magic and power of words.

As the speech begins . . .

• The author describes how his grandfather's stories inspired him.

• He hopes that the books in the library will inspire readers.

READING TIP In this speech, the author uses many Spanish words. Check the footnotes if you need help understanding these terms.

MORE ABOUT . . .

MILKY WAY The Milky Way is a band of stars and gas clouds that can be seen in the night sky.

READING TIP As you read, write down what the author says about his grandfather's stories and books. Use a chart like the one below to organize your ideas.

Grandfather's Stories	Books

WHAT DOES IT MEAN? *Infinite* means "endless" or "countless."

FOCUS

The author recalls his childhood, when he sat under the stars and listened to stories told by old people.

MARK IT UP As you read, underline details that tell what the children learned from the "old ones." An example is highlighted.

A million volumes.
A magic number.
A million books to read, to look at, to hold in one's hand, to learn, to dream. . . .

I have always known there were at least a million stars. In the summer evenings when I was a child, we, all the
10 children of the neighborhood, sat outside under the stars and listened to the stories of the old ones, los viejitos.[1] The stories of the old people taught us to wonder and imagine. Their adivinanzas[2] induced the stirring of our first questioning, our early learning.

I remember my grandfather raising his hand and pointing to the swirl of the Milky Way which swept over us. Then he would whisper his favorite riddle:

Hay un hombre con tanto dinero
20 Que no lo puede contar
Una mujer con una sábana tan grande
Que no la puede doblar.

There is a man with so much money
He cannot count it
A woman with a bedspread so large
She cannot fold it.

We knew the million stars were the coins of the Lord, and the heavens were the bedspread of his mother, and in our minds the sky was a million miles wide. A hundred
30 million. Infinite. Stuff for the imagination. And what was more important, the teachings of the old ones made us see that we were bound to the infinity of that cosmic

---

1. *los viejitos* (lōs vyĕ-hē'tōs) *Spanish*: old ones.

2. *adivinanzas* (ä-dē-vē-nän'säs) *Spanish*: riddles.

WORDS TO KNOW
  induce (ĭn-dōōs') *v.* to bring forth; cause

dance of life[3] which swept around us. Their teachings created in us a thirst for knowledge. Can this library with its million volumes bestow[4] that same inspiration?

I was fortunate to have had those old and wise viejitos as guides into the world of nature and knowledge. They taught me with their stories: they taught me the magic of words. Now the words lie captured in ink, but the magic is still there, the power inherent in each volume. Now with book in hand we can participate in the wisdom of mankind.

Pause & Reflect

FOCUS

The author tells about the power of words. Read to find out more about how his grandfather's words stirred his imagination.

Each person moves from innocence through rites of passage[5] into the knowledge of the world, and so I entered the world of school in search of the magic in the words. The sounds were no longer the soft sounds of Spanish which my grandfather spoke: the words were in English, and with each new awareness came my first steps toward a million volumes. I, who was used to reading my oraciones en español[6] while I sat in the kitchen and answered the <u>litany</u> to the slap of my mother's tortillas,[7] I now stumbled from sound to word to groups of words, head throbbing, painfully aware that each new sound took me deeper into the maze of the new language. Oh, how I clutched the hands of my new guides then!

---

3. **bound to the infinity of that cosmic dance of life:** part of the universe.

4. **bestow** (bĭ-stō′): give.

5. **rites of passage:** rituals marking stages in a person's life.

6. *oraciones en español* (ō-rä-syō′něs ěn ěs-pä-nyōl′) *Spanish:* prayers in Spanish.

7. **tortillas** (tōr-tē′yəz): thin disks of flat cornmeal or wheat-flour bread.

WORDS TO KNOW
litany (lĭt′n-ē) *n.* repetitive recitation

Pause & Reflect

1. What did the author learn from the "old ones"? Check two phrases below. (**Clarify**)
   - ❏ to imagine
   - ❏ to debate
   - ❏ to thirst for knowledge
   - ❏ to read poems

2. What do the stories of the old ones and the books in a library provide? Fill in the missing letters. (**Summarize**)

   w __ __ d __ __ __   and

   k __ __ __ l __ __ __ __ __ .

As the speech continues . . .

- The author explains how he learned about the power of words in books.

- The author remembers the words of his grandfather.

English Learner Support

Language

Metaphor The author uses a metaphor, or comparison, to describe the English language as a confusing network of paths (a *maze*). His *new guides* were the books that helped him learn the language. He *clutched* (held tightly) the "hands" of his guides because he needed their help.

WHAT DOES IT MEAN? To *lisp* is to speak imperfectly or mispronounce certain sounds. *Imbedded in* means "placed firmly in" or "became a part of."

English Learner Support

Language

Simile In lines 75–77, the author compares taking care of the words in his mind to a shepherd who protects sheep.

According to the author, what does each book contain?

Pause & Reflect

1. **MARK IT UP** According to the author's grandfather, what do words become if they are misused? Underline the phrase on this page that tells the answer. **(Clarify)**

2. **MARK IT UP** What details in the boxed passage help you **visualize** the blizzard? Circle those details.

Learn, my mother encouraged me, learn. Be as wise
60 as your grandfather. He could speak many languages. He could speak to the birds and the animals of the field.

Yes, I remember the cuentos[8] of my grandfather, the stories of the people. Words are a way, he said, they hold joy, and they are a deadly power if misused. I clung to each syllable which lisped from his tobacco-stained lips. That was the winter the snow came, he would say, it piled high and we lost many sheep and cattle, and the trees groaned and broke with its weight. I looked across the llano[9] and saw the raging
70 blizzard, the awful destruction of that winter which was imbedded in our people's mind.

And the following summer, he would say, the grass of the llano grew so high we couldn't see the top of the sheep. And I would look and see what was once clean and pure and green. I could see a million sheep and the pastores[10] caring for them, as I now care for the million words that pasture in my mind.

But a million books? How can we see a million books? I don't mean just the books lining the shelves
80 here at the University of New Mexico Library, not just the fine worn covers, the intriguing titles; how can we see the worlds that lie waiting in each book? A million worlds. A million million worlds. And the beauty of it is that each world is related to the next, as was taught to us by the old ones. Perhaps it is easier for a child to see. Perhaps it is easier for a child to ask: How many stars are there in the sky? How many leaves in the trees of the river? How many blades of grass in the llano? How many dreams in a night of dreams?

---

8. *cuentos* (kwĕn'tōs) *Spanish:* stories.

9. *llano* (yä'nō) *Spanish:* plain.

10. *pastores* (päs-tō'rĕs) *Spanish:* shepherds.

FOCUS

The author describes how he felt about reading as a child.

MARK IT UP > As you read, underline details that tell you about his love of reading.

90   So I worked my way into the world of books, but here is the <u>paradox</u>, a book at once quenches the thirst of the imagination and <u>ignites</u> new fires. I learned that as I visited the library of my childhood, the Santa Rosa Library. It was

only a dusty room in those days, a room sitting atop the town's fire department, which was comprised[11] of one
100   dilapidated[12] fire truck used by the town's volunteers only in the direst emergencies. But in that small room I found my shelter and retreat. If there were a hundred books there we were fortunate, but to me there were a million volumes. I trembled in awe when I first entered that library, because I realized that if the books held as much magic as the words of the old ones, then indeed this was a room full of power.

Miss Pansy, the librarian, became my new guide. She fed me books as any mother would nurture her child.
110   She brought me book after book, and I consumed them all. Saturday afternoons disappeared as the time of day dissolved into the time of distant worlds. In a world that occupied most of my other schoolmates with games, I took the time to read. I was a librarian's dream. My tattered library card was my ticket into the same worlds my grandfather had known, worlds of magic that fed the imagination.

Late in the afternoon, when I was satiated[13] with reading, when I could no longer hold in my soul the
120   characters that crowded there, I heard the call of the

---

11. **comprised** (kəm-prīzd′): made up of.
12. **dilapidated** (dĭ-lăp′ĭ-dā′tĭd): in bad condition.
13. **satiated** (sā′shē-ā′tĭd): satisfied.

WORDS TO KNOW
   paradox (păr′ə-dŏks′) *n.* statement that appears to be illogical but may nevertheless be true
   ignite (ĭg-nīt′) *v.* to cause to burn; kindle

As the speech ends . . .

- The author describes visiting a library as a child.
- The author discusses the importance of books.

WHAT DOES IT MEAN?
Quenches means "satisfies a thirst."

English Learner Support
Culture
Community Service In some towns, people take turns as unpaid firefighters. People who work without being paid for it are called *volunteers.*

WHAT DOES IT MEAN? *Direst* means "worst." *Awe* means "wonder." *Nurture* means "care for" or "raise."

READ ALOUD the boxed paragraph. Notice that the author views books as food for the imagination.

READING CHECK What did the author's library card allow him to do?

Folk Tales As a child, the author was told many frightening *cuentos* (stories) about la Llorona, who drowned her children in anger at her husband.

Pause & Reflect

1. Why does the author love reading so much? (**Author's Purpose**)

2. **REREAD** the boxed text. Restate the author's message in your own words. (**Paraphrase**)

CHALLENGE Underline examples of powerful images, or words that appeal to the senses, in this speech. How do these images help the author accomplish his purpose? (**Evaluate**)

llano, the real world of my father's ranchito, the solid, warm world of my mother's kitchen. Then to the surprise and bewilderment of Miss Pansy, I would rush out and race down the streets of our town, books tucked under my shirt, in my pockets, clutched tightly to my breast. Mad with the insanity of books, I would cross the river to get home, shouting my crazy challenge even at la Llorona,[14] and that poor spirit of so many frightening cuentos would wither and

130 withdraw. She was no match for me.

Those of you who have felt the same exhilaration from reading—or from love—will know about what I'm speaking. Alas, the people of the town could only shake their heads and pity my mother. At least one of her sons was a bit touched.[15] Perhaps they were right, for few will trade a snug reality to float on words to other worlds.

And now there are a million volumes for us to read here at the University of New Mexico Library. Books on every imaginable subject, in every field, a history of

140 the thought of the world which we must keep free of <u>censorship</u>, because we treasure our freedoms. It is the word *freedom* which eventually must reflect what this collection, or the collection of any library, is all about. We know that as we preserve and use the literature of all cultures, we preserve and regenerate our own. The old ones knew and taught me this. They eagerly read the few newspapers that were available. They kept their diaries, they wrote décimas[16] and cuentos, and they survived on their oral stories and traditions. ❖

Pause & Reflect

14. *la Llorona* (lä yō-rō'nä) *Spanish:* the Weeping Woman, a ghostly figure of Mexican-American folklore.

15. **a bit touched:** a bit crazy.

16. *décimas* (dā'sē-mäs) *Spanish:* poems written in ten-line stanzas.

WORDS TO KNOW
censorship (sen' sər-ship') *n.* the practice of banning writing, music, or visual material that is considered improper or harmful

Active Reading SkillBuilder

Author's Purpose

Writers choose their topics for a reason. This reason is called the **author's purpose.**
There are four main purposes for writing: to entertain, to inform, to persuade, and to
express opinions. Often a single piece of writing has more than one purpose. Use the
chart below to examine Anaya's purposes for writing "One Million Volumes." For each
purpose, write one or more sentences from the speech that show this purpose.

Purpose for Writing	Sentences That Reveal this Purpose
To Entertain	"Mad with the insanity of books, I would cross the river to get home, shouting my crazy challenge...." "Alas, the people of the town could only shake their heads and pity my mother. At least one of her sons was a bit touched."
To Inform	
To Persuade	
To Express an Opinion	

What do you think was Anaya's **main** purpose for writing this speech? Explain.

Literary Analysis SkillBuilder

Word Choice

Writers choose their words with care in order to express their thoughts and feelings accurately. Through careful **word choice,** a writer can make readers feel a certain way or help readers visualize a scene. As you read "One Million Volumes," think about how certain words affect you as a reader. Use the chart below to record interesting words and phrases and the ideas or feelings they convey.

Words and Phrases	Ideas and Feelings They Convey
"a book at once <u>quenches</u> the thirst of the imagination and <u>ignites</u> new fires"	conveys a passionate love of and need for books
"the stories of <u>the old ones</u>, <u>los viejitos</u>"	creates a sense of history and cultural pride

Follow Up: Write an original paragraph expressing your own thoughts about libraries. You may use some of the words in the chart, or choose your own powerful and precise words. Write your paragraph on a sheet of paper.

Words to Know SkillBuilder

Words to Know

censorship   ignite   induce   litany   paradox

A. Match each definition in the first column with a Word to Know in the second column. Write the letter of that word in the blank.

___ 1. to start a fire   A. induce

___ 2. the banning of books, magazines, and other printed material   B. ignite

___ 3. to bring about or cause something to happen   C. paradox

___ 4. a prayer with repetitive responses   D. censorship

___ 5. a true statement that seems contradictory   E. litany

B. Complete each sentence with one of the Words to Know.

1. Anaya says that stories of his ancestors would _____ the children to think about things more deeply.

2. _____ is the enemy of freedom because it prevents people from reading whatever they want to read.

3. Rudolfo Anaya believes that books _____ the fire of people's curiosity.

4. Anaya says it is a _____ that books quench the thirst of the imagination and ignite new fires at the same time.

5. As a young child, Anaya would recite the _____ as he read the prayers in Spanish.

Academic and Informational Reading

In this section you'll find strategies to help you read all kinds of informational materials. The examples here range from magazines you read for fun to textbooks to bus schedules. Applying these simple and effective techniques will help you be a successful reader of the many texts you encounter every day.

Reading a Magazine Article

A magazine article is designed to catch and hold your interest. Learning how to recognize the items on a magazine page will help you read even the most complicated articles. Look at the sample magazine article as you read each strategy below.

A Read the **title** and other **headings** to get an idea of what the article is about. Frequently, the title presents the article's main topic. The smaller headings introduce subtopics related to the main topic.

B Note text that is set off in some way, such as an **indented paragraph** or a passage in a **different typeface.** This text often summarizes the article.

C Study **visuals**—photos, pictures, maps. Visuals help bring the topic to life and enrich the text.

D Look for **special features,** such as charts, tables, or graphs, that provide more detailed information on the topic or on a subtopic.

E Pay attention to terms in **italics** or **boldface.** Look for definitions or explanations before or after these terms.

MARK IT UP ➤ Use the sample magazine page and the tips above to help you answer the following questions.

1. What is the article's main topic? _____

   What two subtopics does the article cover? _____

2. Draw a star next to the paragraph that summarizes the article.

3. Circle the photo that shows cowboys at work. Put a checkmark beside the one that shows cowboys at play.

4. What is the subject of the chart?

   _____

5. How many boldfaced terms are explained in the chart? _____

6. Underline the sentence that explains what steer wrestling is.

A MODERN COWBOYS

B *If you think cowboys rode off into the sunset in the 1890s, think again. American cowboys are alive and well and living in the western United States and Canada. Although life has changed greatly for cowboys—long cattle drives are a thing of the past, for instance—roping and riding still go with the territory.*

C

A **At Work** Many cowboys today work on cattle ranches. Like the cowboys of the Wild West, modern cowhands work long hours in all kinds of weather. However, unlike old-time cowboys, today's ranchers use machines for many of their jobs. Cowboys still use their horses to rope calves and do other work. But the livestock are often carried in trucks across the large, fenced-in ranches. And when a cow wanders far from the herd, cowboys sometimes use a helicopter to round up the stray.

A **At Play** Rodeos are rooted in the Old West. After working on a cattle drive, cowboys competed and showed off their skills in roping and riding. Today, the rodeo recalls the spirit of these cowboys. The events at a rodeo are divided into two main groups: rough stock events and timed events. Rough stock events include riding bucking horses or bulls. Timed events include calf roping and steer wrestling.

C

D

TYPICAL RODEO EVENTS
Bareback Bronc Riding For 8 seconds, the rider spurs the horse as it bucks.
Saddle Bronc Riding The rider uses a saddle and must stay on the horse for 8 or 10 seconds.
Bull Riding The rider tries to stay on the bull for 8 seconds (no spurring needed).
Calf Roping The rider chases the calf on horseback, ropes it, and then gets off the horse to tie up the calf.
Steer Wrestling The cowboy grabs the steer's horns and wrestles the animal to the ground.
E **Team Roping** A team of two rope and tie a steer.

Reading a Textbook

The first page of a textbook lesson introduces you to a particular topic. The page also provides important information that will guide you through the rest of the lesson. Look at the sample textbook page as you read each strategy below.

A Preview the **title** and other **headings** to find out the lesson's main topic and related subtopics.

B Look for a list of **vocabulary terms.** These words will be identified and defined throughout the lesson.

C Read the **main idea** or **objectives.** These items summarize the lesson and establish a purpose for your reading.

D Notice text on the page that is set off in some way. For example, text placed in a tinted, or colored, box may be from a **primary source** that gives firsthand knowledge about the topic.

E Examine **visuals,** such as photos and drawings, and their **captions.** Visuals can help the topic come alive.

F Find words set in special type, such as **italics** or **boldface.** Also look for material in **parentheses.** Boldface is often used to identify the vocabulary terms in the lesson. Material in parentheses may refer you to another page or visual in the lesson.

MARK IT UP Use the sample textbook page and the tips above to help you answer the following questions.

1. What part of the country does the lesson focus on? _____

2. Circle the vocabulary terms that will be defined in the lesson.

3. Underline the main idea that is developed in the lesson.

4. Put a checkmark beside the excerpt from the primary source. Who wrote the excerpt?

_____

5. Who was Nat Love? _____

6. Circle the vocabulary term that refers to the area from the Missouri River to the Rocky Mountains. Underline the sentence that directs readers to a map on another page.

A

1 Miners, Ranchers, and Cowhands

B **TERMS & NAMES**
frontier
Great Plains
boomtown
long drive
vaquero
vigilante

C | **MAIN IDEA** | **WHY IT MATTERS NOW** |
|---|---|
| Miners, ranchers, and cowhands settled in the West seeking economic opportunities. | The mining and cattle industries that developed then still contribute to American economic growth. |

A **ONE AMERICAN'S STORY**

D Nat Love was born a slave in Tennessee in 1854. After the Civil War, he was one of thousands of African Americans who left the South and went west. In 1869, Love headed for Dodge City, Kansas. He was 15 and now free.

Love's horse taming skills landed him a job as a cowhand. For 20 years, he took part in the cattle drives that brought Texas cattle to Kansas stockyards. He became well known for his expert horsemanship and his rodeo riding and roping. In his 1907 autobiography, Love offered a lively but exaggerated account of his life. He told how he braved hailstorms, fought wild animals, and held off human attackers.

A VOICE FROM THE PAST

D I carry the marks of fourteen bullet wounds on different parts of my body, most any one of which would be sufficient to kill an ordinary man. . . . Horses were shot from under me, men killed around me, but always I escaped with a trifling wound at the worst.

Nat Love, *The Life and Adventures of Nat Love*

As you will read in this section, few cowhands led lives as exciting as that described by Nat Love, but they all helped to open a new chapter in the history of the American West.

Nat Love was an African-American cowhand who became a rodeo star.

E

A Geography and Population of the West

In the mid-1800s, towns such as St. Joseph and Independence, Missouri, were jumping-off places for settlers going west. They were the last cities and towns before the frontier. The **frontier** was the unsettled or sparsely settled area of the country occupied largely by Native Americans.

Many white settlers thought of the **Great Plains**—the area from the Missouri River to the Rocky Mountains—as empty. (See map on page 558.) Few had been attracted to its rolling plains, dry plateaus, and deserts. However, west of the Rockies, on the Pacific Coast, settlers had followed miners streaming into California after the 1849 gold rush. By 1850, California had gained statehood. Oregon followed in 1859.

F

Reading Graphs

Graphs are used to present facts and statistics. Bar graphs and circle graphs are useful for making comparisons. Use the following strategies along with the examples below to help you read graphs.

A Read the **title** to help you understand what the graph is about.

B In bar graphs, look at the data on the horizontal line and the data on the vertical line to find a value or estimate.

C In circle graphs, read the **headings** to learn what each percent number stands for.

D Compare the information from circle graphs and bar graphs to see how they relate. Sometimes they will give the same information. Other times one will give additional information.

E Check the credit to see if the information is up to date and from a respected source.

The following graphs show the results of a survey conducted by *Zillions*, the consumer magazine for children. More than half the participants ages 8 to 14 said they do not get an allowance although some do get spending money. What other observations can you make?

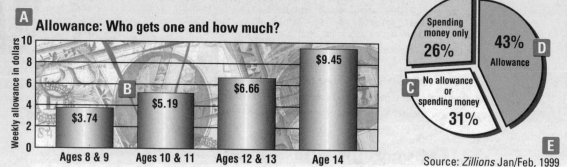

A Allowance: Who gets one and how much?

Weekly allowance in dollars

- Ages 8 & 9 — $3.74
- **B** Ages 10 & 11 — $5.19
- Ages 12 & 13 — $6.66
- Age 14 — $9.45

Percent of Kids Who Get:

- Spending money only **26%**
- **D** **43%** Allowance
- **C** No allowance or spending money **31%**
- **E**

Source: *Zillions* Jan/Feb, 1999

∥ MARK IT UP ⟩ Answer the following questions using the graphs and tips.

1. Draw a box around the graph that shows data on the amount of allowance kids get.

2. How many kids do not get an allowance? Circle your answer.

3. According to the bar graph, how much more allowance does a 13 year-old get than a

   10 year-old? _____

Reading a Transit Map

It's important to know how to read a map so you can find your way around without becoming lost. Look at the example below as you read each strategy in this list.

A Scan the **title** to know the main idea of the map.

B Interpret the **key,** or **legend,** to find out what the symbols on the map stand for.

C Study **geographic labels** to understand specific places on the map.

D Notice the **scale and pointer,** or **compass rose,** to determine distance and direction.

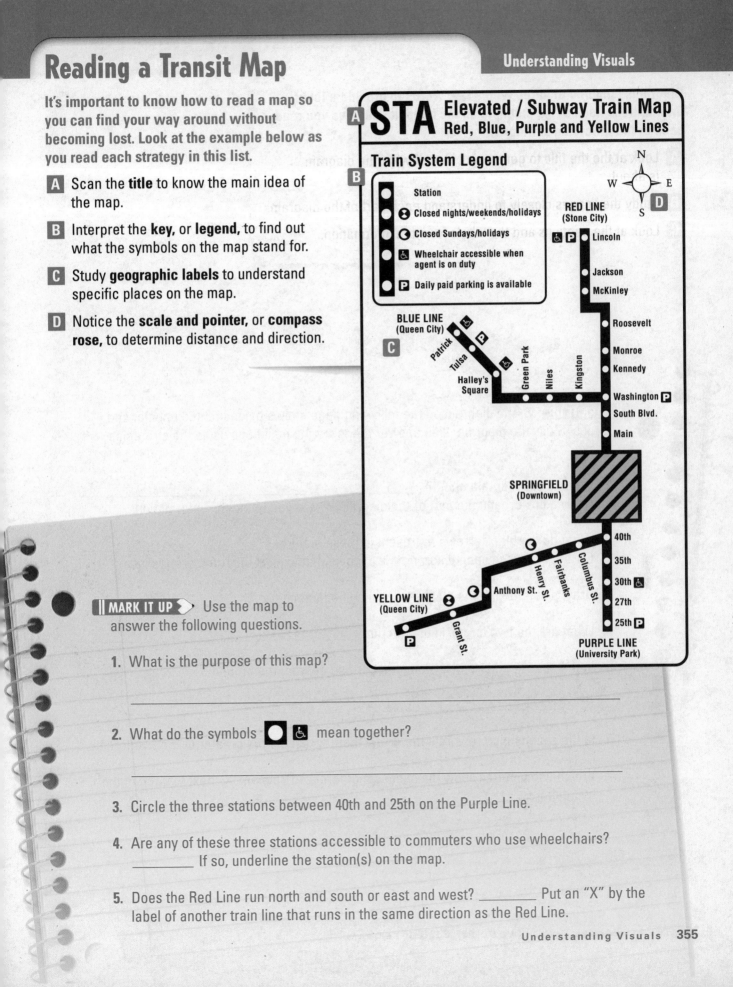

A STA Elevated / Subway Train Map
Red, Blue, Purple and Yellow Lines

B Train System Legend

- ○ Station
- ✕ Closed nights/weekends/holidays
- ☾ Closed Sundays/holidays
- ♿ Wheelchair accessible when agent is on duty
- P Daily paid parking is available

N W E S **D**

RED LINE (Stone City)

♿ P Lincoln

Jackson

McKinley

Roosevelt

Monroe

Kennedy

Washington P

South Blvd.

Main

BLUE LINE (Queen City) **C**

Patrick

Tulsa

Halley's Square

Green Park

Niles

Kingston

SPRINGFIELD (Downtown)

40th

35th

30th ♿

27th

25th P

Henry St.

Fairbanks

Columbus St.

Anthony St.

YELLOW LINE (Queen City)

Grant St.

P

PURPLE LINE (University Park)

|| MARK IT UP Use the map to answer the following questions.

1. What is the purpose of this map?

_____

2. What do the symbols ⬤ ♿ mean together?

_____

3. Circle the three stations between 40th and 25th on the Purple Line.

4. Are any of these three stations accessible to commuters who use wheelchairs? _____ If so, underline the station(s) on the map.

5. Does the Red Line run north and south or east and west? _____ Put an "X" by the label of another train line that runs in the same direction as the Red Line.

Reading a Diagram

Diagrams combine pictures with a few words to provide a lot of information. Look at the example on the opposite page as you read each of the following strategies.

A Look at the the title to get a quick idea of what the diagram is about.

B Study the images closely to understand each part of the diagram.

C Look at the captions and the labels for more information.

|| MARK IT UP The diagram on the following page shows balanced and unbalanced forces. Study the diagram, then answer the following questions using the strategies above.

1. What is this diagram about? _____
Draw a box around the part of the diagram where you found this information.

2. What do the black arrows represent in these pictures? _____
For the arrows in each diagram, write labels that explain what the arrows mean.

3. Draw a star next to the picture showing unbalanced forces.

4. What are the two forces in that picture? _____

5. In the second picture, why does the car rise up from the ground?

_____

6. In the second picture, circle the arrow that represents the greater of the two forces.

7. Which two pictures show the same set of forces? Draw an "X" next to each of the two pictures.

A Balanced and Unbalanced Forces

Newton's First Law of Motion: As long as the forces on an object balance each other, the object's motion will not change.

The force of gravity pulling down on the car is balanced by the force of the ground pushing up on the car. The car remains at rest.

C **Newton's Second Law of Motion: When an unbalanced force acts on an object, the object will accelerate in the direction that the unbalanced force points.**

The force of the crane pulling up on the car is greater than the force of gravity pulling down on it. The car begins to rise.

Once again, the force of gravity pulling down on the car is balanced by the force of the ground pushing up on it. The car is again at rest.

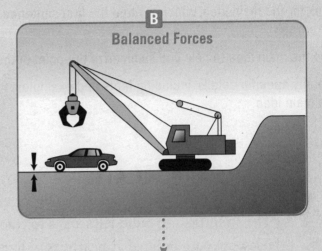

B Balanced Forces

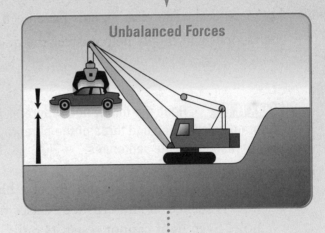

Unbalanced Forces

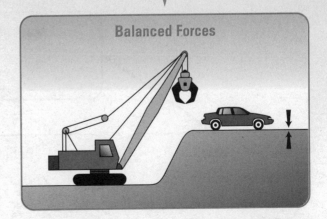

Balanced Forces

Main Idea and Supporting Details

The main idea in a paragraph is its most important point. Details in the paragraph support the main idea. Identifying the main idea will help you focus on the main message the writer wants to communicate. Use the following strategies to help you identify a paragraph's main idea and supporting details.

- Look for the main idea, which is often the first sentence in a paragraph.

- Use the main idea to help you summarize the point of the paragraph.

- Identify specific details, including facts and examples, that support the main idea.

Searching for E.T.

Main idea — Scientists on Project Phoenix search for extraterrestrials—beings from another planet.

Details — The scientists use radio telescopes to track radio signals from outer space. The telescopes are pointed at nearby, sun-like stars that are thought to be orbited by planets. So far, no clear signals have been received. However, scientists hope that the telescopes will finally help answer the question: Is anyone out there?

‖ MARK IT UP > Read the following paragraph. Circle its main idea and write it in the diagram below. Then add three of the paragraph's supporting details to the diagram, using key phrases from the sentences.

Nothing can escape the gravity of a black hole. A meteor passing near the hole is sucked in and crushed. Gases from a dying star are drawn toward the hole. Even light cannot resist its pull.

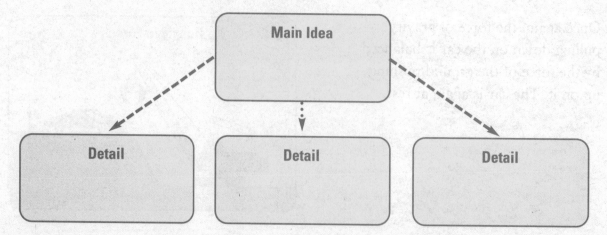

Problem and Solution

Does the proposed solution to a problem make sense? In order to decide, you need to look at each part of the text. Use the following strategies to read the text below.

- Look at the beginning or middle of a paragraph to find the problem.

- Find out why the problem is important.

- Look for the proposed solution.

- Identify the details that support the proposed solution.

- Think about whether the solution is a good one.

A Garden for Market Street?

Statement of problem — Anyone who has walked along Market Street has seen the big empty lot next to the public library. This lot has been empty for two years now, and it is ugly and dangerous. Paper trash and broken bottles cover the ground, and nothing grows there but tough nasty weeds. And who knows what kind of rodents might be crawling around in the dirt?

Explanation of problem — According to the mayor, the owner has long since deserted the property, and no one has any plans to build on it. This is valuable land, and it's right in the middle of town! The citizens should do something with it.

A community nature garden would be a great thing for the city. Teachers and students could share what they've learned about local plant wildlife. Other residents could volunteer to help plant the trees, grasses, and wildflowers. When finished, the garden would be both educational and lovely—a great improvement over the weedy lot!

MARK IT UP > Read the text above and answer the questions.

1. In the third paragraph, underline the proposed solution.

2. Circle at least one detail that supports the solution.

3. Do you agree with the solution? Explain why or why not. _____

Sequence

It's important to understand the *sequence*, or order of events, in what you read. It helps you know what happens and why. Read the tips below to make sure a sequence is clear to you. Then look at the example on the opposite page.

- Read through the passage and think about what its main steps, or stages, are.

- Look for words and phrases that signal time: *today, Saturday, later,* or *9:30*.

- Look for words and phrases that signal order: *first, next, then, before, at last, after,* or *finally*.

The article on the next page describes how a sixteen-year-old spent her day as a movie extra. Use the information from the passage and the tips above to answer the questions.

MARK IT UP

1. Circle words and phrases that signal time.

2. Underline the phrases in the article that signal order.

3. Use the information from the article to complete this time line. Make sure to include signal words in your sentences.

6:45 A.M.	7:45 A.M.	9:30 A.M.	9:50 A.M.–1:30 P.M.	1:30 P.M.
Report to set.				

I Was a Movie Extra

On a recent Saturday, Nicole M., 16, . . . spent the day as a movie extra. . . . She found out that life as an extra isn't exactly glamorous, but she did have fun. Here is her story . . .

I was one of nearly 600 extras who appeared in a fire-drill scene for the movie "Newport South." . . .

At 6:45 A.M. the day of filming, I reported to the set, an abandoned school building. . . . My day started off with registration and wardrobe check. . . . I was assigned to one of four sections: A, B, C or D (I landed in D, along with some of my friends). . . . After that, I was told to find my section and to sit there. My friends and I waited and waited. At 7:45 A.M., caterers arrived with doughnuts, lemonade, coffee, and hot chocolate. After munching down chocolate doughnuts, we

waited again—till 9:30 A.M.

Finally, it was time for our big scene. A guy wearing a headset explained to us what we had to do, then directed us to one of four stairwells. We were smooshed: About 75 people stood shoulder to shoulder. It was 20 minutes before we got the signal to move, and we poured out of the school and headed for the football field. . . .

Before the scene was shot, it was stressed upon us not to look at the cameras. But it was stressed so much it was hard NOT to look. . . .

So, after that first take, we shot the scene two more times, then we got a snack. We had five minutes to use the washroom, eat, and do anything else we needed to. Then it was back to our stairwells. . . .

By 1:30 P.M., the shooting was done, and we all gathered in the gym. . . . I reported to wardrobe and returned my jacket. After standing in line to get paid, my friends and I left—feeling tired, cold, wet, hungry and a bit grouchy.

from *The Chicago Tribune*

Cause and Effect

A cause is an event that brings about another event. An effect is something that happens as a result of the first event. Identifying causes and effects helps you understand how the events are related. The strategies below can help you find causes and effects in any reading.

- Look for an action or event that answers the question "What happened?" This is the effect.

- Look for an action or event that answers the question "Why did it happen?" This is the cause.

- Identify words that signal causes and effects, such as *because, as a result, therefore, cause,* and *since.*

MARK IT UP Use the cause-and-effect passage on the next page to help you answer the following questions. Notice that the first cause and effect in the passage are labeled.

1. Underline the phrase that explains what happened because the *Sultana* was

   carrying so many people. Is this a cause or an effect? _____

2. Circle words in the passage that signal causes and effects. The first one is done for you.

3. Use the causes and effects in the last two paragraphs to complete the following diagram.

Cause: The boat was carrying too many people.	·····>	Effect: The boilers leaked.
Cause:	·····>	Effect:
Cause:	·····>	Effect:

The Sinking of the *Sultana*

On April 25, 1865, about two weeks after the end of the Civil War, a steamboat called the *Sultana* was traveling up the Mississippi River. The ship had set out from Vicksburg, Mississippi, and was going to Cairo, Illinois. Many passengers, including hundreds of ex-prisoners of war, had boarded the ship. Since no one had taken a roll call, the exact number is not known. However, historians guess that there were about 2,300 people on board. That number is about six times as many people as the ship was built to carry. Because the *Sultana* was carrying so many people, it was going slowly.

The load also caused the ship's steam boilers to leak several times over the next two days. The boilers were repaired, but the strain was too much. Early on April 27, the boilers exploded after the ship had sailed just a few miles north of Memphis, Tennessee. As a result of the explosion, hundreds of passengers were killed instantly. Many others drowned or died in the fire that started when hot coals burst from the boiler. Some of the victims who died in the fire were trapped below deck. Others, especially those who had been prisoners of war, were too weak to try to swim in the icy river.

In all, about 1,700 people died. That number is about 200 more than died aboard the *Titanic* 47 years later. The sinking of the *Sultana* was—and still is—the greatest seafaring disaster in American history. However, the newspapers at that time were still covering the death of Abraham Lincoln and his funeral train. Therefore, the tragedy was barely reported.

Signal word

Cause

Effect

Comparison and Contrast

Comparing two things means showing how they are the same. *Contrasting* two things means showing how they are different. Comparisons and contrasts are often used in science and history books to make a subject clearer. Use these tips to help you understand comparison and contrast in reading assignments, such as the article on the opposite page.

- Look for **direct statements** of comparison and contrast: "These things are similar because..." or "One major difference is...."

- Pay attention to **words and phrases that signal comparisons,** such as *also, both, is the same as,* and *in the same way.*

- Notice **words and phrases that signal contrasts.** Some of these are *however, still, but,* and *on the other hand.*

MARK IT UP Read the essay on the opposite page. Then use the information from the essay and the tips above to answer the questions.

1. Circle the words and phrases that signal comparisons. The first one is done for you.

2. Underline the words and phrases that signal contrasts. The first one is done for you.

3. A Venn diagram shows how two subjects are similar and how they are different. Complete this diagram, which uses information from the essay to compare and contrast the United States and Bosnia. Add at least two similarities and two differences.

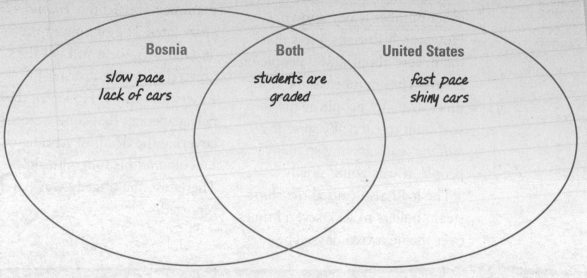

Bosnia
slow pace
lack of cars

Both
students are graded

United States
fast pace
shiny cars

My Two Homes: Bosnia and the U.S.

by Elvisa Pandzic

My family and I came to America because of the war in Bosnia. . . . I had to catch my breath when I first set eyes on Chicago. It was spectacular—like a dream, with its tall buildings and shiny cars. Everything was moving so fast! <u>Still,</u> I often thought of Cazin, where I was born.

I missed the slow pace of small-town life. That and the lack of cars. Most people had no need to travel to a place they couldn't walk to. I especially missed the mountains and hills. Nothing can replace those big beautiful meadows and the forests that took your breath away with their wonderful green smells. . . .

Another big difference is the school system. When I started school in Chicago I was very confused—all the rules were different. In Bosnia, schools are strict and students give their teachers a lot of respect. We used to stand up when a teacher entered the classroom and when we had to answer a question. In American schools, students may talk without even being called on. This is not entirely bad, in my opinion. I like how students can express themselves freely. Another thing that has taken some time getting used to is the grading system. In Bosnia, all the grades are given in numbers, not letters. In Bosnia a grade of A is equal to 5, B to 4, C to 3, D to 2, and F to 1. At least the dress code in my new school is almost the same as in Bosnia. In both places you can wear blue jeans to school. . . .

I have been living in Chicago for about two years and I am adjusting well, but I still miss Bosnia, my first home. I look forward to a time of peace when I can return. I know I will never return to my "old" life, but there is one thing I do know. Wherever I end up, I will celebrate the best of both worlds.

Argument

An argument is an opinion backed up with reasons and facts. Understanding an argument will help you make informed decisions about an issue. Use the following strategies to help you understand an argument.

- Look for words that signal an opinion: *I think; I feel; they claim, argue,* or *disagree.*

- Look for reasons, facts, or expert opinions that support the argument.

- Ask yourself if the argument and reasons make sense.

MARK IT UP Read the argument on the next page, and then answer the questions below.

1. Circle the words that signal an opinion.

2. Underline the two opinions in this argument.

3. Draw a box around the statement that is not supported by reason.

4. The writer gives reasons for and against television. Fill in the chart below using the argument. One answer has been done for you.

1. *Television keeps people informed about current issues and events.*	1.
2.	2.
3.	3.
4.	4.
	5.

Television: Good or Bad?

Many people believe that life before television was happier than life today. In those days, people read books and newspapers for information. Families spent more time together. They talked, ate meals together, and shared chores. Many children used their imaginations to write and tell stories, and they participated in outdoor activities instead of spending hours in front of the television. People were not violent because they did not watch violent programs.

Others disagree. They claim that television has many advantages as an educational tool. It keeps people informed about important current events and issues. Television programs can help children learn valuable social skills such as cooperation and kindness. It can teach children how people live, work, and deal with misfortune. Some public television programs also promote activities such as visits to museums, libraries, bookstores, and zoos.

Both arguments are endless. The only thing we can say for sure is that we need more studies to show whether television is good or bad, or a little bit of both.

Social Studies

Your social studies textbook uses words and graphics to help you learn about people and places today and throughout history. As you read the tips below, look at the sample page on the right.

A First, look at any **headlines** or **subheads** on the page. These give you an idea of what each section covers.

B Carefully read the text and think about **ways the information is organized.** Social studies books are full of sequence, comparison and contrast, and cause and effect.

C Make sure you know the meaning of any boldfaced or underlined **vocabulary terms.** These terms often appear on tests.

D Next, look closely at any **sidebar articles** or **graphics.** Think about how they relate to the main text.

E Read any **study tips** in the margins or at the bottom of the page. These let you check your understanding as you read.

MARK IT UP > The textbook page at right describes some of the effects of the Civil War on Northerners and Southerners. Use information from that page and from the tips above to answer the questions.

1. What two subjects does the page cover? _____

   _____

2. Circle the two vocabulary terms. Then underline the parts of the text that define those terms.

3. What was a Confederate soldier's monthly pay in 1864? Put a star next to the part of the page that gives you this information.

4. What does it mean to *subjugate* someone? _____
   Put a box around the two places that *subjugate* or *subjugation* appear on the page.

5. Complete the diagram.

   | Cause: *Many farmers were in the army.* |

   | Cause: _____ |

   | Cause: _____ |

   | Cause: *Food shortages in South* |

A Economic Effects of the War

Many people suffered economic hardship during the war. The suffering was severe in the South, where most battles were fought, but the North also experienced difficulties.

B Food shortages were very common in the South, partly because so many farmers were fighting in the Confederate army. Moreover, food sometimes could not get to market because trains were now being used to carry war materials. The Confederate army also seized food and other supplies for its own needs.

Another problem, especially in the South, was inflation—an increase in price and decrease in the value of money. The average family food bill in the South increased from $6.65 a month in 1861 to $68 by mid–1863. Over the course of the war, prices rose 9,000 percent in the South.

Inflation in the North was much lower, but prices still rose faster than wages, making life harder for working people. Some people took advantage of wartime demand and sold goods for high prices.

Overall, though, war production boosted Northern industry and fueled the economy. In the short term, this gave the North an economic advantage over the South. In the long term, industry would begin to replace farming as the basis of the national economy.

During the war, the federal government passed two important economic measures. In 1861, it established the C first **income tax**—a tax on earnings. The following year, the government issued a new paper currency, known as **greenbacks** because of their color. The new currency helped the Northern economy by ensuring that people had money to spend. It also helped the Union to pay for the war.

Some Southerners in the border states took advantage of the stronger Union economy by selling cotton to Northern traders, in violation of Confederate law. "Yankee gold," wrote one Confederate officer, "is fast accomplishing what Yankee arms could never achieve—the subjugation of our people."

Resistance by Slaves

Another factor that affected the South was the growing resistance from slaves. To hurt the Southern economy, slaves slowed their pace of work or stopped working altogether. Some carried out sabotage, destroying crops and farm equipment to hurt the plantation economy. When white

_Reading_History
B. Analyzing Causes Why were economic problems particularly bad in the South?
E

Vocabulary
subjugate: to bring under control or to conquer
E

D

daily *life*

INFLATION IN THE SOUTH

During the Civil War, inflation caused hardship in the North and the South. But inflation was especially severe in the Confederacy, where prices could become outrageously high.

The food prices shown below are from 1864. Consider how many days it took a Confederate soldier to earn enough money to buy each of these foods.

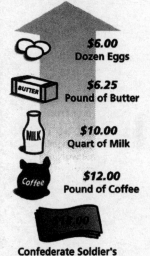

$6.00
Dozen Eggs

$6.25
Pound of Butter

$10.00
Quart of Milk

$12.00
Pound of Coffee

Confederate Soldier's Monthly Pay

Reading in science will be easier when you understand how the explanations, drawings, and special terms work together. Use the strategies below to help you better understand your science textbook. Look at the examples on the opposite page as you read each strategy in this list.

A Preview the **title** and **headings** on the page to see what science concepts will be covered.

B Look for **boldfaced** and **italicized** words that appear in the text. Look for **definitions** of those words.

C Many science textbooks discuss **scientific concepts** in terms of **everyday events or experiences.** Look for these places and consider how they improve your understanding.

D Look for references to numbered **figures** in the text.

E Then look in the margin for these figures, which are **diagrams** or **pictures** with **captions.** See how they illustrate and explain the text.

‖ MARK IT UP ‖ Use the sample science page to help you answer the following questions.

1. What science concept will be covered in this lesson? Where on the page did you find this information?

   _____

2. Circle the key term *light year* and underline its definition.

3. How old is the light from Polaris when it reaches the Earth? _____

4. Draw a star next to the reference to Figure 6-9.

5. In the third paragraph, circle the everyday experience used to help explain parallax.

6. Read the discussion of parallax in the text and look at Figure 6-9. What appears to happen to the close star's position between July and January? What actually happens to the star's position during that time?

   _____

Figure 6-8 The stars in the Big Dipper appear to be the same brightness. Does this mean that all of these stars are the same distance from Earth?

A Star Distances

All of the stars that you see at night are part of the Milky Way galaxy. The Milky Way contains about 200 billion stars. On a clear night, you might think that you can see millions of stars. Actually, you see only about 3000 stars with your **C** unaided eye. To understand why so few stars are visible, think about how you see a flashlight from a distance. At 1 meter, the flashlight is bright. At 50 meters, it appears dimmer. If the flashlight were far enough away, it would be too faint to see. For the same reason, you cannot see most of the stars in the Milky Way because they are too far away.

Astronomers measure distances to stars using the speed of light. Light travels at 300 000 kilometers per second. At this rate, sunlight takes 8 minutes to reach your eyes. Thus, the distance to the sun is 8 light-minutes. Distances to stars are measured in light-years. A **light-year** is the distance that **B** light travels in one year, about 9.5 trillion kilometers. The nearest star, Proxima Centauri, is 4.2 light-years from Earth. The distance to Polaris is 680 light-years. When you look into space, you look into the past. The light you see from Polaris left the star long before Columbus set sail for America.

D Figure 6-9 shows how to measure distance to a star by measuring its parallax. **Parallax** is the apparent shift in an object's position that is caused by the motion of the observer. You can see the parallax of your finger if you look at it only with your left eye and then only with your right eye. Your finger seems to move compared to the background. Try observing the parallax again with your finger closer to your eyes. How does the parallax change? You can observe the parallax of nearby stars with a telescope. The closer a star is, the greater is its parallax.

E **Figure 6-9** In January, the close star appears to be at point *A*. Six months later, when Earth is at the opposite end of its orbit, the close star seems to be at point *B*. This apparent shift is called parallax.

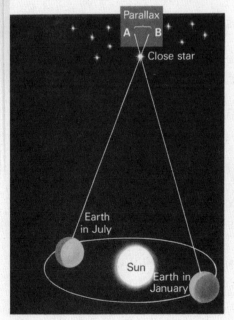

Mathematics

Reading a math textbook requires different skills than reading history, literature, or science. The tips below can help you learn these skills. As you read the tips, look at the sample math page on the right.

A First, look at the lesson **title** and any **subheads** on the page, so you know what topics will be covered.

B Find the **goals** or **objectives** for the lesson. These will tell you the most important points to know.

C Read **explanations** carefully. Sometimes the same concept is explained in more than one way to make sure you understand it.

D Look for **special features** such as study or vocabulary tips. These provide more help or information.

E Study any **worked-out solutions** to sample problems. These are the key to understanding how to do the homework assignment.

|| MARK IT UP Use the sample math page and the tips above to help you answer the following questions.

1. How is a multi-step equation solved? _____

   _____ On the math page, draw a circle around the answer.

2. Draw a box around the vocabulary words that will be studied in this lesson.

3. Where will the question "How hot is Earth's crust?" be answered? _____
   Put a star next to the part of the page that answers this question.

4. How many steps are required to solve and check a linear equation? _____

5. In Example 1, how do you isolate the variable? _____

   _____ Underline the sentence that answers this question.

A Solving Multi-Step Equations

B Goal

Use two or more steps to solve a linear equation.

Key Words

- like terms
- distributive property

How hot is Earth's crust?

Temperatures within Earth's crust can get hot enough to melt rocks. In Example 2 you will see how a multi-step equation can be used to predict the depth at which the temperature of Earth's crust is 114°C.

C Solving a linear equation may require more than one step. Use the steps you already know for transforming an equation. Simplify one or both sides of the equation first, if needed. Then use inverse operations to isolate the variable.

Student Help

D ▶ **VOCABULARY TIP**
The prefix *multi-* means "more than one". A multi-step equation is solved by transforming the equation more than one time.

A EXAMPLE 1 Solve a Linear Equation

Solve $3x + 7 = -8$.

Solution

To isolate the variable, undo the addition and then the multiplication.

E $3x + 7 = -8$	Write original equation.
$3x + 7 - 7 = -8 - 7$	Subtract 7 from each side to undo the addition. (Subtraction Property of Equality)
$3x = -15$	Simplify both sides.
$\dfrac{3x}{3} = \dfrac{-15}{3}$	Divide each side by 3 to undo the multiplication. (Division Property of Equality)
$x = -5$	Simplify.

CHECK ✓ Check by substituting -5 for x in the *original* equation.

$3x + 7 = -8$	Write original equation.
$3(-5) + 7 \stackrel{?}{=} -8$	Substitute -5 for x.
$-15 + 7 \stackrel{?}{=} -8$	Multiply.
$-8 = -8$ ✓	Solution is correct.

Checkpoint ✓ *Solve a Linear Equation*

Solve the equation. Check your solution in the original equation.

1. $6x - 15 = 9$ **2.** $7x - 4 = -11$ **3.** $2y + 5 = 1$

Reading an Application

Reading and understanding an application will help you fill it out correctly and avoid mistakes. Use the following strategies to help you understand any application. Look at the example on the next page as you read each strategy.

A Begin at the top. Scan the application to see what the different sections are.

B Look for special instructions for how to fill out the application.

C Notice any request for materials that must be attached to the application.

D Watch for sections you don't have to fill in or questions you don't have to answer.

E Look for difficult or confusing words or abbreviations. Look them up in a dictionary or ask someone what they mean.

MARK IT UP Imagine that you want to participate in the student science fair. Read the application on the next page. Then answer the following questions.

1. On the application, number the four different sections.

2. What grade levels must students be in to participate in the science fair?

   _____

3. Underline all requests for materials that must be submitted along with the application.

   What are they? _____

4. In the last section, which category number would you write if you had a botany project?

   _____

5. **ASSESSMENT PRACTICE** What name should be written in the Team Member Information section?
   A. your name
   B. your teacher
   C. a competing student
   D. your project partner

6. Invent an idea for a science project. Then fill out the application as best you can.

A **CHICAGO PUBLIC SCHOOLS STUDENT SCIENCE FAIR, INC.**

2000 STUDENT SCIENCE FAIR

Official Entry Form for Region and City Science Fairs

B Fill in the information below. The information must be typewritten or legibly printed (see handbook). Note: information requested for a team member refers to the second pupil on an elementary school project. Students must be in the 7th grade, 8th grade, or high school to participate in the city fair. Age requirements for participation in the state fair are determined by the rules of the Illinois Junior Academy of Science. **A COPY OF THE ABSTRACT MUST BE ATTACHED TO THIS ENTRY FORM.** C

ENTRANT INFORMATION

Entrant Name:

Last   First

Age: **Sex:** **Phone:** ☐☐☐-☐☐☐-☐☐☐☐ **Birth Date:** ☐☐ ☐☐ **1 9** ☐☐

Month Day Year

Address:

Apartment Number   Zip Code

Student Social Security Number: ☐☐☐-☐☐-☐☐☐☐ **Name of Parent or Guardian:** _____

TEAM MEMBER INFORMATION

Name:

Last   First

Age: **Sex:** **Phone:** ☐☐☐-☐☐☐-☐☐☐☐ **Birth Date:** ☐☐ ☐☐ **1 9** ☐☐

Month Day Year

Address:

Apartment Number   Zip Code

Student Social Security Number: ☐☐☐-☐☐-☐☐☐☐ **Name of Parent or Guardian:** _____

SCHOOL INFORMATION

Grade   Unit Number   Region   School   M.R.#

PROJECT INFORMATION

Electricity Required? ☐ ☐
Y N

Check Type of Endorsement(s) Attached*: ☐ Human ☐ Vertebrate Animal ☐ Microbiology ☐ Recombinant DNA

☐ 6th Grade Recognition Luncheon Only

Organism(s) Used in Experiment: _____

E *** A COPY OF THE ENDORSEMENT(S) AND ABSTRACT MUST BE ATTACHED TO THIS ENTRY FORM.**

INSERT THE CORRESPONDING SET OF NUMERALS AND CATEGORY NAME IN THE BOXES PROVIDED.

01 Aero-Space Science	05 Chemistry	09 Engineering Science	13 Mathematics
02 Behavioral Science	06 Computer Science	10 Environmental Science	14 Microbiology
03 Biochemistry	07 Earth Science	11 Health Science	15 Physics
04 Botany	08 Electronics	12 Material Science	16 Zoology

Category Name

Category Number:

Exhibit Title:
Cannot Exceed 45 Spaces

Teacher/ Sponsor Name:

Last   First

☐ **Check here if an interpreter is needed. Indicate which language:** _____

CERTIFICATION:

I hereby certify that this project has been personally inspected and that it fulfills all requirements as described in the Handbooks, including endorsements if applicable.

I hereby certify that I have read all of the above information and that it is accurate.

_____ _____   _____ _____
Region Science Fair Coordinator Signature   Date   Entrant's Signature   Date

83

Reading a Public Notice

Public notices can tell you about events in your community and give you valuable information about safety. When you read a public notice, follow these tips. Each tip relates to a specific part of the notice on the opposite page.

A Read the notice's **title,** if it has one. The title often gives the main idea or purpose of the notice.

B Ask yourself, **"Who should read this notice?"** If the information in it might be important to you or someone you know, then you should pay attention to it.

C Look for **instructions**—things the notice is asking or telling you to do.

D See if there is a logo, credit, or other way of telling **who created the notice.**

E See if there are details that tell you how you can **find out more** on the topic.

F Look for **special features** designed to make the notice easier to understand, such as instructions in more than one language.

‖ MARK IT UP ▷ The notice on the opposite page is from the Web site of a public library. Read it carefully and answer the questions below.

1. Whom is this notice for?

   _____

2. What does the notice ask readers to do?

   _____

3. Underline the part of the notice that explains what "netiquette" is.

4. Circle the parts of the notice that tell who created it.

5. Put a star next to the part that tells where the library is located.

6. **ASSESSMENT PRACTICE** According to the notice, people who do not follow the library's rules for Internet use will
   A. be banned from the library
   B. lose their Internet privileges
   C. receive "flames" from other Internet users
   D. both A and C

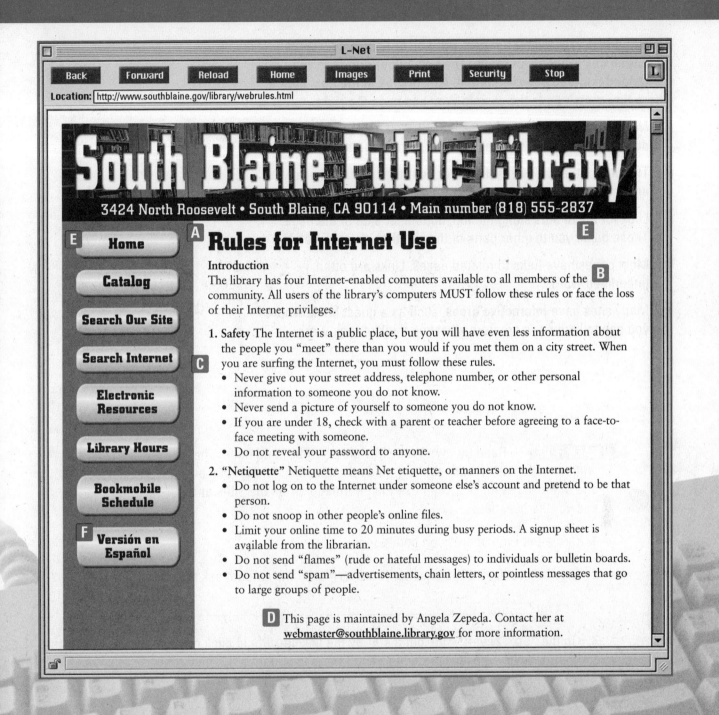

L-Net

Back Forward Reload Home Images Print Security Stop **L**

Location: http://www.southblaine.gov/library/webrules.html

South Blaine Public Library

3424 North Roosevelt • South Blaine, CA 90114 • Main number (818) 555-2837

E Home

Catalog

Search Our Site

Search Internet

Electronic Resources

Library Hours

Bookmobile Schedule

F Versión en Español

A ## Rules for Internet Use

E

Introduction

The library has four Internet-enabled computers available to all members of the **B** community. All users of the library's computers MUST follow these rules or face the loss of their Internet privileges.

C

1. **Safety** The Internet is a public place, but you will have even less information about the people you "meet" there than you would if you met them on a city street. When you are surfing the Internet, you must follow these rules.
   - Never give out your street address, telephone number, or other personal information to someone you do not know.
   - Never send a picture of yourself to someone you do not know.
   - If you are under 18, check with a parent or teacher before agreeing to a face-to-face meeting with someone.
   - Do not reveal your password to anyone.

2. **"Netiquette"** Netiquette means Net etiquette, or manners on the Internet.
   - Do not log on to the Internet under someone else's account and pretend to be that person.
   - Do not snoop in other people's online files.
   - Limit your online time to 20 minutes during busy periods. A signup sheet is available from the librarian.
   - Do not send "flames" (rude or hateful messages) to individuals or bulletin boards.
   - Do not send "spam"—advertisements, chain letters, or pointless messages that go to large groups of people.

D This page is maintained by Angela Zepeda. Contact her at **webmaster@southblaine.library.gov** for more information.

Reading a Web Page

If you need information for a report, project, or hobby, the World Wide Web can probably help you. The tips below will help you understand the Web pages you read. As you look at the tips, notice where they match up to the sample Web pages on the right.

A Notice the page's **Web address,** or URL. You may want to write it down in case you need to access the same page at another time.

B The **title** of the page is usually at or near the top. It will give you an idea of what the page covers.

C Look for **menu bars** along the top, bottom, or side of the page. These guide you to other parts of the site that may be useful.

D Most pages have **links** to related pages. Links are often underlined words.

E Many sites have **interactive areas,** such as a guest book, where you can tell the site's creators what you think of their work.

MARK IT UP > Read the two Web sites on the right-hand page. The top one is a search engine that shows responses to a student's question. The bottom one is a site linked to one of those responses. Then use the information from the sites and the tips above to answer the questions.

1. Circle the Web address on both pages.

2. On the "LookQuick" page, what three terms did the student ask the search engine to

   look for? _____

3. On the "Gold Fever!" site, put a star by the link you would click on if you wanted to learn about people who immigrated to California to take part in the gold rush.

4. Put a box around the link you would click on to tell the creators of "Gold Fever!" your opinion of their site.

5. **ASSESSMENT PRACTICE** Choose the sentence that best summarizes the "Gold Fever!" site.
   A. It describes a dangerous illness called gold fever.
   B. It explains how you can mine for gold in your own backyard.
   C. It is an online museum exhibit about the California gold rush.
   D. none of the above

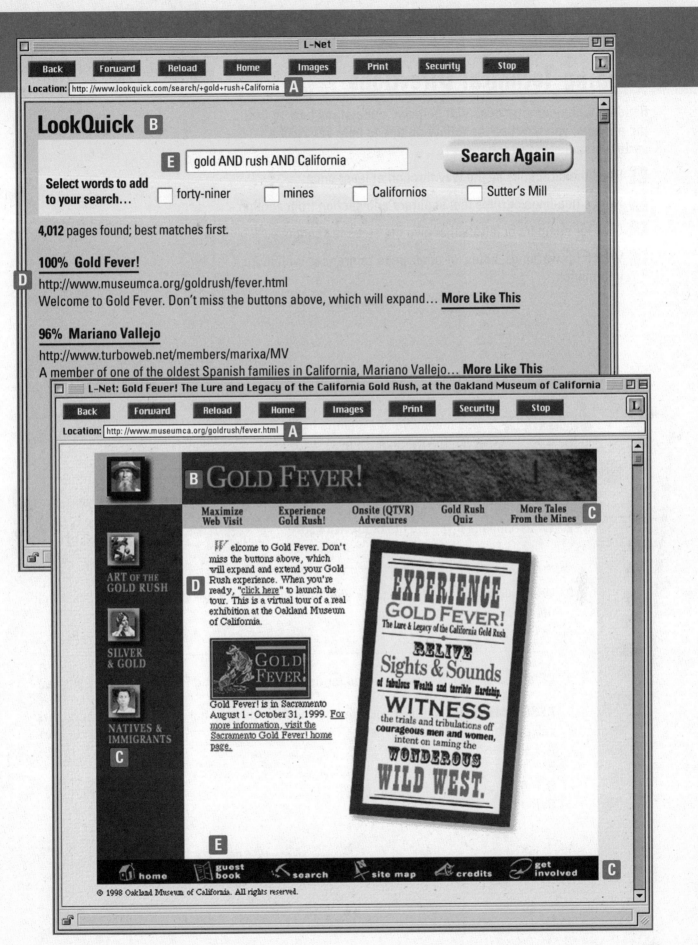

L-Net

Back | Forward | Reload | Home | Images | Print | Security | Stop | **L**

Location: http://www.lookquick.com/search/+gold+rush+California **A**

LookQuick **B**

E gold AND rush AND California   **Search Again**

Select words to add to your search…   ☐ forty-niner   ☐ mines   ☐ Californios   ☐ Sutter's Mill

4,012 pages found; best matches first.

D

100% Gold Fever!

http://www.museumca.org/goldrush/fever.html
Welcome to Gold Fever. Don't miss the buttons above, which will expand… **More Like This**

96% Mariano Vallejo

http://www.turboweb.net/members/marixa/MV
A member of one of the oldest Spanish families in California, Mariano Vallejo… **More Like This**

L-Net: Gold Fever! The Lure and Legacy of the California Gold Rush, at the Oakland Museum of California

Back | Forward | Reload | Home | Images | Print | Security | Stop | **L**

Location: http://www.museumca.org/goldrush/fever.html **A**

B GOLD FEVER!

| Maximize Web Visit | Experience Gold Rush! | Onsite (QTVR) Adventures | Gold Rush Quiz | More Tales From the Mines **C** |

ART OF THE GOLD RUSH

SILVER & GOLD

NATIVES & IMMIGRANTS **C**

D Welcome to Gold Fever. Don't miss the buttons above, which will expand and extend your Gold Rush experience. When you're ready, "click here" to launch the tour. This is a virtual tour of a real exhibition at the Oakland Museum of California.

GOLD FEVER!

Gold Fever! is in Sacramento August 1 - October 31, 1999. For more information, visit the Sacramento Gold Fever! home page.

EXPERIENCE GOLD FEVER!
The Lure & Legacy of the California Gold Rush
RELIVE Sights & Sounds of fabulous Wealth and terrible Hardship.
WITNESS the trials and tribulations off **courageous men and women,** intent on taming the **WONDEROUS WILD WEST.**

E

🏠 home   📖 guest book   🔍 search   🧭 site map   📜 credits   ↪ get involved **C**

© 1998 Oakland Museum of California. All rights reserved.

Reading Technical Directions

Reading technical directions will help you understand how to use the products you buy. Use the following tips to help you read a variety of technical directions.

A Read the directions all the way through at least once.

B Notice headings or rules that separate one section from another.

C Look for numbers or letters that give the steps in sequence.

D Watch for warnings, notes, or other page references with more information.

MARK IT UP Use the above tips and the technical directions on the opposite page to help you answer the following questions.

1. What is the first thing you must do to set the clock? Underline your answer on the next page.

2. What happens if you set the clock at 14:30?

   _____

3. What information can you find on another page? Draw a box around the statement that helps you answer this question.

   _____

4. What power level is recommended for defrosting or thawing food? Circle your answer.

5. **ASSESSMENT PRACTICE** If you are cooking something at full power, which characters will appear on the display?
   A. P-100
   B. P-HI
   C. P-0
   D. P-10

A Microwave Instructions

B Before Operating

1 Plug the power cord into a three-pronged electrical outlet.

C **2** Display panel will light up and flash 88:88.
Touch Stop/Clear pad.

3 Set the clock.
Touch Stop/Clear pad when the oven is first plugged in, or after the electrical power has been interrupted.

Setting the Clock

Procedure

1 Touch Clock pad

2 Enter time of day. For example, if it is 10:30, touch the number pads 1030 and "10:30" will appear.

3 Press the Clock pad again to set the time.

D **Note** You can select any time of the day from 1:00–12:59. To reset Clock, repeat steps 1 through 3 above. If incorrect time (for example, 8:61 or 13:00, etc.) is entered "EE" will appear on display. Touch Stop/Clear pad and program correctly.

Cancelling a Program

• To reset, or cancel, a cooking program as it is being entered, touch Stop/Clear pad once.

• To stop the oven while it is operating, touch Stop/Clear pad once. Do not open the door without pressing Stop/Clear pad.

• An entire cooking program (one stage or multiple stages) can be canceled after the oven has started cooking. This can be done by touching Stop/Clear pad twice.

Note See page 10 to create your own cooking programs.

Power Levels

Most foods can be cooked at full power (P-HI). However, for best results, some foods require a lower cooking power. Some foods such as tender cuts of meat can only be cooked with a lower power. Before setting any power level, the Power Level pad must be touched, followed by desired number. See chart.

1	2	3
4	5	6
7	8	9
POWER LEVEL	0	TIMER CLOCK
STOP CLEAR		START

POWER	Touch Power Level pad, then	Display
100%	Touch Power Level pad once more.	P-HI
90%	Touch number pad 9.	P-90
80%	Touch number pad 8.	P-80
70%	Touch number pad 7.	P-70
60%	Touch number pad 6.	P-60
50%	Touch number pad 5.	P-50
40%	Touch number pad 4.	P-40
30%	Touch number pad 3.	P-30
20%	Touch number pad 2.	P-20
10%	Touch number pad 1.	P-10
0%	Touch number pad 0.	P-0

Note Choose P-30 for thawing or defrosting foods.

Product Information: Warranties

A warranty is a promise that the manufacturer will repair a product for free within a certain time period and under certain conditions. Learning to read a warranty will help you take advantage of the services you're entitled to. Look at the sample limited warranty as you read each strategy below.

A This section explains the services the manufacturer will carry out and the length of time they will be available. "Accessories" are items that are not part of the main product. Accessories that accompany a television may include cables and an antenna.

B In this section, the manufacturer explains the conditions under which the company is not responsible for repairing the product. Note that "acts of God" refers to such natural disasters as floods, earthquakes, and fires.

C The manufacturer may include requirements you must meet to obtain warranty service.

D Manufacturers usually include the phone number and address of their service center. You can contact the service center to find a store that will repair your product.

LIMITED WARRANTY — Color TV

West Electronics Inc. ("West") warrants this Product (including any accessories) against defects in material or workmanship, subject to any conditions set forth as follows:

A A. LABOR: For a period of 90 days from the date of purchase, if this Product is determined to be defective, West will repair or replace the Product, at its option, at no charge, or pay the labor charges to any West authorized service facility. After the Warranty Period, you must pay for all labor charges.

B. PARTS: In addition, West will supply, at no charge, new or rebuilt replacements in exchange for defective parts for a period of one (1) year (color picture tube-two (2) years). After 90 days from the date of purchase, labor for removal and installation is available from West authorized service facilities or a West Service Center at your expense.

C. ACCESSORIES: Parts and labor for all accessories are for one (1) year.

B This warranty does not cover cosmetic damage or damage due to acts of God, accident, misuse, abuse, negligence, commercial use, or modification of, or to any part of the Product, including the antenna.

C Proof of purchase in the form of a bill of sale or receipted invoice which is evidence that the unit is within the Warranty period must be presented to obtain warranty service.

To locate the servicer or dealer nearest you, call:

D **West Service Center**
1-(800)-111-1111
or write to:
West Service Center
1234 Main St.
Westtown, CA 90000

MARK IT UP Read the warranty to help you answer these questions.

1. For how many days after purchase is labor free? _____

2. Underline the conditions not covered by the warranty.

3. What do you need to provide in order to prove that you bought the product within the

   warranty period? _____

4. Circle the phone number you should call to find a store that will repair your product.

5. **ASSESSMENT PRACTICE** How long does the warranty cover accessories?
   A. 90 days
   B. 2 years
   C. 60 days
   D. 1 year

Reading a Train Schedule

Knowing how to read a schedule accurately will help you get to places on time. Look at the example as you read each strategy on this list.

A Scan the **title** to know what the schedule covers.

B Look for **labels** that show **dates** or **days of the week** to help you understand how the weekly or daily schedule works.

C Study **place labels,** such as station names, to help you understand the stopping points on the schedule.

D Look for **expressions of time** to know what hours or minutes are listed on the schedule.

E Look for **train numbers** to help you determine which train stops at certain stations.

A Kenwood to Turner City—Monday through Friday **B**

E STATIONS	300 A.M.	302 A.M.	304 A.M.	306 A.M.	308 A.M.	310 A.M.	312 A.M.	314 —	316 A.M.	318 A.M.	320 A.M.	322 A.M.
C Kenwood LV:	—	—	—	5:55	—	6:17	—	—	6:53	—	—	7:15
North Springs	—	—	—	6:03	—	6:25	—	—	7:02	—	—	7:23
Hollow Lake	—	—	—	6:07	—	6:30	—	7:09	7:06	—	—	7:28
Grant St.	4:58	5:28	5:54	6:17	—	6:39	—	7:12	7:15	7:20	—	7:37
Central St. **D**	5:01	5:31	5:58	6:19	—	6:43	—	7:16	↓	7:24	—	7:42
Main St.	5:05	—	6:02	—	—	6:46	—	—		7:27	—	—
Ft. Peck	5:10	5:37	6:06	6:26	—	6:50	—	7:23	7:24	7:32	—	7:49
River Valley	5:13	5:40	6:10	6:30	—	6:54	—	↓		7:36	—	7:54
Columbus St.	5:16	5:44	6:14	6:35	—	6:59	—		7:32	7:40	—	7:59
Allen Square	5:19	5:47	6:17	6:38	—	7:02	—	7:31	7:36	7:43	—	—
River Falls	5:22	5:50	6:20	6:41	—	7:05	—	7:35	—	7:46	7:53	8:05
Hudson City	5:25	5:53	6:23	6:45	—	7:09	—	↓	7:41	↓	7:57	↓
Santa Ana	—	—	—	—	—	—	—	↓	—	↓	—	↓
Lake Pawnee	5:27	5:55	6:25	6:48	—	7:12	—	7:39	7:43		7:51	
Erie Falls	5:30	5:58	6:28	6:51	—	7:15	—	7:42	—	7:52	8:01	
Turner City AR:	5:33	6:01	6:31	6:54	—	7:18	—		7:48	—	8:06	↓

❙❙ MARK IT UP ▷ Answer the following questions using the train schedule and strategies on this page.

1. Where do the trains on this schedule go? _____

2. What days does this schedule cover? _____

3. Circle three stations where train 304 does not stop.

4. **ASSESSMENT PRACTICE** If you board train 316 from Grant St., what will be the first stop the train will make?
   A. Central St.
   B. Main St.
   C. Ft. Peck
   D. Columbus St.

Test Preparation Strategies

In this section you'll find strategies and practice to help you with many different kinds of standardized tests. The strategies apply to questions based on long and short readings, as well as questions about charts, graphs, and product labels. You'll also find examples and practice for revising-and-editing tests and writing tests. Applying the strategies to the practice materials and thinking through the answers will help you succeed in many formal testing situations.

Test Preparation Strategies

You can prepare for tests in several ways. First, study and understand the content that will be on the test. Second, learn as many test-taking techniques as you can. These techniques will help you better understand the questions and how to answer them. Following are some general suggestions for preparing for and taking tests. Starting on page 390, you'll find more detailed suggestions and test-taking practice.

Successful Test Taking

TUESDAY 4 | Study Content Throughout the Year

1. **Master the content of your language arts class.** The best way to study for tests is to read, understand, and review the content of your language arts class. Read your daily assignments carefully. Study the notes that you have taken in class. Participate in class discussions. Work with classmates in small groups to help one another learn. You might trade writing assignments and comment on your classmates' work.

2. **Use your textbook for practice.** Your textbook includes many different types of questions. Some may ask you to talk about a story you just read. Others may ask you to figure out what's wrong with a sentence or how to make a paragraph sound better. Try answering these questions out loud and in writing. This type of practice can make taking a test much easier.

3. **Learn how to understand the information in charts, maps, and graphic organizers.** One type of test question may ask you to look at a graphic organizer, such as a spider map, and explain something about the information you see there. Another type of question may ask you to look at a map to find a particular place, such as the Klondike setting of the story "The King of Mazy May." You'll find charts, maps, and graphic organizers to study in your literature textbooks. You'll also find charts, maps and graphs in your science, mathematics, and social studies textbook. When you look at these, ask yourself, What information is being presented and why is it important?

4. **Practice taking tests.** Use copies of tests you have taken in the past or in other classes for practice. Every test has a time limit, so set a timer for 15 or 20 minutes and then begin your practice. Try to finish the test in the time you've given yourself.

✔ **Reading Check**

In what practical way can your textbook help you prepare for a test?

5. **Talk about test-taking experiences.** After you've taken a classroom test or quiz, talk about it with your teacher and classmates. Which types of questions were the hardest to understand? What made them difficult? Which questions seemed easiest, and why? When you share test-taking techniques with your classmates, everyone can become a successful test taker.

 ## Use Strategies During the Test

1. **Read the directions carefully.** You can't be a successful test taker unless you know exactly what you are expected to do. Look for key words and phrases, such as *circle the best answer, write a paragraph,* or *choose the word that best completes each sentence.*

2. **Learn how to read test questions.** Test questions can sometimes be difficult to figure out. They may include unfamiliar language or be written in an unfamiliar way. Try rephrasing the question in a simpler way using words you understand. Always ask yourself, What type of information does this question want me to provide?

3. **Pay special attention when using a separate answer sheet.** If you accidentally skip a line on an answer sheet, all the rest of your answers may be wrong! Try one or more of the following techniques:

   - Use a ruler on the answer sheet to make sure you are placing your answers on the correct line.

   - After every five answers, check to make sure you're on the right line.

   - Each time you turn a page of the test booklet, check to make sure the number of the question is the same as the number of the answer line on the answer sheet.

   - If the answer sheet has circles, fill them in neatly. A stray pencil mark might cause the scoring machine to count the answer as incorrect.

4. **If you're not sure of the answer, make your best guess.** Unless you've been told that there is a penalty for guessing, choose the answer that you think is likeliest to be correct.

5. **Keep track of the time.** Answering all the questions on a test usually results in a better score. That's why finishing the test is important. Keep track of the time you have left. At the beginning of the test, figure out how many questions you will have to answer by the halfway point in order to finish in the time given.

☑ Reading Check

What are at least two good ways to avoid skipping lines on an answer sheet?

Understand Types of Test Questions

Most tests include two types of questions: multiple choice and open-ended. Specific strategies will help you understand and correctly answer each type of question.

A **multiple-choice question** has two parts. The first part is the question itself, called the stem. The second part is a series of possible answers. Usually four possible answers are provided, and only one of them is correct. Your task is to choose the correct answer. Here are some strategies to help you do just that.

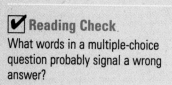

Reading Check

What words in a multiple-choice question probably signal a wrong answer?

1. Read and think about each question carefully before looking at the possible answers.

2. Pay close attention to key words in the question. For example, look for the word *not,* as in "Which of the following is not a cause of the conflict in this story?"

3. Read and think about all of the possible answers before making your choice.

4. Reduce the number of choices by eliminating any answers you know are incorrect. Then, think about why some of the remaining choices might also be incorrect.

   • If two of the choices are pretty much the same, both are probably wrong.

   • Answers that contain any of the following words are usually incorrect: *always, never, none, all,* and *only.*

5. If you're still unsure about an answer, see if any of the following applies:

   • When one choice is longer and more detailed than the others, it is often the correct answer.

   • When a choice repeats a word that is in the question, it may be the correct answer.

   • When two choices are direct opposites, one of them is likely the correct answer.

   • When one choice includes one or more of the other choices, it is often the correct answer.

   • When a choice includes the word *some* or *often,* it may be the correct answer.

- If one of the choices is *All of the above,* make sure that at least two of the other choices seem correct.

- If one of the choices is *None of the above,* make sure that none of the other choices seems correct.

An **open-ended test item** can take many forms. It might ask you to write a word or phrase to complete a sentence. You might be asked to create a chart, draw a map, or fill in a graphic organizer. Sometimes, you will be asked to write one or more paragraphs in response to a writing prompt. Use the following strategies when reading and answering open-ended items:

1. If the item includes directions, read them carefully. Take note of any steps required.

2. Look for key words and phrases in the item as you plan how you will respond. Does the item ask you to identify a cause-and-effect relationship or to compare and contrast two or more things? Are you supposed to provide a sequence of events or make a generalization? Does the item ask you to write an essay in which you state your point of view and then try to persuade others that your view is correct?

3. If you're going to be writing a paragraph or more, plan your answer. Jot down notes and a brief outline of what you want to say before you begin writing.

4. Focus your answer. Don't include everything you can think of, but be sure to include everything the item asks for.

5. If you're creating a chart or drawing a map, make sure your work is as clear as possible.

✔ Reading Check

What are at least three key strategies for answering an open-ended question?

DIRECTIONS Here is a selection entitled "Dolphinspeak" by Aline Alexander Newman. Read the selection carefully. The notes in the side columns will help you prepare for the kinds of questions that are likely to follow readings like this. You might want to preview the questions on pages 392–393 before you begin reading.

Reading Strategies for Assessment

Think about the title. Titles often offer clues about the topic of a selection. Write what you think this article will be about.

Consider the author's purpose. What do these questions suggest about the author's motive for writing this article?

Look for cause-and-effect relationships. Why do scientists believe dolphins can communicate with each other? Circle the reason.

Dolphinspeak
The Incredible Ways Dolphins Communicate with Each Other— and with Us

by Aline Alexander Newman

"Psst, listen up."

A female dolphin was being trained to push paddles to get food. Although she couldn't see her partner, a male dolphin in a separate tank, she kept whistling and chirping to him. Soon he started pushing paddles, too. Did the female "tell" him how to do it?

Squawks, whistles, chirps, and clicks—the racket is earsplitting as groups of bottlenose dolphins zoom around beneath the waves. Scientists have been aware of the dolphins' noisemaking for years. But are the animals talking to each other? If they are, what are they saying?

Where there are dolphins, there are humans who are curious about them. There are dozens of species of dolphins, and they live in oceans all over the world, as well as in some rivers. They live in groups. The ultimate team players, some kinds of dolphins work together to herd fish and then take turns eating their catch. They speed through the water side by side, sometimes making sounds as they swim. They zip along without bumping or banging into each other. Scientists believe the only way dolphins could work together so well and in so many ways is if they're "talking."

That's why marine biologist Kathleen Dudzinski has been eavesdropping on dolphin "conversations" for ten years. By carefully observing dolphin behavior, she hopes eventually to learn their "language." That may take a while. Dolphins are mammals, so they have lungs and must breathe air at the water's surface. But they spend 99 percent of their lives underwater, making them hard to find and study. "It's like trying to put together a giant jigsaw puzzle when you've lost the box lid with the puzzle's picture on it," says Dudzinski.

Dudzinski studies wild dolphins around the world. She films them using a custom-made video camera and recording system. When Dudzinski plays back her tapes, she makes notes of what she sees and hears.

Dolphin communication includes many different kinds of signals: touching each other, body position, movement such as leaping and rolling, and sounds. Sometimes signals are used alone, sometimes in combination. For example, making clicking noises toward each other and then rubbing fins might be the dolphin way of saying "hi."

There is evidence that dolphins call each other "by name." Vincent Janik, a <u>zoologist</u> from the United Kingdom, says that each individual dolphin develops a personal whistle. When the water is so murky that they can't see each other, the dolphins whistle those personal names to stay in touch.

Dudzinski's biggest discovery was recognizing the differences in communication when dolphins play and fight. It was confusing at first, because dolphins whistle loudly and bite each other in both situations. But one day after watching some puppies tumbling about, she realized that the playful dolphins usually do the same thing. They romp and roll and rub each other. Dolphins that are fighting don't do any rubbing, and they tend to get right in each other's faces.

While Dudzinski and Janik do research in the wild, other scientists study captive animals. One pair of captive dolphins knows 50 words in sign language. They even understand the difference between "take the Frisbee to the surfboard" and "take the surfboard to the Frisbee."

Wild dolphins often leap out of the water at the same time. Knowing that, trainers use signals to tell captive dolphins to plan their next move. The animals submerge, "discuss" what they're going to do, and do it—in perfect unison! And that's what humans call cool!

Analyze supporting details. Reread this paragraph to find the details that support the jigsaw puzzle comparison.

Look for clues to the main idea. This paragraph makes a general observation about dolphin communication. Write the main idea of the paragraph in your own words.

Infer meanings from word parts. Circle the word you can see in *zoologist*. Use its meaning to figure out a possible definition for *zoologist*.

Notice comparisons and contrasts. The paragraph that begins, "Dudzinski's biggest discovery . . ." compares and contrasts the behavior of fighting dolphins with that of playing dolphins. Underline the differences she discovered.

Analyze the author's perspective. Circle words that show the author's attitude toward her subject. Are they positive or negative words?

Answer Strategies

Now answer questions 1 through 8. Base your answers on the article "Dolphinspeak." Then check yourself by reading through the side-column notes.

Determine author's purpose.
The key words in this question are *major purpose*. They tell you that the correct answer will refer to the author's main reason for writing the article, not her reason for including some particular facts.

1 The author's major purpose in writing this article is to

    A. compare dolphins with other mammals.

    B. describe how dolphins communicate.

    C. get people interested in training dolphins.

    D. explain how dolphins play.

Look for causes and effects. The word *why* signals that the question involves cause and effect. Find the quoted word in the article. Then choose the answer that matches the reason stated in the text.

2 Why do scientists believe that dolphins "talk"?

    E. They are mammals.

    F. They are able to live in oceans all over the world.

    G. They work together well in many ways.

    H. They make many different kinds of noises.

Infer meanings. Locate the quoted sentence in the passage. Reread the surrounding paragraphs to help you infer the meaning of *zoologist*.

3 Read the following sentence from the article.

> **Vincent Janik, a zoologist from the United Kingdom, says that each individual dolphin develops a personal whistle.**

What is the meaning of the word *zoologist*?

    A. a scientist who studies animals

    B. someone from a foreign country

    C. someone trained to identify whistles

    D. a person who works with captive dolphins

Find contrasts. The question asks for a difference between fighting and playing dolphins. Locate and reread the paragraph that compares and contrasts dolphins' behavior in these two situations.

4 What do fighting dolphins do that is different from what playing dolphins do?

    E. Fighting dolphins whistle loudly.

    F. Fighting dolphins rub each other.

    G. Fighting dolphins get in each other's faces.

    H. Fighting dolphins bite each other.

Identify the main idea. Think about how you would sum up the main idea of the selection in a sentence. Remember that the title often relates to the main idea. Which choice comes closest to your summary?

5 Which statement best summarizes the information in this article?

    A. Dolphins are very noisy mammals.

    B. Dolphins are smarter than people.

    C. Dolphins have a complicated communication system.

    D. We will never understand dolphins.

Answers:
1.B, 2.G, 3.A, 4.G, 5.C

6 If the article needed a new title, which would be best?

E. "Dolphins Call Each Other by Name"

F. "Marine Biologist Kathleen Dudzinski"

G. "Under the Sea"

H. "Can Dolphins Communicate?"

Revisit the title. Consider how the current title reflects the main idea of the article. Eliminate answer choices that are too narrow or too broad. Select the one that is closest in meaning to the actual title.

7 With which statement would the author of "Dolphinspeak" most likely agree?

A. Dolphins are solitary animals.

B. Dolphins should be studied further.

C. Fish can also communicate with each other.

D. Scientists spend too much time studying dolphins.

Identify author's perspective. First eliminate answers that are obviously wrong or irrelevant (A and C). The remaining choices, B and D, express opposite opinions about studying dolphins. Which opinion matches the author's perspective?

8 Read the following sentence from the article.

> **"It's like trying to put together a giant jigsaw puzzle when you've lost the box lid with the puzzle's picture on it," says Dudzinski.**

Explain the meaning of this statement in your own words. Be sure to tell what the scientist is comparing to putting together a jigsaw puzzle and in what ways the two activities are alike.

Plan your response. Underline what the question is asking you to do and what you must include. Then go back to the selection and draw stars next to details that support and develop your answer.

Sample short response for question 8:

The scientist in the article is comparing putting together a jigsaw puzzle to learning about dolphins. She is saying that it's hard to figure out where the pieces of a puzzle go when you don't know what it's supposed to look like. Trying to figure out what dolphins are doing is hard and frustrating in the same way because they spend almost all their time underwater.

Study the response. Notice how the writer states what is being compared in the first sentence. The explanation is then developed with the writer's own thoughts as well as details from the selection.

Answers: 6. H, 7. B

Reading Test Practice
LONG SELECTIONS

DIRECTIONS Now it's time to practice what you've learned about reading test items and choosing the best answers. Read the following selection, "Finding a Bit of History" by Shirley Neitzel. Use the side columns to make notes about the important parts of this selection: main ideas, cause and effect, comparisons and contrasts, difficult vocabulary, supporting details, and so on.

Finding a Bit of History
by Shirley Neitzel

Less than a quarter mile into Maldonado Bay from the dock at Punta del Este, Uruguay, Hector Bado rechecked his instruments and charts. Then he and his crew anchored his ship, the *Surveyor*. This was the place: through earlier exploration he knew what lay on the ocean's bottom here—the remains of the Spanish freighter *Salvador*.

Even though his crew was highly experienced, excitement rippled through them as divers with underwater cameras prepared to enter the murky bay. The divers could see only a few feet through the swirling sand and debris. Maldonado Bay is part of the Río de la Plata, and its sediment has slowly been burying the *Salvador* over 186 years.

In the late 1700s and early 1800s, Spain, Portugal, England, and France waged wars to expand their empires. Spain's South American colonies were occupied at different times by Portuguese and English troops. The colonists were dissatisfied with the rule of their distant king, and in 1810 José Gervasio Artigas led Uruguay in a revolution.

Spain reacted by sending in troops. In April 1812, a battalion of trained soldiers boarded the *Salvador* at Cadiz, Spain, with orders to put down the revolutionaries. On 31 August the ship arrived at the mouth of the Río de la Plata. From there a local naval pilot was to guide it through the treacherous waters into the port of Montevideo. But a *pampero*, a strong wind, was building from the southwest, so the pilot sailed the ship into Maldonado Bay for protection from the storm. The bay proved too shallow for such a large ship, and the *Salvador* struck bottom. The captain was able to free it, but a short time later it struck bottom again.

Although the crew hoped to ride out the storm, the winds were too strong. Sturdy oak planks splintered as each wave smashed the ship's keel onto the bottom of the bay. The *Salvador* listed and heaved. On deck, cannons broke loose from their mounts. Soldiers and crew panicked as the bronze behemoths careened among them. To keep the ship from capsizing, the crew cut the masts. The sails fell, trapping men in the heavy canvas and rigging.

Few of the seven hundred people on board knew how to swim, so they stayed with the ship. Had they known they were only about three hundred meters from shore, more of them might have been able to save themselves. But in the darkness, confusion reigned. The next morning, the *Salvador* lay on the bottom of Maldonado Bay, and most of her troops had gone down with her. Without these soldiers, the Spanish effort to crush the revolution was weakened. By 1816 Spain had lost Uruguay forever.

One of the few survivors of the wreck of the *Salvador* was Antonio De Acosta y Lara, an assistant to the coastal pilots in Montevideo. His handwritten account of that terrible night was found in 1993 by a historian studying in the Naval Archives near Madrid, Spain.

At almost the same time, Hector Bado, diving near Punta del Este, discovered the wreck. The *Salvador* was a wooden sailing vessel, and much of it had rotted away long ago. What's left no longer resembles a ship, and an inexperienced diver might easily have ignored the piles of mussel-covered rubble. But Bado knew the shells could be hiding something interesting. Mussels don't cling to bronze, so with a little investigation, he discovered cannons looking much as they did when the *Salvador* sank. Bado obtained permits from the government of Uruguay to salvage the ship. By the fall of 1998 he was ready.

Most of the items once on board the *Salvador* were hidden by sand and clay. Digging can destroy delicate artifacts, so divers must loosen the sediment by waving their hands like fish tails. It's slow work, but lucky divers may uncover a button, a coin, a bottle, a telescope, or something else from the ship.

A marine archaeologist oversees the salvage. Divers create a grid of string over the wreck site, then carefully explore each square of the grid. Every artifact must be cataloged, cleaned, tagged, photographed, preserved, and stored. A three-dimensional drawing shows where each artifact was found.

On 30 October 1998, the first items—four bronze cannons—were raised from the wreck site. The admiral of the Uruguayan navy, the director of the Historical Museum of Uruguay, and many other officials joined the crew of the *Surveyor* for this historic event, and a navy ship fired a twenty-one-gun salute to the people who died on the *Salvador*.

On the dock at Punta del Este, hundreds of people clapped and cheered as the 1,400-pound cannons were lifted from the *Surveyor*. Each cannon had been cast with its name. These were *Rafael, Piedad, Miguel,* and *Graviel.* Children and adults surrounded the crew of the *Surveyor* and followed the cannons as they were taken by forklift to their preservation site. The salvage of the *Salvador* acknowledges a step toward the formation of the country of Uruguay, and the crowd was eager to see this piece of their history. One old man reached out and touched a cannon, then kissed his fingers. A woman touched a cannon, crossed herself, and fell to her knees.

Afterward, the crew of the *Surveyor* returned to the business of excavating the rest of the wreck. Muskets and swords littered the shallow water, as well as two brass-and-ebony sextants used by the *Salvador*'s navigators to determine their position at sea. Divers also uncovered a tooth extractor, splints, medicine vials, and the surgical tools of the ship's doctor. They found needles, scissors, and thimbles belonging to the ship's tailor, as well as cartons of buttons and bolts of fabric for military uniforms. Careful fanning revealed coins, religious medals, and other personal belongings of the soldiers and crew.

Items uncovered from the shipwreck are being shared equally between the salvage company and the government of Uruguay. Some of the artifacts will go to museums; others will be sold to private collectors. Hector Bado hopes to have any human remains reburied and a memorial erected, either in Uruguay or Spain.

"There are big differences between divers who hunt for treasure and those who are motivated by a desire to learn about naval history and to preserve it," said Bado. "The important thing is to salvage this bit of history."

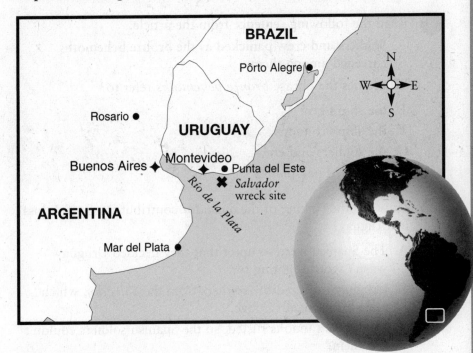

Now answer questions 1 through 10. Base your answers on the article "Finding a Bit of History."

1 What is the author's main purpose in writing this article?

A. to persuade people to study history
B. to explain how the *Salvador* sank in 1812
C. to describe the history and recovery of the *Salvador*
D. to teach people how to dive for sunken treasure

2 The Spanish ship *Salvador* sailed to Uruguay in 1812 to

E. put down a revolution by the colonists.
F. teach Spanish soldiers about life in the colonies.
G. trade with the colonists.
H. see how the ship would handle in shallow water.

3 Using the text and the map, decide which direction the shipwreck was from Montevideo, where the *Salvador* was headed.

A. west

B. east

C. southeast

D. northwest

4 Read the following sentence from the article.

Soldiers and crew panicked as the bronze behemoths careened among them.

What does the phrase *bronze behemoths* refer to?

E. the ship's keel

F. the ship's cannons

G. the soldiers and crew

H. splintered oak planks

5 How did the sinking of the *Salvador* contribute to Spain's loss of Uruguay?

A. The Spanish were so upset that they decided Uruguay wasn't worth fighting for.

B. Uruguay captured the soldiers from the *Salvador,* which gave them the advantage.

C. The ship's cannons rusted, so the Spanish soldiers couldn't fire them.

D. Most of the soldiers on the *Salvador* died, which weakened the Spanish fighting force.

6 What organizational pattern does the author use for the third through the eighth paragraphs?

E. fact and opinion

F. problem and solution

G. chronological order

H. spatial order

7 Which of the following statements best supports the idea that Bado is carefully preserving the *Salvador* artifacts?

    A. Bado's crew works slowly and keeps records of where each item was found.

    B. Bado's crew has found surgical tools used by the ship's doctor.

    C. A historian found a handwritten account of the *Salvador*'s sinking.

    D. The first items to be raised from the site were four bronze cannons.

8 The information in the article "Finding a Bit of History" could best be used for a student research project on

    E. mussels and other animals that live in the ocean.

    F. uncovering lost historical artifacts.

    G. how to avoid being shipwrecked.

    H. the modern government of Uruguay.

9 Read these sentences from the article.

> **One old man reached out and touched a cannon, then kissed his fingers. A woman touched a cannon, crossed herself, and fell to her knees.**

What did the cannons from the *Salvador* mean to these people?

    A. recovery of the lost history of their country

    B. proof that Uruguay can never be defeated by Spain

    C. a wealth of precious bronze metal

    D. pride in the skill of their divers and marine archaeologists

10 Explain how using a grid of string helped divers recover items from the wreck of the *Salvador*. Use details and information from the article to support your answer.

_____

_____

_____

_____

_____

_____

THINKING IT THROUGH

The notes in the side columns will help you think through your answers. See the key at the bottom of the page. How well did you do?

> Keep in mind the key words *main purpose*. Do not be distracted by statements that refer to only one part of the passage.

1 What is the author's main purpose in writing this article?

   A. to persuade people to study history

   B. to explain how the *Salvador* sank in 1812

   C. to describe the history and recovery of the *Salvador*

   D. to teach people how to dive for sunken treasure

> Use the question to help you find the answer. Scan the passage for the date 1812. That is where you will find the reason for the ship's sailing.

2 The Spanish ship *Salvador* sailed to Uruguay in 1812 to

   E. put down a revolution by the colonists.

   F. teach Spanish soldiers about life in the colonies.

   G. trade with the colonists.

   H. see how the ship would handle in shallow water.

> Try rephrasing the question as a fill-in-the-blank statement to be sure you understand what it is asking. "The wreck is located _____ of Montevideo."

3 Using the text and the map, decide which direction the shipwreck was from Montevideo, where the *Salvador* was headed.

   A. west

   B. east

   C. southeast

   D. northwest

> Find this sentence in the selection. Read the sentence preceding it to identify the part of the ship to which *bronze behemoths* refers.

4 Read the following sentence from the article.

   Soldiers and crew panicked as the bronze behemoths careened among them.

What does the phrase *bronze behemoths* refer to?

   E. the ship's keel

   F. the ship's cannons

   G. the soldiers and crew

   H. splintered oak planks

Answers: 1.C, 2.E, 3.C, 4.F

5 How did the sinking of the *Salvador* contribute to Spain's loss of Uruguay?

A. The Spanish were so upset that they decided Uruguay wasn't worth fighting for.

B. Uruguay captured the soldiers from the *Salvador*, which gave them the advantage.

C. The ship's cannons rusted, so the Spanish soldiers couldn't fire them.

D. Most of the soldiers on the *Salvador* died, which weakened the Spanish fighting force.

> Narrow your choices to those that you know contain accurate facts. Then refer back to the passage to determine which one is valid.

6 What organizational pattern does the author use for the third through the eighth paragraphs?

E. fact and opinion

F. problem and solution

G. chronological order

H. spatial order

> Skim the paragraphs listed. What does the frequent use of dates and time-order transitions indicate about the organization?

7 Which of the following statements best supports the idea that Bado is carefully preserving the *Salvador* artifacts?

A. Bado's crew works slowly and keeps records of where each item was found.

B. Bado's crew has found surgical tools used by the ship's doctor.

C. A historian found a handwritten account of the *Salvador*'s sinking.

D. The first items to be raised from the site were four bronze cannons.

> The words *carefully preserving* tell you to eliminate choices that merely state what has been found in the ship or how people learned about the ship.

8 The information in the article "Finding a Bit of History" could best be used for a student research project on

E. mussels and other animals that live in the ocean.

F. uncovering lost historical artifacts.

G. how to avoid being shipwrecked.

H. the modern government of Uruguay.

> Choose the answer most closely related to the central focus of the article as a whole.

Find these sentences in the passage. What reason for these actions is given in the preceding sentence?

9 Read these sentences from the article.

> **One old man reached out and touched a cannon, then kissed his fingers. A woman touched a cannon, crossed herself, and fell to her knees.**

What did the cannons from the *Salvador* mean to these people?

A. recovery of the lost history of their country

B. proof that Uruguay can never be defeated by Spain

C. a wealth of precious bronze metal

D. pride in the skill of their divers and marine archaeologists

10 Explain how using a grid of string helped divers recover items from the wreck of the *Salvador*. Use details and information from the article to support your answer.

> Using a grid of string had a two-fold purpose. First, divers could concentrate on one particular square and thoroughly search it before moving on to the next section of the wreck. In this way, they could be sure they explored the entire area. Second, the grid allowed the divers to keep accurate records of the original location of each artifact. A three-dimensional drawing now shows where each artifact was found.

This response received a top score because it
- explains two uses of the grid.
- uses details from the passage to support the explanation.
- is clearly written.

Reading Test Model
SHORT SELECTIONS

DIRECTIONS This reading selection is a brief e-mail. The strategies you have just used can also help you with this shorter selection. As you read the selection, respond to the notes in the side column.

When you've finished reading, you'll find four multiple-choice questions. Again, use the side-column notes to help you understand what each question is asking and why each answer is correct.

From: Dory Gray <dgray@ourschool.edu>
To: Mr. Storms <jstorms@ourschool.edu>
Date: Mon. Jan 27, 2003, 9:05 a.m.
Subject: Yearbook Plans

Hello Mr. Storms,

   I'm writing on behalf of the yearbook committee to thank you for agreeing to help us with the 2003 *Hoot*. I know we will plan, develop, and <u>creating</u> an outstanding yearbook with your leadership. I've listed below the meeting dates we are planning. Please let me know by reply e-mail whether you can make it at these times.

   Saturdays at 3:00 p.m., school cafeteria

   Tuesdays and Thursdays during lunch period, 3rd floor student lounge

   Fridays during 8th period study hall, library

   We have an exciting idea for how to make this year's *Hoot* a little different. We want to produce an online version. This may be expensive, but it will make Chavez High the first in the city with an electronic yearbook. Let me know what you think.

Thanks,
Dory Gray

Reading Strategies for Assessment

Consider the author's purpose.
Write a sentence explaining what you think is the reason for this e-mail.

Recognize persuasive language.
Underline the sentence that states the main idea of this paragraph. Circle words the writer uses to influence how the reader perceives this main idea.

Analyze sentence structure.
Return to the second sentence and
check the other verbs in the
sentence to decide which answer is
correct.

Analyze persuasive language.
Which choice uses language for the
purpose of appealing to the reader's
sense of pride?

Determine author's purpose. What
is the main reason Dory Gray wrote
the e-mail? Remember that an
effective e-mail usually states the
writer's purpose near the beginning.

Identify the key word. *First* tells
you to look near the beginning of the
e-mail to determine what Mr.
Storms is being asked to do.

1 What is the correct verb form for the underlined word in the
second sentence of the e-mail?

A. creating

B. create

C. created

D. creates

2 Which statement uses a persuasion technique?

E. We want to produce an online version.

F. I've listed below the meeting dates we are planning.

G. It will make Chavez High the first in the city with an
electronic yearbook.

H. Let me know what you think.

3 The author's main purpose in this e-mail is to

A. plan a luncheon with Mr. Storms.

B. involve Mr. Storms in yearbook planning.

C. get publicity for Chavez High.

D. ask Mr. Storms to raise money for the electronic yearbook.

4 According to the e-mail, what is the first response that Mr.
Storms should make?

E. Give permission for an online yearbook.

F. Confirm that he can attend the scheduled meetings.

G. Offer an opinion about the online yearbook.

H. Discuss the project with the principal.

Analyze the poem and answer the two questions that follow. Use the side notes to help you understand what you are reading and what the questions are asking.

The Magnificent Bull

Dinka Traditional

My bull is white like the silver fish in the river
white like the shimmering crane bird on the river bank
white like fresh milk!
His roar is like the thunder to the Turkish cannon on the
   steep shore.
My bull is dark like the raincloud in the storm.   5
He is like summer and winter.
Half of him is dark like the storm cloud,
half of him is light like sunshine.
His back shines like the morning star.
His brow is red like the beak of the Hornbill.   10
His forehead is like a flag, calling the people from
   a distance,
He resembles the rainbow.

I will water him at the river.
With my spear I shall drive my enemies.
Let them water their herds at the well;   15
the river belongs to me and my bull.
Drink, my bull, from the river; I am here
to guard you with my spear.

Reading Strategies for Assessment

Notice similes. The first stanza of this poem is a series of similes that use *like* to link the two parts of each comparison. In each line, underline the part of the bull that precedes *like* and circle what it is being compared to.

Draw conclusions. In the second stanza, what do the words and images suggest about the bull's importance to the speaker?

Answer Strategies

Draw conclusions. A logical conclusion based on evidence in the passage as well as your prior knowledge would be that the bull is very important to the speaker. What further conclusion might reasonably follow?

5 What can you conclude about the speaker's culture?

   A. Fishing is an important activity.
   B. Bulls play a central role in community life.
   C. Warfare is not allowed.
   D. People are encouraged to speak plainly.

Answer: 5. B

Analyze similes. Review the line that says the bull's forehead calls people from a distance. Which answer choice includes words that refer to distance?

6 In line 11, how is the bull's forehead like a flag?

   E. It has the same colors.

   F. It waves in the wind.

   G. It can be seen from far away.

   H. It stands for the community.

Reading Test Practice
SHORT SELECTIONS

DIRECTIONS Use the following selections to practice your skills. Read each passage and circle the key ideas. Then answer the multiple-choice questions that follow.

The Terra Cotta Army
by Victoria C. Nesnick

A group of farmers were searching for water in 1974 and began digging a well. There at Xian (pronounced *SHEE-ahn*), in the center of China, they uncovered something very strange. It was the head of an ancient terra cotta (pottery) statue. The news of their discovery spread, and archaeologists soon appeared on the scene. Continuing the excavation, the scientists found one broken statue after another, until 8,000 life-size clay warriors and horses were finally uncovered. They were the shattered army which had secretly been guarding the tomb of The First Emperor, Qin Shi Huang (pronounced *Chin Sher Wang*), for over 2,200 years.

The Chinese government restored many of the figures and built a hangarlike museum over the site. The *Guinness Book of Records* lists it as the world's largest tomb. French premier Jacques Chirac labeled it "The Eighth Wonder of the World."

The Statues
Some warriors wear armor. Others wear tunics and leggings called puttees. Their hair is tied in a variety of topknots called chignons. Each face is unique. No two are exactly alike. Each horse is also different.

Although the statues appear a solid reddish brown, they were once extremely bright and colorful. Floods, fire, and time have erased much of the ancient hues. What remained was obliterated within hours after the figures were uncovered and exposed to sunlight.

The Weapons

Over 10,000 weapons were found. Although the wooden spear shafts have disintegrated, thousands of bronze arrowheads remain. The most astonishing pieces are the metal swords. After the caked soil was removed, they were still shiny and sharp enough to split a hair. They serve as proof that China, not Europe, was the first to master the technology of the anti-erosion, anti-rust material called chrome.

The Bronze Chariots

In 1981, before archaeologists could release all the soldiers from their cold earthen prison, they made another discovery, a wooden coffin. It contained a set of miniature, horse-drawn chariots made of bronze. Each is a half-size reproduction of the actual sets once used to transport the royal family.

Although they too were found shattered, both sets were carefully restored. They have been labeled "The Champion of the Bronze" and are proof of the metal machinery skills of the Qin Dynasty.

The Workers

Over 720,000 Chinese people labored nearly 40 years, secretly creating the terra cotta army that guards Qin's tomb. After his body and his treasures were in place, the burial chamber was sealed up. The gates were locked, imprisoning all who had worked there. No one was allowed out. This ensured that the location of the tomb would be kept a secret. Crossbows were strategically placed to prevent thieves from stealing the treasures.

The Future

Although Qin's guardian army is now visited by millions of people from around the world, his tomb has not yet been excavated. More time is needed to study the many ancient booby traps that surround it. Archaeologists must also gain the technology necessary to conserve and preserve every item they will uncover. Once the tomb and the anticipated subterranean (underground) kingdom is uncovered, it will be one of the greatest discoveries in Chinese history.

1 The author's purpose in writing this passage is to

   A. entertain people with stories of ancient tombs.
   B. inform people about an important discovery.
   C. persuade people to travel to China.
   D. analyze techniques that archaeologists use to excavate ruins.

2 According to the passage, which might best describe the people of the Qin Dynasty?

   E. lazy and unsophisticated
   F. peace-loving and artistic
   G. hardworking and warlike
   H. cowardly and rebellious

3 What is the meaning of the underlined word in the sentence below?

   What remained was <u>obliterated</u> within hours after the figures were uncovered.

   A. destroyed
   B. brightened
   C. restored
   D. buried

4 Why are the terra cotta figures no longer brightly colored?

   E. The Chinese decided to paint them all reddish-brown.
   F. Paint peels very easily off of terra cotta.
   G. Archaeologists scraped the paint off.
   H. Over the years, water, fire, and sunlight caused the colors to fade.

5 What is one reason why Qin's tomb has not yet been excavated?

   A. The Chinese don't want it to be excavated.
   B. Archaeologists are only interested in the terra cotta army, not the tomb.
   C. Archaeologists need to study the booby traps surrounding it.
   D. Too many tourists visit the site.

6 Which of these statements is an opinion?

    E. Over 10,000 weapons were found.

    F. The most astonishing pieces are the metal swords.

    G. Over 720,000 Chinese labored nearly 40 years, secretly creating the terra cotta army.

    H. Crossbows were strategically placed to prevent thieves from stealing the treasures.

Discord at Danbury

[Setting: the stage of the Danbury School auditorium]

[Characters: Tamara, Jojo, Fred, Jasmine, and Allison stand in a group onstage, talking. Mr. James sits in the first row of the auditorium seats.]

[Enter Dorothy and Anita, walking onstage.]

Dorothy: I hope I get a part in the chorus. I really love to sing.

Anita: Me, too! This is going to be a great play, Dorothy! Wouldn't you rather play the lead, though?

Tamara: OK, now, who's going to direct the play?

[Six hands go up.]

Tamara: We can't all direct! [pause] We should have an election.

Jojo: I nominate myself.

[Tamara makes a face at Jojo.]

Fred: I nominate myself!

Jasmine: I nominate myself!

Allison: I nominate myself!

Tamara:	Then you're all nominated! That's just great. If we can't make any progress on this, how are we ever going to divide up the roles and have rehearsals?
Jasmine:	Never mind, Tamara. I don't really want to be the director.
Tamara:	Well, okay then, let's vote for director.
Jasmine:	I want to be the star!
Tamara:	Mr. James, help!

7 What conclusion can be drawn about Tamara?

A. She likes to take charge.

B. She wants to sing in the chorus.

C. She is shy.

D. She is flirting with Fred.

8 What is most likely the role of Mr. James?

E. He is Tamara's father.

F. He is a student.

G. He is a visitor to the school.

H. He is the teacher in charge of the play.

9 What type of passage is this?

A. a poem

B. a short story

C. a drama

D. an essay

THINKING IT THROUGH

The notes in the side columns will help you think through your answers. Check the key at the bottom of each page. How well did you do?

> The supporting details are factual, indicating that the author wants to share information.

1 The author's purpose in writing this passage is to

    A. entertain people with stories of ancient tombs.

    B. inform people about an important discovery.

    C. persuade people to travel to China.

    D. analyze techniques that archaeologists use to excavate ruins.

> First eliminate the answers in which both adjectives are wrong or unsupported. Then choose the response in which both adjectives are logical inferences based on the forty years of labor and the thousands of weapons found at the site.

2 According to the passage, which might best describe the people of the Qin Dynasty?

    E. lazy and unsophisticated

    F. peace-loving and artistic

    G. hardworking and warlike

    H. cowardly and rebellious

> When two of the possible answers are similar, such as *brightened* and *restored*, usually neither is correct. Use context clues from the paragraph to decide between the other two choices.

3 What is the meaning of the underlined word in the sentence below?

    What remained was <u>obliterated</u> within hours after the figures were uncovered.

    A. destroyed

    B. brightened

    C. restored

    D. buried

> Use the subheadings of the passage to locate the section about the statues and the reasons that the colors faded.

4 Why are the terra cotta figures no longer brightly colored?

    E. The Chinese decided to paint them all reddish-brown.

    F. Paint peels very easily off of terra cotta.

    G. Archaeologists scraped the paint off.

    H. Over the years, water, fire, and sunlight caused the colors to fade.

5 What is one reason why Qin's tomb has not yet been excavated?

A. The Chinese don't want it to be excavated.

B. Archaeologists are only interested in the terra cotta army, not the tomb.

C. Archaeologists need to study the booby traps surrounding it.

D. Too many tourists visit the site.

Find the paragraph in which the excavation of Qin's tomb is discussed. Look for implied or stated cause-and-effect relationships between ideas.

6 Which of these statements is an opinion?

E. Over 10,000 weapons were found.

F. The most astonishing pieces are the metal swords.

G. Over 720,000 Chinese labored nearly 40 years, secretly creating the terra cotta army.

H. Crossbows were strategically placed to prevent thieves from stealing the treasures.

Remember that a *fact* can be proven to be right or wrong, whereas an *opinion* expresses the belief of the writer. Superlatives such as *best, greatest,* and *most* often signal opinions.

7 What conclusion can be drawn about Tamara?

A. She likes to take charge.

B. She wants to sing in the chorus.

C. She is shy.

D. She is flirting with Fred.

Reread Tamara's lines. Only one answer is an accurate conclusion based on what she says.

8 What is most likely the role of Mr. James?

E. He is Tamara's father.

F. He is a student.

G. He is a visitor to the school.

H. He is the teacher in charge of the play.

Think about the setting of the action. Who would most likely be in a school auditorium, familiar with the students, and in a position to give advice?

9 What type of passage is this?

A. a poem

B. a short story

C. a drama

D. an essay

Notice the stage directions, dialogue, and setting.

Answers:
5.C, 6.F, 7.A, 8.H, 9.C

Examine the form. Put one star next to sections that give information. Use two stars to mark sections that may have to be filled out.

Identify important details. In the parts you marked with one star, underline instructions for returning your order.

Functional Reading Test Model

DIRECTIONS Study the following return/exchange form. Then answer the questions that follow.

Return/Exchange Form

DO YOU NEED TO RETURN SOMETHING? IT'S SIMPLE.
- Mail it to us either by UPS or by US Postal Service (insured). If we made a mistake with your order, we'll refund the postage.
- Use the address label provided on the other side of this page when mailing your return back to us.
- We'll process your return right away. Within 2–3 weeks a refund or exchange will be at your door.

IN A HURRY?
Call us now at **1.800.555.1234** and charge your reorder. We'll credit your account when the return arrives at TeenWear.

RETURN REASON CODES
We are always trying to improve, and you can help. Please tell us why you are returning each product by choosing one code number below (one per item). Thanks.

IS IT FIT?

too small		too large
38	Length	39
44	Waist	45
46	Seat/hip	47
49	Chest	48
51	Sleeve	50
52	Neck	53
36	Shoe length	35
19	Shoe width	20

IS IT SATISFACTION?
- 22 Didn't like color
- 9 Didn't like styling
- 79 Didn't like fabric
- 80 Style didn't look good on me
- 16 Quality didn't match price
- 81 Returning matching item
- 83 Ordered multiple sizes for best fit

IS IT QUALITY?
- 5 Fabric too light
- 6 Fabric too heavy
- 10 Fabric poor quality
- 8 Excessive shrinkage
- 21 Not color matched
- 30 Closures/fasteners defective
- 72 Stitching/seams
- 75 Didn't wash well
- 76 Color faded
- 78 Color bled

IS IT SERVICE?
- 2 Arrived too late
- 13 Damaged package or in transit
- 23 Matching items not available
- 26 Photo doesn't represent product
- 29 Wrong item shipped
- 84 Duplicate order

OTHER COMMENTS _____

_____
_____
_____
_____
_____
_____
_____

1. PLEASE TELL US WHAT YOU ARE RETURNING.
(Use the reason codes at the left.)

Reason code	Item Number	Size	Color	Qty	Description	Price

2. PLEASE TELL US WHAT YOU'D LIKE US TO SEND YOU.
(If you already reordered by phone, check here ☐ and do NOT list items.)

Item Number	Size	Color	Alternate Color	Qty	Description	Price

3. WAS THIS A GIFT?   ■ YES   ■ NO
If yes, please check your preference from the following options:
☐ Gift certificate   ☐ Exchange   ☐ I have already reordered by phone.

4. PAYMENT METHOD (Refund will be in the form of original payment.)
If you are ordering more than you returned, please enter payment. Payment method:
☐ Check   ☐ Visa   ☐ MasterCard   ☐ Discover   ☐ AmEx

Credit card number ☐☐☐☐ ☐☐☐☐ ☐☐☐☐ ☐☐☐☐

Expiration date ☐☐☐☐   Signature _____

Follow directions. Write a brief explanation of how and why you would fill out each of these four sections.

1.

2.

3.

4.

Answer Strategies

① What code number would you insert in section 1 if you felt the item to be returned wasn't worth the amount of money you paid for it?

A. 5

B. 16

C. 30

D. 80

◁ On the Return Reason Codes chart, identify the reason represented by each number. Choose the correct one.

② What does a check in section 2 mean?

E. You don't want an item in exchange for the one you're returning.

F. You want a refund.

G. You're not sending your complete order back.

H. You've already reordered your exchange item by phone.

◁ Reread section 2. Which response matches the directions for placing a check?

Answers: 1. B, 2. H

Find the reason represented by code 29. Then review the bulleted directions for sending your item back. What is the policy if the company made the mistake?

3 If 29 is the reason code you used in section 1, what should you expect in addition to your refund or exchange?

   A. a phone call from the company
   B. a postage refund
   C. nothing
   D. a different color of the item

Review the reason for filling out each part of the return form. You are returning an item and requesting an exchange, so sections 1 and 2 must be completed. Section 3 indicates whether the item was a gift. Under what circumstances is section 4 completed?

4 If you return an item that costs $72.50 and order an exchange item for $61.90, which sections should be marked in some way when you send in the form?

   E. 1 and 2
   F. 1, 2, and 3
   G. 1, 2, and 4
   H. all four

Check each choice against the payment options listed in section 4. Which choice is not included?

5 If you are ordering a more expensive item in exchange for the one you are returning, which of the following is NOT a payment option?

   A. cash
   B. American Express
   C. personal check
   D. Discover card

Functional Reading Test Practice

DIRECTIONS Study the directions for placing a classified ad below. Circle the information that you think is the most important. Answer the multiple-choice questions that follow.

Class Ads!

Daily News
Classified Ads
555-1234
or toll free 800-555-1234

Ad packages include free listing online at **DailyNewsClassAds.com**

Please read your ad on the first day of publication. We want you to have the best results possible, and if the copy is not what you wanted, please let us know right away. The publisher reserves the right to accept, reject, or edit any advertising. We will not intentionally misclassify any advertising.

TO PLACE YOUR AD:

By Phone:	**In Person:**	**By Mail:**
Call 555-1234	444 Fleet Street	Classified Advertising
Toll Free 800-555-1234	Sayre, NY	Daily News
M–F 8:30–5:45 p.m.	Lobby hours M–F	P.O. Box 111
	8:30–5:00 p.m.	Sayre, NY 71523

AD DEADLINES
5:45 p.m. one full business day prior to printing
We accept all major credit cards.

HAPPY ADS
Share a special day or accomplishment with the Sayre community! Photos included in ads 3+ inches.
$8.50 per col. inch

RUMMAGE SALES
Single Family 6 lines, 3 days
$15
Group Sale 6 lines, 3 days
$24
Includes rummage sale kit.
Each additional line $1.50 for 3 days

STUFF
Items under $1000
3 lines, 7 days
$10
Items over $1000
3 lines, 7 days
$15
Includes Star symbol Each additional line $2.50

PREMIUM STUFF
3 lines for 21 days
Includes first line bold, symbol, and Hot off the Press.
$25
Includes Star symbol Each additional line $2.50

RENTALS
As low as $1.00 per line available to private party advertisers

1 What information is NOT given that might be helpful for someone wanting to place an ad?

  A. whether the ad can be paid for by credit card

  B. the number of words or letters in a line

  C. the price of a three-line ad for an item worth $1200

  D. the number to call from out-of-town

2 How many inches must a Happy Ad be in order to include a photograph?

  E. at least 1 inch

  F. between 2 and 3 inches

  G. over 3 inches

  H. 8.5 inches

3 Who would NOT be eligible for the rental ad rate of one dollar per line?

  A. a person renting out a room in his or her house

  B. someone renting out his or her beach cottage

  C. someone who wants to lease out his or her recreational vehicle during summer months

  D. an apartment management company

4 If you sold your old bike for $260 as a result of placing a four-line Premium Stuff ad, what would be your profit?

  E. $232.50

  F. $245.00

  G. $247.50

  H. $260.00

5 What kind of ad did you place if you spent $27.00?

  A. 5-line Premium Stuff ad

  B. Group Rummage Sale 8-line ad

  C. Single Family Rummage Sale 6-line ad for 6 days

  D. 4-inch Happy Ad

6 If you want your ad to appear in the Thursday edition and it is already 5:15 p.m. on Tuesday, what should you do?

  E. Send your ad in the mail.

  F. Take your ad to the newspaper office.

  G. Place your ad by telephone.

  H. Visit the Web site.

THINKING IT THROUGH

The notes in the side columns will help you think through your answers. Check the key at the bottom of each page. How well did you do?

1 What information is NOT given that might be helpful for someone wanting to place an ad?

- A. whether the ad can be paid for by credit card
- B. the number of words or letters in a line
- C. the price of a three-line ad for an item worth $1200
- D. the number to call from out-of-town

> Eliminate each choice that does appear in the directions.

2 How many inches must a Happy Ad be in order to include a photograph?

- E. at least 1 inch
- F. between 2 and 3 inches
- G. over 3 inches
- H. 8.5 inches

> Find the Happy Ad. What does it say about including photographs?

3 Who would NOT be eligible for the rental ad rate of one dollar per line?

- A. a person renting out a room in his or her house
- B. someone renting out his or her beach cottage
- C. someone who wants to lease out his or her recreational vehicle during summer months
- D. an apartment management company

> Notice that the rate is valid for private party advertisers only. Three of the answers describe private individuals renting out their property. Which choice does not?

4 If you sold your old bike for $260 as a result of placing a four-line Premium Stuff ad, what would be your profit?

- E. $232.50
- F. $245.00
- G. $247.50
- H. $260.00

> Calculate the price of a four-line Premium Stuff ad, which is $25 plus $2.50, and then subtract that amount from $260 to arrive at the profit.

5 What kind of ad did you place if you spent $27.00?

- A. 5-line Premium Stuff ad
- B. Group Rummage Sale 8-line ad
- C. Single Family Rummage Sale 6-line ad for 6 days
- D. 4-inch Happy Ad

> The best way to approach this question would be to calculate the cost of each kind of ad listed.

Answers:
1.B, 2.G, 3.D, 4.E, 5.B

Test Preparation Strategies **419**

6 If you want your ad to appear in the Thursday edition and it is already 5:15 p.m. on Tuesday, what should you do?

E. Send your ad in the mail.

F. Take your ad to the newspaper office.

G. Place your ad by telephone.

H. Visit the Web site.

Revising-and-Editing Test Model

DIRECTIONS Read the following paragraph carefully. Then answer the multiple-choice questions that follow. After answering the questions, read the material in the side columns to check your answer strategies.

¹ Our river, the Hialeah river, is the most polluted river in the state. ² The level of toxic chemicals in the water are high. ³ The water is not safe to drink. ⁴ The fish are suffering. ⁵ Many more fish live in the river ten years ago. ⁶ Not only are there chemicals in the water; but a greater number of people use the river as a dump than ever before. ⁷ It makes me sad. ⁸ Act now to help save our river.

1 What is the correct capitalization in sentence 1?

A. Our river, the Hialeah river, is the most polluted River in the state.

B. Our river, the Hialeah River, is the most polluted river in the State.

C. Our river, the Hialeah river, is the most polluted river in the state.

D. Our river, the Hialeah River, is the most polluted river in the state.

2 What is the best way to revise sentence 2?

E. The level of toxic chemicals in the water were high.

F. The levels of toxic chemicals in the water is high.

G. The level of toxic chemicals in the water is high.

H. The level of toxic chemical in the water are high.

3 What is the best way to combine sentences 3 and 4?

A. The water is not safe to drink, the fish are suffering.

B. The water is not safe to drink, and the fish are suffering.

C. The water is not safe to drink, but the fish are suffering.

D. The water is not safe to drink, because the fish are suffering.

Reading Strategies for Assessment

Watch for common errors. Highlight or underline errors such as incorrect punctuation, spelling, or capitalization; incomplete or run-on sentences; and missing or misplaced information.

Answer Strategies

Capitalization Capitalize the proper names of geographical features.
For help, see Pupil Edition, pp. R74, R94–R95*
Grammar, Usage, and Mechanics Book, pp. 184–186

Subject-Verb Agreement When determining agreement, ignore prepositional phrases that come between the subject and the verb.
For help, see Pupil Edition, pp. R76–R79
Grammar, Usage, and Mechanics Book, pp. 163–165

Sentence Combining Remember that a compound sentence requires a coordinating conjunction. Which conjunction best expresses the relationship between the two ideas?

Answers: 1.D, 2.G, 3.B

*Pages listed are for the Grammar Handbook in The Language of Literature Pupil Edition and the Grammar, Usage, and Mechanics Book.

Verb Tense *Ten years ago* requires the past tense of the verb.
For help, see Pupil Edition, pp. R84–R85
Grammar, Usage, and Mechanics Book, pp. 94–96

Compound Sentences Two complete thoughts should be connected by a comma and a conjunction or by a semicolon.
For help, see Pupil Edition, p. R96
Grammar, Usage, and Mechanics Book, pp. 193–196

Kinds of Sentences The lack of exclamation points and question marks eliminates exclamatory and interrogative sentences.
For help, see Pupil Edition, p. R102
Grammar, Usage, and Mechanics Book, pp. 16–18

Supporting Details The paragraph is not about the writer but about the pollution of the river. What kind of information would best reinforce this central idea?

4 Which of the following is the correct form of the verb in sentence 5?

   E. had lived

   F. has lived

   G. are living

   H. lived

5 What change should be made in sentence 6?

   A. Change the semicolon to a comma.

   B. Change the semicolon to a period and capitalize *but*.

   C. Change *there* to *their*.

   D. No change

6 What types of sentences does this paragraph include?

   E. declarative and interrogative

   F. declarative and imperative

   G. imperative and interrogative

   H. imperative and exclamatory

7 What information should be added to sentence 7?

   A. how the writer knows that he is sad

   B. how long the writer has been sad

   C. what makes the writer sad

   D. what the writer does when he is sad

Revising-and-Editing Test Practice

DIRECTIONS Read the following paragraph carefully. As you read, circle each error that you find and identify the error in the side column—for example, *misspelled word* or *not a complete sentence*. When you have finished, circle the letter of the correct choice for each question that follows.

¹One day last summer, I saw a car accident. ²It happened on the edge of town. ³It happened on a bright and warm July afternoon. ⁴I set happily on a bench near a main intersection as I waited for a ride home. ⁵Suddenly a loud screeching, noise ripped through the air. ⁶Then the sound of tearing metal and squealing brakes that made a loud noise assaulted my ears. ⁷Soon other people of a building came pouring out. ⁸I edged closer to the scene and peered over people's shoulders. ⁹Waiting to see what would happen.

1 Which resource would most help you find a stronger, more interesting verb to replace *saw* in sentence 1?

A. a thesaurus

B. a dictionary

C. a glossary

D. an index

2 What is the best way to combine sentences 2 and 3?

E. It happened at the edge of town because the July afternoon was bright and warm.

F. It happened at the edge of town; it happened on a bright and warm July afternoon.

G. It happened at the edge of town on a bright and warm July afternoon.

H. It was at the edge of town on a bright and warm July afternoon that it happened.

3 What is the correct form of the main verb in sentence 4?

A. sit

B. was setting

C. had sat

D. sat

4 Where should the comma in sentence 5 be placed?

   E. between *loud* and *screeching*

   F. after *Suddenly*

   G. after *Suddenly* and *loud*

   H. after *noise*

5 What change should be made to sentence 6?

   A. insert a comma after *metal*

   B. insert a comma after *brakes*

   C. delete the phrase *that made a loud noise*

   D. delete the phrase *and squealing brakes*

6 Which modifier in sentence 7 is misplaced?

   E. other

   F. of a building

   G. Soon

   H. out

7 Which sentence in the paragraph is a fragment?

   A. sentence 2

   B. sentence 5

   C. sentence 6

   D. sentence 9

THINKING IT THROUGH

Use the notes in the side columns to help you understand why some answers are correct and others are not. Check the answer key at the bottom of each page. How well did you do?

1 Which resource would most help you find a stronger, more interesting verb to replace *saw* in sentence 1?

   A. a thesaurus

   B. a dictionary

   C. a glossary

   D. an index

> Use the process of elimination. If you know that a dictionary and a glossary give definitions and that an index locates specific references to a topic, then a thesaurus is the only possibility.

2 What is the best way to combine sentences 2 and 3?

   E. It happened at the edge of town because the July afternoon was bright and warm.

   F. It happened at the edge of town; it happened on a bright and warm July afternoon.

   G. It happened at the edge of town on a bright and warm July afternoon.

   H. It was at the edge of town on a bright and warm July afternoon that it happened.

> There is no cause-and-effect relationship, which rules out E. In F, the repetition of the verb is awkward and unnecessary. Of the two remaining sentences, which expresses the idea more concisely?

3 What is the correct form of the main verb in sentence 4?

   A. sit

   B. was setting

   C. had sat

   D. sat

> Remember that *set* means "to place." A person sits. Therefore, you need to choose the correct tense of *sit*.
> *For help, see Pupil Edition, p. R85**

4 Where should the comma in sentence 5 be placed?

   E. between *loud* and *screeching*

   F. after *Suddenly*

   G. after *Suddenly* and *loud*

   H. after *noise*

> Commas set off introductory words and adjectives preceding a noun when each adjective modifies the noun. In this sentence, *loud* modifies *screeching*, not *noise*.
> *For help, see Pupil Edition, p. R96 Grammar, Usage, and Mechanics Book, pp. 193–195*

Answers:
1.A, 2.G, 3.D, 4.F

*Pages listed are for the Grammar Handbook in *The Language of Literature* Pupil Edition and the *Grammar, Usage, and Mechanics Book*.

Try each change suggested. Two of them create errors in the sentence. Which one improves the sentence by deleting a redundant phrase?

5 What change should be made to sentence 6?

   A. insert a comma after *metal*

   B. insert a comma after *brakes*

   C. delete the phrase *that made a loud noise*

   D. delete the phrase *and squealing brakes*

Keep adverbs and adverb phrases as close as possible to the words they modify.

6 Which modifier in sentence 7 is misplaced?

   E. other

   F. of a building

   G. Soon

   H. out

A complete sentence must have a subject and a verb, and it must express a complete thought. Which of the sentences listed does not meet those requirements?
For help, see Pupil Edition, p. R75 Grammar, Usage, and Mechanics Book, pp. 28–30

7 Which sentence in the paragraph is a fragment?

   A. sentence 2

   B. sentence 5

   C. sentence 6

   D. sentence 9

Writing Test Model

DIRECTIONS Many tests ask you to write an essay in response to a writing prompt. A writing prompt is a brief statement that describes a writing situation. Some writing prompts ask you to explain what, why, or how. Others ask you to convince someone about something.

As you analyze the following writing prompts, read and respond to the notes in the side columns. Then look at the response to each prompt. The notes in the side columns will help you understand why each response is considered strong.

Prompt A

Your school's principal is urging families to limit home TV watching to 30 minutes a day. Think about how such a limitation would affect you.

Now write to convince your parents and the principal to accept your point of view on this issue. Be sure to provide support for your argument.

Strong Response

Imagine this. We've finished dinner and the family is all sitting around the living room. I'm doing my homework when all of a sudden, the house is hit by a tornado. In an instant we're sitting in rubble, lucky to be alive. Just one of those things? Not really. If I had been watching TV I would have heard the tornado warning. But that wasn't allowed because I'd already met my half-hour limit.

This may be an extreme example, but you can't deny that television is a major source of information in the world today. Limiting my viewing time to 30 minutes a day will deprive me of important information that might even save all our lives. If TV watching must be limited, at least let me be part of setting the limit.

Analyzing the Prompt

Identify the topic. Underline the subject of the prompt as presented in the first sentence.

Determine requirements. Circle or state in your own words the purpose of your essay, the audience, and the kinds of details you must include.

Answer Strategies

Capture the reader's attention. The writer's hypothetical situation is a dramatic way to begin the essay and make his point.

State your position clearly. This writer's opinion is established early in the essay.

The half-hour limit doesn't make sense for several reasons. First, most TV shows are an hour long. This limit would mean that I couldn't watch even one full program a day. I would miss out on many very good educational, news, and sports broadcasts. And I think I deserve to watch a comedy or other show just for fun once in a while, too. Second, I often need to watch certain programs for school. The series on the Civil War is just one example. I got some wonderful material from that show for my term paper. With a 30-minute limit, I would have missed three-quarters of each episode.

Limiting the total number of programs I watch seems like a better idea. We could set a weekly limit—15 seems reasonable. That's only about two shows a day, which would include required viewing for school. This plan would allow me to take responsibility for my TV watching and to practice organizing my time. And those are two skills I'm told I need to work on.

I'm willing to limit the amount of TV I watch. However, 30 minutes a day will cut me off from a major source of information I need to do well in school and in the world. Please consider these arguments carefully and give me the chance to prove that I can take responsibility for myself.

Prompt B

Everyone has a favorite type of music. Think about which type of music is your favorite. Now explain why you like that type of music the most.

Strong Response

Music has always been a very important part of my life. In fact, my parents insist that I sang my first word rather than just saying it. I've listened to practically every type of music there is from rock to opera. It's nice to know about them all so I can listen to the type that suits my mood. Overall, though, I have to say that I like folk music best.

One of my earliest memories is a concert my parents took me to when I was about five years old. It was just one man singing and playing a guitar, but it was magical. Everyone seemed to know the words and started singing along with him. It was like we were all part of something big and wonderful. I still get that feeling whenever I hear folk music.

So I learned to love folk music before I really knew what it was. Since then I have learned that folk music is the music of the people and I'm one of those people. It is traditional songs that people have sung for centuries and passed along from parent to child. It is also songs that people write to share their hopes and dreams, to protest injustice and hatred in the world, and to remind people that we're not alone.

Not only do folk songs have important messages, but the words can be heard and understood easily. Folk music usually is accompanied by acoustic instruments, such as guitar, banjo, harmonica, and piano, so the singer doesn't

Identify the topic. Circle the topic of the prompt.

Understand what's expected of you. What must be your first step in planning your response? What facts, incidents, or examples will you include in the body of your essay?

Answer Strategies

State the main idea. After making some general observations about music, the writer narrows her focus in a main idea statement that leads into the rest of her essay.

Engage the reader's interest. By including an anecdote, the writer captures the interest of the reader while she explains her liking for folk music.

Offer supporting details. The writer gives specific facts to inform the reader about her topic.

Include transitional words and phrases. Transitional phrases such as *Not only* help unify the essay by showing relationships between ideas in different paragraphs.

have to scream to be heard. You don't leave a folk concert with your eardrums ringing from the aftereffects of amplifiers.

In conclusion, folk music is my favorite kind of music because it helps me be a better person. Its words don't just entertain. They also have important messages about current events and issues that have concerned people for all time. Maybe the most important message of all is that we're all just folks.

Writing Test Practice

DIRECTIONS Read the following writing prompt. Using the strategies you've learned in this section, analyze the prompt, plan your response, and then write an essay explaining your position.

Prompt C

Officials at your school's cafeteria have decided to make school lunches more healthful by eliminating from the menu all fried foods, soda pop, and sweetened desserts.

Think about whether you agree with this policy and why. Now write an essay to convince your principal to accept your point of view. Include support for your position.

Scoring Rubrics

DIRECTIONS Use the following checklist to see whether you have written a strong persuasive essay. You will have succeeded if you can check nearly all of the items.

The Prompt

☐ My response meets all the requirements stated in the prompt.

☐ I have stated my position clearly and supported it with details.

☐ I have addressed the audience appropriately.

☐ My essay fits the type of writing suggested in the prompt (letter to the editor, article for the school paper, and so on).

Reasons

☐ The reasons I offer really support my position.

☐ My audience will find the reasons convincing.

☐ I have stated my reasons clearly.

☐ I have given at least three reasons.

☐ I have supported my reasons with sufficient facts, examples, quotations, and other details.

☐ I have presented and responded to opposing arguments.

☐ My reasoning is sound. I have avoided faulty logic.

Order and Arrangement

☐ I have included a strong introduction.

☐ I have included a strong conclusion.

☐ The reasons are arranged in a logical order.

Word Choice

☐ The language of my essay is appropriate for my audience.

☐ I have used precise, vivid words and persuasive language.

Fluency

☐ I have used sentences of varying lengths and structures.

☐ I have connected ideas with transitions and other devices.

☐ I have used correct spelling, punctuation, and grammar.

Personal Word List

Use these pages to build your personal vocabulary. As you read the selections, take time to mark unfamiliar words. These should be words that seem interesting or important enough to add to your permanent vocabulary. After reading, look up the meanings of these words and record the information below. For each word, write a sentence that shows its correct use.

Review your list from time to time. Try to put these words into use in your writing and conversation.

Word: _____

Selection: _____

Page/Line: _____ / _____

Part of Speech: _____

Definition: _____

_____

_____

Sentence: _____

_____

_____

_____

Word: _____

Selection: _____

Page/Line: _____ / _____

Part of Speech: _____

Definition: _____

_____

_____

Sentence: _____

_____

_____

_____

Word: _____

Selection: _____

Page/Line: _____ / _____

Part of Speech: _____

Definition: _____

_____

_____

Sentence: _____

_____

_____

_____

Word: _____

Selection: _____

Page/Line: _____ / _____

Part of Speech: _____

Definition: _____

_____

_____

Sentence: _____

_____

_____

_____

Word: _____

Selection: _____

Page/Line: _____ / _____

Part of Speech: _____

Definition: _____

_____

_____

Sentence: _____

_____

_____

_____

Word: _____

Selection: _____

Page/Line: _____ / _____

Part of Speech: _____

Definition: _____

_____

_____

Sentence: _____

_____

_____

_____

Word: _____

Selection: _____

Page/Line: _____ / _____

Part of Speech: _____

Definition: _____

_____

_____

Sentence: _____

_____

_____

_____

Personal Word List

Word: _____

Selection: _____

Page/Line: _____ / _____

Part of Speech: _____

Definition: _____

_____

_____

Sentence: _____

_____

_____

_____

Word: _____

Selection: _____

Page/Line: _____ / _____

Part of Speech: _____

Definition: _____

_____

_____

Sentence: _____

_____

_____

_____

Word: _____

Selection: _____

Page/Line: _____ / _____

Part of Speech: _____

Definition: _____

_____

_____

Sentence: _____

_____

_____

_____

Word: _____

Selection: _____

Page/Line: _____ / _____

Part of Speech: _____

Definition: _____

_____

_____

Sentence: _____

_____

_____

_____

Word: _____

Selection: _____

Page/Line: _____ / _____

Part of Speech: _____

Definition: _____

_____

_____

Sentence: _____

_____

_____

_____

Word: _____

Selection: _____

Page/Line: _____ / _____

Part of Speech: _____

Definition: _____

_____

_____

Sentence: _____

_____

_____

_____

Word: _____

Selection: _____

Page/Line: _____ / _____

Part of Speech: _____

Definition: _____

_____

_____

Sentence: _____

_____

_____

_____

Word: _____

Selection: _____

Page/Line: _____ / _____

Part of Speech: _____

Definition: _____

_____

_____

Sentence: _____

_____

_____

_____

Personal Word List

Word: _____

Selection: _____

Page/Line: _____ / _____

Part of Speech: _____

Definition: _____

_____

_____

Sentence: _____

_____

_____

_____

Word: _____

Selection: _____

Page/Line: _____ / _____

Part of Speech: _____

Definition: _____

_____

_____

Sentence: _____

_____

_____

_____

Word: _____

Selection: _____

Page/Line: _____ / _____

Part of Speech: _____

Definition: _____

_____

_____

Sentence: _____

_____

_____

_____

Word: _____

Selection: _____

Page/Line: _____ / _____

Part of Speech: _____

Definition: _____

_____

_____

Sentence: _____

_____

_____

_____

Word: _____

Selection: _____

Page/Line: _____ / _____

Part of Speech: _____

Definition: _____

_____

_____

Sentence: _____

_____

_____

Word: _____

Selection: _____

Page/Line: _____ / _____

Part of Speech: _____

Definition: _____

_____

_____

Sentence: _____

_____

_____

Word: _____

Selection: _____

Page/Line: _____ / _____

Part of Speech: _____

Definition: _____

_____

_____

Sentence: _____

_____

_____

Word: _____

Selection: _____

Page/Line: _____ / _____

Part of Speech: _____

Definition: _____

_____

_____

Sentence: _____

_____

_____

Personal Word List

Word: _____

Selection: _____

Page/Line: _____ / _____

Part of Speech: _____

Definition: _____

_____

_____

Sentence: _____

_____

_____

_____

Word: _____

Selection: _____

Page/Line: _____ / _____

Part of Speech: _____

Definition: _____

_____

_____

Sentence: _____

_____

_____

_____

Word: _____

Selection: _____

Page/Line: _____ / _____

Part of Speech: _____

Definition: _____

_____

_____

Sentence: _____

_____

_____

_____

Word: _____

Selection: _____

Page/Line: _____ / _____

Part of Speech: _____

Definition: _____

_____

_____

Sentence: _____

_____

_____

_____

Word: _____

Selection: _____

Page/Line: _____ / _____

Part of Speech: _____

Definition: _____

_____

_____

Sentence: _____

_____

_____

_____

Word: _____

Selection: _____

Page/Line: _____ / _____

Part of Speech: _____

Definition: _____

_____

_____

Sentence: _____

_____

_____

Word: _____

Selection: _____

Page/Line: _____ / _____

Part of Speech: _____

Definition: _____

_____

_____

Sentence: _____

_____

_____

Word: _____

Selection: _____

Page/Line: _____ / _____

Part of Speech: _____

Definition: _____

_____

_____

Sentence: _____

_____

_____

Personal Word List

Word: _____

Selection: _____

Page/Line: _____ / _____

Part of Speech: _____

Definition: _____

_____

_____

Sentence: _____

_____

_____

_____

Word: _____

Selection: _____

Page/Line: _____ / _____

Part of Speech: _____

Definition: _____

_____

_____

Sentence: _____

_____

_____

_____

Word: _____

Selection: _____

Page/Line: _____ / _____

Part of Speech: _____

Definition: _____

_____

_____

Sentence: _____

_____

_____

_____

Word: _____

Selection: _____

Page/Line: _____ / _____

Part of Speech: _____

Definition: _____

_____

_____

Sentence: _____

_____

_____

_____

Word: _____

Selection: _____

Page/Line: _____ / _____

Part of Speech: _____

Definition: _____

_____

_____

Sentence: _____

_____

_____

_____

Word: _____

Selection: _____

Page/Line: _____ / _____

Part of Speech: _____

Definition: _____

_____

_____

Sentence: _____

_____

_____

_____

Word: _____

Selection: _____

Page/Line: _____ / _____

Part of Speech: _____

Definition: _____

_____

_____

Sentence: _____

_____

_____

_____

Word: _____

Selection: _____

Page/Line: _____ / _____

Part of Speech: _____

Definition: _____

_____

_____

Sentence: _____

_____

_____

_____

Personal Word List

Word: _____

Selection: _____

Page/Line: _____ / _____

Part of Speech: _____

Definition: _____

_____

_____

Sentence: _____

_____

_____

_____

Word: _____

Selection: _____

Page/Line: _____ / _____

Part of Speech: _____

Definition: _____

_____

_____

Sentence: _____

_____

_____

Word: _____

Selection: _____

Page/Line: _____ / _____

Part of Speech: _____

Definition: _____

_____

_____

Sentence: _____

_____

_____

Word: _____

Selection: _____

Page/Line: _____ / _____

Part of Speech: _____

Definition: _____

_____

_____

Sentence: _____

_____

_____

Word: _____

Selection: _____

Page/Line: _____ / _____

Part of Speech: _____

Definition: _____

_____

_____

Sentence: _____

_____

_____

_____

Word: _____

Selection: _____

Page/Line: _____ / _____

Part of Speech: _____

Definition: _____

_____

_____

Sentence: _____

_____

_____

Word: _____

Selection: _____

Page/Line: _____ / _____

Part of Speech: _____

Definition: _____

_____

_____

Sentence: _____

_____

_____

_____

Word: _____

Selection: _____

Page/Line: _____ / _____

Part of Speech: _____

Definition: _____

_____

_____

Sentence: _____

_____

Personal Word List

Word: _____

Selection: _____

Page/Line: _____ / _____

Part of Speech: _____

Definition: _____

_____

_____

Sentence: _____

_____

_____

_____

Word: _____

Selection: _____

Page/Line: _____ / _____

Part of Speech: _____

Definition: _____

_____

_____

Sentence: _____

_____

_____

_____

Word: _____

Selection: _____

Page/Line: _____ / _____

Part of Speech: _____

Definition: _____

_____

_____

Sentence: _____

_____

_____

_____

Word: _____

Selection: _____

Page/Line: _____ / _____

Part of Speech: _____

Definition: _____

_____

_____

Sentence: _____

_____

_____

_____

Word: _____

Selection: _____

Page/Line: _____ / _____

Part of Speech: _____

Definition: _____

_____

_____

Sentence: _____

_____

_____

_____

Word: _____

Selection: _____

Page/Line: _____ / _____

Part of Speech: _____

Definition: _____

_____

_____

Sentence: _____

_____

_____

Word: _____

Selection: _____

Page/Line: _____ / _____

Part of Speech: _____

Definition: _____

_____

_____

Sentence: _____

_____

_____

Word: _____

Selection: _____

Page/Line: _____ / _____

Part of Speech: _____

Definition: _____

_____

_____

Sentence: _____

_____

_____

Personal Word List

Word: _____

Selection: _____

Page/Line: _____ / _____

Part of Speech: _____

Definition: _____

_____

_____

Sentence: _____

_____

_____

_____

Word: _____

Selection: _____

Page/Line: _____ / _____

Part of Speech: _____

Definition: _____

_____

_____

Sentence: _____

_____

_____

_____

Word: _____

Selection: _____

Page/Line: _____ / _____

Part of Speech: _____

Definition: _____

_____

_____

Sentence: _____

_____

_____

_____

Word: _____

Selection: _____

Page/Line: _____ / _____

Part of Speech: _____

Definition: _____

_____

_____

Sentence: _____

_____

_____

_____

Acknowledgments

(Continued from page ii)

Brooks Permissions: "Speech to the Young — Speech to the Progress Toward" from *Blacks* by Gwendolyn Brooks (Chicago: Third World Press). Copyright © 1991 by Gwendolyn Brooks. Reprinted by consent of Brooks Permissions.

Chicago Public Schools: Entry form for Student Science Fair 2000, from the participant handbook. Reprinted by permission of the Chicago Public Schools Student Science Fair.

Consumers Union of U.S.: "Allowance: Who Gets One, and How Much?" (bar graph) and "Percent of Kids Who Get" (pie chart) from *Zillions®*, January/February 1999. Copyright © 1999 by Consumers Union of U.S., Inc., Yonkers, NY 10703-1057, a nonprofit organization. Reprinted with permission from the January/February 1999 issue of Zillions for educational purposes only. No commercial use or photocopying permitted. To learn more about Zillions or Consumers Union, log onto http://www.ConsumerReports.org.

Cricket Magazine Group: "Finding a Bit of History" by Shirley Neitzel, *Cricket,* August 2001, Vol. 28, No. 12, pages 20–24. Copyright © 2001 by Shirley Neitzel. Reprinted by permission of CRICKET magazine.

HarperCollins Publishers: "Legacies," "The Drum," and "Choices," from *The Selected Poems of Nikki Giovanni* by Nikki Giovanni. Copyright © 1996 by Nikki Giovanni. Reprinted by permission of HarperCollins Publishers, Inc.

Henry Holt & Company: "Stopping by Woods on a Snowy Evening" by Robert Frost, from *The Poetry of Robert Frost,* edited by Edward Connery Lathem. Copyright © 1951 by Robert Frost. Copyright 1923, © 1969 by Henry Holt and Company. Copyright 1951 by Robert Frost. Reprinted by permission of Henry Holt and Company, LLC.

Daniel Keyes: "Flowers for Algernon" by Daniel Keyes. Copyright © 1959, 1987 by Daniel Keyes. A book-length version of the story is published by Bantam Books and Harcourt Brace & Company Classic Edition, as well as a companion book, *Reliving "Flowers for Algernon," A Writer's Story*. Reprinted by permission of the author. All rights reserved.

Alfred A. Knopf: "Mother to Son," from *The Collected Poems of Langston Hughes* by Langston Hughes. Copyright © 1994 by The Estate of Langston Hughes. Used by permission of Alfred A. Knopf, a division of Random House, Inc.

National Geographic Society: "Dolphinspeak" by Aline Alexander Newman, *National Geographic World,* August 2001, pages 12–17. Copyright © 2001 by National Geographic Society. Reprinted by permission of National Geographic Society.

Random House: "Raymond's Run," from *Gorilla, My Love* by Toni Cade Bambara. Copyright © 1971 by Toni Cade Bambara. Used by permission of Random House, Inc.

From *The Diary of Anne Frank* by Frances Goodrich and Albert Hackett. Copyright © 1954, 1956 as an unpublished work. Copyright © 1956 by Albert Hackett, Frances Goodrich, and Otto Frank. Reprinted by permission of Random House, Inc.

Caution: *The Diary of Anne Frank* is the sole property of the estate of the dramatists and is fully protected by copyright. It may not be acted by professionals or amateurs without written permission and the payment of a royalty. All rights, including professional, amateur, stock, radio broadcasting, television, motion picture, recitation, lecturing, public reading, and the rights of translation into foreign languages are reserved. All inquiries should be addressed to the agent for the estate of the dramatists: Leah Salisbury, 234 West 44th Street, New York, NY.

Russell & Volkening: Excerpt from *Harriet Tubman: Conductor on the Underground Railroad* by Ann Petry. Copyright © 1955 by Ann Petry. Copyright renewed 1983 by Ann Petry. Reprinted by permission of Russell & Volkening as agents for the author.

Scribner: "A Mother in Mannville," from *When the Whippoorwill* by Marjorie Kinnan Rawlings. Copyright © 1940 by Marjorie Kinnan Rawlings; copyright renewed © 1968 by Norton Baskin. Reprinted with the permission of Scribner, a division of Simon & Schuster Adult Publishing Group.

Illustrations by Todd Graveline

viii, 2, 4, 6, 10, 13, 16, 20, 24, 31, 32, 36, 38, 41, 43, 45, 47, 52, 54, 60, 61, 66, 69, 71, 72, 76, 78, 79, 84, 86, 88, 92, 93, 95, 97, 100, 102, 104, 105, 108, 110, 111, 112, 115, 119, 123, 124, 128, 130, 132, 135, 139, 140, 144, 146, 148, 150, 151, 153, 157, 158, 162, 165, 170, 172, 173, 180, 181, 183, 185, 189, 190, 192, 194, 196, 199, 203, 210, 212, 214, 216, 217, 221, 222, 224, 226, 230, 232, 233, 234, 235, 236, 237, 240, 242, 248, 249, 250, 252, 255, 256, 262, 265, 269, 273, 274, 275, 277, 278, 285, 287, 291, 295, 300, 302, 304, 305, 308, 309, 310, 314, 318, 321, 323, 325, 327, 331, 333, 334, 340, 343, 344.

Art Credits

Cover